THE AMERICAN LAW INSTITUTE

A Concise Restatement
of
TORTS
Third Edition

Compiled
by
ELLEN M. BUBLICK
Dan B. Dobbs Professor of Law

University of Arizona
James E. Rogers College of Law

·A·L·I·

ST. PAUL, MN
AMERICAN LAW INSTITUTE PUBLISHERS
2013

Mat #41431944

ISBN: 978-0-314-61671-5

American Law Institute Publishers has no responsibility for the persistence or accuracy of URLs for external or third-party internet websites referred to in this publication, and does not guarantee that any content on such websites is, or will remain, accurate or appropriate.

DIRECTOR'S FOREWORD

In compiling this Concise Restatement, Professor Ellen Bublick of the University of Arizona has assembled in a compact, convenient, and readily accessible format those portions of these Restatements that an experienced teacher of torts regards as especially pertinent and helpful to an introductory study of the subject.

While assembly of a most manageable study aid entailed the cutting of many relevant Sections, as well as the omission or paring of commentary to many Sections whose black-letter provisions have been included, the material ultimately retained has not been rewritten or changed in substance; its language is precisely that which has been relied upon (and quoted extensively) by the courts and which continues to influence tort-law developments.

The Institute is grateful to Professor Bublick for assembling this excellent compilation and hopeful that it will prove useful both as a supplement to the study of torts and as an introduction to the perennially evolving Torts Restatements.

LANCE LIEBMAN
DIRECTOR
THE AMERICAN LAW INSTITUTE

EDITOR'S FOREWORD

When state and federal courts resolve tort cases, they routinely rely on a small number of persuasive authorities for guidance—chief among these The American Law Institute's Restatement of Torts. A review of the finished projects of the Restatement Third of Torts and the active provisions of the Restatement Second of Torts reveals the reasons for this enduring influence. Comprehensive, well reasoned, carefully illustrated and annotated, the Restatement provisions systematically stake out best practices across the wide range of issues in the field.

As the editor of this concise edition, I have been fortunate to spend time studying the Restatement and mining it for knowledge useful to a first-year Torts course. Having used the book in my own course for several years now, I can say with conviction that students find the Restatement provisions of great value to their studies. To start, Restatement Sections are the only study aid that can assist understanding and be cited in court. Moreover, Restatement Illustrations provide an outstanding vehicle for students to test their grasp of significant tort principles in concrete contexts.

In this third edition, readers will note several changes. The first, and perhaps most dramatic change, is to the book's organization. The Sections in this edition have been drawn from five separate Restatement projects. Thus a Section 1 might be drawn from any of five different works—the Restatement Third of Torts: Liability for Physical and Emotional Harm; the Restatement Third of Torts: Apportionment of Liability; the Restatement Third of Torts: Products Liability; the Restatement Second of Torts; or the Restatement of Agency. While Restatement Section numbers and project names are noted underneath each black-letter provision, Section numbers play a diminished role in this volume. Instead, this book has been organized by topic in a way that corresponds more closely to first-year casebooks. Second, with the completion of the Restatement Third of Torts: Liability for Physical and Emotional Harm and the publication of the second volume of that work, new material concerning direct and vicarious liability and finalized content for Sections concerning emotional harms and land-possessor liability have been introduced into this volume. Third, in response to reader requests, additional Illustrations and commentary have been returned to chapters concerning intentional harm and damages among others. Finally, with the addition of new material, other text has been trimmed to maintain the abbreviated length of the book.

As always, thanks are due to many people. For the privilege of editing this volume and the chance to engage directly with various Restatement of Torts projects, I thank Lance Liebman and Stephanie Middleton of The American Law Institute. Thanks are also due to Ken Abraham who skillfully crafted the first edition of this book, to Ellen Pryor who personally edited the text of her work on Liability of Those Who Hire Independent Contractors, and to other Restatement Third of Torts Reporters for their direct contributions and thoughtful feedback on earlier drafts. Barbara Lopez lent her superb skills to making this manuscript the polished product that it is. Jon Olson at West provided valuable insights into the Concise Restatement series. Marianne Walker and Todd Feldman assisted from the first manuscript drafts on the second edition to the final careful edits of this third edition. Dawn Landers's diligent work and high publishing standards enabled this book to come out well formatted and on time. Particular thanks are also due to my research assistant and project manager Sarah Epperson, whose substantive suggestions and hard work have made this edition the best to date.

A note on editing conventions: the full provisions of the Restatement Third of Torts cover more than a thousand pages. The active provisions of the Restatement Second cover additional print. Of necessity, for this slim volume, editing choices had to be made. To indicate to readers when text of a provision has been omitted, the omission is indicated by ellipses—three dots for omissions internal to a sentence and four dots for other omissions. Cuts that exclude an entire lettered Comment or set of Comments, or cuts that exclude an entire Illustration or set of Illustrations, are not noted by ellipses. The Comment letters and Illustration numbers themselves alert the reader to these omissions. Brackets have been used to insert content necessary to understand omitted material or to identify the subject matter of cross-references. In many instances, rather than add brackets, internal cross-references were deleted to aid clarity. Readers who want to explore the full text of any Section can find that material in the published volumes of the relevant Restatement of Torts project which is noted under each provision.

The American Law Institute has long been an intellectual meeting place for judges, lawyers, and scholars who care about the betterment of the law. Through this volume it is my real pleasure to welcome students to join this discourse.

ELLEN M. BUBLICK
Tucson, Arizona

Summary of Contents

PART VI. STRICT LIABILITY

PART VII. PRODUCTS LIABILITY

PART VIII. NUISANCE

PART IX. APPORTIONMENT OF LIABILITY

PART X. DAMAGES

Table of Contents

PART III. NEGLIGENT HARMS TO PERSONS OR PROPERTY

PART I
INTRODUCTION

CHAPTER 1

AN INTRODUCTION TO THE RESTATEMENT OF TORTS

A. THE AMERICAN LAW INSTITUTE

The American Law Institute was created in 1923 as a private organization of judges, lawyers, and legal scholars seeking to respond to "general dissatisfaction with the administration of justice" by working for improvement of the law. The Institute's primary goal, as stated in its charter, was to "promote the clarification and simplification of the law and its better adaptation to social needs." The incorporators included William Howard Taft and Charles Evans Hughes; Benjamin Cardozo and Learned Hand were among the early leaders.

From the beginning, the ALI worked on "Restatements" of the common law with the goal of helping the systematic development of the law and the pursuit of consistent legal doctrine among the states. The first Restatements were on the subjects of Agency, Conflict of Laws, Contracts, Judgments, Property, Restitution, Security, Torts, and Trusts, all of which have been updated by Second or even Third Restatements. Subsequent Restatement projects have included The Foreign Relations Law of the United States, Unfair Competition, and The Law Governing Lawyers. Other major ALI projects have included the Uniform Commercial Code (for which the ALI has a partner, the Uniform Law Commission), the Model Penal Code, Principles of Corporate Governance, Principles of the Law of Family Dissolution, Principles of the Law of Software Contracts, and Principles of the Law of Aggregate Litigation.

The ALI's working method is to choose for each project one or more experts, usually law professors, as "Reporters" and to subject each of their successive drafts to detailed review by "Advisers" consisting of judges, lawyers, and academics and by a special consultative group of interested Institute members. After appropriate revision, a draft is next submitted for review to the Institute's Council, a governing body of some 60 members drawn widely from the various branches of the legal profession, and then, as a "Tentative Draft," to the membership as a whole at the Institute's Annual Meeting, during which time it is also made generally available for public comment and review. When the project in its entirety has been approved by both the Council and the membership, a process that can take many years, the final, official text is prepared for publication.

The Institute's membership includes judges, practitioners, and law teachers from all areas of the United States as well as many foreign countries, selected on the basis of professional achievement and demonstrated interest in the improvement of the law. Ex officio members include the Chief Justice and Associate Justices of the Supreme Court of the United States, the Chief Judges of the federal courts of appeals and the highest courts of the states, law-school Deans, and the Presidents of the American Bar Association, state bar associations, and other prominent legal organizations.

B. THE RESTATEMENT OF TORTS

Lance Liebman, Director, The American Law Institute

Work on the original Restatement of Torts began in 1923, shortly after the establishment of The American Law Institute earlier that year. Together with the Restatements of Agency and Contracts, it was thus one of the very first undertakings of the Institute. The Reporter with overall responsibility for this work in the ensuing years was Francis H. Bohlen of the University of Pennsylvania, although there were no fewer than seven subsidiary Reporters who drafted various portions of the Restatement, the fourth and final volume of which was published in 1939.

After another 16 years, in 1955, the Institute returned to the subject of torts, revisiting and reconsidering every aspect of the original Restatement, reformulating and frequently expanding its provisions in light of subsequent legal developments. The Restatement Second of Torts, which took 24 years to complete, eventually superseded and entirely replaced its predecessor, no portion of which, therefore, is included in this volume. The Reporters for Torts Second were two of the most eminent torts scholars of the 20th century, William L. Prosser of the University of California's Hastings College of the Law and John W. Wade of Vanderbilt University. The initial drafting was almost entirely the work of Prosser, and the first 19 Chapters were approved by the Institute and published while he was still the Reporter. After Prosser's resignation in 1970, Wade assumed the responsibility of revising Prosser's drafts of the remaining Chapters, presenting them for approval, and overseeing their publication.

By 1991 additional major developments in the law of torts had convinced the Institute that the time had come to begin a Third Restatement of the subject. This time, however, it was decided to concentrate at the outset on the specific areas of tort law most immediately in need of revision or expansion and to proceed by way of specific integrated projects within the broader framework of a complete Restatement of Torts. The initial project, a reexamination of products-liability law, was a particularly appropriate one for the Institute to undertake in light of the extraordinary influence of its previous treatment of this topic. Because of the broad development of the case law in the intervening years, Restatement Third, Torts: Products Liability, which was approved in 1997 and published in 1998, was able to present a far more expansive, nuanced, and sophisticated analysis of this complex and challenging subject than had been possible for the previous Restatement to achieve three decades earlier. Its Reporters were James A. Henderson, Jr., of Cornell University and Aaron D. Twerski of Brooklyn Law School.

The second segment of Torts Third to be undertaken was an analysis of the apportionment of liability in cases in which multiple tortfeasors may be responsible in varying degrees for a single injury, a problem that has become particularly acute and difficult to resolve in comparative-negligence regimes, which may require that the plaintiff's own degree of fault be entered into the equation. The Reporters for Restatement Third, Torts: Apportionment of Liability, which was approved in 1999 and published in 2000, were William C. Powers, Jr., of the University of Texas and Michael D. Green of the University of Iowa.

The third and largest segment of Restatement Third, Torts, is the work on Liability for Physical and Emotional Harm. This was begun by Professor Gary T. Schwartz of the University of California at Los Angeles. After Professor Schwartz's untimely death in 2001, the work was undertaken by Professor Michael Green of Wake Forest University and President William Powers of the University of Texas. That two-volume work is now complete, with the final Chapter completed by Professor Ellen Pryor, currently the Associate Dean for Academic Affairs of the University of North Texas at Dallas College of Law. Dean Ward Farnsworth of the University of Texas is now at work on Torts: Liability for Economic Harm, and Professor Pryor, along with Professor Kenneth Simons of Boston University, will soon begin to draft Sections on Intentional Torts.

In all, the various Torts Restatements have been cited more than 77,000 times by the state and federal courts and have contributed immeasurably to the clarification of tort law throughout the United States.

C. THE RESTATEMENT THIRD OF TORTS: LIABILITY FOR PHYSICAL AND EMOTIONAL HARM

Michael D. Green and William C. Powers, Jr., Reporters,
The Restatement Third of Torts: Liability for
Physical and Emotional Harm

Begun in the mid-1990s, the Restatement Third of Torts: Liability for Physical and Emotional Harm addresses the core principles of liability for physical harm. It provides rules for liability for intentional, negligence, and strict-liability torts that result in physical injury. Later, it was expanded to include liability for emotional harm, and it now encompasses claims for stand-alone emotional harm.

The central concept in this Restatement is the idea of creation of risk. An actor who creates a risk is subject to a presumptive duty of care. An actor who has had no hand in creating the risk that was the source of an injured person's harm is ordinarily not subject to a duty and therefore not subject to liability to that injured person.

What does it mean to create a risk? Every day, each of us creates risks of physical harm to others. We do so when we drive a car, ride a bicycle, hit a baseball, leave a skateboard on a sidewalk, dispose of hazardous waste, or slam a door. All of those acts create risks to others, although thankfully the majority of the time no harm occurs.

Section 7(a) states the principle: an actor must exercise reasonable care with regard to the risks created by that actor. When an actor fails to exercise reasonable care, i.e., acts negligently, that actor is subject to tort liability. By "subject to liability" we mean that it is a necessary but not sufficient condition for liability. (See more below on the other conditions for liability contained in this Restatement.)

But the rule imposing a duty of reasonable care in § 7(a) is not without exceptions. Section 7(b) elaborates that when important reasons of principle or policy require negating or modifying this duty, courts can and should do so. Thus, a court might decide that despite the words that the defendant spoke—publishing a story on self-mutilation by adolescents—thus encouraging "copycat" behavior, First Amendment concerns should override any imposition of tort liability. Or the decision of a police officer to pursue a high-speed chase of a suspected criminal perpetrator might be found too important to subject the decision to engage in such chases to be skewed because of liability concerns. What this Restatement does not do is identify the specific principles or policies that might affect this ordinary duty of reasonable care. Instead it merely exhorts courts to be transparent and articulate the principle or policy that calls for negating or modifying the ordinary duty.

5

Before leaving this concept of duty and proceeding to negligence or reasonable care, two matters justify tarrying. It is often said that "duty" is the first element of a plaintiff's prima facie case and that the plaintiff has the burden of proving it. It is true that duty is an element of a prima facie case for negligence. But it is misleading to say that a plaintiff must "prove" it. Duty, unlike the other four elements of a prima facie case, is a matter of law and therefore for the court to decide. Ordinarily, the facts of the case that are not in dispute (for example, the defendant was driving her car) will be sufficient to establish that a duty existed and so, in that sense, there is no need for evidence to be introduced specifically to prove duty. See § 6, Comment b. Thus, it may be more accurate to say that plaintiff must "establish" the existence of a duty, but of course when the defendant's conduct has created a risk of harm ordinarily there will be no dispute that a duty exists.

A well-established tort-law rule is that there is no duty to rescue another. Thus, even if one could easily and at little risk rescue an infant lying on railroad tracks with a train in the distance, there is no duty to do so and hence no liability for any harm that may befall the child. But several exceptions to this no-duty principle exist, so-called affirmative duties. These affirmative duties are catalogued in Chapter 7 of the Third Restatement and can be found in this book.

Chapter 3 of the Physical and Emotional Harm Restatement rehearses many aspects of negligence, including the role of safety statutes and customary conduct, circumstantial proof of negligence, and the role of disabilities, such as youthfulness, blindness, or mental deficiency in modifying the concept of reasonable care under the circumstances. Chapter 4 spells out the limited bases for strict liability—when liability is imposed although an actor has acted without fault. Strict liability is not absolute liability in the sense that it requires only a showing that the defendant's act caused harm. The conditions for imposing strict liability, for example when engaging in especially dangerous conduct, are also explained in this Chapter.

Causation is the glue that connects the defendant's tortious conduct and the plaintiff's harm. All torts require factual causation. Section 26 contains this requirement, § 27 contains an important supplement, and § 28 addresses on whom the burden of proof is placed. Included in § 28 is a lengthy Comment on proving causation in toxic-substances litigation when a defendant's drug, chemical, or other agent causes disease in others. The need to address causation in this context, a topic which is absent from the Second Restatement, reflects the development of litigation concerning asbestos, cigarettes, prescription drugs, and other chemicals in the latter part of the 20th century. Indeed, the treatment of causation in the Third Restatement is markedly different from its treatment in the Second Restatement.

6

You will, during your study of tort law, confront "proximate cause," which is neither about proximity nor about causation. For that and other reasons the Third Restatement adopts different terminology, "scope of liability," to reflect that even though a defendant breached a duty and caused the plaintiff harm, the defendant still may not be liable. Section 29 is the core provision and other Sections contained in Chapter 6 provide further elaboration and important exceptions.

Tort law is not only about the different bases for liability—intentional, negligent, and strict-liability torts—but also about the protection provided to different interests of potential victims. Protections of bodily integrity and private property are a central interest protected by tort law and hence the Liability for Physical and Emotional Harm Restatement addresses that core—physical harm. Emotional harm is more problematic than physical harm, at least because emotional harm can be so widespread when a calamitous event occurs. Think of the assassination of a well-liked President, the death of a popular performer, or a terrorist attack such as 9/11. Thus, tort law has more carefully cabined liability for causing "stand-alone" emotional harm. Chapter 8 reflects that reduced protection while at the same time recognizing that courts have expanded recovery for emotional harm in the period since the Second Restatement was published.

Chapter 9 reflects the tension between property law with its premise that a person's home (or property) is theirs to do with as they like and tort law, which protects individuals from physical harm. Historically, land possessors were not subject to the same duties to those on private property as those that addressed harm to persons not on private property. Instead, a tiered set of duties was owed to entrants based on the type of entrant who was harmed. As society has changed from being largely agrarian with substantial private ownership of undeveloped land to one with more densely packed and developed land, courts have reformed the categorical duty approach and moved toward a unitary duty of reasonable care by land possessors to those on the land. There is, despite that reform, much devil in the details, which Chapter 9 addresses and attempts to work out in the ALI tradition of coherency and transparency.

Throughout this Restatement, unlike the earlier Restatements, influenced by the formalist approach popular when the first Restatement was drafted, are explanations of the policies that drive the doctrine. In addition, although not included in this volume, documentation of how courts have decided the issue addressed and variances that exist among courts and with the provisions in this Restatement is provided in the Reporters' Notes.

Restatements are not simply a "restatement" of what courts have done. In many cases they attempt to synthesize decisions that seem disparate or confused. Sometimes, they attempt to rationalize a doctrine that has developed by accretion over time. Sometimes they are prescriptive rather than descriptive, providing rules that the Institute believes are an improvement. Herbert Wechsler, at the time the Director of the Institute, explained in words that now grace the wall of the conference room at the Institute: "[W]e should feel obliged in our deliberations to give weight to all of the considerations that the courts, under a proper view of the judicial function, deem it right to weigh in theirs." As you consider the materials in these Restatements, consider whether they appear to be simply descriptive of tort law as you learn it, a synthesis of variations that exist among the states which are free to make tort law as they see fit, or an attempt to lead courts to a more appropriate rule of law.

PART II
INTENTIONAL HARM TO PERSONS OR PROPERTY

CHAPTER 2

INTENTIONAL HARM TO PERSONS

A. GENERAL PRINCIPLES

§ 1. Intent

Restatement of the Law Third, Torts: Liability for Physical and Emotional Harm

A person acts with the intent to produce a consequence if:

    (a) the person acts with the purpose of producing that consequence; or

    (b) the person acts knowing that the consequence is substantially certain to result.

10

Comment:

a. The dual definition. For a variety of reasons, tort law must distinguish between intentional and nonintentional consequences and harms (including harms that may be negligent, reckless, or without fault). Harms that are tortious if caused intentionally may not be tortious if caused unintentionally; affirmative defenses available in negligence cases may not be available when the underlying tort is intentional; the limitation period may vary depending on whether the tort is one of intent or instead one of negligence. . . .

There are obvious differences between the actor who acts with the desire to cause harm and the actor who engages in conduct knowing that harm is substantially certain to happen. There is a clear element of wrongfulness in conduct whose very purpose is to cause harm. . . .

When the actor chooses to engage in conduct with knowledge that harm is certain to follow. . . . [n]ot only does the actor not desire to produce the harmful result, but the actor may be engaging in a generally proper activity for generally proper reasons, even though the activity produces harm as an unavoidable but unwanted byproduct. This can provide an element of justification or reasonableness that is lacking for purposeful harms. . . . [Courts] in particular contexts might want to distinguish between intent in the sense of purpose and intent in the sense of knowledge. . . .

b. Intentional consequences and intentional harms. In general, the intent required in order to show that the defendant's conduct is an intentional tort is the intent to bring about harm (more precisely, to bring about the type of harm to an interest that the particular tort seeks to protect). . . . [T]his Section's Comments focus on intent in the sense of the intent to cause a harmful consequence. In this regard, it can be observed that people all the time voluntarily engage in conduct—swinging a golf club, raising a stick so as to separate two dogs, turning a steering wheel in order to turn a car on a highway, selling a product, transmitting electricity through power lines—that turns out to result in harm. These facts alone do not show that the harm has been intentionally caused for purposes of the law of intentional torts.

Illustration:

1. In a forest area, Ken deliberately pulls the trigger of a rifle. He hopes to hit a wild deer, and he is unaware that any person is in the vicinity. The gun discharges. In fact, Nancy is nearby and is struck by the bullet. Ken has intentionally shot his gun. Yet he has not intentionally caused the harm to Nancy; he did not act with the purpose to produce that harm nor did he know that the harm was substantially certain to occur.

Given the focus of intentional torts on the intention to produce harm, questions sometimes arise when the harm suffered turns out to differ from the harm the actor originally intended. . . .

c. *Purpose and substantially certain knowledge: coverage and relationship.* A purpose to cause harm makes the harm intentional even if harm is not substantially certain to occur. Likewise, knowledge that harm is substantially certain to result is sufficient to show that the harm is intentional even in the absence of a purpose to bring about that harm. Of course, a mere showing that harm is substantially certain to result from the actor's conduct is not sufficient to prove intent; it must also be shown that the actor is aware of this. . . .

Illustrations:

2. Wendy throws a rock at Andrew, someone she dislikes, at a distance of 100 feet, wanting to hit Andrew. Given the distance, it is far from certain Wendy will succeed in this; rather, it is probable that the rock will miss its target. In fact, Wendy's aim is true, and Andrew is struck by the rock. Wendy has purposely, and hence intentionally, caused this harm.

3. The Jones Company runs an aluminum smelter, which emits particulate fluorides as part of the industrial process. Jones knows that these particles, carried by the air, will land on neighboring property, and in doing so will bring about a range of harms. Far from desiring this result, Jones in fact regrets it. Despite its regret, Jones has knowingly, and hence intentionally, caused the resulting harms.

5. Joanne, a physician, provides medication to her patient, Mark. Because Joanne has confused one medication with another, the medication she gives Mark is certain to cause harm to Mark. Such harm ensues. Joanne has not intentionally harmed Mark. While Joanne's conduct was substantially certain to cause him harm, Joanne lacked the knowledge that this would happen.

e. *Substantial certainty: limits.* . . . . The applications of the substantial-certainty test should be limited to situations in which the defendant has knowledge to a substantial certainty that the conduct will bring about harm to a particular victim, or to someone within a small class of potential victims within a localized area. The test loses its persuasiveness when the identity of potential victims becomes vaguer and when, in a related way, the time frame involving the actor's conduct expands and the causal sequence connecting conduct and harm becomes more complex. . . . Moreover, in many situations a defendant's knowledge of substantially certain harms is entirely consistent with the absence of any liability in tort. For example, an owner of land, arranging for the construction of a high-rise building, can confidently

12

predict that some number of workers will be seriously injured in the course of the construction project; the company that runs a railroad can be sure that railroad operations will over time result in a significant number of serious personal injuries; the manufacturer of knives can easily predict that a certain number of persons using its knives will inadvertently cut themselves. Despite their knowledge, these actors do not intentionally cause the injuries that result. . . .

§ 2. Recklessness

Restatement of the Law Third, Torts: Liability for Physical and Emotional Harm

A person acts recklessly in engaging in conduct if:

(a) the person knows of the risk of harm created by the conduct or knows facts that make the risk obvious to another in the person's situation, and

(b) the precaution that would eliminate or reduce the risk involves burdens that are so slight relative to the magnitude of the risk as to render the person's failure to adopt the precaution a demonstration of the person's indifference to the risk.

Comment:

a. Terminology and scope. Terms conveying the idea of wrongdoing that is aggravated—even though falling short of the wrongdoing involved in intentional torts—are common in the discourse of torts. Sometimes, the term used is "gross negligence." Taken at face value, this term simply means negligence that is especially bad. Given this literal interpretation, gross negligence carries a meaning that is less than recklessness. The term "willful or wanton misconduct" is also frequently employed. "Willful misconduct" sometimes refers to conduct involving an intent to cause harm; but "wanton misconduct" is commonly understood to mean recklessness. Frequently, courts refer to conduct that displays a "reckless disregard for risk" or a "reckless indifference to risk." When a person's conduct creates a known risk that can be reduced by relatively modest precautions, to state that the person displays a reckless disregard for risk is equivalent to stating that the person's conduct is reckless. . . .

b. Significance. Not only do several different terms convey the idea of aggravated misconduct, but those terms are themselves deployed in a wide variety of legal contexts. While there are general rules exposing persons to liability who cause harm intentionally (§ 5) or negligently (§ 6), there is no similar general rule subjecting to liability the person who causes harm recklessly. . . .

Furthermore, . . . [w]hile a showing of negligence generally suffices for compensatory damages, the standard for awarding punitive damages commonly refers to the defendant's reckless conduct. . . .

In general, the meaning of a legal term can vary from one legal context to another, as the purposes and policies relating to each context are taken into account. . . .

c. Factors that bear on recklessness: the obviousness of the risk. . . . This Section [ ] requires that the person either have knowledge of the danger or have knowledge of facts that would make the danger obvious to anyone in the actor's situation. If the danger is obvious, then any of three assessments is possible. The first is that the person in fact knew of the risk, even though direct proof of such knowledge may be lacking. . . . The second possible assessment is that the actor—for fear of what might be learned—has, in a studied way, refused to consider the implications of the facts the actor knew. . . . A third assessment is that the actor's denial of actual knowledge of the danger, while sincere, is nevertheless disturbing. . . . Whichever of these three assessments is most pertinent in the individual case, the obviousness of the danger serves to support a finding of recklessness.

The obviousness requirement in Subsection (a) does not require that the risk be obvious to all, but rather obvious to others in the actor's situation. Take the power company that knows that one of its transformers is malfunctioning. Even if people in general would be unaware of the dangers that are involved in a malfunctioning transformer, if those dangers are obvious to power companies generally, Subsection (a) applies. In other cases, those in the actor's situation have less knowledge about risks than the average person, and in such cases it is the knowledge of the former that is taken into account. If, for example, the actor is a 10-year-old child, the question is whether the risk is obvious to other actors of the same age. While inexperience and mental disability are ordinarily not taken into account in assessing whether the actor's conduct is negligent, when the issue is the actor's recklessness the question to be considered is whether the risk would have been obvious to other beginners or others suffering from a like mental disability.

d. The imbalance between the magnitude of the risk and the burden of precautions. Under § 3, negligence is defined in terms of the failure to exercise reasonable care, and reasonable care is explained primarily in terms of the balance between the magnitude of the foreseeable risk and the burden of precautions that can eliminate the risk. The "magnitude" of the risk includes both the likelihood of a harm-causing incident and the severity of the harm that may ensue. If the burden is greater than the magnitude of the risk, the actor who declines to adopt that precaution is generally not negligent. But if the risk is somewhat greater than the burden, the actor is negligent for failing to adopt the precaution.

14

e. Factors that are not decisive: likelihood of harm. . . . [T]he more "probable" the harm, the greater the overall magnitude of the risk created by the actor's conduct . . . but a requirement that harm be "probable" should not be a rigid prerequisite for a finding of recklessness. Consider the driver whose 100-mile-per-hour speeding creates a clear risk of injury; but given the length of the driver's trip, the possibility of harm is by rough estimate no greater than 25 percent. Consider also the person who, hoping to frighten, shoots a gun in the direction of another knowing that there is a live bullet in only one of the six chambers. In neither of these cases is a finding of "probable" harm appropriate; yet in neither case should the absence of such a finding rule out a determination that the actor has been reckless.

If a high probability of harm is not always a necessary condition for a finding of recklessness, neither is it always a sufficient condition for such a finding. . . . Thus a railroad company, knowing that persons will certainly be injured on account of railroad operations, does not for that reason alone bear liability for those injuries; nor does a manufacturer bear liability merely because it produces and distributes a prescription drug, knowing that some number of consumers will suffer adverse reactions.

f. Severity of harm. . . . [A] risk of serious bodily injury is not a firm prerequisite for a finding of recklessness. Such a prerequisite would preclude a finding of recklessness whenever the actor's conduct creates a risk merely of property damage, of moderate personal injury, or of emotional harm. . . . Nevertheless, unless the harm threatened by the actor's conduct is substantial, a finding of recklessness is not appropriate. For example, a person would ordinarily not be found reckless for mishandling, and thereby endangering, a drinking glass owned by another. . . .

§ 5. Liability for Intentional Physical Harm

Restatement of the Law Third, Torts: Liability for Physical and Emotional Harm

An actor who intentionally causes physical harm is subject to liability for that harm.

Comment:

a. An umbrella rule. The rule of liability in this Section does not replace the doctrines for specific intentional torts, such as battery, assault, false imprisonment, and others. Rather, this Section provides a framework that encompasses many specific torts for intentionally caused physical harm. . . .

The general statement of liability in this Section highlights the point that tort law treats the intentional infliction of physical harm differently than it treats the intentional causation of eco-

15

nomic loss or the intentional infliction of emotional harm. In cases involving physical harm, proof of intent provides a basic case for liability, although various affirmative defenses may be available. However, as the focus shifts from physical harm to other forms of harm, the intent to cause harm may be an important but not a sufficient condition for liability. For example, when the defendant intentionally causes the plaintiff to suffer the loss of prospective economic advantage, in order to secure recovery the plaintiff ordinarily must show that the defendant's conduct is not only intentional but also "improper" or wrongful by some measure other than the fact of the interference. When the defendant either intentionally or recklessly causes the plaintiff to suffer emotional harm, to justify a recovery the plaintiff must further establish that the defendant's conduct is "extreme and outrageous" and that the plaintiff's emotional harm is "severe". . . .

As far as the importance of the line between intent and negligence is concerned, the law of torts can be compared to the law of crimes. In the latter, that line is of critical significance. Arson, for example, is a crime that requires more than negligence in initiating the fire. Indeed, the highest grade of arson requires purpose on the part of the defendant; it is not satisfied even by the defendant's recklessness. Tort law, however, recognizes a broad rule of negligence liability in cases involving physical harm. See § 6. In light of this rule, whether the defendant intentionally sets the fire so as to cause harm or is only negligent in its initiation, the defendant is liable in tort for all the harm caused by the fire itself and within the scope of liability. Given the broad standard of liability for physical harm in § 6, in tort law the line between intent and negligence is much less significant than is the same line within the criminal law.

However, in a number of physical-harm cases, the plaintiff's ability to prove intent may benefit the plaintiff in significant respects. It may, for example, eliminate or subordinate certain affirmative defenses, such as assumption of risk and comparative negligence. It may render more generous the rules relating to scope of liability. See § 33. It may also set the stage for the award of punitive damages.

Nevertheless, and somewhat ironically—given that intentional torts are generally deemed considerably more serious than torts of mere negligence—in certain circumstances the plaintiff is worse off if the tort committed against the plaintiff is classified as intentional rather than negligent. In some jurisdictions, for example, the statute of limitations is shorter for intentional torts than for negligent torts. If the tort was committed by an employee of the defendant being sued, classifying the employee's tort as intentional makes it more difficult for the plaintiff to show the tort was committed within the scope of the employee's employment. For reasons somewhat related to vicarious liability, if the plaintiff's suit is against a

16

public entity, a rule of immunity may apply to intentional torts committed by a public employee but not to the employee's negligent torts. In private litigation, the plaintiff may expect that an eventual judgment will be covered by the defendant's insurance policy, and that policy may exclude coverage for intentional torts; accordingly, the plaintiff can be worse off if the tort is intentional rather than negligent.

   b. Subject to liability: the affirmative defenses. The language of "subject to liability" acknowledges the possibility of various affirmative defenses and other liability-limiting doctrines. These may include consent, self-defense, defense of third persons, protection of land and chattels, and privileges relating to discipline. The various affirmative defenses identify those situations in which the law has concluded that the intentional infliction of physical harm is either justifiable or excusable.

§ 33. Scope of Liability for Intentional and Reckless Tortfeasors

Restatement of the Law Third, Torts: Liability for Physical and Emotional Harm

   (a) An actor who intentionally causes harm is subject to liability for that harm even if it was unlikely to occur.

   (b) An actor who intentionally or recklessly causes harm is subject to liability for a broader range of harms than the harms for which that actor would be liable if only acting negligently. In general, the important factors in determining the scope of liability are the moral culpability of the actor, as reflected in the reasons for and intent in committing the tortious acts, the seriousness of harm intended and threatened by those acts, and the degree to which the actor's conduct deviated from appropriate care.

   (c) Notwithstanding Subsections (a) and (b), an actor who intentionally or recklessly causes harm is not subject to liability for harm the risk of which was not increased by the actor's intentional or reckless conduct.

Comment:

   a. The inadequacy of the risk standard. . . . To the extent that scope of liability is employed to prevent a defendant's liability from being out of proportion with the tortfeasor's culpability, the scope of liability for intentional and reckless tortfeasors should be broader than for negligent or strictly liable tortfeasors. . . .

   c. Transferred intent. Another rule expanding the scope of li-

17

ability for intentional tortfeasors beyond that which the risk standard might impose is the doctrine of transferred intent. The doctrine of transferred intent, specific to intentional torts, does some of the work of expanding the scope of liability for an intentional tortfeasor, although it is not formally an aspect of scope of liability. Instead, it is treated as an aspect of whether the intent element is satisfied and provides that, if an actor has the requisite intent to cause harm to one person, that intent will be "transferred" if the actor harms another person, even if that other person is unforeseeable. Transferred intent is particularly applicable in the trespassory torts, which are the intentional torts most likely to involve physical harm, the primary type of injury covered by this Restatement.

e. Expanded scope of liability for unintended harms. . . . For intentional tortfeasors, the factors important for assessing moral culpability include: whether the tortfeasor acted with the purpose to cause harm or only with the knowledge that the harm was substantially certain to occur; the maliciousness of the tortfeasor's intent; and the seriousness of the harm intended. For reckless tortfeasors, the relevant considerations would include the extent to which the tortfeasor knew of and appreciated the danger and the extent of the gap between the harm risked and the precautions required to prevent the harm. . . .

[T]his Comment only addresses the scope of liability for harm factually caused. . . .

Illustration:

2. Mike, who suffered from manic depression, was injured while walking through a high-school parking lot by a bomb that exploded. The homemade bomb was placed there by Dick and Anna with the intent that it explode and harm those in the vicinity. A year after he was injured by the bomb, Mike committed suicide. The administrator of Mike's estate sues Dick and Anna within the applicable limitations period. Damages for Mike's death may be found by the factfinder to be within the scope of Dick's and Anna's liability for their intentional conduct. However, before Dick and Anna may be found liable for Mike's death, the factfinder must determine that the injury from the bomb was a factual cause of Mike's suicide. . . .

f. Tortious conduct did not increase the risk of harm. Just as with scope of liability for nonintentional tortious conduct, intentional and reckless tortfeasors are not liable for harms whose risks were not increased by the tortious conduct, even if that conduct was a factual cause of the harm. . . .

g. Intentional infliction of emotional harm. This Section is

18

limited to determining the scope of liability for intentional and reckless tortfeasors who inflict physical harm upon the plaintiff. The scope of liability for those tortfeasors who intentionally or recklessly inflict pure stand-alone emotional harm is determined according to the requirements found in § 46.

B. BATTERY

§ 13. Battery: Harmful Contact

Restatement of the Law Second, Torts

> **An actor is subject to liability to another for battery if**
>
> > **(a) he acts intending to cause a harmful or offensive contact with the person of the other or a third person, or an imminent apprehension of such a contact, and**
> >
> > **– (b) a harmful contact with the person of the other directly or indirectly results.**

Comment:

   c. If an act is done with the intention described in this Section, it is immaterial that the actor is not inspired by any personal hostility to the other, or a desire to injure him. Thus the fact that the defendant who intentionally inflicts bodily harm upon another does so as a practical joke, does not render him immune from liability so long as the other has not consented. This is true although the actor erroneously believes that the other will regard it as a joke, or that the other has, in fact, consented to it. One who plays dangerous practical jokes on others takes the risk that his victims may not appreciate the humor of his conduct and may not take it in good part. So too, a surgeon who performs an operation upon a patient who has refused to submit to it is not relieved from liability by the fact that he honestly and, indeed, justifiably believes that the operation is necessary to save the patient's life. Indeed, the fact that medical testimony shows that the patient would have died had the operation not been performed and that the operation has effected a complete cure is not enough to relieve the physician from liability.

   d. . . . . [T]he absence of consent is a matter essential to the cause of action, and it is uniformly held that it must be proved by the plaintiff as a necessary part of his case.

§ 16. Character of Intent Necessary *transfer intent*

Restatement of the Law Second, Torts

> **(1) If an act is done with the intention of inflicting upon another an offensive but not a harm-**

19

ful bodily contact, or of putting another in apprehension of either a harmful or offensive bodily contact, and such act causes a bodily contact to the other, the actor is liable to the other for a battery although the act was not done with the intention of bringing about the resulting bodily harm.

(2) If an act is done with the intention of affecting a third person in the manner stated in Subsection (1), but causes a harmful bodily contact to another, the actor is liable to such other as fully as though he intended so to affect him.

Comment on Subsection (1):

a. In order that the actor shall be liable under the rule stated in this Section, it is not necessary that he intend to bring about the harmful contact which results from his act. It is enough that he intends to bring about an offensive contact or an apprehension of either a harmful or offensive contact, and that the bodily harm results as a legal consequence from such offensive contact or from such apprehension. . . .

Illustrations:

1. Intending an offensive contact, A lightly kicks B on the shin. The blow, although offensive, is so slight that it would normally cause no bodily harm. B is suffering from a diseased leg, of which A neither knows nor has reason to know. The slight blow so aggravates the diseased condition as to result in a prolonged and expensive illness, which finally leads to permanent harm to the leg. A is subject to liability to B for the bodily harm caused by his act.

2. A is playing golf. B, his caddie, is inattentive and A becomes angry. Intending to frighten but not to harm B, A aims a blow at him with a golf club which he stops some eight inches from B's head. Owing to the negligence of the club maker from whom A has just bought the club, the rivet which should have secured the head is defective, though A could not have discovered the defect without removing the head. The head of the club flies off and strikes B in the eye, putting it out. A is subject to liability to B for the loss of his eye.

Comment on Subsection (2):

b. The intention which is necessary to make the actor liable under the rule stated in this Section is not necessarily an intention to cause a harmful or offensive contact or an apprehension of such contact to the plaintiff himself or otherwise to cause him bodily harm. It is enough that the actor intends to produce such an effect upon some other person and that his act so intended is the legal cause of a harmful contact to the other. It is not necessary that the actor know or have reason even to suspect that the other is in the vicinity of the third person whom the actor intends to affect and, therefore, that he should recognize that his act, though directed against the third person, involves a risk of causing bodily harm to the other so that the act would be negligent toward him.

Illustration:

3. A and B are trespassers upon C's land. C sees A but does not see B, nor does he know that B is in the neighborhood. C throws a stone at A. Immediately after C has done so, B raises his head above a wall behind which he has been hiding. The stone misses A but strikes B, putting out his eye. C is subject to liability to B.

§ 18. Battery: Offensive Contact

Restatement of the Law Second, Torts

(1) **An actor is subject to liability to another for battery if**

(a) **he acts intending to cause a harmful or offensive contact with the person of the other or a third person, or an imminent apprehension of such a contact, and**

(b) **an offensive contact with the person of the other directly or indirectly results.**

(2) **An act which is not done with the intention stated in Subsection (1, a) does not make the actor liable to the other for a mere offensive contact with the other's person although the act involves an unreasonable risk of inflicting it and, therefore, would be negligent or reckless if the risk threatened bodily harm.**

Comment:

c. Meaning of "contact with another's person." In order to make the actor liable under the rule stated in this Section, it is not necessary that he should bring any part of his own body in contact with another's person. It is enough that he intentionally cause his clothing or anything held or attached to him to come into such contact. So too, he is liable under the rule stated in this Section if he throws a substance, such as water, upon the other or if he sets a dog upon him. . . . All that is necessary is that the actor intend to cause the other, directly or indirectly, to come in contact with a foreign substance in a manner which the other will reasonably regard as offensive. Thus, if the actor daubs with filth a towel which he expects another to use in wiping his face with the expectation that the other will smear his face with it and the other does so, the actor is liable as fully as though he had directly thrown the filth in the other's face or had otherwise smeared his face with it. . . .

Since the essence of the plaintiff's grievance consists in the offense to the dignity involved in the unpermitted and intentional invasion of the inviolability of his person and not in any physical harm done to his body, it is not necessary that the plaintiff's actual body be disturbed. Unpermitted and intentional contacts with anything so connected with the body as to be customarily regarded as part of the other's person and therefore as partaking of its inviolability is actionable as an offensive contact with his person. There are some things such as clothing or a cane or, indeed, anything directly grasped by the hand which are so intimately connected with one's body as to be universally regarded as part of the person. On the other hand, there may be things which are attached to one's body with a connection so slight that they are not so regarded. The line of distinction is very difficult to draw. It is a thing which is felt rather than one to be defined, since it depends upon an emotional reaction. Thus, the ordinary man might well regard a horse upon which he is riding as part of his personality but, a passenger in a public omnibus or other conveyance would clearly not be entitled so to regard the vehicle merely because he was seated in it. . . .

d. Knowledge of contact. In order that the actor may be liable under the statement in this Subsection, it is not necessary that the other should know of the offensive contact which is inflicted upon him at the time when it is inflicted. The actor's liability is based upon his intentional invasion of the other's dignitary interest in the inviolability of his person and the affront to the other's dignity involved therein. This affront is as keenly felt by one who only knows after the event that an indignity has been perpetrated upon him as by one who is conscious of it while it is being perpetrated.

Illustrations:

1. A, a surgeon, while B is under anesthesia, makes an examination of her person to which she has not given her consent. A is subject to liability to B.

2. A kisses B while asleep but does not waken or harm her. A is subject to liability to B.

§ 19. What Constitutes Offensive Contact
Restatement of the Law Second, Torts

A bodily contact is offensive if it offends a reasonable sense of personal dignity.

Caveat:

The Institute expresses no opinion as to whether the actor is liable if he inflicts upon another a contact which he knows will be offensive to another's known but abnormally acute sense of personal dignity.

22

Comment:

a. In order that a contact be offensive to a reasonable sense of personal dignity, it must be one which would offend the ordinary person and as such one not unduly sensitive as to his personal dignity. It must, therefore, be a contact which is unwarranted by the social usages prevalent at the time and place at which it is inflicted.

Illustrations:

1. A flicks a glove in B's face. This is an offensive touching of B.

2. A, while walking in a densely crowded street, deliberately but not discourteously pushes against B in order to pass him. This is not an offensive touching of B.

3. A, who is suffering from a contagious skin disease, touches B's hands, thus putting B in reasonable apprehension of contagion. This is an offensive touching of B.

4. A, a child, becomes sick while riding in B's taxicab. B takes hold of A in order to help her. This is not an offensive touching.

C. Assault

§ 21. Assault

Restatement of the Law Second, Torts

(1) **An actor is subject to liability to another for assault if**

(a) **he acts intending to cause a harmful or offensive contact with the person of the other or a third person, or an imminent apprehension of such a contact, and**

(b) **the other is thereby put in such imminent apprehension.**

(2) **An action which is not done with the intention stated in Subsection (1, a) does not make the actor liable to the other for an apprehension caused thereby although the act involves an unreasonable risk of causing it and, therefore, would be negligent or reckless if the risk threatened bodily harm.**

Comment on Subsection (1):

c. In order that the actor shall be liable under the rule stated in this Section, it is only necessary that his act should cause an apprehension of an immediate contact, whether harmful or merely offensive. It is not necessary that it should directly or indirectly cause any tangible and material harm to the other. If, however, any such harm results to any legally protected interest of the other as a legal consequence of the apprehension, the other may recover damages for such harm as part of the damages recoverable in the action brought for the assault.

d. An act is done with the intention of putting the other in apprehension of an immediate harmful or offensive contact if it is done for the purpose of causing such an apprehension or with knowledge that, to a substantial certainty, such apprehension will result.

Comment on Subsection (2):

f. . . . The interest in freedom from apprehension of a harmful or offensive contact is protected only against acts intended to inflict a bodily contact or to cause an apprehension of such contact, and not against conduct which creates such a risk of it that, had the risk threatened bodily harm, it would constitute negligence.

§ 22.   Attempt Unknown to Other

Restatement of the Law Second, Torts

> **An attempt to inflict a harmful or offensive contact or to cause an apprehension of such contact does not make the actor liable for an assault if the other does not become aware of the attempt before it is terminated.**

Comment:

a. Subsequent knowledge of actor's effort. The rule [concerning assault] deals with liability imposed to protect the actor's interest in freedom from apprehension of immediate and harmful or offensive contacts. It is, therefore, necessary . . . that the act . . . should actually have put the plaintiff in apprehension of an immediate contact. Therefore, the defendant is not liable if his efforts to inflict the bodily contact have been abandoned or frustrated before the other is aware of them. . . .

Illustrations:

1. A, intending to frighten B, discharges a pistol behind his ear. B, who is stone deaf, does not hear the pistol, and does not discover what has happened until later. A is not liable to B.

2. A, standing behind B, points a pistol at him. C overpowers A before he can shoot. B, hearing the noise turns around and for the first time realizes the danger to which he had been subjected. A is not liable to B.

§ 30. Conditional Threat

Restatement of the Law Second, Torts

If the actor intentionally puts another in apprehension of an imminent and harmful or offensive contact, he is subject to liability for an assault although he gives to the other the option to escape the contact by obedience to a command given by the actor, unless the command is one which the actor is privileged to enforce by the infliction of the threatened contact or by a threat to inflict it.

Comment:

a. If the command is one which the actor is privileged to enforce by the infliction of the threatened contact, or by the threat to inflict it, he is not liable by reason of his privilege. If he is not so privileged, he is liable; and it is immaterial whether the other is under a legal duty to comply with the command itself, or whether he does or does not obey it. . . .

Illustrations:

1. A has forced his way into B's house and is making a disturbance. B comes up to A and asks him to leave the house. A refuses to do so. B then comes very close to A saying, "I will give you one minute to leave my house. If you don't, I will put you out." B, being privileged to use force against A's person to eject him from his house, is privileged to threaten to use it.

2. A, in discharging B, a servant, points a pistol at B's head and screams, in a state of great agitation, "Get right out of my house or I will shoot you dead." A is not privileged to enforce his command in this manner, and is subject to liability to B.

§ 31. Threat by Words

Restatement of the Law Second, Torts

Words do not make the actor liable for assault unless together with other acts or circumstances they put the other in reasonable apprehension of an imminent harmful or offensive contact with his person.

Comment:

a. Ordinarily mere words, unaccompanied by some act apparently intended to carry the threat into execution, do not put the other in apprehension of an imminent bodily contact, and so cannot make the actor liable for an assault. . . . For this reason it is commonly said in the decisions that mere words do not constitute an assault, or that some overt act is required. . . .

25

Illustration:

1. A, known to be a resolute and desperate character, threatens to waylay B on his way home on a lonely road on a dark night. A is not liable to B for an assault under the rule stated in § 21. A may, however, be liable to B for the infliction of severe emotional distress by extreme and outrageous conduct. . . .

b. Effect of words as indicating intention. This general rule must, however, be qualified in several respects. While mere words cannot render the speaker liable, words which accompany or precede acts known to the other and understood by him may be decisive evidence of the actor's intention to commit the assault and of the other's apprehension. An act which would normally be construed as indicating a sufficient purpose to inflict an immediate contact to make the actor liable, may be accompanied by words which make it clear that he has no intention to strike the other. Under ordinary circumstances, if the other has heard the actor's words, he must realize that the actor has no intention of striking him and is not put in apprehension of a bodily contact. . . .

c. Likewise, an act which under ordinary circumstances would not be understood as indicating a purpose to inflict a bodily contact may be accompanied or preceded by words or other conduct on the part of the actor which, if known to the other, are sufficient to make the act one which creates not only an apprehension but a reasonable apprehension that he is about to be attacked. In such case, the actor is liable if, knowing that the other is aware of his words or conduct, he does the act with the intention of putting the other in apprehension.

Illustrations:

3. A, during a quarrel with B, reaches for his hip pocket. Whether this act is an assault may depend upon whether A says "I will blow out your brains," or "Wait a minute; I need a handkerchief." It may likewise depend upon whether previous words or acts of A have indicated a desire to do B physical harm. . . .

4. A, a notorious gangster, who is known to have killed other men, telephones B and tells him that he will shoot him on sight. Coming around a corner, B encounters A standing on the sidewalk. Without moving, A says to B, "Your time has come." A is subject to liability to B for an assault.

D. FALSE IMPRISONMENT

§ 35. False Imprisonment

Restatement of the Law Second, Torts

(1) An actor is subject to liability to another for false imprisonment if

(a) he acts intending to confine the other or a third person within boundaries fixed by the actor, and

(b) his act directly or indirectly results in such a confinement of the other, and

(c) the other is conscious of the confinement or is harmed by it.

(2) An act which is not done with the intention stated in Subsection (1, a) does not make the actor liable to the other for a merely transitory or otherwise harmless confinement, although the act involves an unreasonable risk of imposing it and therefore would be negligent or reckless if the risk threatened bodily harm.

Caveat:

The Institute expresses no opinion as to whether the actor may not be subject to liability for conduct which involves an unreasonable risk of causing a confinement of such duration or character as to make the other's loss of freedom a matter of material value. . . .

Comment on Subsection (2):

h. Extent of protection of interest in freedom from confinement. Under this Section the actor is not liable unless his act is done for the purpose of imposing confinement upon the other, or with knowledge that such a confinement will, to a substantial certainty, result from it. It is not enough that the actor realizes or should realize that his actions involve a risk of causing a confinement, so long as the likelihood that it will do so falls short of a substantial certainty.

Illustration [under Subsection (2)]:

2. Just before closing time, A, a shopkeeper, sends B into a cold storage vault to take inventory of the articles therein. Forgetting that he has done so, he locks the door of the vault on leaving the premises. If in a few moments thereafter, he remembers that B is in the vault and immediately goes back and releases B, he is not liable to B for the momentary confinement to which B has been subjected. On the other hand, if he does not remember that B is in the vault until he reaches home and, therefore, although he acts immediately, he cannot release B until B has been confined in the cold vault for so long a time as to bring on a heavy cold which develops into pneumonia, he is subject to liability to B for the illness so caused.

27

§ 36. What Constitutes Confinement

Restatement of the Law Second, Torts

(1) To make the actor liable for false imprisonment, the other's confinement within the boundaries fixed by the actor must be complete.

(2) The confinement is complete although there is a reasonable means of escape, unless the other knows of it.

(3) The actor does not become liable for false imprisonment by intentionally preventing another from going in a particular direction in which he has a right or privilege to go.

Comment:

a. Means of escape. . . . Since the actor has intended to imprison the other, the other is not required to run any risk of harm to his person or to his chattels or of subjecting himself to any substantial liability to a third person. . . . So too, even though there may be a perfectly safe avenue of escape, the other is not required to take it if the circumstances are such as to make it offensive to a reasonable sense of decency or personal dignity.

On the other hand, it is unreasonable for one whom the actor intends to imprison to refuse to utilize a means of escape of which he is himself aware merely because it entails a slight inconvenience or requires him to commit a technical invasion of another's possessory interest in land or chattels which subjects him at most to the risk of an action for nominal damages which in practice is seldom if ever brought.

Illustrations:

1. A locks B, an athletic young man, in a room with an open window at a height of four feet from the floor and from the ground outside. A has not confined B.

2. A locks B, who is suffering from a disease which makes any considerable exertion dangerous to him, in such a room as supposed in Illustration 1. A has confined B.

4. A closes every exit except one, the use of which would involve material harm to B's clothing. A has confined B.

5. A is naked in a Turkish bath. B locks the door into the dressing room but leaves open the door to the general waiting room where persons of both sexes are congregated. B has confined A.

§ 39.   Confinement by Physical Force

Restatement of the Law Second, Torts

The confinement may be by overpowering physical force, or by submission to physical force.

Comment:

a. Under the rule stated in § 35, it is not necessary that the physical force should be such as to overcome the resistance of a man of ordinary strength. It is sufficient that physical force is exercised upon the person of another and that such other is restrained by the force or, without resistance, submits to it.

Illustrations:

1. A lays hold upon B and detains him notwithstanding B's effort to escape. A has confined B.

2. A, a small and weak man, takes hold of B's coat for the purpose of detaining him against his will. B is a much larger man and could, with little exertion, free himself at once. B submits. A has confined B.

§ 40.   Confinement by Threats of Physical Force

Restatement of the Law Second, Torts

The confinement may be by submission to a threat to apply physical force to the other's person immediately upon the other's going or attempting to go beyond the area in which the actor intends to confine him. . . .

Illustrations:

1. B, standing at the door some feet away, says to A, "If you attempt to leave this room, I will knock you down." B makes no threatening gesture. A, in submission to the threat remains in the room. B has confined A. . . .

2. A tells B that if he leaves the room he, A, will shoot him the next time he meets him on the street. B, in submission to the threat, remains in the room. A has not confined B. . . .

3. A threatens B that he will shoot him if he tries to leave the room. B knows that A has no weapon. B stays in the room. A has not confined B. . . .

§ 41. Confinement by Asserted Legal Authority

Restatement of the Law Second, Torts

(1) The confinement may be by taking a person into custody under an asserted legal authority.

(2) The custody is complete if the person against whom and in whose presence the authority is asserted believes it to be valid, or is in doubt as to its validity, and submits to it.

Illustrations:

1. A has in his possession an invalid warrant of arrest. He serves it upon B who, believing it to be valid, submits to it. A has confined B.

2. A, a private citizen, obtains a policeman's uniform and badge. While wearing both, he says to B, "I arrest you," the circumstances being such that a policeman, but not a private citizen, would be privileged to make the arrest. B, believing A to be a policeman, submits. A has confined B.

Comment:

b. Submission to asserted legal authority. It is not necessary that the person asserting an authority shall physically touch the other or take him under his physical control or that submission to the custody be procured by threats or be induced by fear of physical compulsion. If the authority is so asserted as to give the other reason to believe that, if it is not submitted to, physical force will be used to take him into custody under it, submission to the threats which may be inferred from such assertion of authority may constitute a confinement under the rule stated in § 35 even though the other knows the authority to be invalid.

CHAPTER 3

INTENTIONAL HARM TO LAND OR CHATTELS

A. TRESPASS ON LAND

§ 158. Liability for Intentional Intrusions on Land

Restatement of the Law Second, Torts

> One is subject to liability to another for trespass, irrespective of whether he thereby causes harm to any legally protected interest of the other, if he intentionally
>> (a) enters land in the possession of the other, or causes a thing or a third person to do so, or
>> (b) remains on the land, or
>> (c) fails to remove from the land a thing which he is under a duty to remove.

Comment:

b. Meaning of "enters land." Unless the context otherwise indicates, the phrase "enters land" is . . . used . . . to include, not only coming upon land, but also remaining on it, and, in addition, to include the presence upon the land of a third person or thing which the actor has caused to be or to remain there.

e. Conduct which would otherwise constitute a trespass is not a trespass if it is privileged. Such a privilege may be derived from

31

the consent of the possessor, or may be given by law because of the purpose for which the actor acts or refrains from acting.

f. . . . [O]ne whose presence on the land is not caused by any act of his own or by a failure on his part to perform a duty is not a trespasser.

g. A trespass on land may be committed by an intrusion upon the surface of the land or beneath or above the surface.

Comment on Clause (a):

i. Causing entry of a thing. The actor, without himself entering the land, may invade another's interest in its exclusive possession by throwing, propelling, or placing a thing either on or beneath the surface of the land or in the air space above it. Thus, in the absence of the possessor's consent or other privilege to do so, it is an actionable trespass to throw rubbish on another's land, even though he himself uses it as a dump heap, or to fire projectiles or to fly an advertising kite or balloon through the air above it, even though no harm is done to the land or to the possessor's enjoyment of it. . . .

Illustrations:

4. A intentionally drives a stray horse from his pasture into the pasture of his neighbor, B. A is a trespasser. . . .

6. A, on a public lake, intentionally discharges his shotgun over a point of land in B's possession, near the surface. The shot falls into the water on the other side. A is a trespasser.

j. Causing entry of a third person. If, by any act of his, the actor intentionally causes a third person to enter land, he is as fully liable as though he himself enters. . . .

Comment on Clause (b):

l. Failure to leave land. A trespass on land may be by a failure of the actor to leave the land of which the other is in possession, or a part of such land. If the possessor of the land has consented to the actor's presence on the land, his failure to leave after the expiration of the license is a trespass unless his continued presence on the land is otherwise privileged, or unless it amounts to a disseisin. . . .

§ 163. Intended Intrusions Causing No Harm

Restatement of the Law Second, Torts

> **One who intentionally enters land in the possession of another is subject to liability to the possessor for a trespass, although his presence on the**

land causes no harm to the land, its possessor, or to any thing or person in whose security the possessor has a legally protected interest.

Comment:

b. Intention. . . . . The intention which is required to make the actor liable under the rule stated in this Section is an intention to enter upon the particular piece of land in question, irrespective of whether the actor knows or should know that he is not entitled to enter. . . .

c. Purpose or motive. In order that the actor may intentionally enter a particular piece of land, it is not necessary that he act for the purpose of entering. It is enough that he knows that his conduct will result in such an entry, inevitably or to a substantial certainty. . . . Thus it is as much a trespass to enter the land of another without the other's consent or other privilege for the purpose of doing the possessor a favor, as where the actor's purpose is to offend the owner by coming on the land after he has been expressly ordered not to do so.

d. The wrong for which a remedy is given under the rule stated in this Section consists of an interference with the possessor's interest in excluding others from the land. Consequently, even a harmless entry or remaining, if intentional, is a trespass. This is true even though the possessor benefits from the trespass, as where the trespasser tears down a worthless building or prepares a field for cultivation. . . . A common use of the action of trespass is to obtain a determination of a plaintiff's right to exclusive possession.

e. The fact that the actor knows that his entry is without the consent of the possessor and without any other privilege to do so, while not necessary to make him liable, may affect the amount of damages recoverable against him, by showing such a complete disregard of the possessor's legally protected interest in the exclusive possession of his land as to justify the imposition of punitive in addition to nominal damages for even a harmless trespass, or in addition to compensatory damages for one which is harmful.

§ 164. Intrusions Under Mistake

Restatement of the Law Second, Torts

One who intentionally enters land in the possession of another is subject to liability to the possessor of the land as a trespasser, although he acts under a mistaken belief of law or fact, however reasonable, not induced by the conduct of the possessor, that he

(a) is in possession of the land or entitled to it, or

       (b) has the consent of the possessor or of a third person who has the power to give consent on the possessor's behalf, or

       (c) has some other privilege to enter or remain on the land.

Comment:

    a. In order to be liable for a trespass on land . . . it is necessary only that the actor intentionally be upon any part of the land in question. It is not necessary that he intend to invade the possessor's interest in the exclusive possession of his land and, therefore, that he know his entry to be an intrusion. . . .

    b. The actor is not liable for a merely harmless intrusion on land under a mistake induced by the conduct of the possessor. . . .

Illustrations:

    2. A mines coal from under B's land, having mistaken the location of the boundary line. A is subject to liability to B although the mistake is a reasonable one. . . .

    4. A, under a reasonable but mistaken belief that B is the owner and entitled to the possession of Blackacre, obtains from B a conveyance of Blackacre, and enters there. In fact C is the owner in possession of Blackacre. A is subject to liability to C. . . .

    10. A, having obtained from B, who is in possession of Blackacre, permission to enter Blackacre, enters Whiteacre in the reasonable but mistaken belief that Whiteacre is Blackacre. A is subject to liability to the possessor of Whiteacre, even though B is in possession of Whiteacre. . . .

    12. A, who is not a peace officer, mistakenly believing that a felony has been committed and that B has committed it, enters B's land to arrest B. A is subject to liability to B. . . .

    15. A, mistakenly but reasonably believing that B is murdering his wife, breaks into B's house to prevent the supposed murder. A's entry is not a trespass.

B. TRESPASS TO CHATTELS

§ 217. Ways of Committing Trespass to Chattel

Restatement of the Law Second, Torts

    A trespass to a chattel may be committed by intentionally

       (a) dispossessing another of the chattel, or

       (b) using or intermeddling with a chattel in the possession of another.

Comment:

c. *Character of intent necessary.* The intention required to make an actor liable for trespass to a chattel is . . . present when an act is done for the purpose of using or otherwise intermeddling with a chattel or with knowledge that such an intermeddling will, to a substantial certainty, result from the act. It is not necessary that the actor should know or have reason to know that such intermeddling is a violation of the possessory rights of another. Thus, it is immaterial that the actor intermeddles with the chattel under a mistake of law or fact which has led him to believe that he is the possessor of it or that the possessor has consented to his dealing with it. So too, a mistake of law or fact which leads him to believe even upon reasonable grounds that he is privileged to meddle with the chattel without the consent of the possessor does not prevent his act from being a trespass if the privilege is one which does not depend upon his reasonable belief, as where he acts to abate a private nuisance. On the other hand, the greater number of privileges require only the actor's reasonable belief that the necessary facts exist. In such cases, a mistake as to the existence of these facts does not destroy the privilege. Privilege is then based not on the facts but on the belief.

d. *Direct and indirect interference.* . . . [T]he rule stated in this Section is applicable irrespective of whether the intermeddling was the direct or indirect result of an act done by the actor, provided that his misconduct was the legal cause of the harm.

e. *Physical contact with chattel.* "Intermeddling" means intentionally bringing about a physical contact with the chattel. The actor may commit a trespass by an act which brings him into an intended physical contact with a chattel in the possession of another, as when he beats another's horse or dog, or by intentionally directing an object or missile against it, as when the actor throws a stone at another's automobile or intentionally drives his own car against it. So too, a trespass may be committed by causing a third person through duress or fraud to intermeddle with another's chattel. An actor may also commit a trespass by so acting upon a chattel as intentionally to cause it to come in contact with some other object, as when a herd of sheep is deliberately driven or frightened down a declivity. If such intermeddling with another's chattel is done without his consent and without any other privilege, the actor is subject to liability for harm thus caused to the chattel. . . .

§ 218. Liability to Person in Possession

Restatement of the Law Second, Torts

> **One who commits a trespass to a chattel is subject to liability to the possessor of the chattel if, but only if,**

(a) he dispossesses the other of the chattel, or

(b) the chattel is impaired as to its condition, quality, or value, or

(c) the possessor is deprived of the use of the chattel for a substantial time, or

(d) bodily harm is caused to the possessor, or harm is caused to some person or thing in which the possessor has a legally protected interest.

Comment:

a. This Section states the rule as to liability to the possessor of the chattel for a trespass to the chattel . . . The trespasser may also be liable to a person entitled to the immediate possession of the chattel . . . or to one entitled to the future possession of the chattel. . . .

b. . . . If the possessor consents to the actor's trespass, the actor is not liable to him under the rule stated in this Section. . . .

Comment on Clause (a):

d. Where the trespass to the chattel is a dispossession, the action will lie although there has been no impairment of the condition, quality, or value of the chattel, and no other harm to any interest of the possessor. He may recover at least nominal damages for the loss of possession, even though it is of brief duration and he is not deprived of the use of the chattel for any substantial length of time.

Illustration:

1. A, a police officer, has in his possession a writ directing him to levy execution upon the property of B. By mistake A goes to the house of C, and levies execution upon C's automobile, which is standing in C's driveway. A informs C that the car has been taken into the custody of the law, but does not remove it or otherwise interfere with it. An hour later the mistake is discovered, and the execution is discharged. A is subject to liability to C for at least nominal damages.

Comment on Clauses (b) and (c):

e. . . . [O]ne who intentionally intermeddles with another's chattel is subject to liability only if his intermeddling is harmful to the possessor's materially valuable interest in the physical condition, quality, or value of the chattel, or if the possessor is deprived of the use of the chattel for a substantial time, or some other legally protected interest of the possessor is affected as stated in Clause (c). . . .

Illustration:

> 2. A, a child, climbs upon the back of B's large dog and pulls its ears. No harm is done to the dog, or to any other legally protected interest of B. A is not liable to B. . . .

g. Measure of damages. [In general], one in possession of a chattel at the time of another's actionable trespass to it may recover the full amount of the damage or other impairment to the chattel. He is not confined to a recovery for the harm done to his possessory interest in it.

Comment on Clause (b):

h. An unprivileged use or other intermeddling with a chattel which results in actual impairment of its physical condition, quality or value to the possessor makes the actor liable for the loss thus caused. In the great majority of cases, the actor's intermeddling with the chattel impairs the value of it to the possessor, as distinguished from the mere affront to his dignity as possessor, only by some impairment of the physical condition of the chattel. There may, however, be situations in which the value to the owner of a particular type of chattel may be impaired by dealing with it in a manner that does not affect its physical condition. Thus, the use of a toothbrush by someone else may lead a person of ordinary sensibilities to regard the article as utterly incapable of further use by him, and the wearing of an intimate article of clothing may reasonably destroy its value in his eyes. In such a case, the intermeddling is actionable even though the physical condition of the chattel is not impaired.

Comment on Clause (c):

i. The deprivation of use, not amounting to a dispossession, necessary to render the actor liable for his use or other intermeddling with the chattel of another without the other's consent must be for a time so substantial that it is possible to estimate the loss caused thereby. A mere momentary or theoretical deprivation of use is not sufficient unless there is a dispossession. . .

Illustrations:

> 3. A leaves his car parked in front of a store. B releases the brake on A's car and pushes it three or four feet, doing no harm to the car. B is not liable to A.

> 4. A leaves his car parked near the corner. B, desiring to play a joke upon A, pushes the car around the corner where it cannot be easily seen by A. A comes out for his car, and fails to discover it for an hour. B is subject to liability for trespass to A.

Comment on Clause (d):

j. If the actor has committed a trespass . . . he is subject to liability. . . . It is immaterial that the harm so caused was neither intended by the actor nor the result of his negligent or reckless conduct while trespassing.

C. Conversion

§ 222A. What Constitutes Conversion

Restatement of the Law Second, Torts

(1) Conversion is an intentional exercise of dominion or control over a chattel which so seriously interferes with the right of another to control it that the actor may justly be required to pay the other the full value of the chattel.

(2) In determining the seriousness of the interference and the justice of requiring the actor to pay the full value, the following factors are important:

(a) the extent and duration of the actor's exercise of dominion or control;

(b) the actor's intent to assert a right in fact inconsistent with the other's right of control;

(c) the actor's good faith;

(d) the extent and duration of the resulting interference with the other's right of control;

(e) the harm done to the chattel;

(f) the inconvenience and expense caused to the other.

Comment:

c. Recovery of full value of chattel. The importance of the distinction between trespass to chattels and conversion, which has justified its survival long after the forms of action of trespass and trover have become obsolete, lies in the measure of damages. In trespass the plaintiff may recover for the diminished value of his chattel because of any damage to it, or for the damage to his interest in its possession or use. Usually, although not necessarily, such damages are less than the full value of the chattel itself. In conversion the measure of damages is the full value of the chattel, at the time and place of the tort. When the defendant satisfies the judgment in the action for conversion, title to the chattel passes to him, so that he is in effect required to buy it at a forced judicial sale. Conversion is therefore properly limited, and has been limited

38

by the courts, to those serious, major, and important interferences with the right to control the chattel which justify requiring the defendant to pay its full value.

d. No one factor is always predominant in determining the seriousness of the interference, or the justice of requiring the forced purchase at full value. . . . In each case the question to be asked is whether the actor has exercised such dominion and control over the chattel, and has so seriously interfered with the other's right to control it, that in justice he should be required to buy the chattel.

Illustrations:

1. On leaving a restaurant, A by mistake takes B's hat from the rack, believing it to be his own. When he reaches the sidewalk A puts on the hat, discovers his mistake, and immediately re-enters the restaurant and returns the hat to the rack. This is not a conversion.

2. The same facts as in Illustration 1, except that A keeps the hat for three months before discovering his mistake and returning it. This is a conversion.

3. The same facts as in Illustration 1, except that as A reaches the sidewalk and puts on the hat a sudden gust of wind blows it from his head, and it goes down an open manhole and is lost. This is a conversion.

4. Leaving a restaurant, A takes B's hat from the rack, intending to steal it. As he approaches the door he sees a policeman outside, and immediately returns the hat to the rack. This is a conversion. . . .

§ 229. Conversion by Receiving Possession in Consummation of Transaction

Restatement of the Law Second, Torts

> **One who receives possession of a chattel from another with the intent to acquire for himself or for a third person a proprietary interest in the chattel which the other has not the power to transfer is subject to liability for conversion to a third person then entitled to the immediate possession of the chattel.**

Comment:

b. . . . Where there is a sufficiently serious interference, and the transaction is ineffective to give the actor the proprietary interest he intends to acquire, he is subject to liability to a person who is at the time entitled to immediate possession of the chattel, for its conversion. Thus a purported sale, lease, pledge, gift, or bailment which is ineffectual as against the true owner of the chattel makes the purported purchaser, lessee, pledgee, donee, or bailee subject to liability to the owner for conversion.

f. One who has become liable for receiving the possession of a chattel under the rule stated in this Section, may return it and thus reduce the damages recoverable against him if his dealing with it was in good faith and without knowledge or reason to know that he was exercising a dominion inconsistent with another's interest in the chattel, and the physical condition of the chattel is substantially unimpaired, provided the tender of return is made promptly after discovery of the mistake.

g. The rule stated in this Section is applicable only when the actor receives the possession of a chattel with intent to acquire for himself a proprietary interest in it. . . .

h. In a small minority of jurisdictions, the bona fide purchase of stolen goods is held not to be in itself a sufficiently serious interference with the rights of the owner to amount to conversion, and the purchaser does not become liable for conversion until he refuses to surrender the goods to the owner on demand.

CHAPTER 4

DEFENSES OF PERSONS, LAND, AND CHATTELS—PRIVILEGES

A. Self-Defense and Defense of Third Persons

§ 63. Self-Defense by Force Not Threatening Death or Serious Bodily Harm

Restatement of the Law Second, Torts

(1) An actor is privileged to use reasonable force, not intended or likely to cause death or serious bodily harm, to defend himself against unprivileged harmful or offensive contact or other bodily harm which he reasonably believes that another is about to inflict intentionally upon him.

(2) Self-defense is privileged under the conditions stated in Subsection (1), although the actor

41

correctly or reasonably believes that he can avoid the necessity of so defending himself,

(a) by retreating or otherwise giving up a right or privilege, or

(b) by complying with a command with which the actor is under no duty to comply or which the other is not privileged to enforce by the means threatened.

Comment: . . . .

Illustrations:

3. A strikes B with a whip. B by reasonable force disarms A. B is not privileged thereafter to inflict a similar beating upon A.

4. A, a small boy, throws a snowball at B, hitting B in the eye and causing him severe pain. B is not privileged to inflict a beating upon A either as a punishment or as a warning against similar misconduct in the future.

i. Reasonableness of actor's belief. In determining whether the actor's apprehension of the intentional infliction of bodily harm or an offensive contact is reasonable, the circumstances which are known, or should be known, to the actor must be such as would lead a reasonable man to entertain such an apprehension. In this connection, the qualities which primarily characterize a "reasonable man" are ordinary firmness and courage. The other's conduct may put the actor in a reasonable apprehension of bodily harm or an offensive contact, although it is not the sole cause of such apprehension. The acts or statements of third persons may give to the other's conduct so threatening an appearance as to make it capable of causing such an apprehension, though standing by itself, the conduct would not be capable of so doing.

The privilege stated in this Section is conditioned upon the actor's reasonable belief that the other's conduct is both intended and likely to inflict an offensive contact or bodily harm upon him. But it is not necessary that the contact or harm which he apprehends shall be the same as that intended by the other. The actor may know, or reasonably believe in the existence of facts which are unknown to the other, which lead him reasonably to apprehend consequences from the other's threatened conduct not realized by the other. Thus, the actor may be privileged to use force to prevent the other from continuing a course of conduct which is obviously intended only to inflict an offensive contact, but which the actor reasonably believes, because of circumstances unknown to the other, to be likely to go beyond the other's intention and to cause serious bodily harm to the actor.

j. Reasonableness of means employed in self-defense. The

contact or other bodily harm which the actor is privileged to inflict in self-defense must be reasonable; that is, it must not be disproportionate in extent to the harm from which the actor is seeking to protect himself. . . .

Comment on Subsection (2):

m. Actor's duty to retreat. The actor, if he reasonably believes that he is threatened with the intentional imposition of bodily harm, or even of an offensive contact, may stand his ground and repel the attack by the use of reasonable force, which does not threaten serious harm or death, even though he might with absolute certainty of safety avoid the threatened bodily harm or offensive contact by retreating. If one so threatened is privileged to use force in self-defense, although the necessity of so doing can be avoided by relinquishing his privilege to choose his own location, it follows that reasonable force may be used to repel a threatened attack, although the necessity of so doing can be avoided by relinquishing the exercise of any other right or privilege. It also follows that there is a privilege to use force to repel such an attack although the threat to make it is conditioned upon noncompliance with a demand with which the actor is under no legal duty to comply, or which the other is not privileged to enforce by the means which he threatens to employ for that purpose.

On the other hand, if the threatened attack is conditioned upon the actor's non-compliance with the demand made upon him, the actor is not privileged to use force to protect himself against the attack so threatened, if the demand is one with which the actor knows or should know that he is under a legal duty to comply, and the force which the other threatens to apply to him is no greater than the other is privileged to apply for the purpose of securing compliance with his demand. . . .

§ 65. Self-Defense by Force Threatening Death or Serious Bodily Harm

Restatement of the Law Second, Torts

> **(1) Subject to the statement in Subsection (3), an actor is privileged to defend himself against another by force intended or likely to cause death or serious bodily harm, when he reasonably believes that**
>
>> **(a) the other is about to inflict upon him an intentional contact or other bodily harm, and that**
>>
>> **(b) he is thereby put in peril of death or serious bodily harm or ravishment, which can safely be prevented only by the immediate use of such force.**

43

(2) The privilege stated in Subsection (1) exists although the actor correctly or reasonably believes that he can safely avoid the necessity of so defending himself by

(a) retreating if he is attacked within his dwelling place, which is not also the dwelling place of the other, or

(b) permitting the other to intrude upon or dispossess him of his dwelling place, or

(c) abandoning an attempt to effect a lawful arrest.

(3) The privilege stated in Subsection (1) does not exist if the actor correctly or reasonably believes that he can with complete safety avoid the necessity of so defending himself by

(a) retreating if attacked in any place other than his dwelling place, or in a place which is also the dwelling of the other, or

(b) relinquishing the exercise of any right or privilege other than his privilege to prevent intrusion upon or dispossession of his dwelling place or to effect a lawful arrest.

Comment:

   c. The privilege to inflict upon another an offensive contact or bodily harm less than death or serious bodily harm exists if the actor reasonably believes that the other's conduct threatens him with an offensive contact or bodily harm, however great or small, including at the one extreme, death, and at the other, the most trivial scratch. The privilege to use force intended or likely to cause death or serious bodily harm exists if, but only if, the actor reasonably believes that the other's conduct threatens him with death or serious bodily harm or ravishment.

Illustration:

   1. A attempts to slap B's face. B is not privileged to shoot or stab A to prevent him from doing so, although, being much weaker than A, B cannot otherwise prevent A from slapping him.

Comment on Subsection (1):

   f. The use of force intended or likely to cause death or serious bodily harm is not privileged merely to prevent a confinement not itself threatening death or serious bodily harm.

Comment on Subsections (2) and (3):

   g. *Standing one's ground.* As stated in § 63, one whom another

44

threatens to attack may stand his ground and repel the attack with any reasonable force which does not threaten death or serious bodily harm, although he realizes that he can safely retreat and so avoid the necessity of using self-defensive force. But the interest of society in the life and efficiency of its members and in the prevention of the serious breaches of the peace involved in bloody affrays requires one attacked with a deadly weapon, except within his own dwelling place, to retreat before using force intended or likely to inflict death or serious bodily harm upon his assailant, unless he reasonably believes that there is any chance that retreat cannot be safely made. But even the slightest doubt, if reasonable, is enough to justify his standing his ground, and in determining whether his doubt is reasonable every allowance must be made for the predicament in which his assailant has placed him.

Illustrations:

4. A is standing upon a public highway. B points a revolver at him and threatens to shoot him. If A cannot prevent B from shooting him by any other means than by shooting B, he is privileged to do so.

5. A is standing upon a public highway. B, while still some distance away, starts towards A brandishing a razor and threatening to kill him. B is lame, and A knows that he can with perfect safety avoid B's attack by running away. A is not privileged to stand his ground, await B's attack and shoot or stab B to defend himself against it.

i. Standing one's ground in his dwelling place. Under the statement in Subsection (2, a), one attacked in his dwelling place may await his assailant and use deadly force to repel him though he could prevent the assailant from attacking him by closing the door and so excluding the assailant from the premises. But the mere fact that a man is threatened with an attack while he is within his own dwelling place does not justify him in using deadly weapons if he can avoid the necessity of so doing by any alternative other than flight or standing a siege. A man can no more justify using deadly weapons when he is in his own home than he can when he is upon a public highway, if he can avoid the necessity of doing so by complying with a demand, other than a demand that he shall retreat, give up the possession of his dwelling or permit an intrusion into it, or abandon an attempt to make a lawful arrest.

Illustrations:

6. A is standing in the vestibule of his dwelling house. B starts toward A brandishing a razor and threatening to kill him. A is privileged to stand his ground, await B's attack and shoot or stab him, although A could with perfect safety avoid B's attack by retreating to an inner room or by closing and locking the door of the vestibule.

7. A goes to B's dwelling place. Having gained admittance peaceably, he points a revolver at B and threatens to shoot him unless B gives him a watch which B is carrying and which is the property of B, but which A in good faith claims to be his. In determining whether B is privileged to defend himself by shooting A rather than give up the watch, the fact that the demand is made upon him in his own dwelling place instead of upon a public highway is immaterial.

§ 76. Defense of Third Person

Restatement of the Law Second, Torts

The actor is privileged to defend a third person from a harmful or offensive contact or other invasion of his interests of personality under the same conditions and by the same means as those under and by which he is privileged to defend himself if the actor correctly or reasonably believes that

> **(a) the circumstances are such as to give the third person a privilege of self-defense, and**

> **(b) his intervention is necessary for the protection of the third person.**

Comment on Clause (a):

b. The actor is privileged to inflict only such invasions of the other's interests of personality as the third person is, or because of a reasonable mistake of fact is believed by the actor to be, privileged to inflict in his own behalf. The actor, therefore is not privileged to use force likely to cause death or serious bodily harm unless the third person's life or limb is actually or apparently in danger, or to apply any force to the other, or impose any confinement upon him which is in excess of that which is actually or apparently necessary for the third person's protection.

Illustration:

1. A, seeing B apparently about to subject A's daughter C to insulting familiarities, is privileged to use any reasonable means to prevent B from doing so.

c. Under the rule stated in this Section, the actor is privileged to protect a third person by means which he correctly or reasonably believes the third person is privileged to use in his own defense although such third person is not in fact privileged to use such means. . . .

Illustration:

2. A sees B about to strike A's son C. B is in fact privileged to do so to defend himself against an attack made upon him by C. A, who has just come upon the scene, has no

46

reason to believe that his son is the aggressor. A is privileged to use reasonable force to prevent B from striking C.

B. DEFENSES OF LAND AND CHATTELS

§ 77. Defense of Possession by Force Not Threatening Death or Serious Bodily Harm

Restatement of the Law Second, Torts

An actor is privileged to use reasonable force, not intended or likely to cause death or serious bodily harm, to prevent or terminate another's intrusion upon the actor's land or chattels, if

(a) the intrusion is not privileged or the other intentionally or negligently causes the actor to believe that it is not privileged, and

(b) the actor reasonably believes that the intrusion can be prevented or terminated only by the force used, and

(c) the actor has first requested the other to desist and the other has disregarded the request, or the actor reasonably believes that a request will be useless or that substantial harm will be done before it can be made.

Comment:

a. This Section states only the privilege to use force against another for the purpose of preventing or terminating the other's intrusion upon the actor's possession of land or chattels.

c. Purpose of actor. . . . [I]t is not necessary that the actor's sole motive should be his desire to protect his land or chattels from intrusion. If the actor's conduct is for the purpose of defending his exclusive possession of land or chattels, it is privileged although his decision to defend against such intrusion is influenced, no matter how greatly, by personal dislike or hostility to the other. On the other hand, the actor is not privileged, if he uses the other's intrusion as a mere pretext to inflict a harmful contact upon him. Whether the one or the other situation exists may present a difficult question of fact. . . .

Illustrations:

1. A's boat gets adrift and grounds upon B's beach. A storm arises which threatens to carry the boat out to sea. A, being privileged to enter B's land for the purpose of saving his boat, attempts to do so. B is not privileged to use any force to prevent his entry.

2. A finds a highway impassable. He makes a detour over

47

B's field around the obstruction. While so doing, he stops his car for the purpose of taking luncheon. B tells him to move on. A refuses to do so. B may use such force as is reasonable to compel him to obey.

3. A enters B's land under the facts stated in Illustration 1. As he passes B's orchard, he stops to gather fruit growing in it. B is privileged to use such force as is reasonable to expel A from his premises.

e. *Other's incomplete privilege.* . . . [O]ne entering another's premises to preserve his chattel from destruction is not liable for his mere intrusion, but is liable for the damage done to the premises by the exercise of his privilege to enter, no matter how carefully the privilege is exercised. So too, one who uses another's premises as a haven of refuge when his life is threatened by some force of nature is subject to liability for any material harm which he does, although he is not liable for his harmless intrusion. In neither case is the possessor privileged to prevent the intrusion unless he has reasonable grounds to believe that it is likely to cause substantial bodily harm to him or third persons, whether upon the premises or not. Even the certainty that it will cause material harm to the physical condition of the premises is not enough to give him the privilege to exclude the intruder and so sacrifice the intruder's life to save his possession from even material harm.

Illustrations:

4. A, while out sailing with his family in a catboat upon a lake, is overtaken by a sudden squall, and his boat is in danger of being swamped. A puts into B's dock for shelter. B is not privileged to use force to prevent A from taking shelter there, whether A's use of the dock for this purpose does or does not appear likely to cause harm to the dock. But if A harms the dock while taking shelter there, he is subject to liability to B for the harm done to it.

5. A's vessel is moored to B's dock. A violent storm arises which causes the vessel to pound against the dock, threatening to do it substantial harm. A, being confronted with the necessity of putting to sea and imperiling both ship and crew, or securing it to the dock by additional hawsers, adopts the latter alternative. B is not privileged to cast the boat adrift, but A is subject to liability for the damage the boat does to the dock.

§ 84. Use of Mechanical Device Not Threatening Death or Serious Bodily Harm

Restatement of the Law Second, Torts

The actor is so far privileged to employ, for the purpose of protecting his possession of land or chattels from intrusion, a device not intended or likely

to cause death or serious bodily harm that he is not liable for bodily harm done thereby to a deliberate intruder, if

    (a) the use of such a device is reasonably necessary to protect the land or chattels from intrusion, and

    (b) the use of the particular device is reasonable under the circumstances, and

    (c) the device is one customarily used for such a purpose, or reasonable care is taken to make its use known to probable intruders.

Comment:

    c. Barbed wires and spiked walls. A barbed wire fence or spiked railing may be so constructed, located and maintained as to be a reasonable means of protecting the actor's possession of land or chattels from intrusion, and may therefore be privileged in so far as to give immunity from liability to a deliberate intruder; but it may involve an unreasonable risk of harm to persons coming upon, or using or touching his land or chattels with his consent, or in the enjoyment of a privilege, or while lawfully using the highway, none of whom the actor intends the device to affect. The rule stated in this Section does not purport to give the conditions under which there will be liability for the use of a device which, while a legitimate means of protecting land or chattels, creates an unreasonable risk of harm. . . .

    d. . . . This Section deals only with the privilege to protect land or chattels from intrusion by the use of devices which are not likely to cause death or serious bodily harm to intruders, such as barbed wire fences or spiked railings. While these devices are intended to harm one who deliberately persists in intruding, their purpose is not so much to harm intruders, as to protect the actor's possession of land or chattels from intrusion by the deterrent effect which the knowledge of their use, whether derived from observation or the fact that they are customarily used or from a warning, is likely to have upon those who would otherwise intrude. . . .

    e. Reasonableness of device. In order that the actor may be privileged to employ a device which, being a device, is incapable of discriminating between the various classes of intruders and of gauging the amount of force permissible against each, and of making that request which the possessor, if present in person, must make before using any force against the intruder, two conditions must be satisfied. The use of the device must be reasonably necessary and, even if the use of a device is necessary, the device itself must not be unreasonably dangerous. . . .

    f. Necessity of warning. The use of an undiscriminating device is justifiable only because of its probable effectiveness in preventing intrusions. This effect is attained not so much by the harm which is inflicted upon the individuals who are hurt by it while intruding as by the deterrent force exerted upon those who otherwise might intrude by their knowledge that if they do so they will run the risk of harm. Therefore, there is no privilege to use such a device if the fact of its use is concealed from possible intruders or is not reasonably likely to be known by them. . . . If, as is often the case, the use of such device is notoriously customary in the particular neighborhood, the possessor is entitled to assume that the existence of the custom and its notoriety will even on a dark night be sufficient to apprise intending trespassers that such a means of protection may have been installed. . . .

§ 85. Use of Mechanical Device Threatening Death or Serious Bodily Harm

Restatement of the Law Second, Torts

The actor is so far privileged to use a device intended or likely to cause serious bodily harm or death for the purpose of protecting his land or chattels from intrusion that he is not liable for the serious bodily harm or death thereby caused to an intruder whose intrusion is, in fact, such that the actor, were he present, would be privileged to prevent or terminate it by the intentional infliction of such harm.

Comment:

a. Rationale. The actor is privileged to employ deadly force by means of a mechanical device to the same extent to which he is otherwise privileged to use such force. There is no broader privilege, however, to use deadly force by such means. . . .

Illustration:

1. A, who owns a field adjacent to a golf course, is constantly annoyed by caddies coming into his field for balls driven out of bounds. To prevent these intrusions A installs spring guns upon his land. B, a caddy entering in search of a ball, is shot by one of these guns and has his eye put out. A is subject to liability to B whether he has or has not posted warnings or personally warned the caddy who was injured.

C. CONSENT

§ 892. Meaning of Consent

Restatement of the Law Second, Torts

(1) Consent is willingness in fact for conduct

to occur. It may be manifested by action or inaction and need not be communicated to the actor.

(2) If words or conduct are reasonably understood by another to be intended as consent, they constitute apparent consent and are as effective as consent in fact.

Comment:

b. Consent in fact. Consent means that the person concerned is in fact willing for the conduct of another to occur. Normally this willingness is manifested directly to the other by words or acts that are intended to indicate that it exists. It need not, however, be so manifested by words or by affirmative action. It may equally be manifested by silence or inaction, if the circumstances or other evidence indicate that the silence or inaction is intended to give consent. Even without a manifestation, consent may be proved by any competent evidence to exist in fact, and when so proved it is as effective as if manifested.

Illustration:

1. A informs his neighbor, B, that he is glad to have all of his neighbors make use of his swimming pool. C, another neighbor, without any knowledge of A's statement to B, enters the pool and enjoys himself. A brings action against C for trespass to land. On the basis of A's statement to B, it may be found that he has consented to C's entry and that C is not liable.

c. Apparent consent. Even when the person concerned does not in fact agree to the conduct of the other, his words or acts or even his inaction may manifest a consent that will justify the other in acting in reliance upon them. This is true when the words or acts or silence and inaction, would be understood by a reasonable person as intended to indicate consent and they are in fact so understood by the other. This conduct is not merely evidence that consent in fact exists, to be weighed against a denial. It is a manifestation of apparent consent, which justifies the other in acting on the assumption that consent is given and is as effective to prevent liability in tort as if there were consent in fact. On the other hand, if a reasonable person would not understand from the words or conduct that consent is given, the other is not justified in acting upon the assumption that consent is given even though he honestly so believes; and there is then no apparent consent.

Illustration:

2. A, driving along the highway, calls to B, asking permission to take a short cut through B's driveway. B says nothing, but waves his arm in a manner appearing to indicate that A is to go ahead. A does so. Even though B is in fact unwilling for A

to use his driveway and intends his gesture as a denial of permission, A is justified in acting upon the apparent consent and is not liable for trespass.

d. Custom. In determining whether conduct would be understood by a reasonable person as indicating consent, the customs of the community are to be taken into account. This is true particularly of silence or inaction. Thus if it is the custom in wooded or rural areas to permit the public to go hunting on private land or to fish in private lakes or streams, anyone who goes hunting or fishing may reasonably assume, in the absence of a posted notice or other manifestation to the contrary, that there is the customary consent to his entry upon private land to hunt or fish.

§ 168. Conditional or Restricted Consent

Restatement of the Law Second, Torts

A conditional or restricted consent to enter land creates a privilege to do so only in so far as the condition or restriction is complied with.

Comment:

b. A consent restricted to entry for a particular purpose confers no privilege to be on the land for any other purpose.

Illustration:

1. A, the owner of Blackacre, licenses B to drive his cow through Blackacre to B's pasture, lot X. B enters Blackacre to draw gravel from lot X, or to go to lot Y. In either case B's entry is a trespass. . . .

d. One whose presence on land is pursuant to a consent which is restricted to conduct of a certain sort, is a trespasser if he intentionally conducts himself in a different manner, as where one licensed to go on another's land and cut and remove trees not less than six inches in diameter cuts trees four and five inches in diameter. . . .

§ 169. Consent Restricted as to Area

Restatement of the Law Second, Torts

A consent given by a possessor of land to the actor's presence on a part of the land does not create a privilege to enter or remain on any other part.

Illustration:

1. A gives B permission to enter A's kitchen and leave a bottle of milk. B enters the kitchen, leaves the milk on the kitchen table, and then enters A's bedroom. B's entry into the bedroom is a trespass on A's land.

§ 170. Consent Conditioned or Restricted as to Time

Restatement of the Law Second, Torts

> **A consent given by a possessor of land to the actor's presence on the land during a specified period of time does not create a privilege to enter or remain on the land at any other time.**

Comment:

b. . . . . [I]f A licenses B to camp on A's land during the month of September, and B without A's consent enters on August 30th, B is a trespasser on the land.

c. A consent to enter on land for a specified purpose continues for such time and only for such time as is reasonably necessary to accomplish that purpose.

§ 172. Consent Obtained by Duress

Restatement of the Law Second, Torts

> **Consent obtained by duress upon the possessor of land exerted by the actor, or by a third person to the knowledge of the actor, is not effective as a consent to his entry.**

Illustration:

2. A, pointing a gun at B's head, requires B to write out a written license authorizing A to enter on B's land and camp there during the summer. A, going to B's land, presents the written consent to B's custodian, who permits A to enter and camp on the premises. B has in the meantime become desperately ill and is unable to notify his custodian not to recognize the license. A's entry is a trespass.

D. Privileged Entries on Land

§ 196. Public Necessity

Restatement of the Law Second, Torts

complete defense!

> **One is privileged to enter land in the possession of another if it is, or if the actor reasonably believes it to be, necessary for the purpose of averting an imminent public disaster.**

operative *greater good*

Comment:

a. The privilege stated in this Section is conferred upon the actor for the protection of the public. It is essential therefore that the entry be made in order to protect against or repel a public enemy, or to prevent or mitigate the effects of an impending public disaster such as a conflagration, flood, earthquake, or pestilence. . . .

b. Since the privilege stated in this Section is given for the benefit of the public, the actor in the exercise of the privilege may break and enter a dwelling or other structure as well as a fence or other enclosure, and he may use reasonable force against the person, if it reasonably appears to the actor to be necessary to do so in order to accomplish the purpose for which the privilege exists.

Although the actor is subject to liability for harm done in the unreasonable exercise of the privilege . . . in so far as his original entry was privileged, he is not liable for such entry and for acts done prior to such unreasonable conduct. Nor does such misconduct terminate the actor's privilege to be on the land and do acts thereon for the accomplishment of the privilege.

d. . . . [S]ince the privilege is based upon the appearance of necessity, if the actor believes that the impending disaster may be prevented or mitigated in some other reasonable way, and such is the fact, the entry is not privileged.

f. The privilege here stated carries with it the privilege to tear down or destroy buildings, or to remove explosives or other dangerous articles therefrom, or to alter the surface of the soil as by digging ditches, erecting or removing a levee, or doing any other acts on the premises reasonably necessary to effectuate the purpose for which the privilege exists.

§ 197. Private Necessity

Restatement of the Law Second, Torts

> (1) One is privileged to enter or remain on land in the possession of another if it is or reasonably appears to be necessary to prevent serious harm to
>
> (a) the actor, or his land or chattels, or
>
> (b) the other or a third person, or the land or chattels of either, unless the actor knows or has reason to know that the one for whose benefit he enters is unwilling that he shall take such action.
>
> (2) Where the entry is for the benefit of the actor or a third person, he is subject to liability for any harm done in the exercise of the privilege stated in Subsection (1) to any legally protected interest of the possessor in the land or connected with it, except where the threat of harm to avert which the entry is made is caused by the tortious conduct or contributory negligence of the possessor.

54

Comment on Subsection (1):

a. The privilege stated in this Subsection exists only where in an emergency the actor enters land for the purpose of protecting himself or the possessor of the land or a third person or the land or chattels of any such persons. Furthermore, the privilege must be exercised at a reasonable time and in a reasonable manner. Although the actor is subject to liability for harm done in the unreasonable exercise of the privilege stated in this Section in so far as his original entry was privileged, he is [generally] not liable for such entry. . . .

Illustration:

3. A, an aviator, while carefully and skillfully operating his airplane makes a forced landing on B's field in the reasonable belief that it is necessary to do so for the protection of himself and his plane. A is not liable for his mere entry, but under the statement in Subsection (2) is subject to liability for any harm thereby caused to B or to B's buildings, crops or other belongings.

c. Where the actor enters for the protection of himself or his property, it is sufficient for the existence of the privilege that the actor's conduct is necessary or reasonably believed by him to be necessary for the purpose of protecting himself, his land or chattels, and that his entry and the measures taken by him are reasonable in the light of all the circumstances. . . .

Comment on Subsection (2):

j. Where the entry is for the benefit of the possessor of the land, the privilege stated in this Section is a complete one.

In general, where the entry is for the purpose of protecting a legally protected interest of the actor or a third person, the privilege to enter is an incomplete one, in that, although the possessor of the land is not privileged to resist the entry, the actor is subject to liability for all harm to the possessor or to his interest in the land which the actor may cause, whether intentionally, negligently, or accidentally, while exercising his privilege. . . .

k. . . . [W]here the possessor of the land resists such a privileged entry, the actor's use of reasonable force to overcome such resistance to his entry or remaining on the land so long as the necessity continues is completely privileged. Therefore he is not liable for harm so occasioned.

Illustration:

15. While A is canoeing on a navigable river he is suddenly overtaken by a violent storm. To save himself and his canoe from destruction, A seeks to land at B's dock and pull

his canoe up on the dock. B by force attempts to prevent A from so doing, whereupon A uses reasonable force to B's person to effect his entry. A is not liable to B for the harm so occasioned.

PART III
NEGLIGENT HARMS TO PERSONS OR PROPERTY

CHAPTER 5

NEGLIGENCE LIABILITY AND THE ORDINARY DUTY OF CARE

A. GENERAL PRINCIPLES OF NEGLIGENCE LIABILITY FOR PHYSICAL HARMS

§ 3. Negligence

Restatement of the Law Third, Torts: Liability for Physical and Emotional Harm

  A person acts **negligently** if the person does not exercise reasonable care under all the circumstances. Primary factors to consider in ascertaining whether the person's conduct lacks reasonable care are the foreseeable likelihood that the person's conduct will result in harm, the foreseeable severity of any harm that may ensue, and the burden of precautions to eliminate or reduce the risk of harm.

Comment:

  a. Terminology. Conduct that displays reasonable care is the same as conduct that is reasonable, conduct that shows "ordinary care," conduct that avoids creating an "unreasonable risk of harm," and conduct that shows "reasonable prudence." Because a "reasonably careful person" (or a "reasonably prudent person") is one who acts with reasonable care, the "reasonable care" standard for negligence is basically the same as a standard expressed in terms of the "reasonably careful person" (or the "reasonably prudent person").

b. Negligence and contributory negligence. The definition of negligence set forth in this Section applies whether the issue is the negligence of the defendant or the contributory negligence of the plaintiff. There are, however, certain differences in emphasis between negligence and contributory negligence. A defendant is held liable for negligent conduct primarily because that conduct creates a risk of harm to a third party; the plaintiff's contributory negligence serves as at least a partial affirmative defense primarily because it exposes the plaintiff to a risk of harm. . . . In fact, in many cases, the conduct of the defendant that is negligent—for example, a physician's misprescription of medication—creates a risk of harm only to a third party and not to the defendant. Conversely, in many cases the conduct of the plaintiff that is contributorily negligent—for example, carelessly climbing a household ladder—creates a risk only to the plaintiff and not to third parties. However, in many other situations—especially those involving highway traffic—the conduct of the actor imperils both the actor and third parties. In such situations, all the risks foreseeably resulting from the actor's conduct are considered in ascertaining whether the actor has exercised reasonable care.

c. Acts and omissions. A person's negligence often consists of an act as such: for example, making an imprudent left turn while driving. Or it consists of a course of conduct: for example, driving a car at an unreasonable rate of speed. However, this Section makes clear that negligence frequently involves a failure to take a reasonable precaution. Thus, for example, a driver can be negligent for failing to step on the brakes when the driver's car approaches other traffic on the road. Such a failure can be described as an omission, and it hence can be said that the omission is itself negligent. . . . [T]he key point is that the defendant's conduct has created a risk of harm to others. . . .

d. Reasonable care and the primary factors. In many cases the content of reasonable care is explained by the primary factors identified in this Section. However, in particular categories of cases the inquiry into reasonable care, or the conduct of the reasonably prudent person, requires attention to considerations or circumstances that supplement or somewhat subordinate the primary factors. These categories include cases involving emergencies (§ 9), cases involving actors who are children (§ 10), and cases involving actors with disabilities (§ 11). Section 12, addressing the specific knowledge and skills of the actor, and § 13, concerning the role of custom, also supplement the primary factors contained in this Section. . . . [I]n cases in which the actor's alleged negligence

59

consists mainly in the actor's inattentive failure to advert to the risk, explicit consideration of the primary factors is often awkward, and the actor's conduct can best be evaluated by directly applying the standard of the reasonably careful person. See Comment *k*.

   e. Balancing risks and benefits. [T]his Section . . . can be said to suggest a "risk-benefit test" for negligence, where the "risk" is the overall level of the foreseeable risk created by the actor's conduct and the "benefit" is the advantages that the actor or others gain if the actor refrains from taking precautions. . . . Overall, this Section can be referred to as supporting a "balancing approach" to negligence.

   The balancing approach rests on and expresses a simple idea. Conduct is negligent if its disadvantages outweigh its advantages, while conduct is not negligent if its advantages outweigh its disadvantages. The disadvantage in question is the magnitude of risk that the conduct occasions. . . . The "advantages" of the conduct relate to the burden of risk prevention that is avoided when the actor declines to incorporate some precaution. . . . The burden of precautions can take a very wide variety of forms. In many cases it is a financial burden borne originally by the actor, although likely passed on, to a substantial extent, to the actor's customers. In highway cases, the burden can be the delays experienced by motorists in driving more slowly, and the greater level of exertion motorists must make in maintaining a constant lookout. In cases in which a gun owner is held liable for negligently storing a gun, thereby giving access to people who might use the gun improperly, the burden is the greater inconvenience the owner incurs in storing the gun in a more secure way. In cases in which the negligence doctrine is applied to a person who loans a car to a friend with a known deficient driving record, the burden relates to the owner's inability to satisfy the friend's need. In certain situations, if the actor takes steps to reduce one set of injury risks, this would involve the burden or disadvantage of creating a different set of injury risks, and these other risks are included within the burden of precautions. For example, if the motorist takes the precaution of surveying the area next to the highway in order to identify livestock or other animals that might be approaching the highway from adjacent property, the motorist is less able to detect hazards emerging on the highway itself.

   f. Implications. Given a balancing approach to negligence, even if the likelihood of harm stemming from the actor's conduct is small, the actor can be negligent if the severity of the possible harm is great and the burden of precautions is limited. Similarly, even if the severity of expected harm is low, the person can be negligent if the likelihood of harm is high and the burden of risk prevention limited. The greater the burden of precautions facing the actor the less appropriate is a finding of negligence. While

60

judicial opinions sometimes say that an actor who engages in a particularly dangerous activity—for example, the supplying of electricity, or the handling of gasoline or firearms—is subject to a "high degree of care," this language implies no departure from the general approach set forth in this Section. Rather, it signifies that given the great magnitude of the risk, the balancing approach imposes on the actor an obligation of great precautions.

Illustrations:

1. Some time ago the Local Power Company strung electric power lines that travel for a short distance along the bank of the Rogers River. The uninsulated wires are 23 feet above the water level. Over the years, many sailboats have begun using the River for recreational purposes. The metal masts on many of these sailboats exceed 23 feet above water level, though almost always by no more than a foot. Peter is a guest on the sailboat of a friend who is unfamiliar with this segment of the River. The mast of the sailboat reaches 24 feet above water line. As the boat approaches shore, Peter (who did not see the power line) is holding the mast when it came into contact with the line. On account of that contact, Peter suffers severe electric burns. In his suit against Local, he alleges Local's negligence in not having raised the height of the power lines to at least 25 feet once boating on the River had become common. In his suit, the evidence shows that the likelihood of contact between sailboat masts and the power lines at 23 feet is, over time, considerable; the severity of injuries when such contacts occur will probably be extremely serious; the cost to Local of raising the height of the power lines to 25 feet would be moderate. Local can be found negligent for having failed to raise the height of its power lines. . . .

2. Betty is driving on a street during a windstorm when a tree on City property adjacent to the street falls on her car; Betty's car is damaged, and she suffers a personal injury. The tree had been planted by the City 15 years ago, and appeared to be flourishing. It turns out that at the time of the storm there was an internal defect in the tree, which caused it to fall in the pressure of the storm. The City had no actual knowledge of that defect. Within the City's 90 square miles are almost 60,000 trees along city streets. The City inspects each tree annually, by trained staff on a drive-by basis; also, as employees of City departments perform their regular duties, they are under instructions to keep their eyes open for trees in a hazardous condition. Even when a tree goes bad, the chances of it suddenly falling in circumstances likely to produce serious property damage or personal injury are small. Only a much more ambitious inspection program—including an annual 20-minute inspection of each tree—would have succeeded in

61

detecting the defect in the tree that fell on Betty. The City's failure to adopt such a program can be found not negligent. . . .

g. Foreseeable likelihood. . . . In many situations, the likelihood of eventual harm depends in part on the likelihood of various events that may occur between the time of the actor's alleged negligence and the time of the harm itself. Such events commonly include human behavior in all its forms; they can also include the operation of human-made objects, the conduct of animals, and occurrences in nature such as the storm described in Illustration 2. . . .

To establish the actor's negligence, it is not enough that there be a likelihood of harm; the likelihood must be foreseeable to the actor at the time of conduct. Foreseeability often relates to practical considerations concerning the actor's ability to anticipate future events or to understand dangerous conditions that already exist. In such cases, what is foreseeable concerns what the actor "should have known." In some situations it is a person's inattentiveness that basically explains why the person failed to appreciate an existing danger. . . . In other cases, the actor—for example, the City in Illustration 2—could have learned of the danger only by undertaking a considerable effort to gather information. In assessing whether the actor's failure to make that effort indicates that the actor should have known of danger, courts commonly consider the factors included in the negligence balancing approach. That is, they take into account the likely benefit in risk reduction the actor could have achieved by endeavoring to gather more information before engaging in conduct, and also the burden the actor would have borne in making such an effort. . . .

h. Problems of proof and of value and valuation. In most cases only limited information is available as to the foreseeable likelihood of a harmful incident and the actual burden of risk-prevention measures. This is acceptable, and in many cases probably inevitable. . . .

At trial, the plaintiff who alleges the defendant's negligence normally bears the burden, first, of describing the defendant's conduct, and second, of identifying the precaution or precautions the defendant should have adopted. . . .

The harm whose severity should be considered under this Section is not the particular harm suffered by the plaintiff, but whatever harms are rendered more likely by the actor's conduct. There may well be a range of foreseeable harms; and the actual harm suffered by the plaintiff may, depending on the circumstances, be either on the high end or the low end of this range.

Moreover, especially when the anticipated harm is personal or emotional injury, the severity of harm may be difficult if not impossible to quantify; such harms are obviously inherently resistant to quantification. In addition, in many situations the burden of precaution is intangible in a way that perplexes any effort at quantification; an example is the greater exertion required of motorists if they are to maintain a constant lookout and thereby identify potential highway hazards. Moreover, in a number of situations the burden that would be involved by adopting precautions implicates distinctive social values. For example, if a police department is sued for having negligently initiated or conducted a high-speed chase, the burden of risk prevention relates to allowing a person accused of crime possibly to escape apprehension. In a case in which a blood bank is allegedly negligent for failing to inquire into the sexual orientation of potential donors, the burden involves interfering with those donors' privacy.

In most circumstances, negligence law takes into account and credits whatever burdens of risk prevention are actually experienced by the actor and others. While negligence law is concerned with social interests, courts regularly consider private interests, both because society is the protector of private interests and because the general public good is promoted by the protection and advancement of private interests. Nevertheless, in certain negligence cases there may be burdens of risk prevention that courts properly discount or decline to acknowledge. For example, certain motorists—though hoping for and expecting a favorable outcome—may find it exciting to race a railroad train toward a highway crossing. Yet because society may not recognize that excitement as appropriate, it may be ignored by the jury in considering whether the motorist should have driven more conservatively.

For all these reasons, the approach to negligence described in this Section is not one that permits the comparison of common elements or that generates determinate results. Rather, the approach identifies important variables for the jury to take into account in evaluating whether the actor was unreasonable; the jury's responsibility is to render an informed judgment in light of these variables.

i. Risk elimination and risk reduction. In identifying a precaution that should have been adopted, the party alleging negligence need not prove that the precaution would have entirely eliminated the risk of harm. The party can instead prove that the precaution, if implemented, would have reduced that risk. For example, a storekeeper may be aware of a risk of injury occasioned by litter left by customers. The storekeeper can reduce that risk by inspecting every half-hour but can essentially eliminate the risk only by inspecting on a continuous basis. Even though the negligence standard does not require continuous inspections, the failure to maintain a program of half-hour inspections may be negligent. Of course, in order to prevail, the plaintiff must prove not only negligence but also factual causation. Thus, the plaintiff must prove that the reduction in the general risk of harm would have prevented the plaintiff's particular injury: specifically, that an inspection on a half-hour basis would have detected the instance of litter that injured the plaintiff.

j. Negligent precautions and negligent activities. Usually, the precaution identified by a party in seeking to establish the actor's negligence will consist of some way in which the actor could have modified the activity engaged in. In such a case, the burden of precaution relates to how that precaution would have interfered with that activity or rendered it more costly. On some occasions, the party might claim that the actor's very decision to engage in a particular activity created an unreasonable risk of harm. There is no general rule prohibiting such claims. For example, when a person's vision has been impaired by disease, or when the person needs to take medication that produces continuing grogginess, the person can be found negligent for engaging in the activity of driving a car.

Nevertheless, claims of negligence that focus on the actor's entire activity are uncommon. For example, in the 19th century, in many regions expanded canals were possible alternatives to the construction of railroad lines, and canals were much less dangerous than railroads; even so, no company was ever charged with negligence for having constructed a railroad line rather than a canal. The infrequency of negligence claims directed against an entire activity is in part explainable in terms of the heavy burden a party would be required to bear in gathering and presenting the evidence that would be needed to support such a claim. Similarly, a court might reasonably perceive that there would be serious administrative problems in attempting to adjudicate a claim that the actor's entire activity is negligent. If so, the court can consider whether the "duty" considerations described in § 7 justify the rejection of the plaintiff's claim.

In those cases in which a plaintiff does allege negligence in the actor's decision to engage in an activity, the overall utility of the activity is a factor the court needs to consider. For more ordinary negligence claims, however, the utility of the activity is of minimal relevance, if any. Supplying electricity, for example, is of extraordinary value to the community. Even so, the transmission of electricity poses serious risks. If certain precautions can reduce those risks, it is the burden of those precautions, and not the value of the activity itself, that is of relevance in a negligence analysis.

k. Advertence and inadvertence. . . . As defined by tort law, negligence does not include any assumption that the actor has failed to advert to the risk. Rather, the balancing approach to negligence tends to assume that the actor is aware of that risk, but has tolerated that risk on account of the burdens involved by risk-prevention measures. In a significant number of cases . . . the actor's alleged negligence consists of an inattentive failure to perceive or appreciate the risk involved in the actor's conduct. When that conduct is allegedly negligent, the relevant burden of precautions is the burden the actor would have borne by paying more attention in the course of his ordinary affairs. In some cases, there may be evidence that bears on the extent of that burden. In many cases, however, the level of the burden, and hence the reasonableness of the person's inattentiveness, are largely matters of common sense. Accordingly, analyzing the factors highlighted in this Section may be artificial, and the decisionmaker—typically, the jury—can simply consider whether the reasonably careful person *would* have been aware of the risk. For example, the jury can determine whether a pedestrian should have detected, and hence avoided stumbling over, a banana peel located on a crowded sidewalk.

In cases in which the actor allegedly is negligent for not having adverted to the risk, the jury might determine that the reasonably careful person would advert to this risk nine times out of 10. Such a determination acknowledges that such an actor would not notice the risk one time out of 10. The function of the jury is to consider what the reasonably careful person would have done in the particular factual situation, not what that person would do over an extended period of time. Hence, if the probability is 90 percent that the reasonably careful person would have adverted to the particular risk, a finding that the actor was negligent is obligatory. Because the jury focuses on the conduct of the reasonably careful person in each particular case, the fallibility of average persons over a period of time is a reality the jury is not in a position to consider. Accordingly, tort law's case-by-case focus makes it appropriate to say that the reasonably careful person is infallible in a way that ordinary people are not.

l. Act of God. An act of God is a serious and unusual adverse natural event. . . . Several forms of precautions can be relevant in protecting against adverse natural events. The actor can be negligent in building facilities that are unreasonably inadequate in protecting against foreseeable natural events. Thus, there can be negligence in designing or constructing a building that collapses in a severe windstorm or hurricane or in designing or constructing a dam that overflows in a severe rainstorm. In conducting a negligence analysis in such a case, the foreseeable likelihood of harm relates to which adverse natural events can be contemplated during the expected life of the facility. Also, an actor can be negligent for failing to adopt appropriate precautions when an adverse natural event is imminent—for example, for failing to fasten a vessel to a dock as a storm approaches. In such a case, the imminence of the adverse natural event reduces the significance of foreseeable likelihood as a negligence factor, although problems of foreseeability still concern the exact severity of the storm that might arrive. In addition, an actor can be negligent in failing to adopt appropriate precautions when an adverse natural event is already in progress—for example, in failing to drive more slowly when a severe snowstorm has sharply reduced visibility. In such a case, the ongoing natural event eliminates any issue of foreseeability; the only issue is reasonable precautions.

In all, then, cases involving serious and unusual adverse natural events—"acts of God"—essentially call for application of the factors that enter into an ordinary analysis of negligence. . . .

§ 6. Liability for Negligence Causing Physical Harm

Restatement of the Law Third, Torts: Liability for Physical and Emotional Harm /～g5

An actor whose negligence is a factual cause of physical harm is subject to liability for any such harm within the scope of liability, unless the court determines that the ordinary duty of reasonable care is inapplicable.

—Failure to exercise reasonable care

Comment:

b. Elements of a prima facie claim for negligently caused physical harm. This Section includes the five elements of a prima facie case for negligence. The first element, duty, is a question of law for the court to determine, although the court's decision about duty might require the jury to resolve predicate factual disputes upon which a determination of duty rests. Ordinarily, an actor whose conduct creates risks of physical harm to others has a duty to exercise reasonable care. Except in unusual categories of cases in which courts have developed no-duty rules, an actor's duty to exercise reasonable care does not require attention from the court. This Section also contains the four factual elements of a prima facie claim for negligently causing physical harm: (1) failure to exercise reasonable care; (2) factual cause; (3) physical harm; and (4) harm within the scope of liability (which historically has been called "proximate cause"). This Section uses the language "subject to liability" rather than "liable" in recognition that affirmative defenses and other doctrines may avoid liability even when a prima facie case exists.

c. Historical role of negligence as basis for liability. Negligence liability for physical harm has deep roots in the common law. . . . [W]ithin the common-law writ system, negligence was the typical standard of liability when the plaintiff pleaded trespass on the case. Trespass on the case was the appropriate writ for harm that was the indirect consequence of the defendant's conduct. Because employers usually cause harm only indirectly, through the conduct

66

of their employees, employers were typically sued in trespass on the case. For cases brought under the writ of trespass, mid-19th-century opinions resolved ambiguities in the law by positing negligence as the standard of liability. Those decisions also generally placed the burden of proof on the plaintiff. Since the middle of the 19th century, negligence has been widely recognized as the predominant basis for liability for accidentally caused physical harm.

d. Rationales. One justification for imposing liability for negligent conduct that causes physical harm is corrective justice; imposing liability remedies an injustice done by the defendant to the plaintiff. An actor who permits conduct to impose a risk of physical harm on others that exceeds the burden the actor would bear in avoiding that risk impermissibly ranks personal interests ahead of the interests of others. This, in turn, violates an ethical norm of equal consideration when imposing risks on others. Imposing liability remedies this violation.

Another justification for imposing liability for negligence is to give actors appropriate incentives to engage in safe conduct. The actor's adoption of appropriate precautions improves overall social welfare and thereby advances broad economic goals.

e. Implications. A general rule imposing negligence liability for physical harm has affirmative and negative implications. Affirmatively, an actor bears liability for physical harm caused by the actor's negligence. Negatively, an actor does not bear liability for harm caused by the actor unless the harm was caused by the actor's failure to exercise reasonable care. Despite the general rule, other rules of law, such as various rules of strict liability, do sometimes impose liability in the absence of negligence. . . .

f. Duty of reasonable care. The rule stated in § 7 is that an actor ordinarily has a duty to exercise reasonable care. That is equivalent to saying that an actor is subject to liability for negligent conduct that causes physical harm. Thus, in cases involving physical harm, courts ordinarily need not concern themselves with the existence or content of this ordinary duty. They may proceed directly to the elements of liability set forth in this Section. Nevertheless, the duty of reasonable care can be displaced or modified in certain types of cases, as explained in § 7. . . .

Liability for breaching the duty of reasonable care addressed in this Section applies only in cases involving physical and emotional harm, the subject of this Restatement. Liability for negligently caused stand-alone emotional harm (emotional harm that is not derivative of personal injury) is subject to additional duty limitations contained in §§ 47 and 48. Cases involving negligence that causes only economic loss (that is not property damage or derivative of personal injury) are not addressed in this

Restatement and are governed by the principles of the Restatement Second of Torts until additional portions of the Restatement Third of Torts, contained in Torts: Liability for Economic Harm, addressing this matter are approved by the Institute.

g. Unavoidable accident. An "unavoidable accident" is one that the actor could not have avoided by exercising reasonable care. As a legal doctrine, unavoidable accident has a complex common-law history. Originally, it was a defense or offset to strict liability, and in that context its exact meaning was ambiguous. In negligence cases, there is no properly separate doctrine of unavoidable accident, and it does not serve as an affirmative "defense." The "doctrine" is merely a repetition of the general rule that an actor is not liable for harm unless the harm was caused by the actor's failure to exercise reasonable care. . . .

B. THE ORDINARY DUTY OF REASONABLE CARE

§ 7. Duty

Restatement of the Law Third, Torts: Liability for Physical and Emotional Harm

(a) **An actor ordinarily has a duty to exercise reasonable care when the actor's conduct creates a risk of physical harm.**

(b) **In exceptional cases, when an articulated countervailing principle or policy warrants denying or limiting liability in a particular class of cases, a court may decide that the defendant has no duty or that the ordinary duty of reasonable care requires modification.**

Comment:

a. The proper role for duty. . . . [A]ctors engaging in conduct that creates risks to others have a duty to exercise reasonable care to avoid causing physical harm. In most cases, courts . . . need not refer to duty on a case-by-case basis. Nevertheless, in some categories of cases, reasons of principle or policy dictate that liability should not be imposed. In these cases, courts use the rubric of duty to apply general categorical rules withholding liability. For example, a number of modern cases involve efforts to impose liability on social hosts for serving alcohol to their guests. A jury might plausibly find the social host negligent in providing alcohol to a guest who will depart in an automobile. Nevertheless, imposing liability is potentially problematic because of its impact on a substantial slice of social relations. Courts appropriately address whether such liability should be permitted as a matter of duty. Courts may also, for the same reasons, determine that modification of the ordinary duty of reasonable care is required. Thus, courts generally impose on sellers of products that are not defective at the time of sale the limited duty to warn of newly discovered risks, rather than the more general duty of reasonable care, which a jury might find includes a duty to recall and retrofit the product so as to eliminate the risk. Similarly, some courts have modified the general duty of reasonable care for those engaging in competitive sports to a more limited duty to refrain from recklessly dangerous conduct.

There are two different legal doctrines for withholding liability: no-duty rules and scope-of-liability doctrines (often called "proximate cause"). An important difference between them is that no-duty rules are matters of law decided by the courts, while the defendant's scope of liability is a question of fact for the factfinder. When liability depends on factors specific to an individual case, the appropriate rubric is scope of liability. On the other hand, when liability depends on factors applicable to categories of actors or patterns of conduct, the appropriate rubric is duty. No-duty rules are appropriate only when a court can promulgate relatively clear, categorical, bright-line rules of law applicable to a general class of cases.

When addressing duty, courts sometimes are influenced by the relationship between the actor and the person harmed. Thus, courts hold that landowners are free of negligence liability to some trespassers. . . . At other times, courts focus on particular claims of negligence, forbidding some but preserving others. Thus, a court might hold that a landlord has no duty to provide security for rented space in a building, but has a duty of reasonable care in providing security for common areas in the building. Courts also sometimes hold that an actor has a more limited duty than reasonable care, such as an obligation to avoid engaging in reckless conduct that causes physical harm. . . .

The principle or policy that is the basis for modifying or eliminating the ordinary duty of care contained in § 7(a) may be reflected in longstanding precedent and need not be restated each time it is invoked. Thus, the modified duty applicable to medical professionals, which employs customary rather than reasonable care, reflects concerns that a lay jury will not understand what constitutes reasonable care in the complex setting of providing medical care and the special expertise possessed by professionals. At the same time, new concerns may arise that have not previously been the basis for modification of the duty of reasonable care and, when those are invoked, they should be identified and explained.

b. Procedural aspects of duty determination. A defendant has the procedural obligation to raise the issue of whether a no-duty rule or some other modification of the ordinary duty of reasonable care applies in a particular case. . . .

Courts determine legislative facts necessary to decide whether a no-duty rule is appropriate in a particular category of cases. . . . When resolution of disputed adjudicative facts bears on the existence or scope of a duty, the case should be submitted to the jury with alternative instructions. . . .

Illustration:

1. Sadie owns land adjacent to Sam's. She sues Sam, alleging that he failed to exercise reasonable care to prevent a large tree branch on his land from falling on her land and hitting her. Sam claims that Sadie was trespassing on his land when the branch hit her. The law in the applicable jurisdiction imposes a duty on landowners only to avoid wanton or willful injury to trespassers, while also imposing a general duty of reasonable care to avoid causing harm to persons off the land. Sam has the procedural obligation to notify Sadie that he will invoke the limited-duty rule applicable to trespassers. Then, Sadie has the burden to prove that she was injured on her land if she wants to benefit from the more favorable duty rule. If the evidence permits a finding that Sam was wanton or willful, the court should submit the case to the jury with alternative instructions on his duty. If the evidence would not support such a finding, the court should instruct the jury that, if it finds Sam was negligent and Sadie was injured on her land, it should return a verdict for Sadie, but if it finds Sadie was a trespasser, it should return a verdict for Sam.

c. Conflicts with social norms about responsibility. In deciding whether to adopt a no-duty rule, courts often rely on general social norms of responsibility. For example, many courts have held that commercial establishments that serve alcoholic beverages have a duty to use reasonable care to avoid injury to others who might be injured by an intoxicated customer, but that social hosts do not have a similar duty to those who might be injured by their guests. Courts often justify this distinction by referring to commonly held social norms about responsibility. The rule stated in this Section does not endorse or reject this particular set of rules. It does support a court's deciding this issue as a categorical matter under the rubric of duty, and a court's articulating general social norms of responsibility as the basis for this determination.

d. Conflicts with another domain of law. In some cases, negligence-based liability might interfere with important principles reflected in another area of law. For example, one reason the general duty of reasonable care . . . is limited to physical harm is that liability for purely economic harm in commercial cases often raises issues better addressed by contract law or by the tort of misrepresentation. Similarly, no-duty and limited-duty rules in cases involving owners and occupiers of land are influenced by issues that are important in property law. In cases alleging physical harm caused by the content of a publication by a media defendant, some courts have relied on First Amendment concerns in finding that media publishers have no duty or a limited duty. No-duty and limited-duty rules in tort help police the boundaries between these various areas of law.

e. *Relational limitations.* Courts sometimes use the rubric of duty to decide whether an otherwise negligent actor should be liable to a class of persons in a certain relationship. For example, a property owner who creates a hazard might be liable to persons lawfully on the property, but not to a trespasser. Similarly, a home owner who negligently starts a fire might be liable to an adjacent landowner but not to a firefighter. Thus, an actor may have a duty of reasonable care to some persons but not to others.

f. *Institutional competence and administrative difficulties.* Sometimes a particular category of negligence claims would be difficult for courts to adjudicate. Courts may have difficulty gathering evidence or drawing doctrinal lines necessary to adjudicate certain categories of cases. These administrative concerns may support adopting a no-duty rule. For example, when a plaintiff claims that it is negligent merely to engage in the activity of manufacturing a product, the competing social concerns and affected groups would be appropriate considerations for a court in deciding to adopt a no-duty rule.

g. *Deference to discretionary decisions of another branch of government.* Courts employ no-duty rules to defer to discretionary decisions made by officials from other branches of government, especially decisions that allocate resources or make other policy judgments. Courts often use the rubric of duty to hold that it is inappropriate to review these decisions in lawsuits. For example, courts often hold that police have no duty of reasonable care in deciding how to allocate police protection throughout a city. This no-duty limitation requires analysis of whether the challenged action involves a discretionary determination of the sort insulated from review or instead is a ministerial action that does not require deference. This analysis is similar to that under the "discretionary function" exception to the Federal Tort Claims Act.

h. *Plaintiff negligence and no-duty determinations.* Ordinary language makes it awkward to speak of a person having a duty of care to himself or herself. Nevertheless, the rules of comparative responsibility ordinarily diminish the recovery of a plaintiff who has failed to exercise reasonable care to avoid harm to himself or herself. However, cases arise in which courts hold that a plaintiff's recovery should not be affected by the plaintiff's own negligent conduct. Just as special problems of policy may support a no-duty determination for a defendant, similar concerns may support a no-duty determination for plaintiff negligence. . . .

71

i. No duty and no negligence as a matter of law. Sometimes reasonable minds cannot differ about whether an actor exercised reasonable care. . . . In such cases, courts take the question of negligence away from the jury and determine that the party was or was not negligent as a matter of law. Courts sometimes inaptly express this result in terms of duty. Here, the rubric of duty inaccurately conveys the impression that the court's decision is separate from and antecedent to the issue of negligence. In fact, these cases merely reflect the one-sidedness of the facts bearing on negligence, and they should not be misunderstood as cases involving exemption from or modification of the ordinary duty of reasonable care.

In other situations, reasonable minds could differ about the application of the negligence standard to a particular category of recurring facts, but under the rubric of duty courts render a judgment about that category of cases. In conducting its analysis, the court may take into account factors that might escape the jury's attention in a particular case, such as the overall social impact of imposing a significant precautionary obligation on a class of actors. These cases are properly decided as duty or no-duty cases. When no such categorical considerations apply and reasonable minds could differ about the competing risks and burdens or the foreseeability of the risks in a specific case, however, courts should not use duty and no-duty determinations to substitute their evaluation for that of the factfinder.

Thus, in the field of products liability, courts have declared that the warning obligation of prescription-drug manufacturers ordinarily is limited to the prescribing physician and does not extend to warning the patient directly. They reason that the physician can best assess the relevant risk information and determine the appropriate course of treatment. When appropriate, the physician can inform the patient of means by which the patient may minimize the risk of adverse side effects. The physician may also, in appropriate situations, consult with the patient as required by the informed-consent doctrine. Courts have, through this duty limitation, made a categorical determination that having manufacturers provide safety information to physicians, rather than to patients, is the appropriate manner for minimizing the costs of adverse side effects. Such a categorical determination also has the benefit of providing clearer rules of behavior for actors who may be subject to tort liability and who structure their behavior in response to that potential liability. Even when such categorical determinations are adopted, exceptions or limitations may also be appropriate. For example, Restatement Third, Torts: Products Liability § 6(d)(2) contains exceptions to the duty of a drug manufacturer to warn only physicians.

j. The proper role for foreseeability. Foreseeable risk is an element in the determination of negligence. In order to determine whether appropriate care was exercised, the factfinder must assess the foreseeable risk at the time of the defendant's alleged negligence. The extent of foreseeable risk depends on the specific facts of the case and cannot be usefully assessed for a category of cases; small changes in the facts may make a dramatic change in how much risk is foreseeable. Thus . . . courts should leave such determinations to juries unless no reasonable person could differ on the matter.

A no-duty ruling represents a determination, a purely legal question, that no liability should be imposed on actors in a category of cases. Such a ruling should be explained and justified based on articulated policies or principles that justify exempting these actors from liability or modifying the ordinary duty of reasonable care. These reasons of policy and principle do not depend on the foreseeability of harm based on the specific facts of a case. They should be articulated directly without obscuring references to foreseeability. . . .

Despite widespread use of foreseeability in no-duty determinations, this Restatement disapproves that practice and limits no-duty rulings to articulated policy or principle in order to facilitate more transparent explanations of the reasons for a no-duty ruling and to protect the traditional function of the jury as factfinder.

k. Continuing risks of harm. . . . [I]n some cases an actor's conduct may create a continuing risk of harm and the question arises whether the actor has a duty later with regard to that continuing risk. Thus, a person may be exposed to imminent harm by the conduct of an actor many years before in disposing of a live land mine. The duty imposed by this Section requires reasonable care in the initial disposal, and failure to exercise reasonable care in the disposition of the land mine would subject the actor to liability for harms that occur later. . . .

l. Relationship with affirmative duties to act. The general duty rule contained in this Section is conditioned on the actor's having engaged in conduct that creates a risk of physical harm. Section 37 states the obverse of this rule: In the absence of conduct creating a risk of harm to others, an actor ordinarily has no duty of care to another. . . .

m. Relationship with intentionally and negligently inflicted emotional harm. Recovery for stand-alone emotional harm is more circumscribed than when physical harm occurs. These limitations are often reflected in no- (or limited-) duty rules that limit liability. Chapter 8 of this Restatement addresses the special rules for recovery of emotional harm and provides for more limited duties (and liability) when the only harm suffered by the plaintiff is emotional harm than those duties that exist for physical harm. . . .

73

n. *Relationship with duties of landowners and possessors.* As with stand-alone emotional harm, courts have employed different duty rules for land possessors for harm caused to those on the land. Chapter 9 of this Restatement contains the duties owed by land possessors in such circumstances. . . .

o. *Conduct creating risk.* An actor's conduct creates a risk when the actor's conduct or course of conduct results in greater risk to another than the other would have faced absent the conduct. Conduct may create risk by exposing another to natural hazards, as, for example, when a pilot of an airplane flies the plane into an area of thunderstorms. Conduct may also create risk by exposing another to the improper conduct of third parties.

§ 8. Judge and Jury

Restatement of the Law Third, Torts: Liability for Physical and Emotional Harm

(a) **When, in light of all the evidence, reasonable minds can differ as to the facts relating to the actor's conduct, it is the function of the jury to determine those facts.**

(b) **When, in light of all the facts relating to the actor's conduct, reasonable minds can differ as to whether the conduct lacks reasonable care, it is the function of the jury to make that determination.**

Comment:

b. *Explanation and rationale.* . . . In light of the facts relating to the actor's conduct, the question arises whether that conduct is negligent—whether it lacks reasonable care under all the circumstances. Because this is a matter of the law's evaluation of the legal significance of the actor's conduct, such a question could be characterized as a question of law that should be decided by the court. More precisely, it can be characterized as a mixed question of law and fact. . . . The longstanding American practice has been to treat the negligence question as one that is assigned to the jury; to this extent, the question is treated as one that is equivalent to a question of fact. Accordingly, so long as reasonable minds can differ in evaluating whether the actor's conduct lacks reasonable care, the responsibility for making this evaluation rests with the jury. To be sure, in some cases reasonable minds can reach only one conclusion. Accordingly, the rule recognized in this Section permits a directed verdict or judgment as a matter of law—that the actor's conduct must be found negligent, or free of negligence. . . . [R]eaching a decision on the negligence issue requires an exercise of judgment by the jury. The jury is assigned the responsibility of rendering such judgments partly because several minds are better than one, and also because of the desirability of taking advantage of the insight and values of the community, as embodied in the jury, rather than relying on the professional knowledge of the judge.

Illustration:

1. Susan is the mother of Michael, a 23-month-old child. Susan and Michael are visiting at a vacation home owned by their friend Jon. Susan and Michael are in the kitchen; the room is lit by a kerosene lamp on a table. If Susan leaves the kitchen for an hour in order to read a book, and before she returns Michael knocks over the lantern, starting a fire that damages Jon's cabin, a court should find Susan negligent as a matter of law. If Michael knocks the lantern over during a four-second period in which Susan has turned her back in order to take a boiling pot off the stove, the court should find as a matter of law that Susan's turning away is not negligent. If the lantern is knocked over after Susan, wanting to make a quick phone call, leaves the room for one minute, whether Susan's departure is negligent is a question for the jury to decide.

c. *Implications and problems.* A jury decision on the negligence issue is not a precedent for later cases involving different parties and is not even admissible in such later cases as a possible guide to later juries. Jury decisions, then, are generally ad hoc. Most of the time, this ad hoc quality seems inevitable, since the actor's conduct is sufficiently unique as to render largely irrelevant whatever precedent the jury's verdict might set. . . .

Occasionally, however, the need for providing a clear and stable answer to the question of negligence is so overwhelming as to justify a court in withdrawing the negligence evaluation from the jury. In highway-accident cases, for example, the question recurrently arises whether it is contributory negligence not to wear an available seat belt. Granted, the advantages of wearing a seat belt vary to some extent from case to case; the advantage, for example, is greater when the person is riding in a more vulnerable subcompact car. Still, the benefits of having the contributory-negligence question settled in advance are of such force as to make it acceptable for a state's highest court to reach a final, general decision as to whether not wearing seat belts is or is not contributory negligence. . . .

C. PARTICULAR CIRCUMSTANCES RELATED TO THE DUTY OF CARE

§ 9. Emergency

Restatement of the Law Third, Torts: Liability for Physical and Emotional Harm

If an actor is confronted with an unexpected

emergency requiring rapid response, this is a circumstance to be taken into account in determining whether the actor's resulting conduct is that of the reasonably careful person.

Comment:

a. Rationale. . . . If an emergency confronting the actor requires a response in a very brief period of time, this fact should be taken into account in determining whether the response is that of a reasonably careful person. The fact of the emergency may mean that the response is instinctive rather than deliberative; at the least, it indicates that the opportunities for deliberation have been limited by severe time pressures. Reasonable care in conduct and not the actor's mere good faith remains the ultimate criterion for nonnegligence, but the inquiry into reasonableness acknowledges the reality of the emergency situation.

The emergency facing the actor can be created by the conduct of another person, who may or may not be a party to the lawsuit in which the issue of emergency is raised. Or the emergency can be created without human action—for example, by the sudden failure of a car's brakes due entirely to mechanical causes.

Illustration:

1. Sharon, driving a car, approaches Dan's car, and properly steps on the brakes. For reasons unrelated to any negligence on Sharon's part, the brakes fail to function. Sharon's car continues forward. In this emergency, Sharon chooses to step on the brakes again, and they fail again, causing Sharon's car to strike Dan's car, injuring Dan. A calm assessment of the choices facing Sharon indicates that all things considered, a better choice would have been for her to turn the car quickly to the right. Still, the jury can conclude that, in light of the emergency circumstances, Sharon behaved as a reasonably careful person.

d. Prior negligence. In some cases, the emergency faced by the actor—for example, the defendant—is itself due to prior conduct by the defendant that is arguably negligent. Insofar as the plaintiff alleges negligence in the defendant's later choice, the emergency doctrine is applicable in the assessment of this allegation. Yet the plaintiff likely will also allege negligence in the defendant's original conduct. If this allegation is accepted by the jury, the defendant is liable for the plaintiff's harm, notwithstanding the possibility that the defendant's later choice was reasonable; the defendant's original negligence is a factual cause of harm to the plaintiff within the scope of liability.

Illustration:

2. Same facts as Illustration 1, above, except that failure

of the brakes is due to Sharon's negligence in inadequately maintaining the brakes. This negligence renders Sharon liable for the harm Dan suffers in the eventual collision, regardless of how a jury evaluates Sharon's decision to reapply the brakes.

§ 10. Children

Restatement of the Law Third, Torts: Liability for Physical and Emotional Harm

(a) A child's conduct is negligent if it does not conform to that of a reasonably careful person of the same age, intelligence, and experience, except as provided in Subsection (b) or (c).

(b) A child less than five years of age is incapable of negligence.

(c) The special rule in Subsection (a) does not apply when the child is engaging in a dangerous activity that is characteristically undertaken by adults.

Comment:

b. Rationale. Children are less able than adults to maintain an attitude of attentiveness toward the risks their conduct may occasion and the risks to which they may be exposed. Similarly, children are less able than adults to understand risks, to appreciate alternative courses of conduct with respect to risks, and to make appropriate choices from among those alternatives. Acknowledging this, tort law refines the characterization of negligence provided in § 3 to take account of these realities. The negligence question hence concerns whether the child has made reasonable choices and engaged in reasonable behavior, given the limitations that childhood imposes.

All American jurisdictions accept the idea that a person's childhood is a relevant circumstance in negligence determinations. Jurisdictions divide, however, on the best way to take childhood into account. The very substantial majority of all jurisdictions accept the flexible rule set forth in Subsection (a). A considerable minority of jurisdictions pursue a different approach. Under that approach, for children above 14 there is a rebuttable presumption in favor of the child's capacity to commit negligence; for children between seven and 14, there is a rebuttable presumption against capacity; children under the age of seven are deemed incapable of committing negligence.

The difference between the approach taken in Subsection (a) and the minority approach is narrowed by the presence of Subsection (b) providing that children under five years of age are incapable of negligence and by essentially all jurisdictions' acceptance of Subsection (c), providing that children are treated as adults when they engage in dangerous adult activities. . . .

c. Evidence of age, intelligence, and experience. Evidence bearing on the issues identified in Subsection (a) can come from those who know the child, including parents and teachers; it can also come directly from the child. . . . Although the rule for adults set forth in § 11(c) is that mental or emotional disability is a factor not generally taken into account, under the more flexible rules applicable to children any evidence of mental or emotional deficit can be considered. Evidence about experience typically focuses on the child's experience with the particular activity that has given rise to the accident—what the child knows about the activity, how frequently the child has engaged in it, and what instructions the child has received from parents or other adults as to which precautions are needed. For example, the child who has been instructed and reminded by parents not to dart into the street can easily be found contributorily negligent for doing so. . . .

d. Incapacity under age five. . . . [T]he possibility is slight that the conduct of a child under five is either deserving of moral criticism or is capable of being deterred by the application of tort rules. It is therefore appropriate to simplify tort litigation by adopting a rule that regards children under five as incapable of negligent conduct. It would be quite awkward to have a child under five testifying at trial, or being cross-examined, in a case that seeks to raise an issue of the child's negligence or contributory negligence. Of course, when a three-year-old child darts into the street and is struck by a car, the law's denial of the child's contributory negligence does not itself signify that the motorist is liable, either in full or even in part. There remains the need to establish the negligence of the motorist; for example, in driving at an unreasonable speed or in not keeping a proper lookout. Absent such negligence, the motorist bears no liability.

e. Negligence and contributory negligence. The rules relating to children and negligence apply also to children and contributory negligence. . . .

f. Dangerous adult activities. When children choose to engage in dangerous activities characteristically engaged in by adults, no account is taken of their childhood. . . . Examples of dangerous adult activities include driving a car, a tractor, and a motorcycle, and operating other motorized vehicles such as minibikes, motorscooters, dirt bikes, and snowmobiles. Third parties encountering children who are engaging in ordinary youthful activities can typically adjust their own conduct in order to make allowances for the children's proximity. Yet when children engage in adult activities such as motoring, their status as children often cannot be detected, making it impossible for third parties to modify their conduct appropriately. Even if an activity is characteristically engaged in by adults, if it is not distinctly dangerous it is not covered by Subsection (c). For example, baking a meatloaf, although typically an adult activity, ordinarily is not distinctly dangerous. Accordingly, if a child by misusing a kitchen utensil is injured or injures another while assisting a parent in this activity, under Subsection (a) a child standard applies to the evaluation of the child's conduct. . . .

g. Adolescence. In explaining the rule that children who engage in dangerous adult activities such as operating cars and motor scooters are held to an adult standard, it is notable that the children in question are generally older children or teenagers. In considering adolescents who engage in adult activities, it can be observed that adolescents are responsible for a disproportionately high accident rate. If adolescents who engage in dangerous activities such as motoring were held to less than a full standard of care, the result in terms of the noncompensation of victims of substandard conduct would be quite serious. The very high accident rate of 16- and 17-year-old motorists is no doubt partly due to their inexperience. In addition, on account of immature judgment, many adolescents may underestimate the extent of the risks involved in various dangerous activities. Furthermore, it appears that many adolescents display a preference for risk-taking, deriving special pleasure from behaving in certain risky ways; these are pleasures that negligence law tends to disregard.

§ 11. Disability

Restatement of the Law Third, Torts: Liability for Physical and Emotional Harm

(a) **The conduct of an actor with a physical disability is negligent only if the conduct does not conform to that of a reasonably careful person with the same disability.**

(b) **The conduct of an actor during a period of sudden incapacitation or loss of consciousness resulting from physical illness is negligent only if the sudden incapacitation or loss of consciousness was reasonably foreseeable to the actor.**

(c) **An actor's mental or emotional disability is not considered in determining whether conduct is negligent, unless the actor is a child.**

Comment:

a. Disabilities considered. The physical disabilities this Section takes into account generally need to be significant and objectively verifiable. For reasons relating to convenience of administration, it is not worthwhile to attempt to take into account disabilities that are minor or not susceptible to objective verification. Thus, a person's claim of being born clumsy would not be regarded as relevant.

b. Implications. Physical disability can both advantage and disadvantage actors at trial as the possible negligence of their past conduct is considered. It can advantage the actor by establishing that the actor neither knew nor should have known of dangers that would have been known by others. The blind person, for example, is unable to see dangers that would be readily observed by others. Physical disability can also advantage the actor at trial by showing that the actor was unable to adopt a precaution that would be feasible for most persons. The pedestrian with one leg, for example, is not able to run as a speeding car approaches, even though running is a convenient precaution for most pedestrians.

At the same time, persons with particular disabilities can appreciate that some conduct on their part will foreseeably entail a greater risk than the same conduct engaged in by able-bodied persons. Able to foresee this, an actor can be found negligent for not adopting special precautions that can reasonably reduce the special dangers that the actor's conduct involves. For example, it is considerably more dangerous for a blind person to walk over unfamiliar terrain than for a person free of disability. Thus, depending on the circumstances, a blind actor may be found negligent for walking over such terrain without a cane or some other form of assistance.

While it is sometimes said that an actor with a disability must adopt precautions that "compensate" for that disability, obviously complete compensation is often impracticable; what is required is the adoption of reasonable precautions such that their safety advantages outbalance their disadvantages and inconveniences. Yet even with those precautions adopted, there may be a level of risk associated with the activity that makes it negligent for an actor to engage in the activity at all. If, for example, an actor's vision is sufficiently impaired, it is negligent for that person to drive a car. . . .

c. Old age. Old age, as such, is not taken into account in assessing the negligence of an actor's conduct. In many individual cases, however, old age is affiliated with particular physical disabilities. Under Subsection (a), those physical disabilities are taken into account. Thus, an 80-year-old actor who is no longer able to run will not be found negligent in failing to run as a hazard approaches. On the other hand, such an actor may be found negligent for engaging in an activity where running away from dangers is an important precaution.

d. Sudden incapacitation. . . . If an actor has information indicating that an incident of incapacitation may be imminent or is likely to occur in the immediate future, the actor will obviously be unable to show unforeseeability and hence can be found negligent for the subsequent incident of substandard conduct. For that matter, if such an incident is foreseeable in the immediate

80

future, the actor can be found negligent for proceeding to engage at all in a dangerous activity such as driving. For example, if an actor with a diabetic condition feels a hypoglycemic episode approaching, the actor is guilty of negligence in driving a car—or at least in failing to take medication to prevent the episode.

In many cases, however, it is clear that the immediate incident was one that the actor had no ability to foresee. Whether the reasonable-foreseeability standard is satisfied in such a case depends on what information was available to the actor indicating that at some uncertain point in the future the actor might suffer an instance of incapacitation while engaging in a potentially dangerous activity such as driving. Evidence bearing on reasonable foreseeability includes: the number and frequency of episodes of incapacitation in the past; the circumstances of those episodes, insofar as those circumstances bear on the likelihood of a recurrence; the extent to which medical treatment the actor is receiving can be expected to control the underlying medical problem; and whatever advice the actor's physician has provided. Whether the information is significant enough to render the instance of incapacitation reasonably foreseeable is commonly a question to be decided by the jury. In the assessment of reasonable foreseeability, a principal issue to be considered by the jury is whether the prospect of incapacitation is sufficiently foreseeable as to render the actor negligent for choosing to engage in a potentially dangerous activity such as driving.

e. Mental and emotional disability. When the actor is a child, the quite subjective rules concerning children set forth in § 10(a) apply, and any mental or emotional disability suffered by the child is taken into account in determining whether the child has behaved reasonably. For adults, however, such a disability is typically disregarded in considering whether the person has exercised reasonable care. . . . To be sure, modern society is increasingly inclined to treat physical disabilities and mental disabilities similarly, and this inclination is supported by the recognition that many mental disabilities have organic causes. Nevertheless, courts have advanced significant considerations in support of their position. It is useful to distinguish between limited or moderate mental disorders and those disorders that are the most serious, such as psychoses. The former are disregarded partly because they ordinarily are not especially important as an explanation for conduct and also because of the problems of administrability that would be encountered in attempting to identify them and assess their significance. The disregard of more serious mental disorders is also based in part on administrative considerations. The awkwardness experienced by the criminal-justice system in attempting to litigate the insanity defense is at least instructive. Similarly, it can be difficult in many cases to ascertain what the causal connection is between even a serious mental disorder and

81

conduct that appears to be unreasonable. Furthermore, if a person is suffering from a mental disorder so serious as to make it likely that the person will engage in substandard conduct that threatens the safety of others, there can be doubts as to whether the person should be allowed to engage in the normal range of society's activities. While modern society has tended to resolve these doubts in favor of deinstitutionalization, there is nothing especially harsh in at least holding such a person responsible for those harms that the person's clearly substandard conduct causes. The theory of deinstitutionalization implies that even persons with severe mental disorders can adequately comply with society's norms; while reality may fall short of theory, deinstitutionalization becomes more socially acceptable if innocent victims are at least assured of opportunity for compensation when they suffer injury.

In addition, to recognize mental disability as a factor bearing on findings of negligence would be one-sided in a way that recognizing physical disability is not. Under Subsection (a), the physically disabled person, though relieved from doing what the disability prevents the person from doing, is expected to adopt extra precautions to respond to the extra level of risk that the person creates or incurs on account of the disability. Yet when the disability is mental or emotional, the disability directly affects the person's rationality and judgment; because of this, it frequently will be the case that the law cannot expect the person wisely and appropriately to moderate conduct choices so as to take the person's disability into account. . . .

[T]he rule in Subsection (c) that an actor's mental disabilities shall be disregarded applies in the context of the actor's contributory negligence as well as the context of the actor's negligence. . . .

There are, moreover, circumstances . . . that warrant taking actor's emotional disorders into account. The reasoning that ordinarily justifies disregarding those disorders is largely designed to protect the interests and safety of innocent third parties, and to protect even negligent third parties from bearing excessive liabilities. When the plaintiff and the defendant are bound together in an ongoing economic relationship, this reasoning diminishes in force. Thus, if the plaintiff is a health-care professional who has been hired to take care of the person whose emotional disability makes the patient dangerous to others, the plaintiff cannot complain if injured by the very condition that gives rise to the plaintiff's employment. . . .

§ 12.   Knowledge and Skills

Restatement of the Law Third, Torts: Liability for Physical and Emotional Harm

If an actor has skills or knowledge that exceed those possessed by most others, these skills or

82

knowledge are circumstances to be taken into account in determining whether the actor has behaved as a reasonably careful person.

Comment:

a. Rationale. . . . [O]n balance it is best to take persons' actual knowledge and skills into account when the level of their knowledge or skills exceeds the average. In determining which dangers the person knows or should know of, and which precautions the person can appropriately adopt, it simply is not possible to ignore what knowledge the person actually has. For example, if a motorist on a lightly traveled road happens actually to know, because of a recent driving experience, that a deep pothole lurks in the road ahead, the motorist can be found negligent for failing to slow down in approaching that pothole even though the typical motorist would be unaware of its existence. Tort law has always inquired into what the actor "knew or should have known"; so long as the actor has actual knowledge, the source of that knowledge has not been deemed material. . . .

b. Substandard judgment, knowledge, and skills. The fact that a person is below average in judgment, knowledge, or skills is generally ignored in considering whether the person is negligent. . . . A somewhat special case concerns learners or beginners. Just as the law holds teenagers who choose to engage in adult activities to adult standards despite their inexperience, so adults who choose to engage in particular activities can properly be held to general standards, even when they are learners. Yet while an actor's status as a learner is in general ignored, there can be relationships between that actor and the other actor that attach significance to this status. When, for example, the defendant, while learning to drive, receives a lesson from the plaintiff, and when the defendant's inexperienced operation of the car causes an accident that injures the plaintiff, the defendant's status as a beginner is taken into account in considering the defendant's negligence and hence the defendant's liability. That status is ignored, however, if the defendant is sued by a pedestrian injured in the same accident.

c. Intoxication. In a rare case, a person might be the victim of involuntary intoxication: the iced tea the person is drinking may have been spiked with liquor. If the person's resulting intoxication helps explain substandard conduct, this intoxication is taken into account in determining whether the actor has behaved as a reasonably careful person. — liability for negligence depends

Ordinarily, however, intoxication is essentially voluntary in nature. Moreover, intoxication is an important explanation for accidents. A substantial percentage of all highway accidents that produce fatalities involve the consumption of alcohol by the driver of at least one of the vehicles involved. A large percentage of all pedestrians killed in highway accidents are intoxicated at the time of the accidents. Similarly, a substantial fraction of all fatal falls and fatal burns are evidently due to the victims' intoxication.

When an actor's intoxication is voluntary, it is not considered as an excuse for the actor's conduct that is otherwise lacking in reasonable care. Moreover, actors can be found negligent precisely because they consume alcohol knowing that they will shortly be undertaking a dangerous task or because they undertake such a task knowing that they are under the influence of alcohol. . . .

CHAPTER 6

BREACH OF DUTY

A. CUSTOM

§ 13. Custom

Restatement of the Law Third, Torts: Liability for Physical and Emotional Harm

> **(a) An actor's compliance with the custom of the community, or of others in like circumstances, is evidence that the actor's conduct is not negligent but does not preclude a finding of negligence.**
>
> **(b) An actor's departure from the custom of the community, or of others in like circumstances, in a way that increases risk is evidence of the actor's negligence but does not require a finding of negligence.**

Comment:

a. Background. . . . In tort law, negligence is often defined as the lack of "ordinary care." Because complying with custom confirms that the actor has behaved in the ordinary way, one might suppose that proof of compliance with custom would be a complete defense against an allegation of negligence. In this respect, however, the negligence standard, concerned with "reasonable care," is more demanding than a standard understood solely in

85

terms of ordinary care. While the actor is entitled to present to the jury evidence showing that the actor complied with custom, the other party is free to present other evidence, including evidence bearing on the factors identified in § 3, and in doing so seek to establish that the actor's conduct lacks reasonable care.

Illustration:

> 1. Clyde was a guest at the Hilgard Hotel. At nine in the evening, there was a power outage that deprived the hotel of electricity. In his dark room, Clyde fell and injured himself. There was no form of emergency lighting within the hotel room, although flashlights were available at the hotel front desk. At trial, Clyde identified an inexpensive battery-powered lighting fixture that a hotel could install in guest rooms. Had Clyde's room had such a fixture, he would have avoided injury. However, expert testimony makes clear that no hotels provide in-room emergency lighting of this sort. This evidence of Hilgard's compliance with hotel custom is some evidence of its nonnegligence; yet if there is adequate evidence that emergency lighting in hotel rooms is a reasonable precaution with respect to the risk of guests injuring themselves during a power outage, Clyde's claim of negligence can be considered by the jury.

b. Compliance with custom: rationale. Evidence that the actor has complied with custom in adopting certain precautions may bear on whether there were further precautions available to the actor, whether these precautions were feasible, and whether the actor knew or should have known of them. In assessing such evidence, the jury can take into account the fact that almost all others have chosen the same course of conduct as has the actor: "ordinary care" has at least some bearing on "reasonable care." Furthermore, if the actor's conduct represents the custom of those engaging in a certain line of activity, the jury should be aware of this, for it cautions the jury that its ruling on the particular actor's negligence has implications for large numbers of other parties.

The actor's proof of compliance with custom does not, however, conclusively show that the actor was free of negligence in not adopting further precautions. Possibly, the entire community or industry has lagged: all members of the group to which the actor belongs may have been inattentive to new developments or may have been pursuing self-interest in a way that has encouraged the neglect of a reasonable precaution. . . .

c. Departure from custom: rationale. . . . While proof of deviation from custom is only evidence of negligence, this evidence often has significant weight. As a practical matter, the party who has departed from custom can counter the effect of this evidence by questioning the intelligence of the custom, by showing that its

86

operation poses different or less serious risks than those occasioned by others engaging in seemingly similar activities, or by showing that it has adopted an alternative method for reducing or controlling risks that is at least as effective as the customary method. Of course, the actor's departure from custom is initially relevant only if that departure seemingly results in an increase in risk. . . .

Illustration:

2. Carl is a guest in the Finney Hotel. The bathroom in the hotel includes a shower, protected by a sliding door made of ordinary glass. Carl trips while taking a shower and falls on the door. Its glass shatters and lacerates Carl. It is a standard practice among hotels to use shatter-proof tempered safety glass rather than ordinary glass at hazardous locations, such as shower enclosures. Finney's departure from this custom is some evidence of its negligence.

d. Widespread reliance on custom. In some cases, a custom is such that it induces general reliance by virtually all those participating in an activity; to this extent, custom establishes the standard by which those engaging in the activity assume they are bound. For example, rules of the road—such as driving on the right—can develop on private roadways ungoverned by public regulations. An actor's violation of such a custom is often clear proof of negligence.

e. Private standards and public recommendations. In some cases, the actor has complied with or departed from a standard issued by a private organization, or a recommendation issued by a government agency. . . . [S]uch a standard or recommendation can bear on the issue of negligence; often, in an effort to defeat a claim of negligence, a party seeks to show that it has complied with a private organization's standard. Insofar as the standard or the recommendation is understood to be the consensus of leading experts as to desirable or appropriate practices, the evidence rules of the jurisdiction determine the standard's admissibility. . . . Insofar as, in one way or another, the standard or public-agency recommendation is shown to be the equivalent of custom, evidence concerning the standard or recommendation should be treated in accordance with this Section.

f. Actor's departure from own standard. At times a party— typically a large-scale defendant—has adopted standards applicable to its own operations or its own employees. When in the individual case the defendant or its employee departs from that standard, the plaintiff might seek to introduce the standard, and the departure from the standard, as evidence of the defendant's negligence. However, it is quite possible that the defendant's own standard involves a precaution that is more protective than those precautions called for by the general negligence standard. . . . In such a case, allowing the defendant's departure from its own standard to be used against the defendant might seem unfair, since it penalizes the defendant who has voluntarily provided an extra measure of safety. Also, admissibility can discourage defendants from adopting such protective standards; the defendant can readily appreciate that if it adopts such a standard, there will inevitably be occasional lapses, which will expose it to liability.

On the other hand, the existence of the defendant's standard impugns any claim by the defendant that the risk in question is actually unforeseeable or that the safety practice is unfeasible. Moreover, in many cases the plaintiff is a customer of the defendant, or has otherwise entered into a relationship with the defendant, at the time the standard is violated. If so, the plaintiff may well have relied on the defendant's standard (or the defendant's general reputation for safety) in choosing to deal with the defendant; furthermore, the plaintiff may well be paying for at least the general costs of compliance that the standard imposes on the defendant. . . .

[T]he best position is the flexible position that the admissibility of evidence as to the actor's departure from its own standard depends on all the circumstances of the individual case. Of course, even if this evidence is admissible, it does not set a higher standard of care for the actor; rather, it merely bears on the ultimate question of whether the actor has exercised reasonable care.

B. VIOLATION OF STATUTE

§ 14. Statutory Violations as Negligence Per Se

Restatement of the Law Third, Torts: Liability for Physical and Emotional Harm

> **An actor is negligent if, without excuse, the actor violates a statute that is designed to protect against the type of accident the actor's conduct causes, and if the accident victim is within the class of persons the statute is designed to protect.**

Comment:

a. Statutes, regulations, and ordinances. This Section most frequently applies to statutes adopted by state legislatures, but equally applies to regulations adopted by state administrative bodies, ordinances adopted by local councils, and federal statutes as well as regulations promulgated by federal agencies.

b. Express and implied statutory causes of action. Some statutes declare conduct unlawful, impose a public-law penalty on the person whose conduct violates the statute, and also specify that the violator is civilly liable in damages to the victim of the violation. Certain other statutes simply state that, if certain conduct causes harm, the actor is liable to a victim. In considering a suit brought against the violator by a victim of the violation, the responsibility of the court is to enforce the liability right expressly created by the statute. In doing so, the court may need to consider whether traditional tort defenses such as comparative negligence should be deemed impliedly incorporated into the statutory cause of action.

Yet large numbers of statutes, in declaring conduct unlawful and creating a public-law penalty, are silent as to private liability in the event of a statutory violation. In a suit brought by the victim of such a violation, the court, relying on ordinary principles of legislative interpretation, may in appropriate cases infer from the statute a cause of action for damages against the violator. In cases involving conduct that causes physical or emotional harm, courts have not often exercised the authority referred to in this Comment; no doubt this is because the longstanding recognition of the common-law rule affirmed in this Section reduces the significance of an implied statutory cause of action. Beyond implied private causes of action and negligence per se, statutes may also be the basis for finding an affirmative duty.

c. Rationale. The rule in this Section presupposes a statute that declares conduct unlawful but that is silent as to civil liability and that cannot be readily interpreted as impliedly creating a private right of action. . . . [C]ourts, exercising their common-law authority to develop tort doctrine, not only should regard the actor's statutory violation as evidence admissible against the actor, but should treat that violation as actually determining the actor's negligence. An unexcused violation of the statute is thus negligence per se.

There are several rationales for this common-law practice. First, even when the legislature has not chosen to attach a liability provision to the prohibition it has imposed, as a matter of institutional comity it would be awkward for a court in a tort case to commend as reasonable that behavior that the legislature has already condemned as unlawful. Second, in ordinary tort cases, so long as reasonable minds can differ, the responsibility for determining whether a person's conduct is negligent is vested in the jury. One major reason for this is to take advantage of community assessments in making the negligence determination. Yet when the legislature has addressed the issue of what conduct is appropriate, the judgment of the legislature, as the authoritative representative of the community, takes precedence over the views of any one jury.

Third, it must be recognized that the negligence standard encounters difficulty in dealing with problems of recurring conduct. When each jury makes up its own mind as to the negligence of that conduct, there are serious disadvantages in terms of inequality, high litigation costs, and failing to provide clear guidance to persons engaged in primary activity. Because, under § 8(b), courts on their own can only occasionally take negligence determinations away from the jury, these disadvantages of case-by-case decisionmaking remain. In general, statutes address conduct that conspicuously recurs in a way that brings it to the attention of the legislature. Negligence per se hence replaces decisionmaking by juries in categories of cases where the operation of the latter may be least satisfactory.

Furthermore, negligence per se has been settled doctrine in American tort law for many decades. Once settled, the doctrine functions as a default rule in terms of how the judiciary will assess the significance of a statute. The legislature, in enacting a safety statute, can be aware that a party's violation of the statute will result in negligence per se. Aware of this, the legislature can be deemed to accept this result—unless it includes in the statute a specific provision making the statutory violation irrelevant in a common-law action for damages. If the statute does include such a provision, courts should of course honor it and decline to apply this Section.

d. Importance. The doctrine of negligence per se has always been significant in American tort law, and its significance has expanded in recent decades, as the number of statutory and regulatory controls has substantially increased. In particular, the conduct of motorists is extensively dealt with by statutes and regulations; accordingly, in most highway-accident cases, findings of negligence depend on ascertaining which party has violated the relevant provisions of the state's motor-vehicle code. However, for certain other fields of tort law—such as medical malpractice—there is a comparative lack of statutory and regulatory controls. In these areas, negligence per se is of less importance.

f. Type of accident. Negligence per se applies only when the accident that injures the plaintiff is the type of accident that the statute seeks to avert. This statutory-purpose doctrine resembles the scope-of-liability doctrine that is applied in ordinary negligence cases: under the latter, the defendant is liable only if the accident that harmed the plaintiff is the type of accident the jury has taken into account in designating the defendant's conduct as negligent. See Chapter 6.

In determining the purpose of the statute, the court can rely on the ordinary principles of statutory interpretation, including the language or text of the statutory provision, its location within the larger statutory scheme, the more general context of the statute, and indications of specific legislative intent. There is no requirement that the type of accident the plaintiff has suffered be the only type of accident the statute seeks to avert; it suffices if the court can find that avoiding this type of accident is one of the statute's explicit or significant objectives. . . .

Illustrations:

1. A state statute requires that the operator of a truck that becomes disabled on a highway promptly put out a warning sign at least 100 feet behind the truck. When a deflated tire disables Carl's truck, he places a warning sign right next to the truck. Ann, approaching Carl's truck from behind, does not see Carl's warning sign until it is too late for her to stop. Her car strikes the rear of Carl's truck, and she is injured in the collision. Ann would have been able to stop in time had the warning sign been set at the 100-foot distance. In the suit brought by Ann against Carl, Carl's violation of the statute is negligence per se; the basic purpose of the statute is to prevent accidents of this type. In the absence of the statute, Carl's failure to place a warning sign at least 100 feet away from the truck would merely raise a jury question as to Carl's possible negligence.

2. A state administrative regulation requires railroad trains to avoid blocking highway crossings for more than 10 minutes. The Pacific Railway allows one of its trains to remain in a highway crossing for 30 minutes. Fifteen minutes into this 30-minute period, Arthur, driving on the highway, fails to notice the train until it is too late, and collides with it, suffering an injury. Arthur concedes that his absent-minded negligence should reduce his recovery under comparative negligence, but claims that Pacific is negligent per se for violating the regulation. However, a review of the history of the regulation and of the agency's findings that accompany the regulation shows that its only purpose is to encourage the free flow of traffic and prevent traffic delays. Because the prevention of personal injuries is not part of this purpose, Pacific is not negligent per se.

3. A state statute requires that all slow-moving vehicles drive as far to the right on the highway as possible. One of this statute's major purposes is to minimize the safety hazards posed by vehicles whose slow speed can interfere with the flow of highway traffic. Ellen is driving slowly on a highway heading north, yet is violating the statute by driving in the fast lane on the left. Bob is a passenger in Ellen's car. A car coming south on the highway for some reason crosses the highway's median line and strikes Ellen's car, injuring Bob. Had Ellen been in the lane on the far right, her car would have avoided contact with the other car. Bob sues Ellen, and seeks to show her negligence by establishing her violation of the statute. The purpose of the statute is to protect highway safety. However, the statute is designed to prevent accidents between cars mov-

ing in the same direction caused by one car's slow speed, not to prevent accidents between cars moving in opposite directions. Accordingly, Ellen's violation of the statute is not negligence per se.

g. *Class of victims*. To invoke negligence per se, a party must show that the plaintiff was within the class of persons the legislature was endeavoring to protect. . . . The denial [of use of negligence per se when the plaintiff was not a member of the class of victims the legislature was trying to protect] might be subsumed under a type-of-accident analysis, in which the identity of the victim is deemed part of the relevant accident "type." For example, if a statute designed to prevent falls by persons with disabilities requires elaborate railings on the side of stairways, and if a person who is able-bodied is then injured in a fall that such a railing, if present, would have prevented, this fall can be seen as not the type of accident the statute is considering.

However, in certain cases it is exclusively the plaintiff's identity that prevents the accident from being the type anticipated by the legislature. For example, a worksite may contain a plainly dangerous condition that proves the employer's violation of an occupational safety regulation; even so, under this Section negligence per se cannot be invoked if the person suffering injury on account of that dangerous condition turns out to be not a worker but rather a business invitee on the employer's premises. . . .

h. *Factual causation and scope of liability for licensing statutes.* . . . [O]nce the defendant's negligence is established, under other Sections of this Restatement the plaintiff needs to show that the defendant's negligence was a factual cause of the plaintiff's injury and the injury was within the defendant's scope of liability. For example, it may be negligence per se for the defendant to violate a statute by operating a car under the influence of alcohol; but if another motorist rear-ends the defendant, the defendant's negligence in violating the statute is not a factual cause of the plaintiff's injury. Similarly, if the defendant injures a pedestrian while driving in excess of the statutory speed limit, and if an ambulance rushing the pedestrian to the hospital is then struck by lightning so that the plaintiff suffers further injuries, the plaintiff's opportunity to recover from the originally negligent driver for those further injuries depends on the application of scope-of-liability principles. . . .

For a number of activities capable of causing physical and emotional harm, the government requires the licensing of those engaged in the activity. One general purpose of such licensing programs is to protect the public against physical and emotional harm. But in many cases, the immediate reason for the person's lack of a license is unrelated to the state's general safety purpose. For example, a motorist may lack a license only because of a failure to file for license renewal. If this motorist is involved in an accident, the lack of a license has no bearing on the motorist's negligence. Similarly, a physician may lack a license in a state only because the physician has not yet satisfied the state's residency requirement. In these circumstances, the lack of a license does not bear on the physician's possible malpractice in terms of services delivered. In light, then, of the combination of the statutory-purpose doctrine and ordinary principles of scope of liability, the lack of a license is not negligence per se on the part of the actor, nor is it evidence tending to show the actor's negligence.

In other cases, however, this general assessment does not pertain. . . . If a property owner has installed a furnace without securing a permit required by a city ordinance, and if the evidence indicates that the inspector would not have issued the permit because of the furnace's capacity for emitting dangerous gases, then the person who suffers physical harm on account of such emissions can show that the owner's violation of the permit-requiring ordinance is negligence per se. The absence of a license in such a case is a proxy for the owner's violation of the city's substantive safety standards that are enforced through the licensing process.

i. Statutory violation and "duty." This Section primarily applies when the issue is whether the actor's conduct is negligent— whether it lacks reasonable care. . . . The violation of the statute is [also] relevant to a duty analysis, even though the violation does not signify duty per se. . . . [T]he presence of a statutory requirement that is binding on the defendant, and the court's awareness of the legislature's assumptions in imposing that requirement, can be important points for the court to consider in determining whether a duty exists. Consider, for example, a state whose courts have ruled that, under the common law, pharmacists have no tort "duty" directly to warn their customers of the side effects of medications. If, subsequently, a state agency imposes on pharmacists a regulatory duty to warn, the courts should take this regulation significantly into account in reconsidering their earlier ruling; yet the regulation does not require that the courts now recognize a tort duty.

§ 15. Excused Violations

Restatement of the Law Third, Torts: Liability for Physical and Emotional Harm

> **An actor's violation of a statute is excused and not negligence if:**
>
> **(a) the violation is reasonable in light of the actor's childhood, physical disability, or physical incapacitation;**
>
> **(b) the actor exercises reasonable care in attempting to comply with the statute;**

(c) the actor neither knows nor should know of the factual circumstances that render the statute applicable;

(d) the actor's violation of the statute is due to the confusing way in which the requirements of the statute are presented to the public; or

(e) the actor's compliance with the statute would involve a greater risk of physical harm to the actor or to others than noncompliance.

Comment:

a. Background. . . . The excuses recognized by this Section temper what would otherwise be the severity of negligence per se and also reintroduce a significant role for jury assessments in negligence per se cases. One possible problem with the doctrine of negligence per se is that it neglects the point that legislatures, in adopting statutes that prohibit broad categories of private behavior, typically contemplate that public officials will exercise wise discretion in determining which violations of the statutes warrant the initiation of public proceedings. Recognizing excuses under this Section prevents the negligence per se doctrine from being applied in many of those cases in which public officials might well find it inappropriate to prosecute the person who technically is a law violator.

In light of the extensive list of acceptable excuses, it is useful to set forth circumstances that do not count as an excuse. The violation of a statute is not excused by the fact that the person sincerely or reasonably believes that the requirement set by the statute is excessive or unwise; nor is it an excuse if the person is unaware or ignorant of the statutory requirement; nor is it an excuse if there is a custom to depart from the statutory requirement. . . .

b. Childhood and physical disability. Just as an evaluation of ordinary negligence takes into account circumstances such as the childhood of the actor under § 10 and the physical disability of the actor under § 11, so an analysis of negligence per se is modified to take physical disability and childhood into account. Thus, if a motorist violates a statute by crossing over to the wrong side of the highway only because the motorist has been suddenly incapacitated by a heart attack, the motorist is excused from negligence per se. Similarly, if a six-year-old violates a statute by crossing the street outside the marked intersection, the child can be excused from negligence per se if this conduct is consistent with the conduct of other children of the same age, intelligence, and experience. . . .

c. Reasonable efforts to comply. Many statutes seemingly

impose public-law penalties on a strict-liability basis. Thus, a statute may require of all motor-vehicle owners that their vehicles have well-functioning brakes, even though brakes can frequently fail without any negligence on the part of the owner. Other statutes impose requirements that in almost all circumstances can be met by persons who act reasonably—for example, a statute requiring that a car be driven so as to remain on the right side of the road; still, special circumstances—for example, highway emergencies or adverse weather conditions—can result in occasional violations by motorists whose behavior is reasonable.

When the seeming violation of such a statute is relied on as negligence per se, the initial responsibility of the court is to interpret the statute intelligently. Certain statutes that do not set forth any explicit negligence requirement properly can be interpreted as implicitly requiring negligence on the part of the supposed statutory violator. Thus, a statute requiring adequate brakes plausibly can be interpreted as including an implicit requirement that the car owner have some reason to know of the brakes' inadequacy. . . . Similarly, if a statute imposes a strict-liability obligation on motorists to remain on the right side of the road, the motorist whose car crosses the middle of the road because of a sudden tire deflation is excused from negligence per se if the tire deflates despite the motorist's reasonable efforts to prevent this result. . . .

d. Reasonable opportunity to know of factual circumstances. . . . If . . . the actor who violates the statute is unaware of [factors that are not ordinarily present], and if that actor further proves that this ignorance was reasonable, the actor's violation of the statute is excused for purposes of negligence per se. . . . A statute, for example, might prohibit work within 10 feet of a high-voltage power line; if that power line is completely hidden by foliage, and if there are no circumstances that might alert a reasonably careful person to the power line's presence, the actor's violation of the statute is excused.

e. Confusing presentation of the law's requirements. While ignorance of the law does not count as an excuse, for negligence per se to operate fairly the legal system must avoid confusion in its communication of the law's obligations. Accordingly, if a statute is so vague or ambiguous that even the actor aware of the statute would need to guess as to its requirements, the actor who makes a reasonable guess is excused from negligence per se even if a later judicial resolution of the ambiguity reaches a different result. . . . If a sign or signal is such as to confuse the reasonable motorist, negligence per se is not appropriate. . . .

f. Noncompliance is safer. The goal of negligence per se is to encourage conduct that is not negligent—that is, that constitutes

95

reasonable care. Accordingly, an excuse for negligence per se is recognized in unusual cases in which it is proved that the actor's compliance with a statute would create a greater danger than the actor's violation of the statute. The greater danger can be one to which the actor violating the statute would be exposed. Thus, if a statute requires bicyclists to ride on the right side of the road, but expert testimony shows that under the particular traffic circumstances riding on the left side of the road facing traffic is clearly safer, then the bicyclist who violates the statute is excused from negligence per se. Or the danger averted can be one relating to third parties. Thus, a motorist, to avoid striking a child who has darted into the street, might violate a statute by swerving across the middle lane of a highway; if the motorist reasonably concludes that the risks involved in crossing over to the wrong side of the street are less than the risks involved in striking the child, the motorist's violation of the statute is excused. . . .

g. Additional excuses. Although the absence of cases reduces the likelihood of this, there may be further excuses worthy of recognition. For example, there may be a statute, enacted decades ago, that sets forth a 10-mile-per-hour speed limit, and that has never been formally repealed, even though it has been effectively forgotten both by motorists and by law-enforcement officials; the former do not comply with the statute and the latter make no effort to enforce it. In such circumstances, an excuse from negligence per se would be appropriate for the motorist who violates the statute.

C. COMPLIANCE WITH STATUTE

§ 16. Statutory Compliance

Restatement of the Law Third, Torts: Liability for Physical and Emotional Harm

> **(a) An actor's compliance with a pertinent statute, while evidence of nonnegligence, does not preclude a finding that the actor is negligent under § 3 for failing to adopt precautions in addition to those mandated by the statute.**

> **(b) If an actor's adoption of a precaution would require the actor to violate a statute, the actor cannot be found negligent for failing to adopt that precaution.**

Comment:

b. General rule. . . . The rule concerning compliance with statutes may derive partial support from a concern that the lawmaking process can sometimes be insufficiently attentive to the interests of potential victims. . . .

c. Whether the statute specifically addresses the safety problem. A finding that precautions beyond those specified in the statute are called for under this Section is clearly appropriate when the statute does not specifically address the safety problem at issue. Thus, a statute requiring the motorist to signal before turning left does not relate to the motorist's possible negligence in cutting the corner while making the left turn. When tort law finds such a motorist negligent, it in no way questions the judgment rendered by the legislative body. Rather, tort law focuses on a particular precaution the legislators did not themselves consider or did not deem to be a proper object for formal regulation.

d. Statutes that merely set minimum standards. A finding that additional precautions are called for despite the person's compliance with the statute is clearly appropriate if the statute, properly interpreted, undertakes to establish only minimum standards. In requiring additional precautions, tort law recognizes that legislators intended to go part of the way, but not all the way, in identifying those precautions that negligence law generally deems appropriate.

e. Unusual circumstances. A finding that additional precautions are called for despite the actor's compliance with the statute is clearly appropriate if the precaution relates to some unusual situation beyond the generality of situations anticipated by the statute itself. While, for example, a statute may establish a highway speed limit of 55 miles per hour, this statute obviously addresses vehicle speed when highway conditions are essentially ordinary. If adverse weather or heavy traffic makes speeds as high as 55 miles per hour unwise, a finding that the motorist is negligent who drives at 55 miles per hour does not call into question the general judgment rendered by the legislature. . . .

f. Statutory compliance as a limitation on liability. While the Comments above explain the rule to the effect that compliance with statutes is usually no more than evidence of nonnegligence, the observations in the Comments suggest the rule's own limits. When the statute directly addresses the particular safety problem before the court, when the statutory scheme evidently seeks to identify all the precautions called for by the general negligence standards in § 3, and when the particular case involves no unusual circumstances, the court may conclude that the actor's compliance with the statute shows that the actor's conduct does not lack reasonable care. In reaching this conclusion, the court can take into account several factors, including the evident thoroughness of the statute and the desirability of a uniform liability standard that can simplify litigation and provide parties with appropriate guidance as to what precautions are expected of them.

Illustration:

    1. A state statute fixes a speed limit of 55 miles per hour

for a state highway. Linda is driving her car on that highway at a speed of 50 miles per hour. A teenager, Dave, unexpectedly darts from the sidewalk onto the highway. Despite a proper lookout, Linda is unable to stop in time, and strikes Dave, injuring him. Had Linda been driving at 40 miles per hour, she would have been able to avoid hitting Dave. In his lawsuit, Dave alleges that Linda was negligent in driving at a speed faster than 40 miles per hour. At the time the weather had been fine, the road and traffic conditions had been entirely ordinary, and no other circumstances suggested any special danger. A court would be justified in ruling as a matter of law that Linda was not negligent in the speed at which she operated her car.

g. Precautions that would violate statutes. When the absence of a precaution is alleged to be negligent, in a few cases the actor's adoption of that precaution would have required the actor to violate a statute. In such a case, even if § 3 standing on its own might permit a finding that the precaution is an appropriate way to reduce risks, a determination that the actor has been negligent would be improper. This impropriety can be explained in related ways. Many may believe that the values involved in the rule of law—in avoiding clear violations of statutes—take precedence over the values ordinarily associated with avoiding negligence. . . .

If, for example, an administrative agency, exercising powers delegated by statute, prohibits a railroad from installing a certain form of warning device at a highway crossing, the railroad cannot be found negligent for not providing that device. If a statute requires pedestrians or bicyclists to walk or ride with traffic, it would be wrong to find a pedestrian or bicyclist guilty of contributory negligence because of expert testimony that it is safer to walk or ride facing traffic. If traffic is flowing at 80 miles per hour on a highway whose statutory speed limit is 55 miles per hour, the motorist who chooses to drive at 55 may, by doing so, significantly disturb traffic flow in a way that could foreseeably lead to an accident; even so, that motorist cannot be found negligent for declining to drive at an illegal speed. Nevertheless, a court might find that a statute contains an implied exception that would permit deviation from its explicit requirements in an emergency, when a legislature plainly would have preferred that an exception be recognized. Thus, a law mandating a minimum speed on the freeway might be found to contain an implied exception to permit a motorist who is driving at the mandated minimum speed to slow down to avoid hitting a pedestrian if that is the only course of action available to avoid the accident. The jury would then be asked to determine whether such an emergency existed in the particular case and, if so, whether the defendant's failure to slow down constituted negligence. . . .

D. RES IPSA LOQUITUR — any neg. claim

§ 17.   Res Ipsa Loquitur

Restatement of the Law Third, Torts: Liability for Physical and Emotional Harm

> **The factfinder may infer that the defendant has been negligent when the accident causing the plaintiff's harm is a type of accident that ordinarily happens as a result of the negligence of a class of actors of which the defendant is the relevant member.**

Comment:

a. Background. Res ipsa loquitur is an appropriate form of circumstantial evidence enabling the plaintiff in particular cases to establish the defendant's likely negligence. . . . [R]es ipsa loquitur is circumstantial evidence of a quite distinctive form. The doctrine implies that the court does not know, and cannot find out, what actually happened in the individual case. Instead, the finding of likely negligence is derived from knowledge of the causes of the type or category of accidents involved. Assume, for example, that a car driven by the defendant runs off the road, injuring a pedestrian. In considering this category of accidents—cars that run off the road—several possible causes can be identified, including motorist negligence; some mechanical problem with the car; some defect in the roadway; and very adverse weather conditions. If the jury can reasonably believe that motorist negligence is most often the cause when cars run off the road, then, absent further evidence about the particular incident, the jury can reason from the general to the particular and hence properly infer that the defendant motorist was probably negligent.

A risk of error is involved in permitting such an inference; in fact, the motorist might have been free of negligence. But there is a risk of error whenever circumstantial evidence is relied on in reaching findings of negligence. To be sure, res ipsa loquitur does produce an element of discomfort, inasmuch as the defendant can be found negligent without any evidence as to the nature or circumstances of the defendant's actual conduct. This discomfort leads to some circumspection in the application of res ipsa loquitur.

b. Alternative formulations. There are two other methods for articulating the test for res ipsa loquitur. A number of courts adopt a two-step inquiry: step one asks whether the accident is of a type that usually happens because of negligence, while step two asks whether the "instrumentality" inflicting the harm was under the "exclusive control" of the defendant. This formulation, with its emphasis on exclusive control, is unsatisfactory for at least two reasons. One is that the test is sometimes indeterminate, since

99

there may be several instruments that could be deemed the cause of the plaintiff's injury. Another objection is more basic. . . . [F]requently exclusive control functions poorly as [a proxy for the question of which party was probably negligent]. Consider, for example, the consumer who buys a new car; a day after the purchase, the car's brakes fail, and the car strikes a pedestrian who is in a crosswalk. Undeniably, the motorist has exclusive control of the car at the time of the accident. Yet there is no reason to believe that the consumer is the negligent party, and adequate reason to believe that the negligence belongs to the car manufacturer (or, more precisely, that the latter has manufactured a defective product). Accordingly, the injured pedestrian should not have a res ipsa loquitur claim against the consumer, despite the latter's exclusive control; furthermore, the pedestrian might have a res-ipsa-like claim against the manufacturer, despite the latter's lack of exclusive control.

Another two-step formulation for res ipsa loquitur, accepted by some courts, is that res ipsa applies if the type of accident usually happens because of negligence, and if the negligence, when it occurs, is usually that of the defendant, rather than of some other party. This formulation is on the right track; the insight behind it is often basic to a res ipsa analysis. Nevertheless, as a precise test for res ipsa loquitur the formulation is incorrect in one way and unhelpful in another. It is incorrect because the evidence might show that two-thirds of the time accidents of a certain type happen because of negligence, and that two-thirds of the time when negligence does occur the defendant is the negligent party. These showings would satisfy the formulation, even though there is only a four-ninths likelihood that the defendant's negligence caused the accident that injured the plaintiff. Accordingly, the proper result in such a case is to reject res ipsa rather than to accept it. In addition, the formulation is unhelpful because it sets up a two-step inquiry when a one-step inquiry will often be sufficient. For example, assume there are five possible causes of a certain type of accident, each of them of roughly equal frequency; and assume further that only two of the causes are associated with defendant negligence. The formulation would require the jury to ascertain whether the remaining three causes involve the negligence of some party other than the defendant. But this inquiry is unnecessary; given the original information about the five possible causes, res ipsa loquitur should be denied. In a res ipsa case, the jury should be invited to compare those causes of the type of accident that suggest the negligence of the defendant with all other causes (whether negligent or not), and to find in favor of res ipsa if the former predominate.

c. Sources of information. In some cases, the jury can derive its understanding of the circumstances that cause a particular type of accident from the general experience, common knowledge, and common sense of the community. Such experience and knowledge is especially available and helpful when the type of accident is one with which ordinary citizens are generally familiar. It is the function of the court to determine whether there exists a fund of general experience and common knowledge on which the jury can draw.

Frequently, one or both of the parties will offer evidence about the various causes of a type of accident, for example through expert testimony. . . . For a particular type of accident, the court may determine that a fund of common knowledge and experience is lacking; alternatively, commonsense reasoning may run counter to the plaintiff's res ipsa loquitur allegations. In such cases, the plaintiff needs expert testimony in order to escape judgment as a matter of law on the res ipsa claim. . . . [E]xpert testimony is admissible in a medical-malpractice res ipsa loquitur case, and indeed is frequently necessary in order to justify submitting the res ipsa claim to the jury.

Illustration:

1. To deal with a problem of bleeding ulcers, Ronald agrees to surgery. Complications ensue in the course of surgery, which extends its duration from two hours to four hours. After surgery, Ronald ends up with only limited motion in his right arm. Ronald suspects negligence on the part of Dr. Jones, the anesthesiologist, but he has no specific evidence of this. In his suit against Dr. Jones, Ronald seeks to rely on res ipsa loquitur in order to prove Dr. Jones's negligence. Without expert testimony, Ronald's res ipsa loquitur claim against Dr. Jones fails; jurors lack general knowledge as to the possible causes of palsy in the arm after an extended anesthetic of this sort. However, if Dr. Smith, an expert, testifies that such instances of palsy are usually the result of the negligence of the anesthesiologist, Ronald's res ipsa loquitur claim can be considered by the jury. Dr. Jones is of course free to cross-examine Dr. Smith, or to present his own expert to challenge Dr. Smith's testimony.

d. Evidence about other possible causes. In many situations, neither common knowledge nor expert testimony may be available to support the idea that the type of accident ordinarily happens because of the negligence of the defendant. In such situations, res ipsa loquitur can be found applicable only if the plaintiff has offered evidence tending to negate the presence of causes other than the defendant's negligence. That is, if the type of accident is sometimes caused by the defendant's negligence but is more frequently brought about by other causes that are unrelated to the defendant's negligence, res ipsa loquitur can be found applicable only once the plaintiff has presented evidence tending to negate the presence of those other causes. For example, if a product

101

malfunctions six months after being acquired by the purchaser, an inference of the negligence of the manufacturer (or more precisely, a defect in the original product) becomes permissible only if the consumer introduces evidence tending to show that nothing during the six-month period of use explains why the product malfunctioned.

However, in other situations, a jury can reasonably find that the type of accident ordinarily happens because of the negligence of the class of actors whom the defendant represents.

Illustration:

   2. Bruce parks his car at the top of a driveway, which is on an incline. Two minutes later, the car rolls down the incline and injures Janice, on the sidewalk. In suing Bruce, Janice seeks to rely on res ipsa loquitur in order to prove Bruce's negligence. Admittedly, mechanical failure or third-party tampering are at least possible explanations for why the car rolled. Still, the jury's general knowledge can affirm that driver negligence is the usual cause when cars roll so quickly after being parked. Accordingly, the jury may infer that Bruce was negligent.

Evidence may be available about the particular accident that increases or decreases the likelihood of the accident's various possible causes. This evidence can be considered by the court in determining whether res ipsa loquitur is available. . . . For example, in a case involving an airplane crash, the res ipsa analysis acknowledges that certain forms of extremely bad weather, including unexpected wind shear, can be one cause of such crashes. If, on the day of the crash, a large storm was in progress, the possibility of wind shear as a cause of the crash is considerably enhanced. If, on the other hand, the weather was clear on that day, wind shear is eliminated as a possible cause. . . . In Illustration 2, the res ipsa claim would be weaker if there is evidence that vandals had recently been active in the neighborhood and had intruded into cars and released their brakes. . . .

   f. Identity of negligent party: multiple defendants. In cases in which it is clear that someone has been negligent, the remaining question concerns the likelihood that the defendant was the negligent party. If, for example, a product manufactured by one party, purchased and owned by a second party, and then used by a third party malfunctions in a way that causes injury to the plaintiff, it is reasonable to assume that the malfunction was brought about by the negligence on the part of either the manufacturer, the owner, or the user. However, further information is typically needed in order to establish that any one of the three was probably the negligent party. In the absence of such further information, res ipsa claims against any of the parties are properly rejected.

In limited circumstances, however, a group approach to res ipsa loquitur is supportable. If two parties have an ongoing relationship pursuant to which they share responsibility for a dangerous activity, and if an accident happens establishing the negligence of one of the two, imposing res ipsa loquitur liability on both is proper. Consider a building owned and controlled by one party and having an elevator purchased from a second party and serviced by the latter under an exclusive service contract. If the elevator malfunctions, res ipsa loquitur warrants findings of negligence on the part of both parties.

A special rule has developed for patients who suffer harm in the course of surgery. Even if the jury finds that the harm was probably caused by negligence, the jury may be uncertain whether the negligent act was committed by the surgeon, by one of the nurses, or by another medical professional participating in the surgery, such as the anesthesiologist. In such cases, courts permit the plaintiff to assert res ipsa loquitur against all the members of the surgical team. In situations of this sort in which a form of group liability initially applies, any one defendant can escape liability by persuading the jury that the defendant's own conduct was free of negligence. One effective way in which a defendant can accomplish this is by identifying the negligent act of another party that fully explains how the accident happened. This use of res ipsa loquitur is justified by providing incentives to "smoke out" relevant evidence rather than the more common rationale of accepting circumstantial evidence to prove a disputed issue.

g. Specific evidence of nonnegligence or negligence. The defendant may offer evidence showing that the defendant's own conduct was not negligent or that the accident happened for reasons unrelated to the defendant's negligence. If accepted by the jury, such evidence defeats the plaintiff's res ipsa claim. In such cases it can be said that the defendant's evidence prevents the application of res ipsa loquitur; alternatively, it can be said that res ipsa loquitur applies and permits an inference of negligence, but that the defendant's evidence sufficiently negates that inference.

A more difficult question arises when the plaintiff relies on res ipsa loquitur, but seeks in the alternative to assert and prove specific negligence on the defendant's part. . . . [M]ost modern courts find it inappropriate to penalize the plaintiff who seeks to prove specific negligence by preventing the plaintiff from developing and submitting to the jury a res ipsa loquitur argument in the alternative.

In certain cases, the evidence offered by the plaintiff can be properly understood as displacing any res ipsa loquitur claim. . . .

h. Plaintiff contribution. It is sometimes said in res ipsa loquitur cases that the plaintiff needs to exclude the possibility of the plaintiff's own contribution to the accident. A number of modern courts, noting that contributory negligence is no longer a full defense, have ruled that this prerequisite is no longer appropriate. Properly understood, the doctrine concerning plaintiff contribution has a narrow scope, yet survives the shift to comparative responsibility. For example, consider the motorist who parks a car at the top of an incline; a minute later, the car rolls down the incline and runs into a pedestrian, who at the time is carelessly not paying attention. In the pedestrian's suit against the motorist, the plaintiff's own carelessness is relevant as an affirmative defense, although perhaps only a partial defense under comparative responsibility. But the plaintiff's carelessness—even though it has contributed to the accident—in no way diminishes the res ipsa loquitur idea that the car probably rolled because of the motorist's negligence. Hence res ipsa applies, despite the plaintiff's contribution. By contrast, consider the case in which a hotel guest, while taking a shower, is scalded by extremely hot water. In such a case, the plaintiff, in order to establish that the scalding probably happened because of the negligence of the hotel, needs to prove that nothing in the plaintiff's own conduct explains how the incident occurred. In cases fitting this pattern—in which plaintiff contribution as an explanation for what went wrong is an alternative to defendant negligence—. . . . excluding plaintiff contribution is merely a specific aspect of establishing that defendant's negligence is the most probable cause of the accident. . . .

i. Defendant's access to information. . . . The elements of res ipsa loquitur set forth in this Section do not include the defendant's superior access to information. The plaintiff may invoke res ipsa even though the defendant is as ignorant of the facts of the accident as the plaintiff is. For example, in the case of a car that leaves the road and runs over a pedestrian on a sidewalk, the pedestrian may invoke res ipsa loquitur even though the motorist has died in the accident. . . .

j. Judge and jury. Initially, the court determines whether the plaintiff's evidence is sufficient for a reasonable jury to find that res ipsa loquitur is appropriate; that is, whether reasonable minds can infer that the accident is of the type that usually happens because of the negligence of the class of actors to which the defendant belongs. Most jurisdictions employ res ipsa as a permissive inference: an inference of negligence that the jury is entitled to make, but is not required to make. In at least a few jurisdictions, res ipsa loquitur creates a rebuttable presumption, thereby requiring the defendant to come forward with some exculpatory evidence or suffer a judgment as a matter of law. Even in jurisdictions that rely on permissive inferences, the facts of an occasional case may be so compelling in pointing to the defendant's negligence that a court would rule that no reasonable jury could find otherwise and grant judgment as a matter of law. . . .

E. PARTICULAR TYPES OF BREACH

§ 18. Negligent Failure to Warn

Restatement of the Law Third, Torts: Liability for Physical and Emotional Harm

(a) **A defendant whose conduct creates a risk of physical or emotional harm can fail to exercise reasonable care by failing to warn of the danger if:**

(1) **the defendant knows or has reason to know: (a) of that risk; and (b) that those encountering the risk will be unaware of it; and**

(2) **a warning might be effective in reducing the risk of harm.**

(b) **Even if the defendant adequately warns of the risk that the defendant's conduct creates, the defendant can fail to exercise reasonable care by failing to adopt further precautions to protect against the risk if it is foreseeable that despite the warning some risk of harm remains.**

Comment:

a. The wide range of warning circumstances. . . . A warning can often be a useful device for reducing the risk of harm occasioned by the defendant's conduct. The range of defendant conduct that can give rise to the obligation to warn is so broad as to make clear that the failure to warn is a basic form of negligence. The company that sets up power lines can be negligent in failing to warn those who might come into contact with them; a railroad can be negligent for failing to warn a motorist of an approaching train; the proprietor of a retail store can be negligent for failing to warn of dangerous features in its operations. Motorists can be negligent for failing to warn that they are about to make an unexpected driving maneuver; a motorist whose car is blocking a highway can be negligent for failing to warn of the car's presence; a motorist who appreciates that a pedestrian on the road ahead has not noticed the approaching car can be negligent for failing to sound the horn and thereby warn that pedestrian. An employer can be negligent for failing to warn an employee of dangers in job assignments; the party, other than the employer, who creates a hazard in the employee's working area can be negligent for failing to warn the employee of that hazard. A golfer can be negligent in failing to warn nearby golfers of an errant shot; a property owner can be negligent in failing to warn when the structure it owns protrudes into the air in a way that may imperil low-flying airplanes; a public agency that runs a highway system can be negligent in failing to warn of particular features, such as very narrow bridges, low underpasses, or sharp dropoffs, that pose unexpected dangers. A physician can be liable for the failure to warn

105

patients of the possible adverse complications or side effects of surgery or other recommended treatments; and the defendant who is about to come into intimate contact with the plaintiff can be negligent for failing to warn the plaintiff that the defendant suffers from a communicable disease. Persons "supplying" products to others in a variety of circumstances can be liable for failing to warn of dangers in the products. . . .

b. How warnings can be a reasonable measure for reducing risk. Armed with the information provided by a warning, the potential victim may be able conveniently to modify conduct so as to avoid the danger that the defendant's conduct entails. A pilot, for example, can alter the route to avoid a protruding structure; a motorist can maneuver around a stalled vehicle; a motorist can stop the car until the train has passed; persons can keep their hands (or their cranes) away from a power line; motorists can reduce their speed on the highway when approaching a narrow bridge. In other cases, responding to the warning so as to avoid risk would require the potential victim to forsake the otherwise advantageous services the defendant is offering. Thus, having been informed of the risks of surgery, a patient may decline to undergo surgery, or a potential victim may choose not to enter into an intimate relationship with a person who has a communicable disease. Even if a person chooses to accept surgery or to enter into the relationship, the warning given benefits the person by enabling the person to make an informed choice. In some situations, a warning is desirable because it is effective in reducing the likelihood of an accident. Yet, in other situations, a warning is appropriate mainly because it reduces the likely severity of the injuries that such an accident might occasion. For example, by the time one skier is able to warn another, a collision between the two of them may be inevitable; nevertheless, the warning may be effective in reducing the force of the collision and hence in reducing the severity of the resulting injuries. In referring to the "risk of physical or emotional harm," § 18(a) takes into account both avoiding accidents and reducing their consequences when they occur.

In some situations, however, there is little or nothing a potential victim can do even if given a warning. For example, if a golfer's errant shot heads in the direction of a freeway next to the golf course, it would be pointless for the golfer to give a "fore" warning to motorists on the freeway; even if motorists hear the warning, which is unlikely, they would not be able to observe the golf ball and hence maneuver to avoid it. In situations in which a warning would not be of practical value in reducing the risk of harm, the failure to give the warning is not negligent.

c. Causation. To justify liability in a negligent failure-to-warn case, there must be a finding of causation—a finding that the warning, if given, would have prevented the harm that resulted. . . . It may be that the magnitude of the danger to which the warning relates is great and that the plaintiff would have needed to modify conduct only slightly in order to avoid the danger. In such circumstances, it can be reasonable to assume, even without specific evidence, that a warning, if given, would have caused such a change in the plaintiff's behavior; but the jury is not required to make this assumption. . . .

   d. *Failures properly to instruct.* Most claims of failure to warn concern merely the failure to convey information as to the danger entailed by the defendant's activity. In a limited number of cases, the relationship between the defendant and the plaintiff suggests that the defendant in order to exercise reasonable care must properly instruct the plaintiff as to how to proceed safely. A large employer, for example, can be negligent in failing to instruct an employee as to how safely to handle a distinctive job assignment. . . .

   e. *Adequacy of warning.* Even if a warning is provided, a defendant still can be negligent if the warning is not adequate; if its content does not include the relevant information or if its form is not reasonably effective in expressing this information. . . . [W]hen the danger posed by the defendant's particular operations is significantly greater than the dangers involved in other operations of the same general sort, the defendant can be found negligent for failing to give a fuller warning than that which is normally given. For example, when a railroad crossing is unusually hazardous, the warning should be more emphatic than warnings provided at ordinary highway crossings.

   f. *Generally appreciated dangers.* A defendant can be negligent for failing to warn only if the defendant knows or can foresee that potential victims will be unaware of the hazard. Accordingly, there generally is no obligation to warn of a hazard that should be appreciated by persons whose intelligence and experience are within the normal range. When the risk involved in the defendant's conduct is encountered by many persons, it may be foreseeable that some fraction of them will be lacking the intelligence or the experience needed to appreciate the risk. But to require warnings for the sake of such persons would produce such a profusion of warnings as to devalue those warnings serving a more important function.

   However, even though the danger in the defendant's conduct is appreciated by most people, if the defendant is specifically interacting with a particular person—such as a child—whom the defendant knows is lacking in ordinary knowledge, the defendant can be negligent for failing to warn that person. Moreover, even if the hazard is visually obvious, if the conditions are such that persons approaching the hazard will foreseeably be distracted, the defendant can be negligent in failing to warn of the hazard.

g. The defendant who knows, has reason to know, or should know. Negligence in failing to warn can most easily be found when the defendant actually knows of the relevant danger. In these cases, the objective of the law is to induce the defendant properly to share the knowledge the defendant already has.

In other cases, the law's objective relates to the production of knowledge as well as its sharing. Liability can readily be imposed when the defendant has reason to know of the danger entailed by the defendant's activity—when the defendant actually knows facts that should lead a reasonable person to appreciate the danger. Accordingly, the rule in this Section is expressed in terms of dangers of which the defendant knows or has reason to know.

In certain cases, however, the defendant can be negligent for failing to warn when the law concludes that the defendant "should have known" of the danger—that the defendant should have made a reasonable effort to acquire information about the danger. Whether the defendant has an obligation to acquire information— for example, to conduct inspections or engage in research—is initially an issue of duty to be determined by the court. One important criterion is how likely it is that inspections would in fact produce information about dangers of substantial magnitude. Other criteria are the status of the defendant, the relationship between the parties, and the expectations that that relationship occasions. A company engaged in an activity that creates substantial and distinctive dangers—such as the transmission of electric power—operates under an obligation to conduct reasonable inspections of its operations. Similarly, an employer, such as a railroad, that runs a large ongoing operation is expected to acquire the knowledge of safety problems that can enable it to provide employees with appropriate warnings and instructions. By contrast, the owner of a product such as a power saw has no obligation to inspect it before loaning it to a neighbor or turning it over to another for purposes of repair.

h. Warnings and other precautions. . . . In [some] cases, even if a proper warning would enable potential victims to modify their conduct so as to avoid the danger, the defendant may be able to eliminate the danger in the first instance by incorporating precautions that are less burdensome or on balance more reasonable than any conduct modifications available to potential victims. In such a case, the defendant can be negligent in not adopting those precautions; and if the defendant is originally negligent in this way, the fact that the defendant gives a warning of the danger does not eliminate the defendant's liability for that negligence.

Illustration:

1. Paul, while moving his household goods, throws a heavy parcel out of his window onto the street, intending it to

fall into a waiting cart. In doing so, he calls out, "Look out below." He misses his target, and the parcel strikes Andrea, a pedestrian, who does not hear the warning because her attention is directed to other matters. Despite his warning, Paul can be found negligent for dropping the parcel.

§ 19. Conduct That Is Negligent Because of the Prospect of Improper Conduct by the Plaintiff or a Third Party

Restatement of the Law Third, Torts: Liability for Physical and Emotional Harm

The conduct of a defendant can lack reasonable care insofar as it foreseeably combines with or permits the improper conduct of the plaintiff or a third party.

Comment:

a. Scope. . . . [W]hether a defendant's conduct lacks reasonable care and is therefore negligent often depends on the foreseeable likelihood of the actions of other persons. Frequently, these actions—though they may contribute to danger—are themselves normal and proper. Even when the actions are themselves improper, so long as they are foreseeable they remain relevant to the defendant's possible negligence.

The improper action or misconduct in question can take a variety of forms. It can be negligent, reckless, or intentional in its harm-causing quality. It can be either tortious or criminal, or both. Misconduct such as speeding and driving while intoxicated can be criminal even though not intentionally harmful, but instead merely negligent or reckless. An actor's foreseeable negligence may be improper conduct that imperils another person; if so, the foreseeable negligence is tortious. But the actor's foreseeable negligence may consist of conduct that imperils only the actor. If so, then this conduct, while negligent in the sense of lacking reasonable care, might not be regarded as tortious.

b. Foreseeable plaintiff negligence and plaintiff contributory negligence. In many situations, the foreseeable risk that renders the defendant's conduct negligent is the risk that potential victims will act in ways that unreasonably imperil their own safety. Consider, for example, the defendant that, while failing to insulate its power line, locates that line at a certain height, when it is foreseeable that a person holding a long metal object such as a pole might carelessly make contact with the power line, despite its visibility. Such conduct establishes the person's contributory negligence. . . .

Almost all states, however, have now shifted to comparative responsibility as a partial defense, in which the unreasonable conduct of the plaintiff in many cases reduces but does not eliminate the plaintiff's recovery. Accordingly, even if the plaintiff's contributory negligence is conceded, the issue of the defendant's possible negligence remains. . . .

   c. Defendant negligence, third-party misconduct, and scope of liability. . . . [T]he issues of defendant negligence and scope of liability often tend to converge. If the third party's misconduct is among the risks making the defendant's conduct negligent, then ordinarily plaintiff's harm will be within the defendant's scope of liability. For example, if it is negligent to leave keys in one's unlocked car for a period of time in a high-crime area, at least in part because the car may foreseeably be stolen by someone who is likely to operate it negligently or recklessly, then the fact that the car is in fact stolen and driven negligently in a way that injures the plaintiff does not prevent a finding that plaintiff's harm is within the scope of defendant's liability for that negligence. . . .

   d. Rationale. This Section is to a large extent a special case of § 3, and findings of defendant negligence under this Section hence largely depend on consideration of the primary negligence factors set forth in § 3. . . .

   It is sometimes suggested that imposing liability on the defendant for failure to adopt precautions to protect against third-party misconduct unduly diminishes the basic responsibility of the third party. This argument is largely unpersuasive. Insofar as the third party's misconduct is criminal, the third party remains fully subject to whatever criminal punishments the law imposes. If that misconduct is tortious, recognizing the liability of the original defendant does not significantly diminish the potential tort liability of the third party. So long as that party is solvent, the plaintiff will generally much prefer to bring a tort claim against that party directly, since the tortious quality of that party's conduct is typically much easier to recognize and prove than the negligence of the original actor. Moreover, even if the plaintiff both sues and recovers from the originally negligent defendant, that defendant has an appropriate claim for contribution or indemnification against the third party guilty of later misconduct. The more substantial that misconduct, the larger the share of the overall liability the third party will finally bear as a result of the contribution/indemnification claim. It is only when the third party is insolvent that the plaintiff will prefer the claim against the originally negligent defendant, and that defendant will be unable to collect reimbursement from the third party. While third-party insolvency is of course not uncommon, in such situations the third party, as a practical matter, escapes tort liability regardless of whether the law recognizes the liability of the original defendant.

   e. Defendant conduct versus defendant affirmative duties. This

110

Section addresses conduct by defendants that increases the likelihood that the plaintiff will be injured on account of the misconduct of a third party. . . . These cases, in which the defendant's conduct creates or increases the possibility of harm caused by third-party misconduct, can be contrasted to cases in which the defendant merely takes no action to protect the plaintiff against the possibility of third-party misconduct. Because, as a general rule, the law does not impose an obligation to protect or rescue, defendants are liable in such cases only if they are subject to some affirmative duty providing an exception to the general rule.

Illustrations:

1. Judy loans her car for the evening to her friend, Grant, who needs the car for social purposes. Judy knows that Grant's driver's license was suspended a month previously on account of repeated instances of reckless driving. In the course of the evening, Grant drives the car negligently, and injures Eugene, a pedestrian. A jury can find that Judy was negligent in loaning or entrusting her car to Grant.

2. The Nelson Company hires Tom to serve as the janitor in its apartment building. Nelson knows that Tom has a record of inappropriate sexually aggressive conduct toward women. In his role as janitor, Tom has frequent interactions with Carol, one of the building's tenants. One evening, after his workday is over, Tom knocks on Carol's door. Regarding Tom's presence as an ordinary occurrence, Carol lets him in. Once in her apartment, Tom rapes Carol. A jury can find that Nelson was negligent in hiring Tom for a job in which Tom would have access to female tenants within their apartments.

3. Late one night, Richard places his loaded pistol on the coffee table in the family room of his home. The next afternoon, Richard's 10-year-old son, Norm, is spending time in the family room with his friend, Judy. Norm picks up the gun and plays with it; it accidentally discharges and injures Judy. A jury can find that Richard was negligent in providing Norm access to the gun in circumstances in which Norm might use it improperly.

f. Foreseeable likelihood. . . . There are . . . many strong motives operating on actors that generally dissuade them from behaving negligently. Even so, there is a considerable level of negligence in the world; many actors on some occasions conduct themselves unreasonably. To be sure, in many situations the possibility of such negligent conduct is sufficiently slight as to render nonnegligent the actor who fails to modify the actor's own conduct so as to take that possibility into account. Hence, the actor who merely loans a car to an ordinary friend for the evening is not guilty of negligence in entrusting the car, even though there is

111

some abstract possibility that the friend might drive the car negligently or recklessly in the course of the evening. Yet, in other situations, an actor engaging in certain conduct can foresee a considerable risk, either on account of the general prospect of other persons' negligence during the relevant frame of time and place, or because the actor has knowledge of the propensities of the particular person or persons who are in a position to act negligently. For example, if the friend who asks to borrow the actor's car has been drinking at the time of the request, or if the actor knows that the friend's driver's license has been revoked because of a record of deficient driving, the actor can be negligent in lending the car.

The foreseeability of criminal and intentionally harm-causing misconduct invites a more cautious evaluation. The overwhelming majority of persons avoid such conduct almost all the time. Moral codes operate on people in a powerful way; for most people, committing crimes involving personal injury or significant property damage is all but unthinkable. Moreover, the punishments imposed by the criminal law on people convicted of crime produce a powerful deterrent effect. As a general matter, the prospect of criminal conduct is significantly lower than the prospect of negligent conduct. In many situations, the possibility of criminal misconduct is so slight that an actor is not negligent for failing to take the possibility into account.

Illustration:

4. Ajax, a car-rental agency, rents a car to Ron. Ajax has properly inspected the car to make sure it is in sound operating condition. The car turns out to have a bomb in it at the time of the rental; an hour later, the bomb explodes, injuring Ron. While obviously someone deliberately placed the bomb in the car, the circumstances for this remain unclear. Ajax would have discovered the bomb had Ajax conducted an inspection of the car specifically searching for explosive devices before renting the car to Ron. No one knows of any prior incidents in which rental cars have been criminally tampered with in this way. Ajax is not negligent in failing to search the car for explosive devices before renting it.

Nevertheless, there is an unfortunate amount of crime in society. Accordingly, in certain situations criminal misconduct is sufficiently foreseeable as to require a full negligence analysis of the actor's conduct. Moreover, the actor may have sufficient knowledge of the immediate circumstances or the general character of the third party to foresee that party's misconduct. For example, if the owner of a gun who leaves it on a table at home knows that a houseguest has a long record of violent crimes, that knowledge supports the claim that the owner is negligent in giving the guest access to the gun.

112

g. *Burden of precautions.* . . . Third-party misconduct—negligent, reckless, intentional, or criminal—often is sufficiently foreseeable as to render relevant an inquiry into the burden of precautions facing the actor. Yet these burdens can often be extremely high. It is foreseeable, for example, that some number of motorists, while driving on the state's highways, will speed, drive drunk, or fall asleep, and thereby will fail to navigate curves or otherwise allow their cars to leave the highway. However, if the state is liable for the failure to design curves and erect barriers that would protect against such out-of-control vehicles, the overall burden on the state would be excessive, by way of either bearing and defending against liability or redesigning highways. A northbound motorist approaching an intersection in which the stop signs are on the east-west cross-streets can anticipate that motorists from east or west might occasionally run the stop sign and enter the intersection. It is therefore appropriate to impose on the northbound motorist the burden of keeping a lookout; but to expect that motorist to slow down until that person can confirm that other motorists are honoring the person's right-of-way would unduly interfere with ordinary travel. On balance, the law itself must take care to avoid requiring excessive precautions of actors relating to harms that are immediately due to the improper conduct of third parties, even when that improper conduct can be regarded as somewhat foreseeable.

h. *Duty.* In many situations, the conduct by actors that might lead to risks if there is third-party misbehavior is conduct that otherwise is ordinary and normal. Accordingly, claims that the actor is negligent may prompt a public-policy duty review under § 7. For example, commercial displays along the side of highways are commonplace. It may be somewhat foreseeable that an effective display will attract the attention of motorists in a way that results in poor driving by some motorists. If the victim of such poor driving brings suit against the party who has mounted the display, whether that party can be held liable initially raises a question of duty for the court to decide. Similarly, commercial activities such as the retail sale of cars and firearms have traditionally been regarded as socially acceptable. While it may be somewhat foreseeable that some number of persons who purchase cars will drive them irresponsibly and that some number of adults who purchase firearms will use them for improper purposes, it would be troublesome simply to begin sending to juries claims by plaintiffs that the retail store has been negligent in not properly selecting or screening customers; some advance review by judges of the public-policy implications of such categories of claims, under the heading of duty, is therefore appropriate. In conducting such reviews, courts have ruled, for example, that car dealers have no duty to ascertain whether their customers have valid drivers' licenses.

113

CHAPTER 7

PHYSICAL HARM

§ 4. Physical Harm

Restatement of the Law Third, Torts: Liability for Physical and Emotional Harm

> **"Physical harm" means the physical impairment of the human body ("bodily harm") or of real property or tangible personal property ("property damage"). Bodily harm includes physical injury, illness, disease, impairment of bodily function, and death.**

Comment:

a. Definitions. "Property damage" is impairment of tangible personal property or real property. . . .

b. Bodily harm and emotional harm. The definition of bodily harm is meant to preserve the ordinary distinction between bodily harm and emotional harm. Accordingly, if the defendant's negligent conduct (for example, negligent driving) frightens the plaintiff (for example, a pedestrian crossing the street), the harm to the plaintiff's nerve centers caused by this fear does not constitute bodily harm. This distinction is not precise and may be difficult to make in certain cases. . . .

c. The definition of physical harm explained. . . . [A]ny level of physical impairment is sufficient for liability; no minimum amount of physical harm is required. Thus, any detrimental change in the physical condition of a person's body or property counts as a harmful impairment; there is no requirement that the detriment be major. If the defendant by negligent driving scratches the bumper of the plaintiff's car, that scratch, even though minor, is still physical harm. Under this Restatement's Sections on liability, the problem of minor physical harm often will solve itself; most persons who incur such harm are not inclined to sue only to recover a trivial amount of compensation. . . .

d. Claims for emotional harm. Sections 5, 6, and 20-23 of this Restatement are limited to liability for physical harm. The interest in emotional tranquility is addressed in Chapter 8. Once a plaintiff satisfies the threshold requirement for recovery for emotional harm contained in that Chapter, the remaining provisions of this Restatement, including Chapters 1, 3-7, and 9 apply to the claim. Nevertheless, when emotional harm results from bodily harm that is recoverable under §§ 5, 6, and 20-23, damages for the emotional harm may be recovered without satisfying the additional requirements of Chapter 8. See § 46, Comment *b*. . . .

When an actor's tortious conduct causes emotional harm to another and that emotional harm then causes bodily harm to the other, recovery for both is governed by §§ 5, 6, and 20-23 of this Restatement, just as emotional harm that is caused by bodily harm is recoverable under those Sections, independent of the requirements of Chapter 8. That emotional harm plays a role in the causal mechanism that produces bodily injury does not affect liability for the bodily injury.

Illustration:

3. [After a negligent and erroneous report by Liz Labs to the Tarheel Medical Society that a physician, Dr. Kate, recently used illegal drugs], Dr. Kate becomes so distraught at the false-positive report that she commits suicide. A tort action by Dr. Kate's administrator against Liz Labs is governed by §§ 5, 6, and 20-23; Dr. Kate's administrator need not satisfy the requirements of §§ 46-48 to recover for the harm.

e. Claims for property damage. Property damage as defined in this Section provides a basis for a claim of negligence (under § 6) or strict liability (under the rules in §§ 20-23). However, one category of property damage does not provide a basis for such claims. An actor might provide a claimant with real property or tangible personal property that has a latent physical problem; however, this is not a basis for a negligence or strict-liability claim unless the latent physical problem causes bodily harm or property damage to other property. For further statement of this rule as applied in products-liability actions—along with explanation, examples, and an exception for asbestos removal—see Restatement Third, Torts: Products Liability § 21(c) and Comments *d* and *e*.

CHAPTER 8

FACTUAL CAUSE

A. BUT-FOR CAUSE

§ 26. Factual Cause

Restatement of the Law Third, Torts: Liability for Physical and Emotional Harm

Tortious conduct must be a factual cause of harm for liability to be imposed. Conduct is a factual cause of harm when the harm would not have occurred absent the conduct. Tortious conduct may also be a factual cause of harm under § 27.

Comment:

a. Nomenclature and history. Both the Restatement Second of Torts and the Restatement of Torts employed the term "legal cause" to encompass two distinct inquiries: factual cause and proximate cause. . . . Despite the venerability of the "legal cause" term in Restatement history, it has not been widely adopted in judicial and legal discourse, nor is it helpful in explicating the ground that it covers. Both because it is not well-entrenched and because of the importance of distinguishing clearly between "factual cause" and "proximate cause," this Restatement employs different terminology to address these two requirements for liability in tort. "Factual cause" is addressed in this Chapter and "proximate cause" in [a later Chapter], where it is instead denominated "scope of liability." . . . .

b. "But-for" standard for factual cause. The standard for factual causation in this Section is familiarly referred to as the "but-for" test, as well as a *sine qua non* test. Both express the same concept: an act is a factual cause of an outcome if, in the absence of the act, the outcome would not have occurred. With recognition that there are multiple factual causes of an event, see

116

Comment *c*, a factual cause can also be described as a necessary condition for the outcome. . . .

An act can also be a factual cause in accelerating an outcome that otherwise would have occurred at a later time. Thus, an electrocution due to a faulty ground-fault interrupter causes an acceleration in the death of the victim from natural causes. The loss of the victim's remaining years of life caused by the electrocution provides the framework for determining the damages that would be recoverable in a wrongful-death action. Acceleration may occur for harms other than death as well.

c. Tortious conduct need only be one of the factual causes of harm. An actor's tortious conduct need only be *a* factual cause of the other's harm. The existence of other causes of the harm does not affect whether specified tortious conduct was a necessary condition for the harm to occur. Those other causes may be innocent or tortious, known or unknown, influenced by the tortious conduct or independent of it, but so long as the harm would not have occurred absent the tortious conduct, the tortious conduct is a factual cause. Recognition of multiple causes does not require modifying or abandoning the but-for standard in this Section. Tortious conduct by an actor need be only one of the causes of another's harm. When there are multiple sufficient causes (see Comment *i*), each of which is itself sufficient to cause the plaintiff's harm, supplementation of the but-for standard is appropriate.

A useful model for understanding factual causation is to conceive of a set made up of each of the necessary conditions for the plaintiff's harm. Absent any one of the elements of the set, the plaintiff's harm would not have occurred. Thus, there will always be multiple (some say, infinite) factual causes of a harm, although most will not be of significance for tort law and many will be unidentified. That there are a large number of causes of an event does not mean that everything is a cause of an event. The vast majority of acts, omissions, and other factors play no role in causing any discrete event.

This causal-set model does not imply any chronological relationship among the causal elements involved, although all causes must precede the plaintiff's harm. An actor's tortious conduct may occur well before the other person suffers harm and may require a number of subsequent events to produce the harm. Thus, a gas valve negligently constructed may not fail for many years. Toxic substances may be sold without adequate warnings but not produce harm for decades. Conversely, the tortious conduct may occur after a number of other necessary events have already occurred, but close in time to the occurrence of harm. Nor does this model imply any relationship among the causal elements; causal elements may operate independently, as when a property owner neglects a patch of ice on a sidewalk and a careless pedestrian fails to notice the condition, producing a fall.

117

In some cases, two causal sets may exist, one or the other of which was the cause of harm. Thus, for example, in a case in which the plaintiff claims that a vaccination caused subsequent seizures, and the defendant claims that the seizures were caused not by the vaccination, but by a preexisting traumatic injury to the plaintiff, the causal set including the vaccination and the causal set including the traumatic injury are such alternative causes. If sufficient evidence to support each of these causal sets is introduced, the factfinder will have to determine which one is better supported by the evidence. On the other hand, if the evidence revealed that a traumatic injury and a vaccination can interact and cause seizures, then the vaccination and the trauma may each be a factual cause (both elements of the causal set) of the plaintiff's seizures. . . .

d. Causes and conditions. Because many of the causes necessary for an outcome regularly exist as background conditions and are unimportant for legal or other purposes, some would distinguish them from causes and describe them as conditions. Historically, many courts sought to distinguish certain events that were thought to be unimportant or inappropriate for the imposition of liability as conditions rather than causes. This distinction is common also in nonlegal discourse, and there is thus some awkwardness in describing oxygen and fuel as causes of the destruction of a building, along with the arsonist who provided the source of ignition. Nevertheless, providing criteria to distinguish causes from conditions, which inevitably entails ambiguity and uncertainty, is unnecessary for legal purposes. Further, to emphasize the empirical nature of factual causal determinations, all necessary elements for an outcome are described as causes in this Restatement. Thus, this Restatement refers to tortious conduct as *a* cause of harm and refers to a causal set, of which the tortious conduct was one necessary condition, as *the* cause of harm. On occasion, this Restatement refers to all of the routine, background causes that complete the necessary causal set as "background causes."

e. Counterfactual inquiry for factual cause. The requirement that the actor's tortious conduct be necessary for the harm to occur requires a counterfactual inquiry. One must ask what would have occurred if the actor had not engaged in the tortious conduct. In some cases, in which the tortious conduct consists of the entirety of an act, this inquiry may not be difficult. Thus, if a driver falls asleep and that driver's car crashes into another's home, assessing what would have occurred if the actor had not fallen asleep poses little difficulty. In other cases, especially those in which the tortious conduct consisted of marginally more risky conduct than is acceptable or in which the actor failed to take a precaution that would have reduced the risk to another, such as by warning of a danger, the counterfactual inquiry may pose difficult problems of proof.

118

f. Framework for causal analysis. Before the causal inquiry required by this Section can be conducted, it must be framed. Framing requires two steps: the initial step is to identify the relevant, legally cognizable harm for which recovery is sought. Often this step will be straightforward, but there are times when courts recognize new, unusual, or reconceptualized harms, which change the causal inquiry. See Comment *n* ("Lost opportunity or lost chance as harm").

Illustration:

1. During surgery to correct a congenital anomaly, Culver, a 19-month-old child, suffered a serious injury because of an overdose of anesthesia. Culver's anesthesiologist explained that she believed the overdose occurred because a vaporizer, a component of an anesthesia machine, malfunctioned. St. Maria's Hospital, the hospital where the surgery took place, took possession of the anesthesia machine after Culver's injury as a part of its internal investigation. At the time, St. Maria's assured Culver's representative that it would preserve the machine. Two months later, when Culver's attorneys were preparing to file suit against the anesthesia machine's manufacturer, St. Maria's informed Culver's attorneys that it had lost the anesthesia machine. Although St. Maria's negligence in failing to preserve the anesthesia machine is not a factual cause of Culver's injury, its negligence is a cause of Culver's inability to pursue a claim against the machine's manufacturer. In a jurisdiction that recognizes negligent spoliation of evidence as a cause of action, St. Maria's negligence is a factual cause of harm to Culver.

As explained in Comment *b*, sometimes the harm may be a period of time by which the harm was accelerated. Thus, an actor may accelerate the occurrence of a disease in a person who, through natural causes, would have contracted the disease some years later. The additional period of time by which the onset of disease is accelerated is the legally cognizable harm for which the person may recover.

The second framing step requires determination of the conduct of the actor alleged to be tortious, which also entails identifying the alternative conduct that would not have been tortious. Again, this identification and application to the causal inquiry is often routine. A driver exceeding the speed limit by 20 miles per hour on a divided highway is not a cause of harm when another driver on the opposite side of the highway two miles away hits a pedestrian. Similarly, the negligence of a driver who crosses the center lane of a two-lane highway and collides with another automobile traveling in the opposite direction is a factual cause of all harm suffered by those in the other automobile as a result of the collision. Nevertheless, in some instances, especially when the actor's conduct is tor-

119

tious only because it is marginally more risky than nontortious conduct, the causal inquiry must be framed by the incremental risk of the tortious conduct, as distinguished from the risk posed by the entirety of the conduct. Thus, the causal inquiry asks whether the harm would have occurred if the actor had not acted tortiously.

Illustration:

> 2. While driving 57 miles per hour on a road with a 50-miles-per-hour speed limit, Ken ran into Melanie, a pedestrian. Ken is not subject to liability for negligence in speeding unless he would not have hit Melanie or would have caused her less harm if he had been driving 50 miles per hour. (Ken may be subject to liability to Melanie for negligence unrelated to his speeding.)

g. Distinct aspects of the causal inquiry. In many cases, the factual-cause inquiry requires only a straightforward examination of the connection between an act or omission and subsequent harm to a person. However, in some cases there can be several distinct inquiries that require consideration. For example, there may be no doubt that an actor's agent or instrumentality caused another's harm, but there may be a dispute about whether the tortious aspect of the actor's conduct was a cause of the harm. This is often the case when the injured person claims that the actor was negligent in providing warnings; any improved warnings would have had to prevent harm to the injured person. Also, this is often the case when the actor's tortious conduct consists of some marginally riskier conduct, such as speeding. In other cases, causation may be in dispute because the actor's connection to the tortious conduct is in doubt. . . . In toxic-substances cases, the causal inquiry is modified by the limits of and available forms of scientific evidence. That inquiry often must address whether the agent for which the actor is responsible is capable of causing the disease from which another suffers (known as general causation). In addition, the question whether the agent caused the specific plaintiff's disease (known as specific causation) is confronted. In addition, a person's exposure to the actor's agent is another necessary aspect for factual cause to exist. Each of these distinct inquiries is a component of the factual-cause inquiry.

h. Tortious conduct. . . . [T]ortious conduct includes entire acts, such as leaving an obstruction on an unlit sidewalk; marginal conduct, such as driving at a speed in excess of a reasonable one; or omissions with regard to existing risks, such as ignoring a slippery condition in the public area of a retail business. . . .

i. Multiple causes distinguished from multiple sufficient causes. . . . Frequently, plaintiffs allege that multiple tortious acts or omissions caused their harm. . . . So long as the factfinder determines that any one of the alleged acts was tortious and a but-for cause of the harm, that is sufficient to subject the actor to liability.

In a few cases, especially ones in which the plaintiff alleges multiple omissions by a single defendant, doubt may exist whether each of the defendant's acts or omissions was, independent of the others, a but-for cause of the plaintiff's harm. . . . For purposes of applying the but-for standard in this Section, the factfinder may consider all such tortious acts or omissions by a defendant in determining whether, in their absence, the plaintiff's harm would not have occurred.

Illustration:

> 3. David's airplane was seriously damaged when he was forced to land the plane without the retractable gear in the down position. David sues Chaser Aircraft, the manufacturer of the plane. David claims that Chaser neglected to include instructions in its service manual of the need to be sure of a minimum clearance between two parts in the landing-gear as-sembly when reassembling the gear after routine servicing. David's plane was serviced at Chaser because Chaser needed to complete unrelated warranty work to the aircraft. The Chaser mechanic who worked on David's plane was fired shortly after the work was completed for repeatedly failing to consult service manuals when working on a plane, and David includes a claim based on the mechanic's negligence. Neither the omitted instruction nor the mechanic's negligence in fail-ing to consult the manual is, by itself, a but-for cause of the harm to David's plane because neither one alone would have produced the harm to David's plane. See § 27, Comment *i.* Nevertheless, if the factfinder determines that a company providing a service manual with the omitted instruction and the same company with a mechanic who properly consulted the service manual would have prevented the damage to David's plane, Chaser's multiple negligent acts are a factual cause of the plane damage.

j. Substantial factor. The "substantial-factor" test as the rou-tine standard for factual cause originated in the Restatement of Torts and was replicated in the Restatement Second of Torts. Its primary function was to permit the factfinder to decide that factual cause existed when there were multiple sufficient causes—each of two separate causal chains sufficient to bring about the plaintiff's harm, thereby rendering neither a but-for cause. See § 27. The substantial-factor test has not, however, withstood the test of time, as it has proved confusing and been misused.

The "substantial factor" rubric is employed alternately to impose a more rigorous standard for factual cause or to provide a more lenient standard. Thus, for example, comparative-responsibility jurisdictions improperly employ the substantial-factor test to suggest to a jury that it should find the plaintiff's "substantial" contributory negligence, rather than the defendant's tortious conduct, to be "the" cause of harm. Conversely, some courts have accepted the proposition that, although the plaintiff cannot show the defendant's tortious conduct was a but-for cause of harm by a preponderance of the evidence, the plaintiff may still prevail by showing that the tortious conduct was a substantial factor in causing the harm. That proposition is inconsistent with the substantial-factor standard adopted in the Restatement Second of Torts, and is inconsistent with this Section as well. To be sure, courts may decide, based on the availability of evidence and on policy grounds, to modify or shift the burden of proof for factual cause, as they have when multiple tortfeasors act negligently toward another but only one causes the harm. See § 28(b). Courts may, for similar reasons, decide to permit recovery for unconventional types of harm, such as a lost opportunity to avoid an adverse outcome. Nevertheless, the substantial-factor rubric tends to obscure, rather than to assist, explanation and clarification of the basis of these decisions. The element that must be established, by whatever standard of proof, is the but-for or necessary-condition standard of this Section. Section 27 provides a rule for finding each of two acts that are elements of sufficient competing causal sets to be factual causes without employing the substantial-factor language of the prior Torts Restatements. There is no question of degree for either of these concepts.

The substantial-factor standard has also been employed in enhanced-injury cases when proof of the amount of harm caused by the second actor is uncertain. Courts are understandably reluctant to impose a rigorous burden of production on those who are injured by serial tortfeasors to show how much harm was caused by each of the tortious acts. See § 28, Comment d. Thus, courts state that so long as a plaintiff proves that the second tortfeasor's conduct was a substantial factor in causing the enhanced harm, the burden of proof on the magnitude of harm is on the defendants. The invocation of the substantial-factor test is unnecessary to this end; courts can state more clearly that so long as the second tortfeasor's conduct was a but-for cause of *some* enhanced harm, the burden of proof shifts to that tortfeasor on its magnitude. Apportionment of liability among tortfeasors is addressed in Restatement Third, Torts: Apportionment of Liability.

k. Preemptive causes and duplicative factors. After a person suffers harm, another causal set may exist that, had the initial cause not existed, would have caused the same harm. Thus, this might occur when one hunter negligently fires a rifle, killing a hiker, and, shortly thereafter, another hunter negligently fires, and the second shot would have been sufficient to cause the hiker's death, except that the death had already occurred. An act or omission cannot be a factual cause of an outcome that has already occurred. The first hunter's negligence is a cause of the hiker's death and preempts any causal role in the hiker's death of the second hunter's negligence. A duplicative factor, such as the second hunter's shot, need not arise after harm has occurred. Thus, if the hiker had terminal cancer at the time the first hunter's bullet killed the hiker, the hunter's negligence is a factual cause of the hiker's death, while the cancer is not. However, the hiker's cancer is relevant to the measure of damages for which the hunter is liable.

l. Burden of proof. The burden of proof in civil actions requires proof by a preponderance of the evidence. Consistent with § 28, a plaintiff must prove that it is more likely than not that, if the defendant had not acted tortiously, the plaintiff's harm would not have occurred. Consistent with Comment *c*, the plaintiff need not prove that the defendant's tortious conduct was the predominant or primary cause of the harm. So long as the defendant's tortious conduct was more likely than not *a* factual cause of the harm, the plaintiff has established the element of factual cause.

Illustrations:

4. Cain, a two-year-old child suffering from a bacterial infection, received a routine childhood vaccination with a vaccine manufactured by Vacso. Shortly after receiving the vaccine, Cain spiked a very high fever, went into respiratory arrest, and died. Cain's estate provides competent evidence that Cain died because of the infection and the vaccine; if either Cain had not had an infection or if Cain had not been vaccinated, death would not have ensued. Cain's estate has satisfied its burden of production to show that the vaccine was a factual cause of Cain's death.

5. Same facts as Illustration 4, except that in its defense, Vacso introduces competent evidence that the biological mechanism of infections and adverse drug reactions are entirely independent; therefore, either the vaccine or the infection caused Cain's death, but not the two in combination. If the factfinder accepts this evidence and finds that the infection was more likely (or equally likely) a cause of death than an adverse vaccine reaction, Cain's estate has failed to satisfy its burden of persuasion that the vaccine was a cause of Cain's death.

m. Plaintiff's conduct. Throughout this Section, reference has been made to the determination of whether "tortious conduct" is a factual cause of the plaintiff's harm. The same rules for factual cause that apply to defendants' tortious conduct also apply to determine whether a plaintiff's contributory negligence is a factual cause of harm suffered by the plaintiff.

n. Lost opportunity or lost chance as harm. A number of courts have recognized a lost opportunity (or lost chance) for cure of a medical condition as a legally cognizable harm. This new characterization of harm permits recovery when adherence to traditional categories of legally cognizable harm and rules of proof of causation would not. Under the preponderance-of-the-evidence standard, plaintiffs fail in their burden of proving factual causation if they do not introduce evidence that proper care more likely than not would have cured or otherwise improved their medical condition. Thus, courts traditionally have required that a plaintiff show that the probability of a better outcome was in excess of 50 percent. Plaintiffs who do provide such proof, of course, recover the entirety of their damages.

Concomitant with this reconceptualization of the harm for a plaintiff unable to show a probability in excess of 50 percent is an adjustment of the damages to which the plaintiff is entitled. Rather than full damages for the adverse outcome, the plaintiff is only compensated for the lost opportunity. The lost opportunity may be thought of as the adverse outcome discounted by the difference between the ex ante probability of the outcome in light of the defendant's negligence and the probability of the outcome absent the defendant's negligence. These decisions are a response to inadequate (and unavailable) information about what would have been the course of a specific patient's medical condition if negligence, typically in failing to diagnose, refer, or otherwise provide proper treatment, had not occurred. Lost chance thus serves to ameliorate what would otherwise be insurmountable problems of proof, i.e., proving what would have happened to the plaintiff or plaintiff's decedent if proper medical care had been provided. Among courts that are inclined to modify the law in this area in response to the difficulties of proof, recognizing lost opportunity as harm is preferable to employing a diluted substantial-factor or other factual-causation test, thereby leaving recovery to the unconstrained inclination of any given jury and providing some fortunate plaintiffs with a full measure of damages for their physical harm while denying any recovery to others. . . .

The lost-opportunity development has been halting, as courts have sought to find appropriate limits for this reconceptualization of legally cognizable harm. Without limits, this reform is of potentially enormous scope, implicating a large swath of tortious conduct in which there is uncertainty about factual cause, including failures to warn, to provide rescue or safety equipment, and otherwise to take precautions to protect a person from a risk of harm that exists. To date, the courts that have accepted lost opportunity as cognizable harm have almost universally limited its recognition to medical-malpractice cases. Three features of that context are significant: (1) a contractual relationship exists between patient and physician (or physician's employer), in which the raison d'être of the contract is that the physician will take every reasonable measure to obtain an optimal outcome for the patient; (2) reasonably good empirical evidence is often available about the general statistical probability of the lost opportunity; and (3) frequently the consequences of the physician's negligence will deprive the patient of a less-than-50-percent chance for recovery. Whether there are appropriate areas beyond the medical-malpractice area to which lost opportunity might appropriately be extended is a matter that the Institute leaves to future development.

Recognizing a lost opportunity for cure is not strictly a matter of factual causation; rather, it reconceptualizes the harm. Once the harm is reconceptualized as the lost opportunity, the factual-cause inquiry changes. Both because the lost-opportunity doctrine is one involving the definition of legally cognizable harm and because it has been confined to medical malpractice, a specialized area of negligence liability outside the scope of this Restatement, the Institute takes no position on this matter, leaving it for future development and future Restatements.

B. MULTIPLE SUFFICIENT CAUSES

§ 27. **Multiple Sufficient Causes** ← Anderson p. 356

Restatement of the Law Third, Torts: Liability for Physical and Emotional Harm

> **If multiple acts occur, each of which under § 26 alone would have been a factual cause of the physical harm at the same time in the absence of the other act(s), each act is regarded as a factual cause of the harm.**

Comment:

a. Multiple sufficient causes generally. This Section applies whenever there are two or more competing causes, each of which is sufficient without the other to cause the harm and each of which is in operation at the time the plaintiff's harm occurs. When an actor's tortious conduct is such a cause, it nevertheless would not be a factual cause if factual causes were limited to the definition in § 26: even without that tortious conduct, the harm would still have occurred because of the competing cause. Nevertheless, courts have long imposed liability when a tortfeasor's conduct, while not necessary for the outcome, would have been a factual cause if the other competing cause had not been operating.

Illustration:

1. Rosaria and Vincenzo were independently camping in a heavily forested campground. Each one had a campfire, and

each negligently failed to ensure that the fire was extinguished upon retiring for the night. Due to unusually dry forest conditions and a stiff wind, both campfires escaped their sites and began a forest fire. The two fires, burning out of control, joined together and engulfed Centurion Company's hunting lodge, destroying it. Either fire alone would have destroyed the lodge. Each of Rosaria's and Vincenzo's negligence is a factual cause of the destruction of Centurion's hunting lodge.

In many cases, multiple sufficient causes will each, along with background causes, be capable of causing the harm, as in Illustration 1. This Restatement thus refers to causes such as Rosaria's and Vincenzo's negligence as multiple sufficient causes. . . .

b. History and terminology. Courts and scholars have long recognized the problem of overdetermined harm—harm produced by multiple sufficient causes—and the inadequacy of the but-for standard for this situation. . . . [C]ases invoking the concept are rare. . . .

This Restatement's § 26 and Comment *j* eliminate any discretion to reject insubstantial factual causes, and this Section does the same for multiple sufficient causes. There is no apparent reason for providing the factfinder discretion on normative or evaluative grounds to pick and choose among tortious acts that are independently (with other background circumstances) sufficient to cause the harm. . . . When the tortious conduct is not itself sufficient, and its contribution is relatively trivial in comparison to the other causes, limitations are appropriate. . . .

c. Rationale. A number of justifications exist for the rule in this Section. A defendant whose tortious act was fully capable of causing the plaintiff's harm should not escape liability merely because of the fortuity of another sufficient cause. That justification is not entirely satisfactory. Tortious acts occur, with some frequency, that fortuitously do not cause harm. Nevertheless, the actors committing these acts are not held liable in tort. When two tortious multiple sufficient causes exist, to deny liability would make the plaintiff worse off due to multiple tortfeasors than would have been the case if only one of the tortfeasors had existed. Perhaps most significant is the recognition that, while the but-for standard provided in § 26 is a helpful method for identifying causes, it is not the exclusive means for determining a factual cause. Multiple sufficient causes are also factual causes because we recognize them as such in our common understanding of causation, even if the but-for standard does not. Thus, the standard for causation in this Section comports with deep-seated intuitions about causation and fairness in attributing responsibility.

d. One cause tortious, the other innocent. This Section applies in a case of multiple sufficient causes, regardless of whether the competing cause involves tortious conduct or consists only of innocent conduct. So long as each of the competing causes was sufficient to produce the same harm as the defendant's tortious conduct, this Section is applicable. Conduct is a factual cause of harm regardless of whether it is tortious or innocent and regardless of any other cause with which it concurs to produce overdetermined harm.

When one of multiple sufficient causes is not tortious, the question of damages is a different matter from the causal question. The question of what (if any) damages should be awarded against these tortfeasors properly belongs to the law of damages and is not addressed in this Restatement. . . .

  e. *Alternative causes.* In some cases, a defendant may contend that the acts of another were the cause of the plaintiff's harm and thus that defendant's tortious conduct was not a cause of the plaintiff's harm. Whether that claim implicates the rule in this Section depends on whether the other forces were operating and sufficient to cause the harm contemporaneously with the defendant's tortious conduct or, alternatively, were the factual cause of the harm *instead of* the defendant's tortious conduct. If the evidence supports the former finding, then this Section is applicable. If the evidence supports the latter finding, then the applicable standard for factual causation is that stated in § 26.

Illustration:
  2. Trent is the guardian ad litem and father of Lakeesha, an infant born with a birth defect. Trent sues Pharmco, a pharmaceutical company, alleging both that Pharmco's drug caused Lakeesha's birth defect and that Pharmco was negligent for its failure to warn that its drug was teratogenic. Trent introduces sufficient evidence for the factfinder to find that Pharmco's failure to warn was negligent, that the drug was a cause of Lakeesha's birth defect, and that an adequate warning would have prevented the birth defect. Pharmco contends that its drug did not cause Lakeesha's birth defect. Rather, Pharmco contends, Lakeesha's birth defect was caused by a genetic condition wholly independent of Pharmco's drug. Pharmco introduces sufficient evidence in support of its claims. The factfinder must determine if the drug, absent Lakeesha's genetic condition, would have caused the birth defect. The factfinder must also determine if, absent the drug, Lakeesha's genetic condition would have caused the birth defect. If the factfinder determines that either the drug or the genetic condition would have, in the absence of the other, caused Lakeesha's birth defect at the same time then each is a factual cause pursuant to this Section. If the factfinder determines that either the drug or the genetic condition played no role in the birth defect, then the other's causal status is determined under the but-for standard of § 26.

The appropriate rule may depend on resolution of a factual question, as demonstrated in Illustration 2. Thus, the court may have to provide contingent instructions that ask the jury first to determine whether it finds that only one cause was operating, or that both were operating. Then, alternative instructions must be provided to correspond with the jury's finding. In most cases, however, this will not be necessary, as there will not be a dispute about whether the other forces are an alternative or a multiple sufficient cause.

f. Multiple sufficient causal sets. In some cases, tortious conduct by one actor is insufficient, even with other background causes, to cause the plaintiff's harm. Nevertheless, when combined with conduct by other persons, the conduct overdetermines the harm, i.e., is more than sufficient to cause the harm. This circumstance thus creates the multiple-sufficient-causal-set situation addressed in this Comment. The fact that an actor's conduct requires other conduct to be sufficient to cause another's harm does not obviate the applicability of this Section. See § 26, Comment *c*. Moreover, the fact that the other person's conduct is sufficient to cause the harm does not prevent the actor's conduct from being a factual cause of harm pursuant to this Section, if the actor's conduct is necessary to at least one causal set. Sometimes, one actor's contribution may be sufficient to bring about the harm while another actor's contribution is only sufficient when combined with some portion of the first actor's contribution. Whether the second actor's contribution can be so combined into a sufficient causal set is a matter on which this Restatement takes no position and leaves to future development in the courts. See Comment *i*.

Illustration:

3. Able, Baker, and Charlie, acting independently but simultaneously, each negligently lean on Paul's car, which is parked at a scenic overlook at the edge of a mountain. Their combined force results in the car rolling over the edge of a diminutive curbstone and plummeting down the mountain to its destruction. The force exerted by each of Able, Baker, and Charlie would have been insufficient to propel Paul's car past the curbstone, but the combined force of any two of them is sufficient. Able, Baker, and Charlie are each a factual cause of the destruction of Paul's car.

That there are common elements in each of the sufficient causal sets does not prevent each of the sets from being a factual cause pursuant to this Section.

Illustration:

4. Jonathan raises salmon in a pond on his property. Due to an unusual rainfall, a chemical, potentially toxic to salmon, leaks into the pond from natural deposits some distance from

128

Jonathan's property. However, the chemical concentration in the pond remains below the threshold that causes harm to salmon. Shelley and Mia, who engage in industrial operations near Jonathan's property, each negligently allow the escape of the same chemical from their operations. Shelley's and Mia's chemical is deposited in Jonathan's pond at the same time; each is sufficient with the existing contamination to raise the chemical concentration of the pond to a level that kills all of the salmon. Each of Shelley's and Mia's negligence is a factual cause of Jonathan's loss of salmon.

With the explanation provided in this Comment about the scope of this Section, a more precise, if also more complicated version of the black letter in this Section might be stated as:

When an actor's tortious conduct is not a factual cause of harm under the standard in § 26 only because one or more other causal sets exist that are also sufficient to cause the harm at the same time, the actor's tortious conduct is a factual cause of the harm.

g. *Toxic substances and disease.* . . . When a person contracts a disease such as cancer, and sues multiple actors claiming that each provided some dose of a toxic substance that caused the disease, the question of the causal role of each defendant's toxic substance arises. Assuming that there is some threshold dose sufficient to cause the disease, the person may have been exposed to doses in excess of the threshold before contracting the disease. Thus, some or all of the person's exposures may not have been but-for causes of the disease. Nevertheless, each of the exposures prior to the person's contracting the disease (or the time at which the disease was determined, see § 26, Comment *k*) is a factual cause of the person's disease under the rule in this Section. Whether there are some exposures that are sufficiently de minimis that the actor should not be held liable is a matter not of factual causation, but rather of policy, and is addressed in § 36 [trivial contributions to multiple sufficient causes].

h. *Preempted tortious conduct.* This Section does not apply to tortious conduct that only could have caused harm at some time after the harm actually occurred. A clear example is when a negligent driver hits a body already dead due to being hit earlier by another negligent driver. . . . Once the harm has occurred, any other cause that remains incomplete is not a cause of harm. . . .

Illustration:

6. Emma, who was employed as an asbestos insulation installer for many years, is killed when a defect in a ground-fault interrupter (GFI) in her bathroom fails. The GFI failed to break the electrical circuit after an electrical razor fell in the bathtub, resulting in Emma's electrocution. The autopsy

reveals that Emma was in the early stages of mesothelioma, an almost invariably fatal form of cancer, due to her asbestos exposure. The defect in the GFI is the factual cause of Emma's death, and her exposure to asbestos is not a factual cause of her death. Whether the damages recoverable from the GFI manufacturer are diminished because of Emma's mesothelioma and, if so, by how much, are beyond the scope of this Restatement. . . .

i. Special cases involving multiple sufficient causal sets and preempted conditions. Results in some cases are difficult to explain under the rules stated in this Section and its Comments. Sometimes, one candidate for a multiple sufficient cause appears de minimis, as when a match is thrown into an already raging fire. Another such situation occurs when an element of a potentially sufficient set requires additional elements and the additional contribution that occurs is greater than necessary to cause the harm. For example, a negligently constructed dam that would have collapsed in an ordinary flood may be overwhelmed by a flood so large and unforeseeable that no dam would have controlled it. Other times, two candidates for multiple sufficient causes may be two omissions that fail to prevent harm and each is dependent on the nonexistence of the other to be a but-for cause, as when a motorist fails to apply brakes that, because of earlier failures during repair, would not have worked, or when a consumer fails to read a product label that omitted a warning.

Both the match and the negligent construction of the dam could be characterized as causes if one conceptualizes them as combining with something less than the actual events that occurred. Thus, a fire that needed just the additional amount of heat of a match to destroy a home and a flood of normal proportions make the match and dam factual causes. Nevertheless, courts often decline to hold the de minimis candidate a cause and thus dismiss the negligent construction of the dam as not a cause of any flooding damage. That conclusion may be affected by the fact that the flood is a nontortious competing cause. See Comment *d.* Similarly, courts often conclude that the earlier of two multiple-sufficient-cause candidates, separated in time, that failed to prevent harm was not a cause. Indeed, courts routinely hold that an inadequate warning, which would not have prevented an injury even if read, is not a cause of an injury if an adequate warning would not have been read. Those courts may also be tempted to dismiss the later candidate as noncausal because it is not a but-for cause of the harm; they may also be influenced when the later candidate does not involve tortious conduct. These results seem to depend on intuitions that are not captured in the purely conceptual general rule that each of two sufficient sets of conditions to bring about an injury is treated as a cause. . . .

[S]ome of the cases involving multiple failures to prevent harm

130

appear to involve the intuitive notion that one of the candidates has preempted the other, thereby preventing the other from being a factual cause. Thus, the failure to apply the brakes might be thought to preempt the negligence in repairing the brakes as a factual cause. These cases present difficult problems at the intersection of preemption and multiple sufficient causes. Unlike negligently running over a dead body, in which preemption is clear, the special cases addressed in this Comment present much more ambiguous instances of preemption. . . .

[D]ecided cases do not support clear rules. Thus, this Restatement does not provide a set of rules to resolve these cases. Instead, it highlights the disagreements that these cases raise, and leaves their resolution to further case-law development of rules or to case-by-case resolution under specific factual settings.

C. Burden of Proof

§ 28. Burden of Proof

Restatement of the Law Third, Torts: Liability for Physical and Emotional Harm

(a) **Subject to Subsection (b), the plaintiff has the burden to prove that the defendant's tortious conduct was a factual cause of the plaintiff's harm.**

(b) **When the plaintiff sues all of multiple actors and proves that each engaged in tortious conduct that exposed the plaintiff to a risk of harm and that the tortious conduct of one or more of them caused the plaintiff's harm but the plaintiff cannot reasonably be expected to prove which actor or actors caused the harm, the burden of proof, including both production and persuasion, on factual causation is shifted to the defendants.**

Comment on Subsection (a):

b. Reasonable inference and speculation in proving causation. To isolate and determine whether an act was a factual cause of an outcome requires consideration of whether that outcome would have occurred without the act's having taken place. As philosophers have taught, factual cause is not a phenomenon that can be seen or perceived; instead, it is an inference drawn from prior experience and some, often limited, understanding of the other causal factors—the causal mechanism—required for the outcome. Thus, all causal determinations require inferential reasoning. In some cases, the inference is quite powerful, as when a pilot, who failed to obtain an adequate briefing about the weather, flies into a storm and crashes, killing the passengers. In other cases, the inference may be quite weak, as when a person exposed to a suspected toxic substance develops a common form of cancer. Sometimes the inferences are submerged in the testimony of what appears to be a percipient witness, as, for example, when an eyewitness testifies that she observed the defendant crush the plaintiff's skull with a baseball bat. Sometimes the inferential reasoning required is quite evident, as when a child is found drowned in a pool that did not have a lifeguard present. Reasonable inferences are matters left to the jury's collective experience and common sense. But courts continue to regulate the cases that are submitted to juries by requiring that sufficient evidence be introduced to justify drawing a reasonable inference of factual causation. When the inferential leap from the evidence to the conclusion is too great, courts intervene to declare that juries may not speculate, and the matter is removed from the province of the jury. This procedure is not unique to factual causation, but exemplifies the procedural requirement of sufficient proof of each factual element of a claim. . . .

[T]he plaintiff need not prove the defendant's tortious conduct was a cause of the harm with a high degree of certainty. The civil burden of proof merely requires a preponderance of the evidence, and the existence of other, plausible causal sets that cannot be ruled out does not, by itself, preclude the plaintiff from satisfying the burden of proof on causation. The difficulty is often that evidence does not provide any reasoned method for determining what the respective probabilities are for the potential causes. It is in cases of this genre that the court's approach toward the degree of freedom afforded juries to make a reasonable judgment in the face of uncertainty is critical.

In cases in which the defendant's tortious conduct is clear, many courts are lenient about the plaintiff's proof of causation, especially if the plaintiff has done all that is reasonably possible by way of gathering and presenting evidence of causation. Some cases ease the plaintiff's burden on factual causation by employing a presumption of causation in negligence per se cases. Other courts have adopted a presumption of causation when the defendant fails to warn or provides an inadequate warning in products-liability cases. The use of presumptions in negligence per se and warnings cases is by no means universal, but it does reflect some courts' willingness to adapt the burden of proof depending on the type of tortious conduct and the difficulties of proof the plaintiff faces.

Beyond negligence per se and warnings cases, in unusual circumstances in addition to those in Subsection (b), courts may shift the burden of proof on causation to defendants. Courts have shifted the burden of proof on the aspect of causation that requires identification of the actor who committed the tortious conduct— there being adequate evidence that the tortious conduct caused the plaintiff's harm. These rare cases are characterized by a close relationship among the actors who potentially caused the other's harm, the actors having superior knowledge of the relevant circumstances, and the person harmed having no reasonable prospect for obtaining evidence of causation. . . .

In the end, the line between permissible inference for the jury and impermissible speculation is one that must be determined based on the specific facts of the case and the court's approach to the allocation of decisionmaking authority between judge and jury.

c. Toxic substances and disease

(1). *Introduction.* Cases involving toxic substances often pose difficult problems of proof of factual causation. These problems can also arise in cases involving activities that may cause disease, such as continued repetitive motion. Sometimes it is difficult to prove which defendant was connected to the toxic agent, or whether an adequate warning would have prevented the plaintiff's harm. The special problem in these cases, however, is proving the connection between a substance and development of a specific disease. In all of these cases, the requirement to prove factual causation remains the same; the plaintiff must prove it by a preponderance of the evidence, and the standards for factual causation set forth in §§ 26-27 continue to apply.

In most traumatic-injury cases, the plaintiff can prove the causal role of the defendant's tortious conduct by observation, based upon reasonable inferences drawn from everyday experience and a close temporal and spatial connection between that conduct and the harm. Often, no other potential causes of injury exist. When a passenger in an automobile collision suffers a broken limb, potential causal explanations other than the collision are easily ruled out; common experience reveals that the forces generated in a serious automobile collision are capable of causing a fracture. By contrast, the causes of some diseases, especially those with significant latency periods, are generally much less well understood. Even known causes for certain diseases may explain only a fraction of the incidence of such diseases, with the remainder due to unknown causes. Causal agents are often identified in group (epidemiologic) studies that reveal an increase in disease incidence among a group exposed to the agent as compared to a group not exposed. Biological mechanisms for disease development—i.e., a series of causally linked physiological changes from exposure to disease development—are frequently complicated and difficult to observe. Science continues to develop a better understanding of the biological steps in the development of diseases, but current knowledge in this respect is considerably more modest than for traumatic injury. As a consequence, courts in toxic-substances cases often must assess various alternative methods proffered with regard to factual causation. . . .

Most causation issues are resolved under the "but-for" standard for factual cause. See § 26. The plaintiff must prove by a preponderance of the evidence that, but for the defendant's tortious conduct with respect to the toxic substance, the plaintiff would not have suffered harm. When group-based statistical evidence is proffered in a case, this means that the substance must be capable of causing the disease ("general causation") and that the substance must have caused the plaintiff's disease ("specific causation"). In other cases, when group-based evidence is unavailable or inconclusive, and other forms of evidence are used, the general and specific causation issues may merge into a single inquiry. In any case, plaintiff's exposure to the toxic agent must be established. . . .

(5). *Multiple exposures and synergistic interactions.* In some cases, a person may be exposed to two or more toxic agents, each of which is known to be capable of causing (general causation) the person's disease. The two agents may operate independently, in which case the incidence of disease in a group exposed to both will be additive—the excess incidence due to the first agent along with the excess incidence due to the second agent. . . . If the toxic agents are attributable to the tortious conduct of separate actors, courts then face the question whether to apply the rule developed for multiple exposures in asbestos cases. This rule permits finding each actor's asbestos products to which the person was exposed to be a factual cause of the person's disease. See § 27, Comment g. Alternatively, courts might employ the traditional rule, requiring proof of which of the multiple exposures was a cause of the harm. At least where the biological mechanism by which disease develops is unknown, the asbestos rule is quite analogous and attractive as a means for adapting proof requirements to the available scientific knowledge. Apportionment of liability among those actors held liable is based on the comparative-responsibility rules in Restatement Third, Torts: Apportionment of Liability §§ 1-25. The alternative—the more traditional requirement of proof of which of the two toxic exposures was *the* cause of the disease—would require proof that does not exist, except on a probabilistic basis. . . .

Illustrations:

1. Abby was exposed to two different solvents while working in a laboratory. Each solvent contained a toxic chemical; one contained brion, and the other contained choron. After developing a disease, myeplopia, several years later, she sues the manufacturers of each solvent, claiming that the manufacturers were negligent for including a toxic chemical in their solvents. Abby's evidence, presented by competent expert testimony based on valid scientific evidence, reveals that the increased risk of contracting myeplopia from the dose of brion to which she was exposed is insufficient to permit a finding of factual causation. Similarly, the increased risk of myeplopia from exposure to choron is insufficient to permit a finding of factual causation. However, Abby's evidence reveals that, while choron and brion operate independently (those exposed to both are only subject to an increased risk of the additive risks of each), the combined risk of contracting myeplopia due to

134

exposure to both is sufficient to permit a finding of factual causation. Each of the manufacturers is subject to liability. See § 26, Comment c. Apportionment of liability between the manufacturers is governed by Restatement Third, Torts: Apportionment of Liability.

2. Same facts as Illustration 1, except that competent evidence shows that choron exposure increases the risk of myeplopia by 10 times, as does brion exposure. Competent evidence also reveals that the mechanism by which myeplopia develops is different for choron exposure and for brion exposure and that exposure to one or the other, but not both, is the most likely explanation for Abby's myeplopia. Abby cannot prove, however, whether choron or brion caused her myeplopia. Pursuant to § 28(b), the burden of proof on agent-disease causation is shifted to the manufacturers of choron and brion.

3. Same facts as Illustration 2, except that competent evidence reveals that choron and brion operate in precisely the same physiologic manner in the human body; they are interchangeable in their role in causing myeplopia. Exposure to each of choron and brion is a factual cause of Abby's myeplopia. See § 27, Comment g.

In some cases, as, for example, asbestos workers who smoke cigarettes, the two toxic agents together have a synergistic effect. This means that the excess incidence of disease among those exposed to both agents will be greater than the sum of the excess incidences found in those exposed to each separate agent. If the synergistic effect is sufficiently large, the excess incidence of disease due to the synergistic effect will be greater than the excess incidence due to each of the agents separately. In such circumstances, factfinders may infer that the combined exposure is a cause of the plaintiff's disease. . . .

d. Burden of proof on magnitude of divisible harm. . . .

(1). Apportioning harm caused by the legally culpable conduct of multiple parties. When two or more actors (perhaps including the plaintiff) contribute to causing the harm, the question of how much harm each actor caused arises. . . . [T]here are cases in which the evidence introduced by the plaintiff does not readily reveal how much of the harm was caused by each defendant's tortious act, although the evidence reveals that each such defendant contributed to causing at least some harm to the plaintiff. A modern example is "crashworthiness" cases in which the plaintiff, involved in an automobile accident caused by one tortfeasor, suffers enhanced injury due to a defect in the automobile that makes it uncrashworthy. . . .

[T]his Comment provides that the plaintiff need not prove the precise magnitude of harm caused by each defendant in order to make out a prima facie case: so long as the plaintiff proves that each defendant's tortious conduct caused some harm, the plaintiff has satisfied the burden of proof on factual cause. Conversely, a defendant who establishes that the plaintiff's contributory negligence caused some of the plaintiff's harm need not prove the precise magnitude of damages attributable to that component of harm. This reciprocal treatment of plaintiff negligence is consistent with the overall approach of Restatement Third, Torts: Apportionment of Liability. . . .

(2). Apportioning harm between tortious conduct and innocent causes or nonparty actors. By contrast with Comment *d(1)*, causal apportionment of a plaintiff's harm may be required when a plaintiff had a preexisting symptomatic condition and the extent of enhanced injury is uncertain. Thus, a defendant whose tortious conduct aggravates a plaintiff's preexisting back problem and causes greater pain is liable only for the harm caused by the aggravation and not for any harm due to the original condition. Such apportionment may also be required when the plaintiff suffers enhanced injury before trial for which the defendant is not liable, and the enhanced injury is not caused by tortious conduct or, if it is, the responsible actor is not a defendant in the suit.

The preexisting condition (or enhanced harm) may be the result of entirely innocent forces, as when a plaintiff is born with a congenital susceptibility to harm or develops such a susceptibility later in life. The condition may be the result of a lifestyle choice of the plaintiff, such as obesity from overeating or emphysema from cigarette smoking, or even the result of contributory negligence by the plaintiff. The condition may be the result of prior tortious conduct by a nonparty. The plaintiff may have already sued for and recovered damages for the preexisting condition from a nonparty.

Given the variety of circumstances and the predictable schism among the courts about how to allocate the burden of proof, the Institute takes no position on who should bear the burden of proof. The equities for imposing this burden on the plaintiff recede as: (1) the relative seriousness of the preexisting condition compared to the aggravation is small; (2) the preexisting condition was the product of innocent causes; (3) even when the preexisting condition was not the product of an innocent cause, the plaintiff has been unable to recover from anyone else for the preexisting condition; (4) the plaintiff was not contributorily negligent in causing the aggravation; and (5) the plaintiff is in no better position to prove the extent of aggravation than is the defendant. Regardless of how the burden of proof is allocated, the preferred approach is to employ a modest threshold for the party with the burden of proof to satisfy the burden of production on the magnitude of harm. So long as there is some modicum of evidence that would permit the fact-finder to make a causal apportionment, that course is preferable to making whichever party bears the burden of proof bear the entirety of the loss. . . .

Comment on Subsection (b):

f. Burden shifting when plaintiff cannot reasonably demonstrate which of several tortfeasors caused the harm. Subsection (b) is based on the well-known case of Summers v. Tice, and its adoption in § 433B(3) of the Restatement Second of Torts. This burden-shifting rule is commonly known as "alternative liability.". . . . [C]ourts have generally accepted the alternative-liability principle of § 433B(3), while fleshing out its limits. . . .

g. Rationale. The rationale for shifting the burden of proof to defendants whose tortious conduct exposed the plaintiff to a risk of harm is that, as between two culpable defendants and an innocent plaintiff, it is preferable to put the risk of error on the culpable defendants. In at least some cases, it appears that the defendants' better access to proof and doubts about the plaintiff's ability to extract that evidence from the defendants, even with modern discovery, have influenced the courts to employ burden shifting. Conversely, when the plaintiff had a reasonable opportunity to identify the person whose tortious conduct caused the harm and did not diligently pursue that opportunity, courts have been disinclined to permit a plaintiff to invoke alternative liability. . . .

h. Joinder of all defendants. Courts have insisted that all persons whose tortious acts exposed the plaintiff to a risk of harm be joined as defendants as a condition for alternative liability. . . .

i. Each defendant acted tortiously. Unless all of the actors who may have harmed the plaintiff acted tortiously, the rationale for invoking alternative liability is absent. Courts continue, without exception, to turn away plaintiffs who are unable to establish this element.

Illustration:

6. Reed, a pedestrian, was injured by a sofa that was negligently or intentionally thrown from an upper-story hotel room during the celebration of an NCAA basketball championship. Reed sues all of the occupants of the 47 rooms from which the sofa might have been thrown. Reed must prove which of the defendants was responsible for throwing the sofa; the burden shifting provided in this Subsection is unavailable to Reed in his suit because he has not shown that the occupants of each of the 47 rooms acted tortiously.

The result would be the same if two sofas fell simultaneously, one thrown negligently or intentionally from one room and the other not due to negligence of the occupant of the other room, and Reed, not knowing from where the sofa that fell on him came, sued the occupants of both rooms. Each of the possible causes of harm must be tortious for this Subsection to be invoked.

j. Exposing plaintiff to the risk of harm. In Summers v. Tice, the connection between the defendants' tortious conduct and the plaintiff's harm was quite tight, regardless of the actual causal relationship. Both defendants were physically present, fired their guns in the direction of the plaintiff, and by doing so created an imminent risk to the plaintiff. Similarly, in many alternative-liability cases, a close connection exists between the risk of harm created by the defendants' tortious conduct and the harm suffered by the plaintiff. As that connection becomes more tenuous, even while each defendant remains a *possible* cause of the plaintiff's harm, the basis for the rule in this Subsection is diminished. Thus, for example, when a defective product injures a person who cannot identify which of several manufacturers made the specific product, courts refuse to invoke alternative liability against all manufacturers of the product. . . .

Illustrations:

7. Ken was hit by a taxi late one night after a substantial snowstorm. The skid marks left by the taxi revealed that after the driver slammed on the brakes and began skidding, the brakes failed. A nearby witness confirmed that the driver of the taxi appeared to be pumping the brakes furiously while the vehicle continued to roll. Because of the hour and lack of light, neither Ken nor the witness could identify the company name of the taxi. There are five different taxicab companies that operate in the community; each has a single cab. Examination of the five cabs reveals that each one has the same brake problem, caused by negligent maintenance, which permits the brakes to fail when a substantial amount of snow accumulates around them. The burden of proof on which taxicab company's vehicle ran into Ken remains with Ken because the other taxicab companies' negligence was too far removed to have exposed Ken to a risk of harm.

8. Five taxicabs were driven on city streets crowded with automobiles and pedestrians. The five taxi drivers, operating independently, were negligently weaving in and out of traffic on the same street at the same time, narrowly averting collisions among themselves and with others. One of the taxicabs nicked Ken, a pedestrian, breaking his leg, while swerving to avert a collision with another vehicle. In the confusion, no witness could identify the taxi that hit Ken. The burden of proof on which taxicab company's vehicle hit Ken is shifted to the taxicab companies, if Ken joins all of them in his suit.

k. Multiple actors and nonsimultaneous tortious conduct. . . . There is a stronger intuitive appeal to alternative liability when there are only two defendants, and each is equally likely to have been the factual cause of another's harm, thereby leaving a plaintiff just a bit short of the evidence required to prove that one was the cause of harm by a preponderance of the evidence. Nevertheless, the rationale for alternative liability—shifting the burden of proof to the culpable parties who exposed an innocent person to risk— applies as well when there are more than two such culpable parties. . . .

Although simultaneous tortious conduct (or nearly so) existed in many of the early alternative-liability cases, no good reason exists for requiring simultaneity as a condition for shifting the burden of proof. . . .

l. One or more defendants' tortious conduct caused plaintiff's harm. Alternative liability is limited to those cases in which fewer than all defendants caused the plaintiff's harm, and the plaintiff is unable to prove which one(s). When multiple actors are each a cause of all of another's harm, all such actors are liable for that harm; the form of that liability and apportionment among them is based on Restatement Third, Torts: Apportionment of Liability. . . .

Illustration:

10. Phil, a passenger in an automobile passing through an intersection, was injured when first Elizabeth, and then, several seconds later, Joshua, driving in opposite directions on the intersecting road, went through a red light, and each collided with the car in which Phil was a passenger. After the collisions, Phil had a severely fractured hip, which required several reconstructive surgeries. In Phil's suit against Joshua and Elizabeth, uncontradicted evidence shows that Joshua would have collided with Phil's car, because of its slow speed, in virtually identical fashion, whether or not Elizabeth had first hit Phil's car. The evidence, however, is conflicting on whether Phil's harm occurred due to the first collision alone or the second collision alone, and on whether its severity was a consequence of both collisions. The jury should be instructed that, if it can find that one or the other of the collisions alone was the factual cause of Phil's harm, the verdict should be against the defendant responsible for that collision. If the jury finds that the severity of the fracture was a result of both collisions, both defendants would be liable for the entirety of the harm, pursuant to Comment *d*, unless one was able to show a basis for causal apportionment. Finally, if the jury finds that Phil's harm was caused either by Joshua or Elizabeth, but not by both, and cannot determine which, Subsection (b) shifts the burden of proof on causation to Joshua and Elizabeth. Unless one or both has introduced sufficient evidence to satisfy this burden, both are liable for Phil's harm. . . .

p. Market-share liability. In a narrow range of cases, courts have been confronted with plaintiffs who have similar proof problems to those who seek to invoke alternative liability. These cases involve exposure to a toxic substance and the plaintiff's understandable inability to prove which manufacturer sold the product, often many years or decades before any disease becomes clinically evident. The prototype for this kind of case is the drug diethylstilbestrol (DES), a drug prescribed in the middle part of the 20th century to prevent miscarriage. DES, because it was not patented, was manufactured by hundreds of pharmaceutical companies. DES caused disease in the offspring of the mothers who took the drug, typically 20 years after exposure, and at a time when evidence of which manufacturer produced the DES the mother had consumed was, quite often, unavailable. . . .

A number of courts [ ] adopted a new "market share" theory that permitted apportionment of liability among defendant-manufacturers based on each one's share of the relevant market for DES. Many of the details of the specific market-share theory adopted vary from court to court, but common to all is that liability is several, rather than joint and several, and is limited to the market share of each defendant, so that in theory each will pay roughly the amount that represents the overall harm caused by that defendant's DES. A roughly equal number of courts have declined to craft a new theory for DES plaintiffs, expressing concern that to do so would rend too great a chasm in the tort-law requirement of factual causation. . . . Virtually all courts that have considered the question have declined to apply a market-share liability theory to products that are not fungible and, therefore, do not pose equivalent risks to all of those exposed to the products.

Market-share liability, when the product is fungible and, therefore, poses equivalent risks, is attractive both from a compensatory and deterrence standpoint. If plaintiffs can demonstrate that the marketing and sale of a product was tortious and that the product caused their harm, they have a strong claim for compensation. More importantly, deterrence is better served by making manufacturers of toxic substances responsible for harm caused by defective products, even when the passage of time makes identification of the connection between manufacturer and plaintiff impossible. Using market share to determine each manufacturer's several liability provides an appropriate deterrent to tortious conduct because it imposes liability for approximately the amount of harm caused by each manufacturer's defective product. Market-share liability is more difficult to justify from a corrective-justice standpoint, but at least some commentators find corrective justice compatible with liability for imposing risk.

Even when serving compensation and deterrence goals, there are two difficulties with market-share liability. First, the administrative costs of determining each defendant's market share have been distressingly disproportionate to the compensation provided.

Part of the reason was the natural intuition to seek the local market most particular to the plaintiff, thereby increasing the likelihood that the manufacturer that provided the drug that harmed the plaintiff is among those held liable and facilitating the opportunity for defendants who did not provide the drug that harmed the plaintiff to exculpate themselves. Narrowly defined markets, however, require relitigation of the appropriate market repeatedly. Later courts, appreciating this experience, employed broader, even national, markets to keep administrative costs within reason. Even then, concern about the existence and accuracy of market-share data is another aspect of administrative costs.

A second concern counseling against adopting a market-share theory is institutional capacity. Crafting a coherent market-share scheme that both relaxes the traditional tort requirement of factual causation and provides a workable market-share system is much more the type of lawmaking traditionally, and appropriately, a matter for legislative action than for common-law decisionmaking.

When market-share liability is limited to fungible products that pose equivalent risks to users who have no reasonable means to prove which manufacturer provided the product that caused the plaintiff's harm, it has an exceedingly limited reach. . . . Even among jurisdictions accepting a pure market-share theory, it has very rarely been applied outside of DES cases.

Because of the nearly even split among jurisdictions and the lack of an emerging consensus or trend, Restatement Third, Torts: Products Liability, explained the important considerations in crafting a market-share system and left the matter to the developing law. . . .

CHAPTER 9

SCOPE OF LIABILITY (PROXIMATE CAUSE)

Special Note on Proximate Cause: . . . .

Although the term "proximate cause" has been in widespread use in judicial opinions, treatises, casebooks, and scholarship, the term is not generally employed in this Chapter because it is an especially poor one to describe the idea to which it is connected. See § 29, Comment *b*. Hence, this Chapter is entitled, "Scope of Liability." That terminology more accurately describes the concerns of this Chapter: Tort law does not impose liability on an actor for all harm factually caused by the actor's tortious conduct. With the exception of no- and limited-duty rules and affirmative defenses, limitations on liability are contained in this Chapter. . . .

This Restatement omits "legal cause" terminology for three reasons. As explained in § 26, Comment *a*, and § 29, Comment *g*, this Restatement separates factual cause from scope-of-liability limitations and, to further that end, no longer employs an umbrella term to encompass both concepts. Second, legal cause contributes to the misleading impression that limitations on liability somehow are about factual cause. Finally, despite 75 years of Torts Restatement commitment to legal cause, its acceptance in the vocabulary of tort law is quite limited.

A. Harms Risked by the Tortious Conduct

§ 29. Limitations on Liability for Tortious Conduct

Restatement of the Law Third, Torts: Liability for Physical and Emotional Harm

An actor's liability is limited to those harms that result from the risks that made the actor's conduct tortious.

Comment:

a. History. No serious question exists that some limit on the scope of liability for tortious conduct that causes harm is required. The difficulties arise in working out the framework for this limit, both between no-duty limitations and scope-of-liability limits, and in the form that scope-of-liability rules take. . . .

b. Proximate-cause terminology and instructions to the jury. As mentioned in the Special Note at the outset of this Chapter, the term "proximate cause" is a poor one to describe limits on the scope of liability. . . . Courts should craft instructions that inform the jury that, for liability to be imposed, the harm that occurred must be one that results from the hazards that made the defendant's conduct tortious in the first place. Employing the term "proximate cause" implies that there is but one cause—the cause nearest in time or geography to the plaintiff's harm—and that factual causation bears on the issue of scope of liability. Neither of those implications is correct. Multiple factual causes always exist, see § 26, Comment *c*, and multiple proximate causes are often present. An actor's tortious conduct need not be close in space or time to the plaintiff's harm to be a proximate cause. And proximate cause is only remotely related to factual causation. Thus, the term "causation" should not be employed when explaining this concept to a jury.

Unfortunately, most standard jury instructions use the term "proximate cause" and include within it instructions on both factual cause and scope of liability. . . . Jury instructions that separate these two components of the case facilitate focus on the appropriate matter. Even in cases in which both issues are disputed, separate instructions and separate consideration of each issue should clarify the requisite inquiries for the jury. . . .

c. Scope. This Restatement covers liability for physical and emotional harm, and this Chapter provides limits on the scope of liability for such cases. . . .

d. Harm different from the harms risked by the tortious conduct. Central to the limitation on liability of this Section is the idea that an actor should be held liable only for harm that was

143

among the potential harms—the risks—that made the actor's conduct tortious. The term "scope of liability" is employed to distinguish those harms that fall within this standard and, thus, for which the defendant is subject to liability and, on the other hand, those harms for which the defendant is not liable. This limit on liability serves the purpose of avoiding what might be unjustified or enormous liability by confining liability's scope to the reasons for holding the actor liable in the first place. To apply this rule requires consideration, at an appropriate level of generality, see Comment *i*, of: (a) the risks that made the actor's conduct tortious, and (b) whether the harm for which recovery is sought was a result of any of those risks. . . .

Thus, the jury should be told that, in deciding whether the plaintiff's harm is within the scope of liability, it should go back to the reasons for finding the defendant engaged in negligent or other tortious conduct. If the harms risked by that tortious conduct include the general sort of harm suffered by the plaintiff, the defendant is subject to liability for the plaintiff's harm. When defendants move for a determination that the plaintiff's harm is beyond the scope of liability as a matter of law, courts must initially consider all of the range of harms risked by the defendant's conduct that the jury *could* find as the basis for determining that conduct tortious. Then, the court can compare the plaintiff's harm with the range of harms risked by the defendant to determine whether a reasonable jury might find the former among the latter.

The standard imposed by this Section is often referred to as the requirement that the harm be "within the scope of the risk," or some similar phrase, for liability to be imposed. For the sake of convenience, this limitation on liability is referred to in the remainder of this Chapter as the "risk standard."

Illustrations:

3. Richard, a hunter, finishes his day in the field and stops at a friend's house while walking home. His friend's nine-year-old daughter, Kim, greets Richard, who hands his loaded shotgun to her as he enters the house. Kim drops the shotgun, which lands on her toe, breaking it. Although Richard is negligent for giving Kim his shotgun, the risk that makes Richard negligent is that Kim might shoot someone with the gun, not that she would drop it and hurt herself (the gun was neither especially heavy nor unwieldy). Kim's broken toe is outside the scope of Richard's liability, even though Richard's tortious conduct was a factual cause of Kim's harm.

4. James Transport Co. provides a company-owned automobile to Henry for personal and business use. While driving on vacation, Henry is speeding, loses control of the vehicle, and destroys a roadside billboard owned by Nannouncements, Inc. Nannouncements sues James Transport, claiming that it

negligently entrusted an automobile to Henry, despite his history of several speeding and other moving violations, as well as a number of recent accidents, all of which were known by James. If the factfinder determines that James was negligent in providing the vehicle to Henry, Nannouncement's harm is within the scope of James's liability for its negligence, as a matter of law, because the risk that made James negligent was that Henry would drive poorly and cause an accident. . . .

Tortious conduct may be wrongful because of a variety of risks to a number of different classes of persons. Thus, driving a vehicle negligently poses risks to persons and property who might foreseeably be harmed in a number of ways—by a collision with another vehicle or pedestrian, by the vehicle leaving the road, by the consequences of a narrowly averted collision, by the confusion and distraction of an accident scene, or by other consequences. Some of those risks may be more prominent than others, but all are relevant in determining whether the harm is within the scope of liability of the actor's tortious conduct.

Illustration:

> 6. Parker's automobile is run off a narrow, hilly road by Wilson, who is driving a semitrailer negligently. Because the accident scene involves an unusual configuration of the semitrailer and Parker's vehicle, Deborah, who is driving by, stops her car at the side of the road to observe the scene. While parked at the side of the road, Deborah is hit by another vehicle driven carelessly into Deborah's car. Whether Deborah's harm is within the scope of liability created by Wilson's negligence in causing the accident with Parker is a question for the factfinder.

Determining the risks that made the defendant's conduct tortious may require consideration of whether that conduct includes risks also posed by the tortious conduct of another person. Thus, identical injuries, if they occur in different ways or at different times, may be treated differently under this Section, despite the general rule contained in Comment o.

Illustrations:

> 7. Arthur owns a convenience store located within an exclusive, gated community. Sandy, who lives in the community, tripped on a curbstone in the store's parking lot one night after emerging from the store. Sandy suffered a skull fracture in the fall. Sandy sues Arthur for negligence in failing to have light to illuminate the parking lot, which is otherwise pitch dark. If the factfinder determines that Arthur's failure to light the parking lot was negligent and a factual cause of Sandy's harm, Sandy's harm is within the scope of Arthur's liability, because the risk of someone falling in the parking lot

145

due to darkness is among the risks that made Arthur negligent for failing to provide lighting in the parking lot.

8. Same facts as Illustration 7, except that Sheldon, a thief, to gain entrance to the grounds, digs a tunnel underneath a fence, owned and maintained by the homeowners' association, that surrounds Sandy's community. Sheldon sees Sandy emerge from Arthur's store. As Sandy walks through the parking lot, Sheldon is able to approach Sandy undetected because of the darkness. Sheldon trips Sandy from behind, and in the resulting fall, Sandy suffers a skull fracture. No prior assaults had occurred at Arthur's store. Sheldon's role in causing Sandy's harm is relevant to whether that harm is outside the scope of Arthur's liability for Arthur's failing to light the parking lot. The factfinder may decide that the harm Sandy suffered arose from the risk of a criminal attack due to darkness and that this was not a foreseeable risk that made Arthur's failure to provide lighting negligent because it occurred in a gated community without any previous criminal history.

Many jurisdictions are sensitive to imposing liability for failing to protect others from the risk of criminal attacks and often require some prior criminal actions before permitting liability to be imposed. Those jurisdictions might decide that Sandy's harm is outside the scope of Arthur's liability as a matter of law. Even in those jurisdictions that would not decide Arthur's scope of liability as a matter of law, Sheldon's role in causing the harm would be appropriate for argument by the attorneys and consideration by the factfinder with regard to Arthur's scope of liability. Thus, Illustrations 7 and 8 reveal the fact-intensive nature of the scope-of-liability issue. In each case, the inquiry requires assessment, based on the particular circumstances of the case, of the legally cognizable risks that existed and that made the actor's acts or omissions with regard to those risks tortious. In a negligence action, prior incidents or other facts evidencing risks may make certain risks foreseeable that otherwise were not, thereby changing the scope-of-liability analysis.

e. Rationale. Limiting liability to harm arising from the risks created by the tortious conduct has the virtue of relative simplicity. It also provides a more refined analytical standard than a foreseeability standard or an amorphous direct-consequences test. Furthermore, the standard adopted in this Section imposes limits on liability by reference to the reasons for holding an actor liable for tortious conduct in the first place. The risk standard appeals to intuitive notions of fairness and proportionality by limiting liability to harms that result from risks created by the actor's wrongful conduct, but for no others. It also provides sufficient flexibility to accommodate fairness concerns raised by the specific facts of a case.

146

Critiques of the over- and underbreadth of the risk standard as the limit on scope of liability have been voiced, as has the criticism that the risk standard is indeterminate for a significant class of cases. Nevertheless, the indeterminacy—which might also be characterized as flexibility—in the risk standard can be understood as a virtue that assists in ameliorating the over- and underbreadth criticism. The risk standard can be employed to do justice in a wide range of cases in which the particular facts require careful consideration and thereby resist any rule-like formulation. Yet it does so within an understandable and coherent framework that avoids standardless determinations. Finally, some of the inadequacies of the risk standard are addressed in other Sections and Comments in this Chapter, which identify specific areas in which courts have modified the standard contained in this Section.

Courts have increasingly moved toward adopting a foreseeability test for scope of liability in negligence cases. Currently, virtually all jurisdictions employ a foreseeability (or risk) standard for some range of scope-of-liability issues in negligence cases. When properly understood and framed, the foreseeability standard is congruent with the risk standard adopted by this Section for negligence cases. At least some courts have employed language that veers closer to the formulation of the risk standard provided in this Section than does a foreseeability test. The risk standard nevertheless is preferable to a foreseeability standard. . . .

f. Relationship with duty limitations. This Chapter is about limits on the liability of an actor whose tortious conduct is a factual cause of harm. There are two primary legal doctrines for limiting liability: duty and scope of liability. . . . One significant difference between these two doctrines is helpful in determining their appropriate spheres of application. Duty is a question of law for the court, while scope of liability, although very much an evaluative matter, is treated as a question of fact for the factfinder. Hence, duty is a preferable means for addressing limits on liability when those limitations are clear, when they are based on relatively bright lines, when they are of general application, when they do not usually require resort to disputed facts in a case, when they implicate policy concerns that apply to a class of cases that may not be fully appreciated by a jury deciding a specific case, and when they are employed in cases in which early resolution of liability is particularly desirable. Duty is usefully employed when a court seeks to make a telling pronouncement about when actors may or, on the other hand, may not be held liable. Thus, the liability of social hosts for providing alcohol to their guests is best treated as a duty issue, rather than as a matter of scope of liability. On the other hand, when the limits imposed require careful attention to the specific facts of a case, and difficult, often amorphous evaluative judgments for which modest differences in the factual circumstances may change the outcome, scope of liability is a more

147

flexible and preferable device for placing limits on liability. Its use is also consistent with the role of the jury in tort cases. . . .

Limitations of liability based on the specific facts of a case—for example, the relationship of the actor's tortious conduct to the victim's harm or the unusual, wanton, or extraordinary way in which the harm occurred—are matters courts denominate as proximate cause and are addressed as scope-of-liability limits. . . .

g. Decoupling legal cause. . . . This Restatement, by contrast, treats factual cause and scope of liability separately for several reasons. . . . [C]learly differentiating the predominantly historical question of factual cause from the evaluative question of scope of liability makes for a clearer, more focused analysis. Finally, separation enables courts to employ instructions that avoid causal language when explaining scope-of-liability limitations to the jury.

Thus, common instructions on proximate cause that employ language requiring that the tortious conduct cause the harm in a "natural and continuous sequence," sometimes accompanied with the additional requirement that the causal sequence "be unbroken by any efficient intervening cause," do not reflect the risk standard adopted in this Section. . . .

h. Risk to particular interests. . . . [T]he question is whether the harm that occurred is among the harms the risks of which made the actor's conduct tortious. Thus, if in Illustration 3, Kim had dropped Richard's gun on Alphonso, Kim's father who was standing nearby, Richard would not be liable to Alphonso despite Richard's negligence in entrusting the gun to Kim, which posed a risk of an accidental shooting to Alphonso. And, if Kim had dropped the gun on a box containing fragile crystal, breaking it, and the gun went off injuring Alphonso, the owner of the crystal could not recover for its loss, even if Alphonso owned it and even though Alphonso could recover for his personal injury. Indeed, in Illustrations 7 and 8, Arthur is negligent toward Sandy and Sandy suffers the same physical injury in both Illustrations, yet Arthur may not be subject to liability for the injury in Illustration 8 and is subject to liability in Illustration 7. In assessing whether the scope of an actor's liability extends to a given harm, the critical matter is the context in which the actor is tortious, including the facts establishing the risks that exist at the time of the actor's conduct and the manner in which the actor's conduct was deficient. . . .

[W]henever an injured person is exposed to risk within the scope of the harm and suffers other harm outside the scope, the question of the appropriate level of generality to describe the risks and harms occurs. . . .

i. Understanding and characterizing the risk of harm. The risk standard is defined with respect to risks of harm, while the "type of harm" can be described at varying levels of generality. It can

148

also be described by including some degree of detail about how the harm occurred. In [ ] Illustration 2, . . . the risk of harm might have been described generally as a risk of personal injury. Alternatively, it might have been described more specifically—. . . as a broken toe due to the force of a dropped shotgun that fell onto the toe in Illustration 3. . . . Illustration 3 employs a narrower characterization, closer to the one provided in this Comment.

No rule can be provided about the appropriate level of generality or specificity to employ in characterizing the type of harm for purposes of this Section. . . . Courts often respond to efforts by advocates to employ excessive detail in characterizing the type of harm in order to make it appear more unforeseeable with the dictum that the manner of harm is irrelevant. Factfinders, no doubt, respond to these efforts with their own judgment and common sense to decide the appropriate specificity with which to assess the scope of liability. Conversely, in Illustration 3, characterizing the type of harm as merely physical harm and therefore arising from the risks posed by negligently entrusting a gun to a child fails to acknowledge the more limited risks posed by the negligent act—namely, those that might occur due to an accidental firing of the gun within the geographic range in which any bullet might travel. Different types of harm may be threatened by different tortious acts; a risk of a gunshot wound is different from a risk of a chemical burning, a traumatic collision, an electrical shock, or a snarling pit bull.

In addition to the difficulty of determining the appropriate level of generality with which to describe the type of harm, courts also confront the problem that the risks that are encompassed within the actor's tortious conduct may not be readily apparent. . . . [T]he negligence standard is quite general in the risks that it addresses. Thus, greater uncertainty and difficulty occur in negligence cases in determining whether the harm that resulted arose from the risks that made the actor's conduct unreasonable.

Many cases will pose straightforward or manageable determinations of whether the type of harm that occurred was one of those risked by the tortious conduct. Yet in others, there will be contending plausible characterizations that lead to different outcomes and require the drawing of an evaluative and somewhat arbitrary line. Those cases are left to the community judgment and common sense provided by the jury. Certain recurring factual circumstances are sometimes dealt with by a legal rule. . . .

j. Connection with reasonable foreseeability as a limit on liability. Many jurisdictions employ a "foreseeability" test for proximate cause, and in negligence actions such a rule is essentially consistent with the standard set forth in this Section. Properly understood, both the risk standard and a foreseeability test exclude liability for harms that were sufficiently unforeseeable at the time of the actor's tortious conduct that they were not among the risks—potential harms—that made the actor negligent. Negligence limits the requirement of reasonable care to those risks that are foreseeable. Thus, when scope of liability arises in a negligence case, the risks that make an actor negligent are limited to foreseeable ones, and the factfinder must determine whether the type of harm that occurred is among those reasonably foreseeable potential harms that made the actor's conduct negligent.

Although the risk standard in this Section is comparable to the foreseeability standard in actions based on negligence, the risk standard contained in this Section is preferable because it provides greater clarity, facilitates clearer analysis in a given case, and better reveals the reason for its existence. The risk standard provides greater clarity and facilitates analysis because it focuses attention on the particular circumstances that existed at the time of the actor's conduct and the risks that were posed by that conduct. Risks may be foreseeable in context, as when an extraordinary storm is forecast, requiring precautions against the risks posed by it, that might otherwise be thought of, out of context, as exceedingly unlikely and therefore unforeseeable. The risk standard focuses on the appropriate context, although a foreseeability standard, properly explained, could do this also. The risk standard provides better understanding about the reasons for its existence by appealing to the intuition that it is fair for an actor's liability to be limited to those risks that made the conduct wrongful. Thus, factfinders can apply the risk standard with more sensitivity to the underlying rationale than they might muster with an unadorned foreseeable-harm standard.

A foreseeability test for negligence cases risks being misunderstood because of uncertainty about what must be foreseen, by whom, and at what time. When courts pose the foreseeability inquiry as whether the harm was foreseeable at the time the defendant acted or as whether an intervening act was foreseeable, attention is deflected from the crux of the risk-standard inquiry. Moreover, the risk standard deals more comfortably with scope of liability when the defendant is an actor for whom the law modifies the objective standard of care. Thus, the risk standard would adapt the scope of liability for a child who is not expected to anticipate the same scope of harms as an adult.

For the strict-liability bases for liability, the standard in this Section is more cogently applied than a foreseeability standard. The greater generality and therefore flexibility of the risk standard contained in this Section make it readily adaptable to cases in which the tort does not require that the harm is foreseeable. Thus, for wild animals, in the rare case in which the owner is justifiably ignorant and reasonably believes the animal tame, the risk standard can be applied without any modification; if the dangerous quality of the animal is the cause of harm, liability exists. . . .

k. Consistency with negligence per se. The risk standard in this Section is congruent, as well, with scope-of-liability limitations employed for statutory violations that constitute negligence per se. Liability for statutory violations is limited to harms that the statute was enacted to prevent and to persons who were intended to be protected from those harms. See § 14, Comments *f* and *g*. As the latter Comment explains, for most cases in which the scope of liability for a statutory violation is at issue, attention to the safety concerns the statute addresses will also be sufficient to exclude liability to plaintiffs who were not within the class protected. Thus, scope-of-liability limitations for statutory violations, while focused on the more specific harms addressed by the legislature, employ the same framework of inquiry.

l. Strict liability. The principle set forth in this Section is equally applicable to scope-of-liability limits on strict liability. . . . Thus, even if it is assumed that the defendant, in storing packages of explosives, is carrying on an abnormally dangerous activity, should the stored packages tumble and land on the plaintiff, injuring the plaintiff without exploding, the plaintiff cannot recover in strict liability. . . . In addition, consider the defendant whose blasting activity produces vibrations that, in turn, induce mother minks in a nearby mink farm to destroy their offspring. Because harm such as this is no part of the characteristic risk that leads the law to regard the activity of blasting as abnormally dangerous, the defendant blaster does not bear strict liability for that harm. . . .

In each of these two examples, the denial of strict liability leaves open the possibility of negligence liability. The defendant may be negligent, for example, in how the packages of explosives have been stacked. Moreover, if the prospective blaster knows that a mink farm is nearby, negligence law may oblige the defendant to notify the mink-farm owner of its blasting plans, so that the owner can take appropriate precautions: for example, temporarily separating mother minks from their offspring. . . .

m. Additional limits on scope of liability. . . . In addition to others described in this Chapter, there are cases in which the scope of liability would be too vast, in light of the circumstances of the tortious conduct, if a risk standard governed liability. One example of this situation would be a negligent jailer who permitted a dangerous criminal to escape. While liability might extend to some of the escaped criminal's immediate victims, courts would be loathe to extend the jailer's liability to include hundreds or thousands of victims across the country over a period of decades, if the criminal were not recaptured. . . . Whatever verbal formulation is employed in these rare cases of unacceptably overwhelming liability in light of the tortious conduct, courts should appreciate that there are such occasions when the risk principle may require supplementation.

At the same time, some tortious conduct may threaten, in a very clear way, massive harm and merely the fact that the scope of liability is huge is not, of itself, a ground for imposing limits on it. Asbestos-products manufacturers exposed hundreds of thousands to asbestos fibers, but no court has suggested the manufacturers' scope of liability should be confined because of the number of injured claimants or the magnitude of the aggregate damages. Similarly, a negligent operator of a nuclear plant would not have its liability limited based on the number of persons who were exposed to an escape of radiation or the magnitude of the damages, in the absence of legislation imposing such limits.

n. Unforeseeable plaintiffs. No express limitation in this Section places harm to unforeseeable plaintiffs outside the scope of an actor's liability. . . . Ordinarily, the risk standard contained in this Section will, without requiring any separate reference to the foreseeability of the plaintiff, preclude liability for harm to such plaintiffs.

Illustration:

9. Betsy, a passenger on the Xavier Railroad company, is attempting to board a train while carrying a bulky and apparently fragile package. Bob, an employee of Xavier, attempts to assist Betsy in boarding a crowded train and does so in a careless fashion that creates a likelihood Betsy will drop the package or otherwise damage it. Betsy does drop the package, which contains explosives, although there is nothing in the appearance of the package that would have so indicated. The package explodes upon impact, and the force of the explosion knocks over a platform scale 30 feet away. The scale falls on a waiting passenger, Heather, injuring her. Heather's harm is not within the scope of Bob's liability for his negligence as a matter of law; neither Bob nor Xavier is liable to Heather.

While Heather might be characterized as an unforeseeable plaintiff, a straightforward application of the risk standard in this Section reveals that that characterization is unnecessary to the outcome. The risks posed by Bob's negligence do not include the results of concussive forces due to an explosion; any harm that was posed by Bob's negligence was to the package, due to its apparent fragility and the consequences of it falling to the ground, or perhaps, physical injury to Betsy.

Generally, application of the risk standard should avoid much of the need for consideration of unforeseeable plaintiffs, as revealed above. In those cases in which the plaintiff was, because of time or geography, truly beyond being subject to harm of the type risked by the tortious conduct, but the plaintiff somehow suffers such harm, the defendant is not liable to that plaintiff for the harm.

o. Manner of harm. Courts commonly state that the manner in which the harm occurs is irrelevant to scope of liability so long as the harm is foreseeable or within the risk standard. Properly understood, this is a helpful guideline, but it must be appreciated in conjunction with the risk standard. Some aspects of the manner in which the harm occurs *are* relevant to a determination of the scope of an actor's liability. Thus, for example, that the harm occurred through an explosion in Illustration 9 is critical to the harm being beyond the scope-of-liability, given that there was no foreseeable risk from explosives when Bob was careless about the package falling. Similarly, in Illustrations 7 and 8, the tortious conduct and harm in each are identical, but there is a critical difference in the manner in which the harm occurred: in one case the skull fracture was due to a fall caused by a lack of light, while in the other, the harm was caused by an intentional tort by an intruder. Thus, the manner of harm can be of critical importance in determining whether the harm is within the scope of liability even though in both cases the victim's skull injury was made possible by a lack of light.

Nevertheless, in many cases there is value to the common wisdom about the unimportance of the manner of harm. Every outcome is a unique combination of many causes that concur to bring it about. Many varied, odd, and extraordinary acts, forces, and events may concur to produce a given harm, such that it can readily be said that the manner of harm was unusual, extraordinary, or unforeseeable. Such a statement is unhelpful in a scope-of-liability analysis, which focuses on the risks that make the conduct tortious and on the type of harm. Mechanisms are important so long as they bear, in a general and reasonable way, on the risks that were created by the tortious conduct in the circumstances that existed at the time. Beyond that, details of the causal forces that concurred to cause the harm and their individual or combinational foreseeability are unimportant to the inquiry on the scope of liability.

p. Extent of harm. If the type of harm that occurs is within the scope of the risk, the defendant is liable for all such harm caused, regardless of its extent. Even when a foreseeability standard is employed for scope of liability, the fact that the actor neither foresaw nor should have foreseen the extent of harm caused by the tortious conduct does not affect the actor's liability for the harm. One of the primary applications of this rule occurs when the injured person has a preexisting condition creating an unusual susceptibility. In some such cases, the extent of the harm is unforeseeable; the actor is nevertheless subject to liability for the full extent of the harm. . . .

q. Judge and jury. Scope of liability is a mixed question of fact and law, much like negligence. As with negligence, the court's role

153

is to instruct the jury on the standard for scope of liability when reasonable minds can differ as to whether the type of harm suffered by the plaintiff is among the harms whose risks made the defendant's conduct tortious, and it is the function of the jury to determine whether the harm is within the defendant's scope of liability.

s. *Scope of plaintiff responsibility.* The rules contained in this Section regarding the scope of liability for tortious conduct are the same for determining when a plaintiff's contributory negligence will reduce the recovery based on comparative responsibility. Thus, even if a plaintiff's contributory negligence is a factual cause of harm, if the risks posed by the plaintiff's negligence are different from the type of risk that produced the plaintiff's harm, no apportionment of liability is made to the plaintiff.

§ 30. Risk of Harm Not Generally Increased by Tortious Conduct

Restatement of the Law Third, Torts: Liability for Physical and Emotional Harm

An actor is not liable for harm when the tortious aspect of the actor's conduct was of a type that does not generally increase the risk of that harm.

Comment:

a. *Tortious conduct did not increase risk of harm.* An actor's tortious conduct may be a factual cause of harm under § 26 but not be of a type such as to affect the probability of such harm occurring. This situation arises when the risk created by the actor's tortious conduct did not increase the risk of the harm suffered by the other person. To put the point slightly differently, greater care by the actor would not reduce the frequency of such accidents. When tortious conduct does not generally increase the risk of the type of harm that occurred, the wrongful aspect of the actor's conduct is merely serendipitous or coincidental in causing the harm. While § 29 contains the primary limitation on liability, this Section creates another limit on the scope of liability.

Illustration:

1. Gordie is driving 35 miles per hour on a city street with a speed limit of 25 miles per hour with Nathan as his passenger. Without warning, a tree crashes on Gordie's car, injuring Nathan. Gordie's speeding is a factual cause of Nathan's harm because, if Gordie had not been traveling at 35 miles per hour, he would not have arrived at the location where the tree fell at the precise time that it fell. Gordie is not liable to Nathan because Gordie's speeding did not increase the risk

of the type of harm suffered by Nathan. The speeding merely put Gordie at the place and time at which the tree fell. This is true even if the type of harm suffered by Nathan might be found to be one of the risks arising from speeding in an automobile.

Many would respond to Illustration 1 with the intuitive reaction that Gordie's speeding was not a factual cause of Nathan's harm. That intuition can be expressed in a more analytical framework: the *risks* occasioned by speeding did not cause Nathan's harm. This may be understood by appreciating that Gordie's speeding was as likely to put him in a position away from the tree as it was to put Gordie in the position he was in at the time the tree fell—the accident occurred because of the luck of the draw, not because of the risks of speeding. Nevertheless, Gordie's speeding was a but-for cause of Nathan's harm in Illustration 1. To prevent confusion, this increased-risk requirement is addressed as a matter of scope of liability.

Application of the principle in this Section may require careful attention to, and description of, the risks created by the actor's tortious conduct. Whether the tortious conduct increased the risk of harm may depend on the circumstances and time frame in which the harm occurs. The critical inquiry is whether the risks posed by the tortious conduct of the actor would, if repeated, make it more likely that harm such as that suffered by the other person would also occur. If the harm is no more likely to occur than if the actor desisted from the tortious conduct, the harm is not within the scope of the actor's liability pursuant to this Section.

Illustration:

2. While driving on a country road, Joe lost control of his car because Sander, driving a semitrailer in the opposite direction, negligently crossed over the center line of the road and did not leave enough room for Joe to stay on the road. Several cars stopped, creating a hazard at the site, particularly because a curve in the road obscured the site and approaching traffic had little advance warning that the road was blocked. Betty, Joe's passenger, went down the road to warn approaching traffic of the hazardous condition ahead and the need to slow down. After a tow truck returned Joe's car to the road, he and Betty drove off. A few miles from the scene, Betty decided to pick wildflowers by the side of the road, and Joe stopped his car just off the road. While picking flowers, Betty was struck by an automobile when the driver failed to keep an adequate lookout. Although Sander's negligence is a factual cause of Betty's injury, her injury is outside the scope of Sander's liability because the risks created by Sander's negligence did not increase the risk of Betty being struck when she decided to get out of her car and pick wildflowers at the side of the road.

The limitations on scope of liability contained in this Section are also applicable to a plaintiff's contributory negligence, and to whether such negligence will reduce the plaintiff's recovery. . . .

b. Rationale. This limitation on scope of liability contributes both to appropriate incentives for deterrence and to affirming corrective-justice concerns. Limiting liability to instances in which the tortious conduct increased the risk of harm is essential for appropriate incentives in a tort system that retains a factual-cause requirement. Deterrence, it is true, can be obtained by criminal and regulatory systems, but those devices remain outside the tort system. From a corrective-justice perspective, a merely serendipitous causal connection between the tortious aspect of the actor's conduct and the other's harm provides little reason for requiring the defendant to correct for that which has been wrongfully taken from the plaintiff.

B. UNFORESEEABLE HARM

§ 31. Preexisting Conditions and Unforeseeable Harm

Restatement of the Law Third, Torts: Liability for Physical and Emotional Harm

When an actor's tortious conduct causes harm to a person that, because of a preexisting physical or mental condition or other characteristics of the person, is of a greater magnitude or different type than might reasonably be expected, the actor is nevertheless subject to liability for all such harm to the person.

Comment:

a. History. Known colloquially as the "thin-skull" or "eggshell plaintiff" rule, and described often as the "defendant takes the victim as found," this Section adopts and extends § 461 of the Restatement Second of Torts. . . . This Section [applies to] all preexisting conditions of an injured person and harm that results from that condition that might itself be characterized as unforeseeable.

b. Relationship to general scope-of-liability principles. . . . In many cases, this rule simply reflects the outcome of application of a general approach, such as the risk standard contained in § 29. . . . Thus, although the type of harm that occurs is unexceptional, the magnitude of the damages is extraordinary because of a peculiar characteristic of the injured person. . . .

Illustrations:

1. Gino, who worked as a concessionaire at a sports

stadium, negligently collided with Maddy, a fan attending the game, and knocked her to the ground. Maddy had an asymptomatic herniated disc that resulted in her suffering serious back injury and pain as a result of Gino's negligence. All of Maddy's harm is within Gino's scope of liability for his negligence, as a matter of law.

2. Tom, a passenger in an automobile, suffered modest physical injuries in an accident in which Katherine drove across the center line of the road and sideswiped the automobile in which Tom was riding. During treatment for his injuries, Tom's doctors prescribed narcotic painkillers because of the severe pain from which Tom was suffering. Tom became addicted to the painkillers and remained addicted for approximately a year before he was able, after attending a detoxification program, to overcome his addiction. Tom had a history of drug dependence, and Katherine seeks to introduce evidence of Tom's drug dependence to ameliorate the damages to which he would otherwise be entitled to recover for his drug addiction. Tom's predisposition to becoming addicted constitutes a preexisting condition within the meaning of this Section. That condition is irrelevant to the damages to which he is entitled, unless Katherine can show that Tom's predisposition would have resulted in his independently becoming addicted at some time during the year even if he had not had narcotic painkillers because of the accident.

Similarly, when the damages that occur are of a greater magnitude than might be expected, all of those damages are within the scope of liability. The risk standard would produce this result in any case, but in jurisdictions that employ a foreseeability test, this Section and Comment foreclose an argument that the extent of damages suffered was unforeseeable.

Illustration:

3. Jennifer was driving her automobile, manufactured by Benessere Motor Co., on an Interstate highway when the voltage regulator in the car failed due to negligent installation. The failure caused the battery fluid to boil, which produced toxic fumes that reached the interior of the car. Jennifer suffered chronic vocal-cord dysfunction as a result. Jennifer was a popular vocal performer who earned several million dollars each year. All of Jennifer's lost earnings due to her vocal-cord injury are within the scope of Benessere's liability for its negligence, as a matter of law.

The thin-skull rule is applicable to all forms of tortious conduct, whether accidental or intentional.

Illustration:

4. Gary was born with a genetic predisposition to heart

157

disease. While leaving a tavern late one night, he was accosted by Jeffrey, who ordered Gary to hand over his wallet. When Gary resisted, Jeffrey hit Gary in the chest with his fist, which resulted in Gary suffering a heart attack. Gary's harm resulting from the heart attack is within the scope of Jeffrey's liability, as a matter of law.

As earlier language in this Comment implies, a plaintiff need not have a preexisting condition to recover for physical or emotional harm that is of unforeseeable magnitude. This Section exists to respond to claims by defendants that an unusual characteristic of the plaintiff has produced unforeseeable harm that is therefore outside the defendant's scope of liability. It is not; neither is physical or emotional harm that is of an unforeseeable magnitude when no preexisting condition exists.

c. Distinction from factual causation. The preexisting-condition rule, which addresses the scope of liability when the extent of harm is unusual or greater than might be anticipated, must be distinguished from the requirement of factual cause, which limits an actor's liability to the injuries caused by the tortious conduct. When a person has a preexisting condition or injury that has already caused or is causing harm of some degree, the actor is only liable for any enhancement of the harm caused by the tortious conduct. This Section applies equally to any such enhanced harm: the unforeseeability of the harm due to the condition of the person does not negate the actor's liability for the enhanced harm. The questions of the burden of proof on showing enhancement of injury and its magnitude, and of apportionment of liability among the parties, are addressed in § 28, Comment *d*, and Restatement Third, Torts: Apportionment of Liability.

Illustration:

5. Same facts as Illustration 1, except that at the time Gino collided with Maddy, she had a mild level of chronic back pain. After the accident with Gino, Maddy suffered severe back pain. Gino is subject to liability for the enhanced injury to Maddy; he is not liable for the pain from which Maddy was suffering at the time of the accident.

In some cases, the actor's tortious conduct may merely accelerate the time when the other person suffers harm. Thus, an individual may have a predisposition to contracting a type of cancer. An environmental exposure triggers the occurrence of cancer in that individual, who would nevertheless have contracted the cancer at some time in the future. The damages to which the person is entitled when this situation arises are not addressed in this Restatement.

d. Property damage. The rule stated in this Section is applicable to property, as well. When harm to property is of a greater

158

magnitude or different type than might be expected because of a characteristic of the property, the harm is within the scope of the actor's liability.

§ 32. Rescuers

Restatement of the Law Third, Torts: Liability for Physical and Emotional Harm

Notwithstanding § 29 or § 34, if an actor's tortious conduct imperils another or the property of another, the scope of the actor's liability includes any harm to a person resulting from that person's efforts to aid or to protect the imperiled person or property, so long as the harm arises from a risk that inheres in the effort to provide aid.

Comment:

a. History. The seminal case imposing liability on a tortfeasor for harm suffered by a person who came to the rescue of another is Wagner v. Int'l Ry. Co., 133 N.E. 437 (N.Y. 1921), authored by Judge Cardozo. . . .

b. Scope of the "rescue doctrine." The "rescue doctrine" addresses a mélange of issues that arise when a rescuer is injured in attempting to assist another. These issues include duty, scope of liability, superseding cause, contributory negligence, and assumption of risk. The aspect relevant to scope of liability provides that an actor, whose tortious conduct puts the actor or another at risk, is subject to liability to a third person who is injured while attempting to come to the aid of the actor or of the other imperiled person. This Section is also applicable to a rescuer of imperiled property, whether that property is owned by another or by the rescuer. The actor is subject to liability regardless of whether the rescuer might be thought foreseeable or whether harm to the rescuer might be thought within the risk standard. Thus, while harm to a rescuer might be found unforeseeable or the rescuer's decision to aid another might be characterized as a superseding cause, scope of liability does not prevent a rescuer from recovering for injuries suffered as a result of the rescue. Similarly, in those jurisdictions that rely on duty to address unforeseeable plaintiffs, actors owe a duty of care to rescuers, independent of the duty owed to others who are foreseeably put at risk by the actor's conduct. . . .

Illustration:

1. Middlesex County maintained a nature park that included paths along its canyons and gorges. Denis, employed as a park ranger by Middlesex County, became aware that a stream had dangerously eroded the support for a path, but ne-

glected to close the path or to post warnings. A group of campers pitched camp after dark near the path. Two of the campers, Anne and Craig, left the group to go on a walk. Anne and Craig fell into a gorge when the weakness in the support for the path gave way. The other members of the camping party heard what sounded like a falling object and called out to Anne and Craig, but received no response. Steve and Larry proceeded with a flashlight to investigate and discovered that Craig and Anne had fallen into the bottom of the gorge and appeared to be unconscious. In his attempt to descend to the bottom of the gorge, Larry lost his footing, fell, and suffered harm. Middlesex County and Denis are subject to liability to Larry for the harm he suffered in attempting to rescue Anne and Craig. . . .

When the rescue doctrine is applicable, the jury should be instructed that it may find the defendant liable to the rescuer based on tortious conduct putting another at risk and on the harm to the other being within the scope of the risk created by the tortious conduct. The factfinder need not be instructed about, nor address, whether the harm to the rescuer was among the risks that made the actor's conduct tortious.

The rescue doctrine is equally applicable when a person is put at risk by another's tortious conduct but has not suffered any harm at the time of the attempted rescue. . . .

c. Limits on the scope of liability to rescuers. The rescue doctrine does not obviate all scope-of-liability limitations on a tortious actor's liability. Analogously to § 29, when the harm suffered by the rescuer is different from the harms whose risks would be expected to arise in the rescue, the actor is not liable because the harm is outside the scope of liability. Thus, when an unusual type of harm occurs in a rescue, the inquiry is whether, at the outset of that particular rescue, the risk of such harm would reasonably be anticipated. . . .

Professional rescuers are often treated differently under what is colloquially known as the "firefighter rule." Under its modern incarnation, that rule is based on a mélange of public-policy considerations and dealt with under the rubric of duty.

d. The impact of comparative responsibility. Historically, one of the reasons for the rescue doctrine was to prevent a rescuer from being barred from recovery because of a finding that the rescuer was contributorily negligent. However, liability to rescuers was limited to those who did not proceed in a reckless, wanton, or rash manner. With the adoption of comparative responsibility, many courts appropriately have applied that doctrine to rescuers, permitting the factfinder to assign comparative responsibility to a rescuer who acts unreasonably in undertaking or conducting a rescue. The social value and altruistic motivation of rescuers is relevant both to whether a rescuer acts unreasonably and to apportioning comparative responsibility in this situation. The logic of this adjustment to the rescuer doctrine to permit comparative responsibility to be apportioned to a negligent rescuer also suggests that comparative responsibility be apportioned when a rescuer proceeds in a reckless or wanton manner, rather than relying on the former rule that would bar recovery.

C. INTERVENING, SUBSEQUENT, AND DUPLICATIVE ACTS

§ 34. Intervening Acts and Superseding Causes

Restatement of the Law Third, Torts: Liability for Physical and Emotional Harm

> **When a force of nature or an independent act is also a factual cause of harm, an actor's liability is limited to those harms that result from the risks that made the actor's conduct tortious.**

Comment:

a. History and introduction. . . . The rule stated in this Section . . . recognizes that other human acts and forces of nature may concur with tortious conduct to cause harm. Were it not for the long history of intervening and superseding causes playing a significant role in limiting the scope of liability, this Section would not be necessary. However, to address the substantial body of law on this subject and to explain the bases for its declining importance, this Section is necessary. . . .

b. Intervening acts and superseding causes. . . . These terms ["intervening acts" and "superseding causes"] are only conclusory labels. A reasoning and normative process is required in order to separate background causes from intervening forces and to decide which intervening forces under what circumstances are superseding, thus avoiding the liability of an actor who engaged in tortious conduct.

c. The impact of comparative responsibility on superseding causes. Historically, the legal environment in which the doctrine of superseding cause and proximate cause arose was quite different from the environment in the 21st century. First, contributory negligence barred a plaintiff from recovery. Thus, a plaintiff's negligence served, in effect, as a superseding cause as a matter of law. . . . Second, there was no right to contribution among joint tortfeasors until the middle of the 20th century. Thus, the law regarding intervening acts and superseding causes reflected in the Restatement of Torts was developed at a time when negligent tortfeasors could not obtain contribution from another negligent tortfeasor or even from an intentional tortfeasor. The no-

161

contribution rule could produce substantial unfairness on those occasions when multiple tortfeasors were held liable. . . .

Just as comparative responsibility has obviated the need for a number of legal rules designed to ameliorate the harshness of contributory negligence . . . the advent of comparative principles has reduced the role for superseding cause. This is most evident when courts consider a plaintiff's conduct as an intervening act and possible superseding cause. At the time when contributory negligence barred a claim, it did not make much difference if the basis for the plaintiff's losing the case was proximate cause or contributory negligence. The former gave courts a bit more control over juries that might have been inclined to ameliorate the harshness of contributory negligence with a discounted verdict. But employing superseding cause to bar a plaintiff's recovery based on the plaintiff's conduct is difficult to reconcile with modern notions of comparative responsibility. Indeed, in most cases it constitutes negating the principles of comparative responsibility and returning to a regime of contributory negligence as a complete bar to recovery. There may be instances in which the plaintiff's intervening conduct produces harm that is different from the harms whose risks made the defendant's conduct tortious, but those cases are sufficiently infrequent that courts should be very cautious about invoking superseding cause based on a plaintiff's act to hold the harm outside the defendant's scope of liability.

Even when third persons, rather than plaintiffs, are negligent or commit intentional torts, the need for aggressive use of superseding cause to absolve a tortfeasor from liability has subsided in light of the modification of joint and several liability and of the trend toward permitting comparative responsibility to be apportioned among negligent and intentional tortfeasors. Comparative responsibility permits liability to be apportioned among multiple tortfeasors and to take account of the causal relationship between each tortfeasor's conduct and the harm as well as the culpability of each tortfeasor.

d. Intervening act the source of the risk making the conduct tortious. In some instances, the risks posed by even an extraordinary force of nature or by a culpable (or, a fortiori, nonculpable) human act may be precisely the risks that render tortious an actor's failure to adopt adequate precautions. . . . Similarly, an actor may be found negligent for failing to take appropriate precautions against the hazards posed by an extraordinary force of nature. When an actor is found negligent precisely because of the failure to adopt adequate precaution against the risk of harm created by another's acts or omissions, or by an extraordinary force of nature, there is no scope-of-liability limitation on the actor's liability.

Illustration:

1. Laurie was a guest at the Rogers Motor Inn, which

was located in a neighborhood where significant violent crime existed. After Laurie returned to her room, David was able to gain entrance to Laurie's room because the lock on the door was of the simple residential type that could be easily defeated with a credit card. After gaining entrance to Laurie's room, David sexually assaulted her. Laurie sues Rogers claiming negligence in providing inadequate locks for guest rooms. David's criminal acts are not a superseding cause of Laurie's harm, as a matter of law, and, consequently, Laurie's harm is within the scope of Rogers's liability for its negligence.

e. Unforeseeable, unusual, or highly culpable intervening acts. In some cases, the risk that makes conduct tortious is one created by another person's conduct. Thus, in Illustration 1, Rogers is negligent because of the risk of an assault on one of its guests. In such cases, the intervening act and the attendant harm are within the scope of the defendant's liability, and those cases are not addressed in this Comment. However, in other cases, the risk is one that exists independently of human intervention, although causes in addition to the defendant's tortious conduct are required for the harm to occur. When those other causes—intervening acts—are unforeseeable, unusual, or highly culpable they may bear on whether the harm is within the scope of the risk.

Illustrations:

2. Carol undertakes a substantial excavation in a crowded public sidewalk and leaves it without putting concrete barriers around the excavation, creating a risk that a pedestrian on the sidewalk will fall into the excavation. Barbara, passing Gary on the sidewalk, negligently bumps into him, knocking Gary into the excavation. Carol is subject to liability to Gary, as Gary's harm is within the scope of Carol's liability for her negligence. . . .

4. Same facts as Illustration 2, except that Barbara deliberately shoves Gary into the excavation. Whether Gary's harm is within the scope of Carol's liability for her negligence is an issue for the factfinder. The factfinder will have to determine whether the appropriate characterization of the harm to Gary is falling into an unguarded excavation site or being deliberately pushed into an unguarded excavation site and, if the latter, whether it is among the risks that made Carol negligent. . . .

In some cases the intervening act may be an omission. Thus, once an actor creates a risk, that risk may be avoided or ameliorated by another who, notified or aware of the danger, can be expected to take steps to do so. When the other person fails to take such action, as when an employer, informed of the need to modify a dangerous aspect of industrial machinery, fails to do so, that omission may justify finding the harm beyond the actor's scope of liability, especially if the original actor could not reasonably foresee the failure.

✕ *f. Sole proximate cause.* Courts sometimes employ the doctrine of "sole proximate cause" to limit the liability of a defendant. Such use covers a variety of quite different ideas. Courts have employed sole proximate cause to deny a negligent plaintiff recovery. Courts also use sole proximate cause to mean that a defendant was not negligent or that any negligence by a defendant was not a proximate cause of the harm. The most common usage of sole proximate cause is as an alternative to superseding cause. But there is no meaning distinct to sole proximate cause. Sole-proximate-cause terminology is confusing for two reasons: (1) it incorrectly implies that there can be only one proximate cause of harm; and (2) it obscures a more direct and precise explanation for denying liability. In light of the confusion it can generate, and of the availability of more precise explanations for denying liability, it is a term best avoided.

g. Harm outside the scope of the risk. When the harm that occurs arises from a risk other than one that was among those that made the actor's conduct tortious, the actor is not liable. That there are intervening acts that also are a cause of the harm does not affect this result. As with § 30, tortious conduct that does not increase the risk of the harm in a general way does not subject the actor to liability for harm caused, regardless of the existence of an intervening act.

Illustrations:

6. David, a private security guard, personally purchased a walkie-talkie designed for children as a toy and manufactured by the Hohe Toy Co. David took one of the receivers to work and left the other with his brother, Gary. One night, while inspecting an empty warehouse whose door was left open, David was accosted by several thieves. David attempted to contact Gary to call for help, but a defective switch in the walkie-talkie prevented David from contacting Gary. The thieves attacked and injured David, who sues Hohe for the harm he suffered in the attack. Despite the defect in Hohe's walkie-talkie, Hohe is not liable for David's harm as a matter of law, because the attack by the thieves produced harm that was not among the risks that one might consider in determining that, at the time of manufacture, the walkie-talkie was defective.

7. Same facts as Illustration 6, except that the walkie-talkie is manufactured by Stand Tall, Inc., a company that specializes in security equipment for law-enforcement personnel, and the walkie-talkie was designed and marketed for use by law-enforcement officials. Stand Tall's liability for selling a

defective walkie-talkie includes the harm suffered by David in the attack by the thieves, as a matter of law. . . .

§ 35. Enhanced Harm Due to Efforts to Render Medical or Other Aid

Restatement of the Law Third, Torts: Liability for Physical and Emotional Harm

An actor whose tortious conduct is a factual cause of harm to another is subject to liability for any enhanced harm the other suffers due to the efforts of third persons to render aid reasonably required by the other's injury, so long as the enhanced harm arises from a risk that inheres in the effort to render aid.

Comment:

a. Liability for enhanced harm from efforts to aid an injured person. . . . The Restatement Second of Torts provided that a negligent actor was liable for enhanced harm caused by third persons in rendering aid reasonably required by the injured person, regardless of whether the third person acted negligently. This Section reiterates that rule, which retains virtually unanimous acceptance, and expands it to cover other tortious conduct. Negligence in medical treatment of a tortiously caused injury is the most common invocation of the rule in this Section.

Illustration:

1. Harriet, a diabetic, required special orthopedic shoes. Walter, the podiatrist who fitted Harriet for her shoes, did so negligently. The improperly fitted shoes caused blistering on Harriet's feet. Harriet saw Yael, her physician, about the blistering, but Yael decided nothing need be done. Because of her diabetic condition, Harriet developed gangrene and had to have her leg amputated. Harriet sued Walter for negligence, seeking to recover damages for her amputation. Walter contends that if Yael had not been negligent in failing to take prompt action to treat Harriet's blistering, she would not have lost her leg. Whether Yael's treatment was negligent or not, Harriet's amputation is within the scope of Walter's liability for his negligence in fitting Harriet for special shoes.

This Section includes harm that results from a rescuer's efforts that are objectively reasonably required based on the plaintiff's condition and circumstances, as well as those efforts that a rescuer reasonably believes are required, even if the rescuer is incorrect in that judgment.

b. Rationale. The reasons for this rule are various and may apply differentially, depending on the circumstances of the case. In

165

the context of enhanced harm due to medical care, the inherent risks of non-negligently-provided treatment are plainly within the scope of the actor's liability. If the rule were different for negligently enhanced injury, defendants would have a strong incentive regularly to claim that enhanced harm was due to medical malpractice. Thus, the rule in this Section avoids the administrative costs of litigating the collateral issue of medical malpractice every time a defendant might claim such enhanced injury. The predictable incidence of medical malpractice, however prevalent as a cause of enhanced injury, has often led courts to note its foreseeability. Finally, in the medical-care context, the rule in this Section obviates the need for injured persons to pursue a medical-malpractice claim when a defendant claims that some portion of the harm was caused by a health-care provider's negligence. Defendants are free to assert contribution claims against medical professionals for malpractice in enhancing the plaintiff's injury. More broadly, the risk of enhanced injury to a person suffering harm due to efforts of others to aid the person is one that should be anticipated as arising from conduct posing risks of harm to others. Indeed, it would be the rare case in which enhanced harm covered by this Section would not be within the scope of the original tortfeasor's liability under the general standard. . . . Nevertheless, the specificity contained in the rule in this Section may assist courts in resolving the enhanced-harm issue addressed here.

c. *Harm different from harms whose risks are incident to normal efforts to render aid.* An actor is not liable for all enhanced harms that occur from efforts to render aid. Only those enhanced harms whose risks are created by normal efforts to render aid are within the scope of the actor's liability. The actor is not subject to liability for enhanced harm caused by extraordinary or unusual acts that create risks of harm different from those normally created by efforts to render aid. . . .

Illustration:

2. Susan, a pedestrian on a busy promenade, negligently failed to keep a lookout. She ran into and knocked down Amy, another pedestrian. Amy suffered several bruises and cuts in the fall and was rendered unconscious. None of Amy's injuries required anything more than ordinary first aid. Harvey, a passerby who was not a physician and who had no health-care training, stopped to help Amy. Harvey decided that to reduce the risk of infection, he should enlarge one of Amy's cuts with his penknife so as to enhance the flow of blood. When he did so, he cut off the tip of Amy's finger. Susan is not subject to liability for the enhanced harm caused by Harvey's efforts to aid Amy. . . .

d. *Effect of adoption of comparative responsibility or modifica-*

166

tion of joint and several liability. . . . When two or more defendants are liable for the enhanced harm suffered by a plaintiff, as may occur under this Section, and the governing law imposes several liability, each of the defendants is held liable for the amount of damages reflecting the enhanced harm discounted by the comparative share of responsibility assigned by the factfinder to that defendant.

Illustration:

4. Same facts as Illustration 1, except Harriet sues both Walter and Yael. The jury finds Walter liable for Harriet's blistering and Walter and Yael liable for Harriet's amputation. The jury awards $300,000 in damages to Harriet for her amputation and finds that Walter is 10 percent and Yael is 90 percent comparatively responsible for the amputation. In a jurisdiction in which several liability is the applicable rule, the judgment against Walter would be $30,000 for the amputation and $270,000 against Yael. Walter would also be liable for all the damages awarded for Harriet's blistering.

§ 36. Trivial Contributions to Multiple Sufficient Causes

Restatement of the Law Third, Torts: Liability for Physical and Emotional Harm

When an actor's negligent conduct constitutes only a trivial contribution to a causal set that is a factual cause of harm under § 27, the harm is not within the scope of the actor's liability.

Comment:

a. History. . . . There are [ ] a class of cases in which the actor's negligence, while a member of a causal set sufficient to produce the harm, pales by comparison to the other contributions to that causal set. While the conduct still constitutes a factual cause under § 27 and Comment *f*, this Section preserves the limitation on liability that the substantial-factor requirement in the prior Restatements might have played in this situation.

b. Trivial contributions to overdetermined outcomes. To preserve the largely objective inquiry . . . on factual cause, the limit on liability provided by this Section is located in this Chapter on scope of liability. . . . The exception applies only when there are multiple sufficient causes and the tortious conduct at issue constitutes a trivial contribution to any sufficient causal set. In general, this limitation will apply when the causal contribution of various actors is susceptible to being compared on a common metric, such as quantity of comparable pollution or of toxic substances. It may be particularly appropriate when another tortious actor's conduct is sufficient (with background causes) to cause the harm, and the actor's tortious conduct can only be characterized as an element of a sufficient causal set by disaggregating the other's tortious contribution.

In some cases, the contribution of an actor claiming the benefit of this Section will require submission of the case to the factfinder to decide if the actor's contribution was sufficiently trivial so as to be beyond the actor's scope of liability. In other cases, the contribution may be sufficiently de minimis that the court can rule as a matter of law.

Illustration:

1. Jerry worked for 40 years as an asbestos-insulation installer. During that time, he was exposed to asbestos fibers from insulation manufactured by a dozen manufacturers. In the case of most of the manufacturers, Jerry was exposed to their products on a daily basis for years. Jerry's 40 years of substantial exposure to asbestos was considerably more than required to cause Jerry's mesothelioma. Jerry's exposure to the product of one manufacturer, Centurion Company, however, occurred at a commercial construction site where other installers were using a Centurion product. Centurion's product was installed in a single day, on a different floor of the building from where Jerry worked that day. Competent and reliable expert testimony was introduced that explained that Jerry would have inhaled some fibers from Centurion's product during that day, but the amount would be minuscule compared to Jerry's exposure to other defendants' asbestos products. Centurion is not subject to liability to Jerry, despite any tortious conduct by it in manufacturing and selling its asbestos product.

The limitation on the scope of liability provided in this Section is not applicable if the trivial contributing cause is necessary for the outcome; this Section is only applicable when the outcome is overdetermined. By contrast, the actor who negligently provides the straw that breaks the camel's back is subject to liability for the broken back. . . .

CHAPTER 10

DEFENSES

A. ASSUMPTION OF THE RISK

§ 2. Contractual Limitations on Liability

Restatement of the Law Third, Torts: Apportionment of Liability

When permitted by contract law, substantive law governing the claim, and applicable rules of construction, a contract between the plaintiff and another person absolving the person from liability for future harm bars the plaintiff's recovery from that person for the harm. Unlike a plaintiff's negligence, a valid contractual limitation on liability does not provide an occasion for the factfinder to assign a percentage of responsibility to any party or other person.

Comment:

b. Rationale and effect. . . . A valid contractual limitation on liability does not provide an occasion for the factfinder to assign a percentage of responsibility to any party or other person. In these respects, a valid contractual limitation on liability differs from a plaintiff's negligence, which merely reduces a plaintiff's recovery by the percentage of responsibility the factfinder assigns to the plaintiff. See § 7.

c. Method of forming contractual limitations on liability. A contractual limitation on liability may occur by written agreement, express oral agreement, or conduct that creates an implied-in-fact contract. See Comment *d*. Whether there is such a contract is determined by the applicable rules of contract law. The essential element of a contractual limitation on liability is that each party agrees that the defendant is under no obligation to protect the plaintiff and shall not be liable to the plaintiff for the consequences of conduct that would otherwise be tortious. . . .

d. Burden of proof and strict construction of contracts. A party invoking a contractual limitation on liability must prove the existence and application of the contract. Normally, a contract is effective if it is consistent with the understanding of a reasonable person in the plaintiff's position. A contract that limits liability must be expressed in clear, definite, and unambiguous language and cannot be inferred from general language. Generally, contracts absolving a party from intentional or reckless conduct are disfavored. When an individual plaintiff passively accepts a contract drafted by the defendant, the contract is construed strictly, favoring reasonable interpretations against the defendant. A contract is not unenforceable merely because it fails to use specific language naming the causes of action to which it applies. In a written consumer contract, the fact that language is in small print or otherwise is not conspicuous is a factor in determining whether the agreement is enforceable.

e. Other unenforceable contracts. Some contracts for assumption of risk are unenforceable as a matter of public policy. Whether a contractual limitation on liability is unenforceable depends on the nature of the parties and their relationship to each other, including whether one party is in a position of dependency; the nature of the conduct or service provided by the party seeking exculpation, including whether the conduct or service is laden with "public interest"; the extent of the exculpation; the economic setting of the transaction; whether the document is a standardized contract of adhesion; and whether the party seeking exculpation was willing to provide greater protection against tortious conduct for a reasonable, additional fee. A contractual limitation on liability may be unenforceable on contract principles, such as fraud, misrepresentation, duress, undue influence, or mistake. . . .

f. Relation to consent. Any agreement by words or conduct that would constitute consent to an intentional tort constitutes a defense under the rule stated in this Section.

g. Reckless conduct and intentional torts. Subject to the restrictions in Comments *d*, *e*, and *h*, the rule stated in this Section applies to claims based on a defendant's intentional or reckless conduct.

h. Contractual limitations on liability. Substantive rules preclude disclaimers, exculpatory contracts, or other forms of contractual limitation on liability in various circumstances. For example, disclaimers for personal injury are unenforceable in products-liability cases. They are restricted in breach-of-warranty cases governed by the Uniform Commercial Code. If a contractual limitation on liability is effective for one cause of action but not for another, the plaintiff can recover for the other cause of action but not for the first.

i. Implied assumption of risk distinguished. This Section does not apply when a plaintiff's conduct demonstrates merely that the plaintiff was aware of a risk and voluntarily confronted it. That type of conduct, which is usually called "implied assumption of risk," does not otherwise constitute a defense unless it constitutes consent to an intentional tort. . . .

k. Effect of a contractual limitation on liability on defendants not parties to the contract. A contractual limitation on liability bars a plaintiff's recovery only against a defendant who made the contract, who under normal principles of contract law is a third-party beneficiary, or who succeeds in such an interest. The contract does not bar a plaintiff from recovering from other tortfeasors. . . .

B. PLAINTIFF FAULT

§ 3. Ameliorative Doctrines for Defining Plaintiff's Negligence Abolished

Restatement of the Law Third, Torts: Apportionment of Liability

Plaintiff's negligence is defined by the applicable standard for a defendant's negligence. Special ameliorative doctrines for defining plaintiff's negligence are abolished.

Comment:

a. Standard for plaintiff's negligence same as standard for defendant's negligence. . . . This Section applies the standard of negligence, however defined, to plaintiffs. It also abolishes certain ameliorative doctrines that were designed to avoid the harsh effects of contributory negligence as an absolute bar to a plaintiff's recovery. These doctrines are no longer appropriate when, under comparative responsibility, a plaintiff's negligence only reduces his or her recovery.

The standard of negligence employed to evaluate a plaintiff's conduct is the same as the standard of negligence employed to evaluate a defendant's conduct. It applies to conduct that imposes risks on the plaintiff or on other persons to the same extent that the standard employed to evaluate a defendant also applies to conduct that imposes risks on the defendant and on others. A

171

plaintiff's conduct that imposes risks on other persons may be valued differently from conduct that imposes risks only on the plaintiff. Plaintiff's negligence can include conduct that is reckless, grossly negligent, or intentional.

Whether a plaintiff's personal characteristics (such as age, knowledge, mental ability, and physical characteristics) are taken into account is determined by the same rules that determine whether a defendant's personal characteristics are taken into account. . . .

Whether a plaintiff's conduct violates or complies with a statute or industry custom, or occurs in an emergency, is taken into account in the same way it is taken into account when evaluating a defendant's conduct. . . .

b. Timing of the plaintiff's and defendant's conduct: last clear chance, mitigation of damages, and avoidable consequences. . . . [T]his Section applies to all types of plaintiff's conduct, regardless of the relative timing of the defendant's conduct, the plaintiff's conduct, and the accident. . . . No last-clear-chance rule categorically forgives a plaintiff for conduct that would otherwise constitute negligence.

This Section applies to a plaintiff's unreasonable conduct that aggravates the plaintiff's injuries. No rule about mitigation of damages or avoidable consequences categorically forgives a plaintiff of this type of conduct or categorically excludes recovery. . . .

The timing of the plaintiff's and defendant's conduct may be relevant to the degree of responsibility the factfinder assigns to a plaintiff. It may also be relevant to whether the plaintiff's injury was within the scope of liability of either the plaintiff's or defendant's conduct.

Illustrations:

1. A negligently runs out of gasoline on the highway. B sees A's automobile but negligently fails to avoid hitting it with his own automobile, injuring A. A is not forgiven his own negligence under the last-clear-chance rule. In assigning percentages of responsibility, the factfinder may take into account that B knew of A's peril and was subsequently negligent.

2. Same facts as Illustration 1, except B drives recklessly. A is not forgiven his own negligence under the last-clear-chance rule. In assigning percentages of responsibility, the factfinder may take into account the fact that B knew of A's peril and subsequently acted recklessly. . . .

3. A negligently fails to wear a seat belt. B drives an automobile negligently, causing it to crash into A's automobile. A is thrown through the windshield and severely injured. Un-

less there is a statute precluding consideration of seat-belt use, A's conduct in failing to wear a seat belt is relevant in determining whether A was negligent and, if so, in assigning percentages of responsibility for the portion of the plaintiff's injuries caused by the failure to wear the seat belt.

4. A negligently breaks B's leg. B negligently (or deliberately) fails to follow his doctor's orders about taking anti-inflammatory medication. This failure causes B's leg to heal more slowly, which in turn causes B to miss two extra weeks of work. B's failure to take his medicine affects his percentage of responsibility for and thereby reduces his recovery of damages caused by the two-week delay. It does not, however, bar him entirely from recovering those damages or cause them to be excluded from the damage finding. . . .

5. A negligently breaks B's leg. B negligently goes skiing on the broken leg one week after it is set. This reinjures B's leg, delaying B's return to work by two weeks. B's conduct in skiing on the broken leg affects his percentage of responsibility for the damages related to the two-week delay. Damages caused by B's decision to ski on the broken leg are not, however, excluded in their entirety from B's damages. A fact-finder may find that B's decision to ski on a broken leg was unforeseeable and beyond the scope of the risk created by A's negligence. . . .

c. Relationship to implied assumption of risk and defendant's negligence. This Section applies to a plaintiff's negligence even when the plaintiff is actually aware of a risk and voluntarily undertakes it. Except as provided in § 2, no jury instruction is given on assumption of risk.

A plaintiff who is actually aware of a *reasonable* risk and voluntarily undertakes it, as when a parent tries to rescue a child from a fire, is not negligent. The parent may, however, be negligent for other reasons, such as the manner of the rescue. When a plaintiff is negligent, the plaintiff's awareness of a risk is relevant to the plaintiff's degree of responsibility.

Whether the defendant reasonably believes that the plaintiff is aware of a risk and voluntarily undertakes it may be relevant to whether the defendant acted reasonably. The defendant might reasonably have relied on the plaintiff to avoid the known risk, or other policy considerations may dictate that the defendant has no duty or a limited duty to the plaintiff. Whether the plaintiff is aware of a risk and voluntarily assumes it may also be relevant to whether the plaintiff's conduct is a superseding cause. . . .

Illustration:

6. A attends a baseball game at B's ballpark. A sits in a portion of the stands beyond the point where the screen

173

prevents balls from entering the seats. A is aware that balls occasionally are hit into the stands. The fact that A knew balls are occasionally hit into the stands does not constitute assumption of risk. The fact that A knew balls occasionally are hit into the stands is relevant in evaluating whether A acted reasonably by engaging in particular types of conduct while sitting in the stands (sitting in the stands would not itself constitute unreasonable conduct). If the factfinder concludes that A did not act reasonably under the circumstances, A's knowledge of the risk is relevant to the percentage of responsibility the factfinder assigns to A. If B could reasonably assume that A and other fans are aware that balls are occasionally hit into the stands, this fact is also relevant to whether B acted reasonably in relying on A to watch out for balls instead of constructing a screen or providing warnings.

d. Substantive rules of legal liability with respect to plaintiff's negligence, including plaintiffs who own real property and plaintiffs injured by intentional tortfeasors. Substantive rules of liability sometimes do not require defendants to exercise reasonable care. This is often done under the rubric of "no duty" or other nomenclature. For example, owners and occupiers of land sometimes are not required to exercise reasonable care to avoid injuring an undiscovered trespasser. Bystanders are typically not required to exercise reasonable care to rescue someone in peril. If such a rule would apply to a person as a defendant, it also applies to that person as a plaintiff.

Illustrations:

8. A trespasses on B's land without B's knowledge and damages B's flowers. In a suit by B against A, A argues that B failed to use reasonable care because he did not protect his flowers. B's recovery against A is not diminished by B's conduct if the substantive rule of law does not require B to exercise reasonable care to protect an undiscovered trespasser from a condition on the land.

9. A injures B in an automobile accident. B requires medical treatment but refuses a blood transfusion on religious grounds. Whether B must exercise reasonable care with respect to permitting the transfusion and whether B's refusal is outside the scope of the risk created by A's negligence are determined by the applicable substantive law, not by the rule stated in this Section.

Substantive rules establishing that an actor had "no duty" as a matter of law normally apply equally to plaintiffs and defendants. However, in some jurisdictions a plaintiff's negligence does not reduce recovery from an intentional tortfeasor, even though it does reduce recovery from other tortfeasors. . . .

§ 4. Proof of Plaintiff's Negligence and Legal Causation

Restatement of the Law Third, Torts: Apportionment of Liability

The defendant has the burden to prove plaintiff's negligence, and may use any of the methods a plaintiff may use to prove defendant's negligence. Except as otherwise provided in Topic 5, the defendant also has the burden to prove that the plaintiff's negligence, if any, was a legal cause of the plaintiff's damages.

Comment:

a. Burden of proof. . . . The burden to prove plaintiff's negligence rests on the defendant or, in a case with more than one defendant, on any defendant who seeks to benefit from a finding that the plaintiff was negligent. Except as otherwise provided in Topic 5, the defendant or defendants also have the burden to prove that the plaintiff's negligence was a legal cause of any portion of the plaintiff's injuries or damages for which the defendant seeks relief or reduction under § 7. If the defendant has met these burdens, the defendant has no further burden to produce particular evidence about the precise percentage of responsibility the factfinder should assign to the plaintiff.

Illustration:

1. A, who is driving an automobile, hits B, who is a pedestrian, in a parking lot. B sues A for negligently failing to keep a lookout and for speeding. A claims that B's damages should be reduced because B failed to use reasonable care in watching for automobiles. B has the burden to prove that A failed to use reasonable care and that this failure was a legal cause of B's damages. A has the burden to prove that B failed to use reasonable care and that this failure was a legal cause of B's damages. If A and B meet their burdens of proof on these issues, they do not have any further burden to produce particular evidence about the precise percentage of responsibility the factfinder should assign to A.

b. Methods of proving a plaintiff's negligence. A defendant seeking to prove plaintiff's negligence may employ any method of proof that, under similar circumstances, would be available to a plaintiff to prove that a defendant was negligent. These methods include circumstantial evidence, statute or regulation . . . and industry custom.

§ 7. Effect of Plaintiff's Negligence When Plaintiff Suffers an Indivisible Injury

Restatement of the Law Third, Torts: Apportionment of Liability

Plaintiff's negligence (or the negligence of an-

Pure comparative fault

other person for whose negligence the plaintiff is responsible) that is a legal cause of an indivisible injury to the plaintiff reduces the plaintiff's recovery in proportion to the share of responsibility the factfinder assigns to the plaintiff (or other person for whose negligence the plaintiff is responsible).

Comment:

a. History and definitions. This Section provides the basic principle of comparative responsibility. It replaces the rule of contributory negligence as an absolute bar to a plaintiff's recovery under Restatement Second, Torts § 467.

Some systems bar recovery when the plaintiff's percentage of responsibility is at or above 50 percent or 51 percent. These systems are generally known as modified-comparative-responsibility (50% bar or 51% bar) systems. Other systems bar recovery only when the plaintiff's percentage of responsibility is 100 percent. They are generally known as pure comparative-responsibility systems. This Section provides for a pure comparative-responsibility system.

b. Scope. This Section applies even though the conduct of a defendant was reckless or is governed by strict liability. . . . Whether a plaintiff's negligence reduces his or her recovery against an intentional tortfeasor is not governed by this Restatement.

e. Indivisible injury. This Section applies to an indivisible injury to the plaintiff. An injury is indivisible if, according to the applicable rules of causation, the plaintiff and each relevant person caused the entire injury. . . .

f. Legal cause. A plaintiff's negligence does not affect the plaintiff's recovery unless it was a legal cause of the plaintiff's injury.

Illustration:

3. A, who is driving while intoxicated, is stopped at a red light. B negligently fails to stop and hits A's car in a rear-end collision. A sues B for personal injuries suffered in the collision. A's own negligence of being intoxicated does not affect A's recovery, because it did not cause A's injuries.

g. Calculation of plaintiff's recovery. Percentages of responsibility are assigned by special verdict to any plaintiff, defendant, settlor, immune person, or other relevant person, see Topic 2, whose negligence or other legally culpable conduct was a legal cause of the plaintiff's injury. The percentages of responsibility must total 100 percent. The factfinder makes a separate finding of the plaintiff's total damages. Those damages are reduced by the percentage of responsibility the factfinder assigns to the plaintiff. The resulting amount constitutes the plaintiff's "recoverable damages." Whether any particular defendant is liable for more than its own share of the recoverable damages is governed by Topic 2.

Illustration:

4. A sues B. The factfinder assigns 40 percent responsibility to A and 60 percent responsibility to B. The factfinder finds that A's damages are $100,000. A's recovery is reduced from $100,000 to $60,000, which constitute the plaintiff's "recoverable damages."

h. Judicial reallocation of responsibility when an assignment of responsibility is legally erroneous. After the verdict, the trial or appellate court may determine that the factfinder erroneously assigned a percentage of responsibility to a party or other person submitted to the factfinder under Topic 2 ("nonliable person"). For example, the nonliable person may have been immune from liability or owed no duty of care, or there may have been insufficient evidence to support any assignment of comparative responsibility to that person. One remedy is for the court to reallocate the nonliable person's share of comparative responsibility proportionately to the remaining persons. This process has the advantage of avoiding a new trial. Nevertheless, interests of justice may sometimes require a new trial. The factors relevant to whether a new trial is required include: (1) whether eliminating the nonliable person from the factfinder's consideration might have substantially altered the jury deliberations, such as when the nonliable person was assigned the vast majority of responsibility and the remaining persons only very small percentages; (2) whether reallocation would put a party on the other side of a discontinuity in the jurisdiction's joint-and-several-liability rules, see Topic 2, or modified-comparative-responsibility rule, see Comment *n*; and (3) whether the jurisdiction permits argument and instruction to the jury about those discontinuities.

i. Judicial adjustment of shares of responsibility to avoid a new trial. When a court determines that the factfinder's assignment cannot be upheld in light of the evidence, a procedure similar to remittitur and additur is a reasonable mechanism for judicial adjustment of the factfinder's assignments. . . .

m. Plaintiff's negligence when the defendant undertakes to treat or repair a condition caused by the plaintiff's negligence or otherwise to protect the plaintiff from his or her negligence. Notwithstanding § 3, Comment *b*, in a case involving negligent rendition of a service, including medical services, a factfinder does not consider any plaintiff's conduct that created the condition the service was employed to remedy. . . .

177

Illustrations:

8. A negligently injures himself in an automobile accident. A seeks medical treatment from B, who negligently aggravates A's injury. In a suit in which A seeks to recover from B for the part of A's injuries caused by B's medical malpractice, the factfinder does not consider A's negligence in causing the accident. A's negligence produced the very condition B undertook to treat.

10. A seeks medical treatment from B. B aggravates A's condition because B negligently fails to properly diagnose A's problem. B's failure to diagnose A's condition was due in part to A's negligent failure to provide accurate answers to B's questions. In a suit in which A seeks to recover from B the part of A's injuries caused by B's negligence, the factfinder does consider A's negligence in failing to accurately answer B's questions. That conduct was not a cause of the condition B undertook to treat.

12. A negligently damages his own automobile and takes it to B for repair. B negligently repairs the automobile. The faulty repairs cause the automobile to crash, injuring A. A sues B. The factfinder does not consider A's original negligence in damaging the automobile.

Sometimes a defendant has a legal obligation to protect the plaintiff from the plaintiff's own conduct, such as a caretaker of a child or insane person. Using the plaintiff's negligence to reduce the plaintiff's recovery against such a defendant may be inconsistent with the basis of the defendant's liability. That question, however, is one of the scope of a defendant's legal obligations. Consequently, it is not addressed by this Restatement.

n. Modified comparative responsibility. Under modified comparative responsibility, a plaintiff is barred from recovery only if the factfinder assigns the plaintiff a percentage of responsibility greater than (51% bar) or equal to or greater than (50% bar) that of all of the defendants and other relevant persons to whom a percentage of responsibility is assigned. The plaintiff is not barred because the factfinder assigns a percentage of responsibility to the plaintiff that is equal to or greater than that of an individual defendant.

Illustration:

15. A sues B and C. The factfinder assigns 40 percent responsibility to A, 40 percent responsibility to B, and 20 percent responsibility to C, and finds that A's damages are $100,000. In a jurisdiction that has adopted a pure comparative-responsibility system, A recovers a total of $60,000 from B and C. In a jurisdiction that has adopted a modified-comparative-responsibility system (51% bar), A recov-

ers a total of $60,000 from B and C. A is not barred from recovering from C merely because A's percentage of responsibility is greater than C's percentage of responsibility. In a jurisdiction that has adopted a modified-comparative-responsibility system (50% bar), A recovers a total of $60,000 from B and C. A is not barred from recovering from B or C merely because A's percentage of responsibility is greater than C's percentage of responsibility and equal to B's percentage of responsibility.

C. ASSIGNING SHARES OF RESPONSIBILITY

§ 8. Factors for Assigning Shares of Responsibility

Restatement of the Law Third, Torts: Apportionment of Liability

Factors for assigning percentages of responsibility to each person whose legal responsibility has been established include

(a) the nature of the person's risk-creating conduct, including any awareness or indifference with respect to the risks created by the conduct and any intent with respect to the harm created by the conduct; and

(b) the strength of the causal connection between the person's risk-creating conduct and the harm.

Comment:

a. Assigning shares of responsibility. The factfinder assigns comparative percentages of "responsibility" to parties and other relevant persons whose negligence or other legally culpable conduct was a legal cause of the plaintiff's injury. The factfinder does not assign percentages of "fault," "negligence," or "causation."

"Responsibility" is a general and neutral term. Assigning shares of "fault" or "negligence" can be misleading because some causes of action are not based on negligence or fault. Assigning shares of "causation" wrongly suggests that indivisible injuries jointly caused by two or more actors can be divided on the basis of causation. Assigning shares of "culpability" could be misleading if it were not made clear that "culpability" refers to "legal culpability," which may include strict liability.

Of course, it is not possible to precisely compare conduct that falls into different categories, such as intentional conduct, negligent conduct, and conduct governed by strict liability, because the various theories of recovery are incommensurate. However, courts routinely compare seemingly incommensurate values, such as when they balance safety and productivity in negligence or products liability law. . . .

b. Causation and scope of liability. Conduct is relevant for

179

determining percentage shares of responsibility only when it caused the harm and when the harm is within the scope of the person's liability.

Illustration:

1. A rear-ends B's automobile when B is stopped at a red light at night. B sues A, alleging that A was not watching the road. A claims that B was negligent for failing to have working taillights and for being drunk. In assigning a percentage of responsibility to B, the factfinder considers B's failure to have working taillights if the factfinder finds that the absence of working taillights was a legal cause of the collision; the factfinder does not consider B's drunkenness if the factfinder concludes that the same accident would have happened even if B had been sober and thus that B's drunkenness was not a legal cause of the collision.

c. *Factors in assigning shares of responsibility.* The relevant factors for assigning percentages of responsibility include the nature of each person's risk-creating conduct and the comparative strength of the causal connection between each person's risk-creating conduct and the harm. The nature of each person's risk-creating conduct includes such things as how unreasonable the conduct was under the circumstances, the extent to which the conduct failed to meet the applicable legal standard, the circumstances surrounding the conduct, each person's abilities and disabilities, and each person's awareness, intent, or indifference with respect to the risks. The comparative strength of the causal connection between the conduct and the harm depends on how attenuated the causal connection is, the timing of each person's conduct in causing the harm, and a comparison of the risks created by the conduct and the actual harm suffered by the plaintiff. . . .

Illustrations:

2. A is injured when A's and B's automobiles collide at an intersection with a four-way stop. In A's lawsuit against B, A is found negligent for taking his eyes off the road to attend to a child in the back seat, and B is found negligent for purposefully trying to beat A's automobile across the intersection after seeing it approaching. A's conduct and B's conduct are each found to have caused A's indivisible injury. The factfinder would be justified in assigning a higher percentage of responsibility to B because, between A and B, (a) B's conduct deviated more significantly from the legally required norm, (b) B had a more culpable state of mind, and (c) the other circumstances surrounding A's conduct were more forgivable.

7. E is injured when E's and F's automobiles collide at an intersection. In E's lawsuit against F, E and F are both found

to be negligent. F is mentally impaired. In assigning percentages of responsibility to the parties, the factfinder may take F's mental impairment into account, even though the impairment is not relevant to F's legal culpability under the applicable objective legal standard for negligence. The court has discretion, where appropriate, to limit inquiry into F's mental state on the ground that it would be too prejudicial, confusing, or misleading or would cause undue delay. If the evidence is admitted, a limiting instruction may be appropriate to instruct the jury that F's mental state is not relevant to the question of whether F is negligent, but may only be considered for assigning percentages of responsibilities.

CHAPTER 11

AFFIRMATIVE DUTIES

A. GENERAL RULE

Scope Note: Section 7 states the general principle that an actor has a duty to exercise reasonable care when the actor's conduct creates a risk of harm. This Chapter addresses an actor's duties when the actor's conduct does not pose a risk of harm but, nevertheless, a person is at risk of harm due to other forces. It begins with the basic proposition that an actor whose conduct has not created a risk of harm does not have a duty to another person. It then sets forth exceptions to this no-duty rule. . . .

§ 37. No Duty of Care with Respect to Risks Not Created by Actor

Restatement of the Law Third, Torts: Liability for Physical and Emotional Harm

> An actor whose conduct has not created a risk of physical or emotional harm to another has no duty of care to the other unless a court determines that one of the affirmative duties provided in §§ 38-44 is applicable.

Comment:

b. Relationship to ordinary duty of reasonable care when creating a risk of harm. Section 7 of this Restatement states the general principle that an actor has a duty of reasonable care when the actor's conduct creates a risk of physical harm to others. This Section states a complementary principle: there is no duty of care when another is at risk for reasons other than the conduct of the actor, even though the actor may be in a position to help. As with any no-duty rule, this one pretermits consideration of an actor's negligence. In the absence of a duty, the actor cannot be held liable. As with the no-duty rules addressed in § 7, the no-duty rule in this Section is based on policy. . . .

There are several exceptions to this Section's no-duty rule. They are set forth in the remainder of this Chapter. These exceptions impose a duty to take action to prevent or ameliorate the risk of harm created by others. When one or more of the exceptions is applicable, breach of duty, factual causation, and scope of liability must also be addressed before determining the actor's liability. As with the special relationships identified in §§ 40–41, the affirmative duties identified in this Chapter are not an exclusive list; courts may identify additional areas for affirmative duties in the future, just as courts may decide, for reasons of policy or principle, that additional no-duty rules should be recognized. See § 7(b).

c. Misfeasance and nonfeasance. Misfeasance and nonfeasance have a long history as concepts used to explain the distinction between affirmatively creating risk and merely failing to prevent harm. However, this distinction can be misleading. The proper question is not whether an actor's failure to exercise reasonable care entails the commission or omission of a specific act. Instead, it is whether the actor's entire conduct created a risk of harm. For example, a failure to employ an automobile's brakes or a failure to warn about a latent danger in one's product is not a case of nonfeasance governed by the rules in this Chapter, because in these cases the entirety of the actor's conduct (driving an automobile or selling a product) created a risk of harm. This is so even though the specific conduct alleged to be a *breach* of the duty of reasonable care was itself an omission.

Illustrations:

1. Pleasant Valley Insurance Company provides workers'-compensation insurance to Green Acres Rest Home. Pleasant Valley periodically inspects Green Acres to identify risks to Green Acres' employees. During an inspection, Pleasant Valley's employee neglects to inspect Green Acres' heating system and, therefore, fails to identify a faulty valve that emitted carbon monoxide. Later, Colleen, a Green Acres employee, is overcome by leaking carbon monoxide. Because Pleasant Val-

ley's conduct did not create a risk of harm to Colleen, whether Pleasant Valley has a duty of care to Colleen is governed by the provisions of this Chapter, not § 7. See § 42.

2. Same facts as Illustration 1, except that during an inspection, Pleasant Valley's employee removes and inspects a valve in Green Acres' heating system. The employee neglects to replace the valve, which permits carbon monoxide to leak from the heating system. Colleen is overcome by the leaking gas. Because the conduct of Pleasant Valley's employee created a risk of harm, whether Pleasant Valley had a duty of care to Colleen is governed by § 7, not by this Chapter, even though the specific claim of negligence is that Pleasant Valley's employee *omitted* to replace the valve.

In the absence of the rules provided in this Chapter, it is sometimes difficult to determine whether an actor's conduct created a risk of harm. It would be necessary to explore, hypothetically, whether the same risk of harm would have existed even if the actor had not engaged in the conduct. Thus, a retail store that operates in a dangerous and isolated neighborhood might be characterized as creating a risk of criminal activity to patrons. If that characterization were accepted, § 7 would impose a duty of reasonable care to provide security for patrons and employees on the site. However, determining whether the retail store has created a risk of criminal activity requires consideration of what would have happened if the store had not been in operation. Would the patron have been subject to an equivalent risk of attack elsewhere? Or would the patron have forgone late-night shopping if the store had not been there? Fortunately, specific rules addressing the duty question exist for many of the common patterns in which these difficult cases arise and are contained in §§ 39-44. . . .

d. *Natural risks, third-party risks, and conduct that increases the magnitude of natural or third-party risks.* This Section applies to all risks of physical or emotional harm. It applies to risks due to natural forces, such as the threat to a swimmer who is drowning or a hiker who is caught in an unexpected mountain storm. It also applies to risks that result from the conduct of a third person, whether innocent, negligent, or intentional. Thus, absent an exception provided later in this Chapter, a bystander owes no duty of care to an individual being assaulted on a public street. On the other hand, an actor's conduct may increase the natural or third-party risk—such as by inciting a swimmer to swim despite a dangerous riptide or by providing a weapon or alcohol to an assaulter. Similarly, an actor's business operations might provide a fertile location for natural risks or third-party misconduct that creates risks that would not have occurred in the absence of the business. In these cases, the actor's conduct creates risks of its own and, therefore, is governed by the ordinary duty of reasonable care contained in § 7. Section 19 specifically addresses the duty of reasonable care when an actor's conduct increases the risk of third-party conduct that causes harm. . . .

e. Rationale. Several justifications have been offered for the no-duty rule provided in this Section. The most common relies on the distinction between placing limits on conduct and requiring affirmative conduct. This distinction in turn relies on the liberal tradition of individual freedom and autonomy. Classical liberalism is wary of laws that regulate conduct that does not infringe on the freedom of others. Some commentators have argued that mandating a duty to rescue might cheapen acts of Good Samaritans. Some commentators also argue that it might be difficult to limit an affirmative duty to aid others in peril from becoming a general duty of self-sacrifice. And in those instances when there are many potential rescuers, there may be no basis for choosing one on whom to place a rescue duty. At the opposite extreme, it is doubtful that a legal duty to rescue would have a significant impact on the incidence of easy rescues, given the effect of nonlegal influences in such circumstances. Finally, determining factual causation tends to be more difficult when the tortious act entails a failure to prevent harm from occurring.

On the other hand, by not imposing a duty to rescue, the law may be understood to convey the message that it condones an actor's failure to assist another in mortal peril when the actor could do so at little or no cost, a proposition that is morally repugnant. The tension between the no-duty rule and these values about humanitarian conduct is reflected in exceptions to the no-duty rule that are addressed in §§ 38-44.

f. The role of foreseeability. Section 7, Comment *j*, rejects unforeseeability as a ground for deciding that no duty exists. Conversely, foreseeable harm, even highly foreseeable harm, does not affect the no-duty rule in this Section. . . .

Judicial reliance on foreseeability under specific facts occurs more frequently and aggressively in cases involving the allegation that an affirmative duty exists than in other cases. This suggests that courts more carefully supervise affirmative-duty cases than cases in which the actor's conduct creates a risk of harm. This tendency is even more pronounced when the alleged duty is to protect the plaintiff from third parties, especially the criminal acts of third parties. Sometimes, courts develop specific rules or balancing tests about the quantity, quality, and similarity of prior episodes required to satisfy foreseeability. Many courts use similar techniques to limit liability for failing to protect a plaintiff from self-inflicted harms. In addition, courts aggressively employ no duty when it is dubious that any precaution an actor-defendant might have taken would have prevented the plaintiff's harm.

Courts have other devices to limit liability when they are

persuaded that the defendant should not be liable. The court can determine, as a matter of law, that there is insufficient evidence of a necessary element or that, given the overwhelming weight of the evidence, no reasonable jury could make a required finding. Finding no duty is the more comfortable route for a court in this situation because duty is a question of law. By contrast, a determination of no breach as a matter of law more accurately reflects that the court is pretermitting jury consideration of an element of the case traditionally left to the jury. Regardless of which device is employed, the court should be aware that each constitutes an incursion on the role of the jury as factfinder and as the repository of commonsense normative wisdom in individual cases. That is a different endeavor from determining the legal rules that apply to classes of cases.

g. Limitations on and expansion of affirmative duties. The remainder of this Chapter provides a variety of exceptions to the rule in this Section that an actor has no duty to another when the actor has played no role in creating the risk of harm to the other. However, those exceptions remain subject to a court deciding, based on special problems of principle or policy that warrant denying liability, see § 7, that no duty should be imposed on the actor. . . .

A court may also decide to expand the scope of the affirmative duties provided in this Chapter. The Sections recognizing certain relationships as imposing an affirmative duty are stated nonexclusively, leaving to the courts whether to recognize additional relationships as sufficient to impose an affirmative duty.

h. Duty of reasonable care. The affirmative duties provided in the remainder of this Chapter are of reasonable care under the circumstances. Those circumstances include the fact that the affirmative duty is imposed even though the actor played no role in creating the risk of harm.

i. Affirmative duties of public entities. The imposition of affirmative duties on public entities poses two distinct problems. First, there is the concern that the judicial branch give appropriate deference to a coordinate branch of government when a decision allocates resources or involves other significant political, social, or economic determinations. The "public duty" doctrine, which denies a tort-law duty to provide police, fire, and other protective services to members of the public generally, reflects this concern. Second, unlike private persons and entities, governmental entities exist, in significant part, to protect the public from risks that are created by others. Law enforcement, fire protection, building inspection, and social services are only a few of the many governmental operations that provide a significant protective function. The limitless potential liability that might be visited on government entities if

186

affirmative duties were imposed on them for every undertaking has influenced courts in limiting the existence and scope of affirmative duties to which government entities are subject. Some courts insist on a "special relationship" between the plaintiff and a public entity that distinguishes the plaintiff from the public at large before imposing an affirmative duty. The "special relationship" invoked by these courts should be distinguished from the special relationships described in §§ 40 and 41.

j. Limited duties. In some cases, courts recognize a duty more limited than the general duty of reasonable care. . . .

B. EXCEPTIONS

§ 38. Affirmative Duty Based on Statutory Provisions Imposing Obligations to Protect Another

Restatement of the Law Third, Torts: Liability for Physical and Emotional Harm

When a statute requires an actor to act for the protection of another, the court may rely on the statute to decide that an affirmative duty exists and to determine the scope of the duty.

Comment:

b. Statutes, regulations, and ordinances. As with § 14 (Statutory Violations as Negligence Per Se), this Section includes statutes enacted by state and federal legislatures, as well as regulations promulgated by state and federal administrative agencies, and ordinances adopted by local governments.

Both federal and state courts may rely on federal statutes or regulations to recognize an affirmative duty in tort law. When they do so, they are determining state law, as there is no general federal common law. The use of a federal enactment to find a state-law affirmative duty is permissible so long as the federal provision does not preempt state tort-law liability. . . .

c. Express and implied statutory causes of action. Some statutes that impose an obligation to protect others expressly provide for a private cause of action. Even without such a provision, courts may find that a private cause of action is implied. On the other hand, sometimes statutes expressly or implicitly bar a private cause of action. This Section addresses the interstices left when statutes neither provide for nor negate private rights of action. When the legislature has not provided a remedy, but the interest protected is physical or emotional harm, courts may consider the legislative purpose and the values reflected in the statute to decide that the purpose and values justify adopting a duty that the common law had not previously recognized. . . .

Illustrations:

1. Steven rents an apartment from Garber Realty. After he moves in, the lock on the rear door of the apartment breaks, and despite several requests from Steven, Garber does not repair the lock. One night when Steven is away, a burglar enters Steven's apartment through the rear door and steals a substantial amount of Steven's personal property. Steven sues Garber for the value of the stolen property, asserting negligence in failing to keep the apartment locks operational. A municipal ordinance requires landlords to provide and maintain locks on all rental properties but states nothing about any private rights that might exist for violations of the ordinance. A court in a jurisdiction that has not previously recognized a common-law duty of landlords to exercise reasonable care for the safety of its tenants should take the ordinance into account in determining whether Garber has a common-law duty of reasonable care to maintain locks on its apartments.

2. A statute requires all public schools to test all students for scoliosis, an abnormal curvature of the spine. The Spartan school district neglects to comply with this requirement, and the diagnosis of scoliosis in Elizabeth, a student in the Spartan school district, is delayed. Elizabeth sues Spartan for her enhanced harm due to the delayed diagnosis, and Spartan responds that it owed Elizabeth no duty.

The statute does not explicitly provide a private right of action for persons who suffer from violations of the statute nor is there any indication that the legislature thought such a claim under the statute should exist. A provision in the statute providing for administrative enforcement makes plain that the legislature sought to minimize the expense incurred by school districts, including school districts that did not comply with their statutory obligations. Based on this analysis, the court decides that no implied right of action exists under the statute. The legislature's concern about preserving school districts' financial resources counsels against the court finding that Spartan had an affirmative duty to Elizabeth with regard to scoliosis testing.

d. *Relationship with negligence per se.* A statute providing for an affirmative duty in tort is different from the principle of negligence per se for statutory violations. Negligence per se relies on a specific statutory standard to pretermit reference to the more general reasonable-care standard for adjudicating the question of breach of duty. But even without reliance on the statute, the actor is subject to a duty of reasonable care and to potential tort liability. On the other hand, employing a statute to provide a tort duty where none previously existed creates a new basis for liability not previously recognized by tort law. This Section is limited to

188

statutes that impose obligations to act for the safety of others where tort law otherwise would not have so provided because of the no-duty rule in § 37.

e. *Considerations in determining the role of a statute in recognizing an affirmative duty.* . . . There are several good reasons why a statute might support an affirmative duty. The legislature's decision to impose the obligation imbues it with official recognition and commitment. The statute itself can be used to limit the duty, thereby mitigating the problem of drawing lines. Statutes also provide the public with notice of the obligations they impose. Finally, tort law can serve an enforcement role when the policy reflected in the statute is important, but the statute does not contain adequate enforcement provisions.

On the other hand, when a court finds that permitting tort actions would be inconsistent with the statute's design or purpose, imposing a tort duty is improper. A statute's enforcement may best be left to public officials exercising discretion informed by broader concerns than a private party might consider. A statute that imposes no penalty or a very modest penalty might be designed to play a hortatory role and is, therefore, not appropriate as a basis for an affirmative tort duty. A statute may also contain indications that the potentially large monetary damages employed by tort law should not be imposed on those to whom the statutory obligation is directed.

f. *Breach of affirmative duties based on statutes.* If a court determines that a statute creates an affirmative tort duty, a determination that the duty was breached often follows without further consideration. If the statute contains specific prescriptions that the actor violated, there is no independent breach inquiry. In these instances, the statute provides the basis for an affirmative duty, and violation of the statute's prescribed conduct is negligence per se. . . .

§ 39. Duty Based on Prior Conduct Creating a Risk of Physical Harm

Restatement of the Law Third, Torts: Liability for Physical and Emotional Harm

When an actor's prior conduct, even though not tortious, creates a continuing risk of physical harm of a type characteristic of the conduct, the actor has a duty to exercise reasonable care to prevent or minimize the harm.

Comment:

c. *Risk of a type characteristic of conduct.* The duty imposed by this Section is conditioned on the creation of a continuing risk

189

characteristic of the actor's conduct. . . . [A] college student who transports several classmates during spring break to a seaside resort is a factual cause of a variety of risks of future harms that might occur at the resort. However, none of the harms that might result from those risks, e.g., injuries from a mugging, sexually transmitted diseases, or alcohol-induced injuries, has a sufficient relationship to transporting passengers on spring break to support an affirmative duty under this Section. Even if the driver later sees one of the passengers being mugged in a dark alley, the driver has no duty to the passenger under this Section. Of course, transporting passengers does create risks to them, and the driver is subject to a duty of reasonable care to the passengers for those risks under § 7.

Illustration:

3. Randall, while on a bridge spanning a river, decides to jump from the bridge into the water, an action barred by no law. Randall carefully canvasses the area below before jumping but does not realize that Cheri is treading water directly under the bridge. As Randall jumps, Cheri swims out from under the bridge. Randall lands on top of Cheri, knocking her unconscious. While not subject to liability for her initial injuries, Randall has a duty of reasonable care to Cheri to mitigate the extent of the harm she suffers. . . .

d. *Relationship to ordinary duty of reasonable care when creating a risk of harm.* . . . In cases falling under this Section, the actor's risk-creating conduct has ceased, but the risk to the other person continues. For example, someone might unwittingly lend adulterated food to a neighbor and only later learn about the danger. The conduct of lending the food has ceased, but the risk to the neighbor continues. This Section makes clear that the lender has a duty to use reasonable care to warn the neighbor or otherwise mitigate the risk. . . . Consequently, this Section is most often invoked when an actor engages in a discrete, nontortious act that creates a continuing risk of harm and causes harm at a later time. For example, an automobile driver who collides with another (negligently or nonnegligently) has a duty to use reasonable care to prevent further harm to the other. . . .

e. *Helplessness not required.* . . . This Section does not require that the injured person be rendered helpless. Of course, the injured person's condition is relevant in determining what care is reasonable. If the injured person is as capable as the actor of taking steps to mitigate further harm, the actor does not breach the duty of reasonable care by failing to take those steps. But if the actor is better situated to render aid than the injured person, reasonable care may require the actor to do so, regardless of the injured individual's physical condition.

Illustration:

    5. Vince, while motoring on an isolated mountain road, nonnegligently drives into Jane, who was hiking on the side of the road. Jane is injured but remains lucid. Jane, who does not have a cell phone, asks Vince to use his cell phone to call for aid. Vince refuses and drives off. Vince owes a duty to Jane to use reasonable care to mitigate further harm and is subject to liability for any enhanced harm suffered by Jane due to delay caused by Vince's negligent failure to use his cell phone to summon assistance for Jane.

    g. Impact of comparative responsibility. Subsequent negligent conduct by an actor may aggravate an initial injury also caused by the actor. The actor may have acted either negligently or innocently in causing the initial injury. If the plaintiff's own negligence was also a cause of the original injury or the aggravated injury, comparative responsibility is employed to apportion liability. . . .

§ 40. Duty Based on Special Relationship with Another

Restatement of the Law Third, Torts: Liability for Physical and Emotional Harm

    (a) An actor in a special relationship with another owes the other a duty of reasonable care with regard to risks that arise within the scope of the relationship.

    (b) Special relationships giving rise to the duty provided in Subsection (a) include:

        (1) a common carrier with its passengers,

        (2) an innkeeper with its guests,

        (3) a business or other possessor of land that holds its premises open to the public with those who are lawfully on the premises,

        (4) an employer with its employees who, while at work, are:

            (a) in imminent danger; or

            (b) injured or ill and thereby rendered helpless,

        (5) a school with its students,

        (6) a landlord with its tenants, and

        (7) a custodian with those in its custody,

    if:

        (a) the custodian is required by law to take custody or voluntarily takes custody of the other; and

        (b) the custodian has a superior ability to protect the other.

Comment:

c. Relationship to ordinary duty of reasonable care when creating a risk of harm. In some cases, the duty imposed by this Section is a pure affirmative duty because the actor had no role in creating the risk of harm to the other, as in Illustration 1 below. In other cases, the actor's conduct might have played a role in creating the risk to the injured party, such as by hiring an employee with known dangerous propensities. In these cases, the source of the duty of reasonable care is § 7. . . .

d. Duty of reasonable care. . . . [T]he duty imposed requires only *reasonable* care under the circumstances. One of the relevant circumstances to be considered is whether a pure affirmative duty as described in Comment *c* is involved. For example, an individual with an incipient heart attack does not impose the burden of paying for necessary medical care on a hotel by checking into the hotel. In the case of illnesses, actors will frequently satisfy their duty by ascertaining that no emergency requiring immediate attention exists and by summoning appropriate medical care. . . .

f. Scope of the duty. The duty imposed in this Section applies to dangers that arise within the confines of the relationship and does not extend to other risks. Generally, the relationships in this Section are bounded by geography and time. Thus, this Section imposes no affirmative duty on a common carrier to a person who left the vehicle and is no longer a passenger. Similarly, an innkeeper is ordinarily under no duty to a guest who is injured or endangered while off the premises. Of course, if the relationship is extended—such as by a cruise ship conducting an onshore tour—an affirmative duty pursuant to this Section might be appropriate.

Illustrations:

1. While eating lunch alone at the Walkalong restaurant, Joe suddenly suffers a severe asthma attack. Several waiters at the restaurant recognize that Joe is suffering an asthma attack. All of them ignore Joe, and another 10 minutes pass before another patron observes Joe and summons medical care. The delay results in Joe suffering more serious injury than if he had received medical attention promptly after the waiters observed his plight. The Walkalong restaurant is subject to liability to Joe for his enhanced injury due to the delay in his receiving medical care.

2. Same facts as Illustration 1, except Joe suffers his asthma attack after finishing his meal at Walkalong and departing. Rich, a waiter at Walkalong, sees Joe through a window and appreciates that he is suffering an asthma attack but does nothing, thereby delaying appropriate medical care for Joe. Walkalong is not subject to liability for any enhanced

injury to Joe due to the delay in his receiving medical care because Joe's asthma attack occurred outside the scope of the relationship he had with Walkalong.

g. Risks within the scope of the duty of care. The duty described in this Section applies regardless of the source of the risk. Thus, it applies to risks created by the individual at risk as well as those created by a third party's conduct, whether innocent, negligent, or intentional. . . .

h. Rationale. . . . [R]equiring actors to exercise reasonable care to avoid harming others is justified by deterrence and corrective-justice policies. . . . No algorithm exists to provide clear guidance about which policies in which proportions justify the imposition of an affirmative duty based on a relationship. . . . A relationship identifies a specific person to be protected and thus provides a more limited and justified incursion on autonomy, especially when the relationship is entered into voluntarily. In addition, some relationships necessarily compromise a person's ability to self-protect, while leaving the actor in a superior position to protect that person. Many of the relationships also benefit the actor. Finally, for those cases in which it is unclear whether the risk is one created by the actor's conduct, see Comment *c*, this Section avoids the need to engage in the difficult inquiry into what would have happened if the actor had never engaged in its business or other operations. . . .

j. Duty of business or other possessor of land who holds its premises open to the public. . . . This Section imposes an affirmative duty on a subset of land possessors for certain risks that do not arise from conditions or activities on the land. Businesses and other possessors of land who hold their land open to the public owe a duty of reasonable care to persons lawfully on their land who become ill or endangered by risks created by third parties. . . .

k. Duty of employers. Workers' compensation has displaced most common-law occupational tort claims. Where workers' compensation is applicable, it governs employer liability for employees' occupational injuries. In those limited instances in which it is inapplicable, § 7 provides the ordinary duty of reasonable care owed by employers to employees based on risks created by the employment environment. This Subsection provides for a limited affirmative duty owed by employers based on the employment relationship.

The circumstances in which the affirmative duty imposed in this Subsection might apply have been largely limited to the risk to an employee of a criminal attack by a third party that occurs at the place of employment, an illness or injury suffered by an employee while at work (but not resulting from employment) that renders the employee helpless and in need of emergency care or assistance, and the occasional case that falls through the cracks of workers'-compensation coverage and implicates an affirmative duty as opposed to the ordinary duty imposed by § 7. . . .

l. Duty of schools. The affirmative duty imposed on schools in this Section is in addition to the ordinary duty of a school to exercise reasonable care in its operations for the safety of its students and the duties . . . to entrants on the land. The relationship between a school and its students parallels aspects of several other special relationships—it is a custodian of students, it is a land possessor who opens the premises to a significant public population, and it acts partially in the place of parents. . . . As with the other duties imposed by this Section, it is only applicable to risks that occur while the student is at school or otherwise engaged in school activities. And because of the wide range of students to which it is applicable, what constitutes reasonable care is contextual—the extent and type of supervision required of young elementary-school pupils is substantially different from reasonable care for college students.

m. Duty of landlords. . . . [T]he rationale for imposing a duty on landlords is similar to the rationale for other special relationships in this Section. In addition, the landlord has control over common areas, has superior means for providing security, and derives commercial advantage from the relationship. The landlord also has an ongoing contractual relationship with the tenant, and the lease itself could allocate responsibility for exercising care. Because the landlord usually is in a better position than individual tenants to exercise control over common areas and, with respect to individual units, to provide locks and other security devices, imposing a duty on the landlord replicates the result that might be reached if landlords and tenants with similar bargaining power addressed this matter.

Reasonable care cannot prevent every breach of security. Courts have been protective of landlords in these circumstances, often by employing no-duty rulings based on the particular circumstances of the case. These decisions do not undermine the general duty imposed by this Section but are better understood as a determination by the court that no reasonable jury could find negligence under the particular circumstances. . . .

n. Duty of custodians. . . . This Section retains the general affirmative duty owed by custodians to persons in their custody. The custodial relationships that courts have recognized as imposing an affirmative duty include day-care centers and the children for whom they care, hospitals and their patients, nursing homes with their residents, camps and their campers, parents and their dependent minor children, and, of course, the classic jailer–inmate relationship. Section 41 imposes a duty of reasonable care on custodians to protect others from risks created by those in custody. In addition to state tort law, federal constitutional provisions provide affirmative duties on behalf of those who are involuntarily in the custody of governmental officials. . . .

o. Nonexclusivity of relationships. The list of special relationships provided in this Section is not exclusive. Courts may, as they have since the Second Restatement, identify additional relationships that justify exceptions to the no-duty rule contained in § 37.

One likely candidate for an addition to recognized special relationships is the one among family members. . . .

§ 41. Duty to Third Parties Based on Special Relationship with Person Posing Risks

Restatement of the Law Third, Torts: Liability for Physical and Emotional Harm

(a) An actor in a special relationship with another owes a duty of reasonable care to third parties with regard to risks posed by the other that arise within the scope of the relationship.

(b) Special relationships giving rise to the duty provided in Subsection (a) include:

(1) a parent with dependent children,

(2) a custodian with those in its custody,

(3) an employer with employees when the employment facilitates the employee's causing harm to third parties, and

(4) a mental-health professional with patients. Tarasoff

Comment:

c. Duty of reasonable care. The duty imposed by this Section is to exercise reasonable care under the circumstances. It is not to ensure that the other person is controlled. If the other person poses a risk of harm to third parties, the actor must take reasonable steps, in light of the foreseeable probability and magnitude of any harm, to prevent it from occurring. In addition, the relationships identified in this Section are ones in which the actor has some degree of control over the other person. The extent of that control also bears on whether the actor exercised reasonable care.

If the actor neither knows nor should know of a risk of harm, no action is required. Thus, if a person in custody appears to pose no risk to others, the custodian is not negligent if the person in custody harms another. . . .

The duty imposed by this Section subjects an actor to liability for the actor's own tortious conduct. Liability for breach of the

195

duty provided in this Section is not vicarious and does not depend on whether the third party also committed a tort.

d. Duty of parent of dependent children. The basis of the parents' duty with regard to dependent children is the parents' responsibility for child-rearing, their control over their children, and the incapacity of some children to understand, appreciate, or engage in appropriate conduct. As children reach adolescence, courts recognize that the process of gaining independence is an important consideration in determining what constitutes reasonable care on the part of parents. When children reach majority or are no longer dependent, parents no longer have control, and the duty no longer exists.

Parents often will have no reasonable warning that their child is about to engage in conduct that causes physical harm. Even parents of children who have displayed a propensity toward dangerous conduct may have no reasonable or practical method for ameliorating many of the dangers. These are issues that affect a determination of reasonable care.

A number of cases involve parents who furnish or provide access to alcohol to minor children. Those cases do not engage the affirmative duty addressed in this Section. Instead, they are cases of an actor creating a risk of harm to others. . . .

e. Duty of employers. The duty provided in Subsection (b)(3) encompasses the employer's duty to exercise reasonable care in the hiring, training, supervision, and retention of employees. . . . Employment facilitates harm to others when the employment provides the employee access to physical locations, such as the place of employment, or to instrumentalities, such as a concealed weapon that a police officer is required to carry while off duty, or other means by which to cause harm that would otherwise not be available to the employee.

Illustration:

    1. Welch Repair Service knows that its employee Don had several episodes of assault in his previous employment. Don goes to Traci's residence, where he had previously been dispatched by Welch to perform repairs, and misrepresents to Traci that he is there on Welch business to check those repairs. After Traci admits Don to her home, he assaults her. Welch is subject to a duty under this Subsection with regard to Don's assault on Traci.

f. Duty of custodians. Custodians of those who pose risks to others have long owed a duty of reasonable care to prevent the person in custody from harming others. The classic custodian under this Section is a jailer of a dangerous criminal. Other well-established custodial relationships include hospitals for the mentally ill and for those with contagious diseases. Custodial relationships imposing a duty of care are limited to those relationships that exist, in significant part, for the protection of others from risks posed by the person in custody. . . .

Courts have been reluctant to impose a duty on actors who make discretionary determinations about parole or prerelease programs, even though these decisions arise in a custodial relationship. Imposing such a duty, thereby creating concern about potential liability, might detrimentally affect the decisionmaking of parole boards and others making similar determinations. By contrast, those who supervise parolees, probationers, or others in prerelease programs engage in more ministerial functions, and they are held to an affirmative duty of reasonable care. . . .

g. *Duty of mental-health professionals.* The seminal case of *Tarasoff v. Regents of the University of California,* 551 P.2d 334 (Cal. 1976), recognized a special relationship between a psychotherapist and an outpatient, and a corresponding duty of care on the part of the psychotherapist to third parties whom the patient might harm. . . . The core holding of *Tarasoff* has been widely embraced, but courts often disagree about specifics. . . .

A mental-health professional has a duty to use customary care in determining whether a patient poses a risk of harm. Once such a patient is identified, the duty imposed by reasonable care depends on the circumstances: reasonable care may require providing appropriate treatment, warning others of the risks posed by the patient, seeking the patient's agreement to a voluntary commitment, making efforts to commit the patient involuntarily, or taking other steps to ameliorate the risk posed by the patient. In some cases, reasonable care may require a warning to someone other than the potential victim, such as parents, law-enforcement officials, or other appropriate government officials. . . .

Illustrations:

3. Steve, a 14-year-old having adolescent adjustment difficulties, is referred to Dr. Cress, a psychologist. Dr. Cress treats Steve for several months, concluding that Steve suffers from mild depression and deficits in peer social skills. Steve occasionally expresses generalized anger at his circumstances in life but never blames others or gives any other indication that he might act violently, and Dr. Cress has no reason to think that Steve poses a risk of harm to others. Steve hacks his parents to death with a scythe. Dr. Cress had no duty to Steve's parents and is not subject to liability to the administrators of their estates.

4. Dr. Strand, a clinical psychologist, becomes aware, during the course of counseling, that a patient, Lester, is sexually abusing his eight-year-old stepdaughter, Kelly. Dr. Strand

does not communicate this information to Kelly's mother or to appropriate officials of the state Department of Social Services, or take any other steps to prevent Lester from continuing his sexual assaults on Kelly. Dr. Strand owes a duty of reasonable care to Kelly and is subject to liability for the harm due to Lester's continuing abuse of her. . . .

h. Duty of non-mental-health physicians to third parties. . . . The physician–patient relationship is not among the relationships listed in this Section as creating an affirmative duty. That does not mean that physicians have no affirmative duty to third parties. Some of the obligations of physicians to third parties, such as with patients who are HIV-infected, have been addressed by legislatures. In other areas, the case law is sufficiently mixed, the factual circumstances sufficiently varied, and the policies sufficiently balanced, that this Restatement leaves to further development the question of when physicians have a duty to use reasonable care or some more limited duty—such as to warn only the patient—to protect third parties. . . .

If a court does impose an affirmative duty on physicians to nonpatients, it must address both the content of the duty and the question of who can recover. For example, a court might limit the scope of a physician's duty to warning the patient of risks that the patient poses to others. A court might then hold that the physician's liability extends to any person harmed by the patient's condition or to a more limited class based on relationship with the patient, time, or place.

i. Nonexclusivity of relationships. As with § 40, the list of special relationships provided in this Section is not exclusive. . . .

§ 42. Duty Based on Undertaking

Restatement of the Law Third, Torts: Liability for Physical and Emotional Harm

> An actor who undertakes to render services to another and who knows or should know that the services will reduce the risk of physical harm to the other has a duty of reasonable care to the other in conducting the undertaking if:
>
> (a) the failure to exercise such care increases the risk of harm beyond that which existed without the undertaking, or
>
> (b) the person to whom the services are rendered or another relies on the actor's exercising reasonable care in the undertaking.

Comment:

c. Ordinary duty of reasonable care and affirmative duty based on undertaking. An actor who engages in an undertaking is subject to the ordinary duty of reasonable care provided in § 7 for risks created by the undertaking. In that case, no inquiry into affirmative duties is necessary. This Section, by contrast, addresses an actor's liability for harm arising from other risks when the actor undertakes to eliminate or ameliorate those risks.

Illustrations:

1. Caryn and David purchase a new natural-gas furnace for their home. They hire Jillian to install the furnace, and she does so. She does not follow the manufacturer's minimum requirements for venting the furnace, and as a result, both Caryn and David suffer carbon-monoxide poisoning. Danielle, their friend, finds them unconscious in their home due to the carbon-monoxide poisoning. Danielle drags them to another room but does not call for help. Caryn and David suffer harm that could have been avoided if Danielle had summoned help. Whether Danielle is subject to a duty to Caryn and David for harm that could have been avoided is governed by this Section, not § 7, because Danielle's conduct did not itself create the risk that caused the harm.

2. Same facts as described in Illustration 1. Jillian owes a duty of reasonable care as provided in § 7 to Caryn and David for the harm due to carbon-monoxide poisoning, without reference to this Section, because Jillian's conduct in installing the furnace created the risk that caused harm to Caryn and David.

The duty provided in this Section is one of reasonable care. It may be breached either by an act of commission (misfeasance) or by an act of omission (nonfeasance). . . .

d. Threshold for an undertaking. An undertaking entails an actor voluntarily rendering a service, gratuitously or pursuant to contract, on behalf of another. The undertaking may be on behalf of a specific individual or a class of persons. The actor's knowledge that the undertaking serves to reduce the risk of harm to another, or of circumstances that would lead a reasonable person to the same conclusion, is a prerequisite for an undertaking under this Section. The actor need not act for the purpose of protecting the other; this Section is equally applicable to those who act altruistically and to those who act nonaltruistically, as is often the case when an undertaking is the result of a contractual arrangement. While knowledge that the undertaking will reduce the risk of harm to another is necessary for the existence of an undertaking, knowledge that the other will rely on the undertaking is not. . . .

e. Promises as undertakings. . . . If contract law provides a remedy for mere promises, tort law should also do so when breach of the promise causes personal injury or property damage. The crux of a duty based on a promise is that the actor engage in behavior that leads another to forgo available alternatives for protection. . . .

f. Increasing the risk of harm. The requirement that the actor increase the risk of harm means that the risk to the other person is increased beyond that which existed in the absence of the actor's undertaking.

This requirement is often met because the plaintiff or another relied on the actor's performing the undertaking in a nonnegligent manner and declined to pursue an alternative means for protection. . . . [R]eliance is merely a specific manner of increasing the risk of harm to another. . . .

Illustration:

3. Ahmed's neighbor, Meena, agrees to make daily visits to Ahmed's house to care for Ahmed's cat and dog while he is out of town. Meena forgets to do so. Meena owes a duty of reasonable care to Ahmed because he relied on Meena to attend to his pets. Meena is subject to liability for harm caused by her negligent failure to visit Ahmed's home and attend to his pets. . . .

g. Scope of the undertaking. In some cases, a question arises about whether the risk that caused the harm or the actor's negligence (typically an omission), was within the scope of the undertaking. The scope of an undertaking can be determined only from the facts and circumstances of the case. When reasonable minds can differ about whether the risk or negligence was within the scope of the undertaking, it is a question of fact for the factfinder.

Illustrations:

4. Lindsay hires Margaret to fix a leaking plumbing fixture in a second-floor apartment. Margaret repairs the leak in a nonnegligent manner. After completing the repairs, Margaret realizes that water that had leaked earlier from the fixture then had run from the apartment onto an adjacent alley. When returning home that evening, Lindsay slips and falls on ice that formed in the alley from the runoff. Lindsay sues Margaret, claiming that she had a duty of reasonable care with regard to the water that leaked out of the fixture. The risks posed by the water that had previously escaped from the fixture are beyond the scope of Margaret's undertaking to repair the fixture as a matter of law, and Margaret is not subject to liability for Lindsay's harm.

5. The River City School District provides school crossing guards at the three most dangerous intersections for each school in the district. While walking to school and crossing one

of those intersections, Alphonso, a seven-year-old, is hit by an automobile and injured because no crossing guard is present. Alphonso's guardian sues the School District, claiming that its negligence caused Alphonso's harm. The duty of the School District encompasses reasonable care at the intersection at which Alphonso was injured, as a matter of law, and the School District is subject to liability for Alphonso's harm.

Acts that comprise an undertaking are often ambiguous with respect to the scope of the undertaking. When reliance is the basis for the increased risk, fairness suggests that the scope of the undertaking be interpreted from the perspective of those who might reasonably have relied on the undertaking. When an undertaking involves a promise, the promise might provide probative evidence about the scope of the undertaking.

h. Termination. While an actor who engages in a gratuitous undertaking need not continue the undertaking indefinitely, the actor may not unreasonably terminate the undertaking. In most nonemergency, gratuitous undertakings, providing reasonable notice that the actor is terminating the undertaking suffices. Notice of termination is also probative on the question of reliance. . . .

i. Undertakings to provide public utilities. Similar to their reluctance to impose affirmative duties on government entities, courts have been reluctant to impose tort duties on providers of public utilities. . . .

The [best] explanation for limitations on the duty of public utilities . . . is concern about the huge magnitude of liability to which a utility might be exposed from a single failure to provide service that affects hundreds, thousands, or, in the case of an electrical blackout, millions of people. In addition, when the harm is property damage, often the plaintiff will have first-party insurance that covers the loss. . . .

§ 43. Duty to Third Parties Based on Undertaking to Another

Restatement of the Law Third, Torts: Liability for Physical and Emotional Harm

An actor who undertakes to render services to another and who knows or should know that the services will reduce the risk of physical harm to which a third person is exposed has a duty of reasonable care to the third person in conducting the undertaking if:

(a) the failure to exercise reasonable care increases the risk of harm beyond that which existed without the undertaking,

(b) the actor has undertaken to perform

201

a duty owed by the other to the third person, or

(c) the person to whom the services are rendered, the third party, or another relies on the actor's exercising reasonable care in the undertaking.

Comment:

c. *Relationship to § 42.* This Section parallels § 42 but extends to third parties the duty that is owed. . . .

e. *Reliance.* Reliance on an undertaking is another way in which the risk of harm may be increased. An undertaking may create an appearance of safety or make alternative arrangements appear unnecessary. . . .

Illustration:

1. Rick, while piloting a small plane with his spouse, Steve, as a passenger, detects smoke in the cockpit. Rick radios the Pleasant Flying Service located at one of several nearby airports to determine if firefighting equipment is available. Upon being told that it is, Rick informs Pleasant that he is going to land at the airport because of a suspected fire and will need emergency firefighting equipment. Sheila, an employee of Pleasant, promises to provide such equipment and proceeds to retrieve the airport fire truck and move it to the runway. In her haste, Sheila negligently fails to unlock the garage door before actuating the motor for the door opener, jamming the door and preventing her from moving the truck out of the garage and onto the runway. After Rick lands, a fire breaks out that burns Steve. Pleasant owes a duty of reasonable care to Steve based on its undertaking to provide firefighting equipment and on Rick's reliance on Pleasant's undertaking. . . .

f. *Threshold for an undertaking.* . . . The actor need not know who the third person is who is subject to risk. The knowledge requirement is satisfied if the actor knows or should know that the undertaking reduces the risk of harm to a class of persons that includes the third-person victim. Thus, an actor who undertakes an inspection of a home heating system has a duty not only to the homeowner hiring the actor (pursuant to § 42) but also, pursuant to this Section, to subsequent owners and occupants for risks that should have been revealed through the exercise of reasonable care during the inspection.

g. *Undertaking a duty owed by another to a third person.* When an actor undertakes to perform a duty that another person owes to a third person, the actor is subject to a duty of reasonable care. . . .

Illustration:

2. Phillip's Ribs, a restaurant, hires Lyndsey, an independent contractor, to keep its sidewalks clear of ice and snow. After a particularly bad storm, Lyndsey fails to clear the restaurant's sidewalks. Luther, a customer of Phillip's, falls on the sidewalk and suffers injury. Lyndsey has a duty of reasonable care to Luther because Lyndsey undertook a duty owed by Phillip's to Luther. . . .

h. Relationship to contractual duties. The duty imposed by this Section is independent of any contractual obligations. The duty of reasonable care imposed by this Section protects against physical or emotional harm and exists regardless of whether there is a contract, whether a claim for breach of contract is available, or whether the plaintiff is a third-party beneficiary of the contract. . . .

§ 44. Duty to Another Based on Taking Charge of the Other

Restatement of the Law Third, Torts: Liability for Physical and Emotional Harm

(a) **An actor who, despite no duty to do so, takes charge of another who reasonably appears to be:**

(1) **imperiled; and**

(2) **helpless or unable to protect himself or herself**

has a duty to exercise reasonable care while the other is within the actor's charge.

(b) **An actor who discontinues aid or protection is subject to a duty of reasonable care to refrain from putting the other in a worse position than existed before the actor took charge of the other and, if the other reasonably appears to be in imminent peril of serious physical harm at the time of termination, to exercise reasonable care with regard to the peril before terminating the rescue.**

Comment:

c. Distinctive feature of rescuer affirmative duty. This Section is limited to instances in which an actor takes steps to engage in a rescue by taking charge of another who is imperiled and unable adequately to protect himself or herself. The duty is limited in scope and duration to the peril to which the other is exposed and requires that the actor voluntarily undertake a rescue and actually take charge of the other. The actor must have a purpose of benefiting the other. . . .

d. Rationale. The rationale for the duty imposed by this Section is primarily that the justifications for the no-duty-to-rescue rule do not apply. Because the actor has voluntarily chosen to engage in a rescue, imposing a duty of reasonable care does little harm to the freedom and autonomy of the rescuer. The actor has singled himself or herself out, thereby obviating concerns about a duty to rescue when there are many persons who might perform the rescue equally well. The "taking charge" requirement eliminates much of the difficult line-drawing that might be required to determine whether preliminary steps by an actor amount to a "rescue" that imposes the duty provided in this Section. That the rescuer voluntarily undertook the rescue also eliminates any need to distinguish between "easy" rescues and those that impose substantial burdens. By taking charge of the other, the rescuer may have prevented others from rescuing, but neither reliance nor increased risk need be proved for this Section to be applicable. Finally, the duty imposed by this Section is confined in time and in scope by the specific peril to which the other is exposed and, therefore, does not create a protracted and burdensome obligation.

e. Relationship to ordinary duty of reasonable care when creating a risk of harm. When a rescuer injures another in the course of a rescue, the ordinary duty of reasonable care provided in § 7 is applicable. Thus, if an actor, having observed a pedestrian run down by a hit-and-run driver and bleeding badly, takes the pedestrian in an automobile and hits a tree en route to the hospital, breaking the pedestrian's nose, the rescuer is subject to the ordinary duty of reasonable care. Reference to this Section is unnecessary because the rescuer's conduct in driving the pedestrian created a risk of harm, requiring the exercise of reasonable care. That the harm occurred in the course of a rescue, rather than on some other occasion, does not affect the ordinary duty of care. On the other hand, if the rescuer, while driving the pedestrian to the hospital, decides to make a stop at a local tavern, the rescuer is subject to liability for any enhanced harm caused by the delay pursuant to this Section, even if the pedestrian would not have arrived at the hospital any earlier if the actor had declined to rescue.

f. Duty of reasonable care. The rescuer need only exercise reasonable care under the circumstances. Those circumstances include the fact that the rescuer is acting gratuitously. An actor who undertakes a rescue does not thereby acquire an obligation to pay the other's hospital bill, even if the actor is in a better financial position to do so than the other.

g. Taking charge of one who is helpless. The rule stated in this Section is applicable whenever a rescuer takes charge of another who is imperiled and incapable of taking adequate care. The rule is equally applicable to one who is rendered helpless by his or her own conduct, including intoxication; by the tortious or innocent conduct of others; or by a force of nature. The rule, however, requires that the rescuer take charge of the helpless individual with the intent of providing assistance in confronting the then-existing peril.

h. Termination. Having undertaken a rescue, a rescuer must exercise reasonable care not to cause the other to be in a worse position than existed before the rescue. . . . [W]hen a person is in imminent peril of serious bodily injury, the rescuer must exercise reasonable care in deciding whether to discontinue the rescue. Thus, a rescuer of a drowning swimmer may not indiscriminately cease rescue efforts after towing the swimmer halfway to shore. In addition, once having secured the safety of the other, the rescuer may not then return the other to peril, even if the peril is no greater than that which existed at the time the actor initiated the rescue. Thus, one who rescues a drowning swimmer and brings the swimmer to shore may not leave the swimmer in the middle of a busy highway. This does not mean that a rescuer cannot leave the other in a worse state than the other was in at some point *during* the rescue. A Good Samaritan who "rescues" a homeless person who is suffering from severe malnutrition by taking the person home and feeding the person is not thereby obliged to continue feeding the person for life.

i. Good Samaritan statutes. Beginning in 1959, most states enacted Good Samaritan statutes designed to encourage voluntary emergency care by providing a measure of protection from civil liability for those who render aid. Many of these statutes limit or disallow the liability that would otherwise exist under this Section. . . .

CHAPTER 12

DUTY OF LAND POSSESSORS

A. DEFINITIONS

Scope Note: This Chapter addresses the special case of the duty owed by land possessors. . . . [T]his Chapter addresses an area in which courts have modified the ordinary duty of reasonable care. . . .

[T]his Chapter provides a general duty of reasonable care by land possessors for risks created by possessors to those on the land. It then recognizes that a land possessor's right to exclusive use and possession of the land represents a countervailing principle that requires accommodation by tort law in the case of certain trespassers on the land. . . . The duty of land possessors is covered here, in a dedicated Chapter, primarily because land possessors' duties have historically been treated separately. . . .

§ 49. Possessor of Land Defined

Restatement of the Law Third, Torts: Liability for Physical and Emotional Harm

A possessor of land is

(a) a person who occupies the land and controls it;

(b) a person entitled to immediate occupation and control of the land, if no other person is a possessor of the land under Subsection (a); or

(c) a person who had occupied the land and controlled it, if no other person subsequently became a possessor under Subsection (a) or (b).

Comment:

b. *Owners.* In many instances, the owner of real property will be its possessor for purposes of this Chapter. It is the owner who ordinarily has control over the premises and occupies them. However, the critical issue is occupation and control rather than ownership. Owners who cede exclusive possession and control of the land to others do not have a duty to entrants on the land under this Chapter. Thus, an owner who sells property to another on a long-term contract that provides for the buyer to occupy the land until the full purchase price is paid is not a land possessor and is not subject to the provisions in this Chapter. . . .

c. *Control.* A person is in control of the land if that person has the authority and ability to take precautions to reduce the risk of harm to entrants on the land, which is the reason for imposing the duties contained in this Chapter on land possessors. . . .

d. *Multiple possessors.* Possession of land may be divided among several actors, as, for example, when a lessor leases portions of a building to several tenants but retains possession of common areas. . . . In such cases, each actor has the duty provided in this Chapter with respect to the portion of the premises controlled by that actor. Agents of a principal who are provided and assume possession of a portion of the land are possessors under this Section and thus subject to the same duties as the principal-possessor. . . .

e. *Nonpossessory actor present on the land.* A nonpossessory actor has a duty of reasonable care under § 7 for conduct that creates risks to others on private property. However, such an actor is not subject to the duties provided in this Chapter, unless engaged as an agent for the possessor and acting for the benefit of the possessor. . . .

Illustration:

1. Kyle is a guest in Meeren's home and, after some prompting by other guests, agrees to demonstrate magic tricks. While demonstrating a trick involving an open flame, he ignites the clothing of Sarah, another guest, burning her. Kyle owes Sarah a duty of reasonable care pursuant to § 7; this Chapter is inapplicable to the duty owed by Kyle, because he is not in possession of the premises.

f. *Contractors engaged in work on the land.* For purposes of this Chapter, a contractor employed by the possessor to perform work on the land, whether an employee or independent contractor, is treated as a land possessor. . . .

207

g. Contractors who have completed work on the land. A contractor who has completed work on the land on behalf of the possessor is. . . . subject to the ordinary duty of reasonable care under § 7 for risks created by the work but is not subject to any duty with regard to other conditions or activities on the land because the contractor is no longer a land possessor, having ceased activity on the land and relinquished possession of it.

h. Former possessors. A person who has relinquished possession and control of land to another is [generally] not subject to the duties provided in this Chapter. . . .

§ 50. Trespasser Defined

Restatement of the Law Third, Torts: Liability for Physical and Emotional Harm

A trespasser is a person who enters or remains on land in the possession of another without the possessor's consent or other legal privilege.

Comment:

b. Consent. Consent exists when, regardless of the intent of the possessor, a reasonable person would understand the words, conduct, or inaction of the possessor to constitute consent. Consent to enter may be limited by time or space and may be terminated by the land possessor. Consent given under duress, substantial mistake, misrepresentation, or fraud may be ineffective.

c. Other legal privilege. A person may have legal privilege to enter on the land of another despite lack of consent by the land possessor. The circumstances providing for such privilege include the right to enter to avoid an imminent public disaster; to prevent serious harm to oneself, a land possessor, or a third person; to reclaim goods; to abate a public nuisance; and to permit certain law-enforcement activities. In addition, if a landowner withdraws consent to enter from others, including lessees, suddenly and without advance notice, those whose right to enter has been rescinded have legal privilege to remain for a reasonable time and to remove personal property before leaving the land.

d. Nontrespassing entrants. All persons on another's land who do not fit the definition of trespasser provided in this Section are nontrespassing entrants. No distinction is made among nontrespassing entrants in this Chapter. . . .

B. GENERAL DUTY OF LAND POSSESSORS

§ 51. General Duty of Land Possessors

Restatement of the Law Third, Torts: Liability for Physical and Emotional Harm

Subject to § 52, a land possessor owes a duty of reasonable care to entrants on the land with regard to:

(a) conduct by the land possessor that creates risks to entrants on the land;

(b) artificial conditions on the land that pose risks to entrants on the land;

(c) natural conditions on the land that pose risks to entrants on the land; and

(d) other risks to entrants on the land when any of the affirmative duties provided in Chapter 7 is applicable.

Comment:

a. History and scope. Largely for historical reasons, the duty of a land possessor has not been a general duty of reasonable care but, instead, has consisted of differing duties depending on the status of the person on the land. At the time these status-based duties were developed, no general duty of care existed, and duties were based on relationships or specific activities. Thus, the status-based duties imposed on land possessors were consistent with basic negligence law and were the basis for imposing *any* duty on land possessors. However, with the evolution of a general duty of reasonable care to avoid physical harm as recognized in § 7, the status-based duties for land possessors are not in harmony with modern tort law. This Section rejects the status-based duty rules and adopts a unitary duty of reasonable care to entrants on the land. At the same time, § 52 reflects a policy-based modification of the duty of land possessors to those on the land whose presence is antithetical to the rights of the land possessor or owner. . . .

b. Relationship with the remainder of this Restatement. . . . [A] default duty of reasonable care for risks created by the land possessor is provided in this Section, as well as an affirmative duty for natural conditions. . . .

c. Reasons for an integrated duty of reasonable care. There are several reasons for the imposition of a unitary duty of reasonable care on land possessors, applicable to all entrants on the land.

(1). Boundary ambiguity causing compromised certainty; increased complexity producing confusion. As bright-line rules, the status-based system of land-possessor duties promised certainty of

209

outcome with administrative efficiency. In some cases, that system performed according to promise. In other cases, however, the certainty advantage was compromised by ambiguity about the boundaries of the categories. In yet other cases, such as when young children were lured onto property by an attractive danger and were injured, the certainty advantage had a concomitant disadvantage of producing results that were felt to be unfair. The combination of ambiguity about boundaries and the perceived unfairness of some outcomes led to adoption of new interstitial categories and exceptions. The resulting "semantic morass," . . . proved confusing and difficult to administer and thus susceptible to different outcomes in similar cases.

(2). *Converging similarity with a unitary standard.* The subcategories and exceptions that courts developed to the general duty rules for trespassers and for licensees produced an overall result closer to the reasonable-care duty imposed by this Section than to a no-duty or a limited-duty rule such as that adopted in § 52 for flagrant trespassers.

(3). *Trespassers impose no greater burden of precaution.* Land possessors must take reasonable care on behalf of invitees. Generally, exercising reasonable care on behalf of trespassers as well will impose no additional burden of precaution on land possessors. Thus, it is difficult to find good reasons to treat licensees and ordinary trespassers differently from invitees.

Illustration:

1. Ed and Margaret carpool together to work. Unable to find a place on the street to park, Margaret pulled into a parking lot owned by the Viner Hospital that is restricted to hospital visitors. After parking, Ed decides to go into the hospital to visit his brother, while Margaret, who has no business at the hospital, walks toward her office in a nearby building. Both Ed and Margaret slip and fall on an accumulation of ice while walking across the sloping parking lot. Under applicable law, Margaret is a trespasser while Ed, having decided to visit his brother, is an invitee. Viner Hospital owes both Ed and Margaret a duty of reasonable care for the condition of the parking lot. Under the circumstances provided in this Illustration, determination as to whether the duty was breached is for the factfinder.

(4). *Differences between contemporary society and historical conditions in which the status-based system developed.* The status-based duties imposed on land possessors were influenced by a time when land was the predominant form of wealth and large tracts of land were held by a powerful few. Those conditions have changed in modern times.

e. *Artificial conditions.* Artificial conditions on the premises

210

can be categorized into those that the possessor has personally constructed or had constructed by an agent and those that the possessor inherited from a former possessor. . . .

[T]here are good grounds for imposing [a duty of care with respect to artificial conditions that existed on the premises when the possessor acquired it] on the current possessor. The current possessor is the only person with the legal authority to eliminate or ameliorate the risks posed by the artificial condition. Imposition of this duty does not implicate a concern about who has the duty, as would a general duty to rescue. This duty does not pose difficult line-drawing problems, as would a duty of easy rescue. Finally, although the possessor has not created the risk, the possessor has, by inviting or permitting persons to enter the land, played a role in the risk confronted by those entrants.

A land possessor has a duty to identify risks that exist on the land. However, some risks cannot reasonably be discovered, and the land possessor is not subject to liability for those risks. . . . Thus, if a former possessor created an artificial condition on the land that the subsequent possessor does not know of and could not reasonably know of, the subsequent possessor is not in breach of the duty of reasonable care with regard to that condition. As provided in this Section, the duty of a land possessor is independent of the duty and liability of a former possessor of the same land who created the artificial condition and its attendant risk and who is subject to a duty of reasonable care in connection with that conduct.

f. Natural conditions. A natural condition is a condition on the land that has not been created or modified by the conduct of any person. It includes the unmodified topography of the land, natural bodies of water present, undomesticated animals not brought or attracted thereon, and the growth of plants, weeds, and trees that are on the land through no human agency. Trees and other landscaping that are planted by anyone and changes in the surface through excavation or other human agency are not natural conditions.

The duty of reasonable care imposed on a land possessor includes risks arising from natural conditions. Although the land possessor did not create those risks, land possessors nevertheless are charged with this duty for much the same reasons as discussed in Comment *e* regarding artificial conditions created by predecessor possessors.

g. Summary of land-possessor duties. A land possessor owes a duty of reasonable care to entrants on the land with regard to all risks that exist on the land. This duty of reasonable care extends to the entrant and any personal property that accompanies the entrant onto the land. Ordinarily, a possessor of land does not owe

211

a duty of reasonable care for risks arising from the conduct of transients and independent contractors while on the possessor's land. However, the affirmative duties . . . may impose a duty on the possessor for such risks. Thus, a business that opens its premises to the public owes an affirmative duty to those lawfully on the premises, and a school owes an affirmative duty to its students. . . .

h. Durable precautions and transient precautions. Precautions may be of two general types, durable and transient. Transient precautions are exemplified by oral warnings, which are issued at a given place and time and then vanish. Durable precautions, by contrast, remain in place and thus eliminate or reduce risk over a lengthier period of time. Whether a land possessor has breached a duty of reasonable care may depend on whether the precaution the plaintiff alleges that the defendant failed to adopt is durable or transient. Transient precautions can only be provided and effective when the presence of the entrant is known or foreseeable; consequently, they are not required when the circumstances do not suggest a foreseeable risk. Thus, whether an entrant was unanticipated is an important issue of fact bearing on breach when the claim is that a land possessor was negligent for failing to provide an oral warning. Durable precautions are generally more burdensome and are not required unless the risk of harm exceeds the burden of taking the durable precaution.

Illustrations:

2. Marc owns a home and stores anhydrous ammonia in a garden shed on the property. Anhydrous ammonia, which can cause severe chemical burns if handled improperly, is used as a fertilizer. It is also used as an ingredient in methamphetamine, an illegal drug. Betty, a police officer investigating a report of a strong chemical smell in the neighborhood, obtains Marc's permission to search the premises. During the search, Betty enters the shed and examines a container. Its lid pops off, and the contents, under pressure, spray onto her and burn her. Marc, who is aware of the possibility of the sudden and unintended escape of the chemical, is subject to liability for failing to warn Betty that anhydrous ammonia was kept under pressure in the shed.

3. Same facts as Illustration 2, except Marc is not present when Betty comes to investigate. Upon realizing that no one is home, Betty searches the land and the shed, which is unlocked, and she is injured in the same fashion. Marc is not subject to liability for failing to warn Betty. Marc, however, may be subject to liability to Betty for failing to take precautions to more securely store the chemicals in the shed.

j. Duty of reasonable care to trespassers. This Section, in conjunction with § 52, requires land possessors to exercise reasonable care on behalf of trespassers (save for flagrant trespassers) for risks created by the possessor and those posed by artificial and natural conditions. . . .

Illustration:

7. Virginia and her daughter, Jeanne, a two-year-old, temporarily reside with a friend, Euclid, and her young daughter, because Virginia lost her job and can no longer afford her apartment's rent. Euclid's lease specifies that she cannot have anyone but herself and related family residing in her apartment, making Virginia and Jeanne trespassers. The balcony off Euclid's apartment is missing several of the vertical posts required to make the railing safe. Hoover, Euclid's lessor, has been notified of the condition, but has failed over a two-month time period to repair the railing. Hoover is subject to liability for the physical harm Jeanne suffers when she falls through the opening in the railing.

k. Open and obvious dangers. . . . Known or obvious dangers pose less of a risk than comparable latent dangers because those exposed can take precautions to protect themselves. Nevertheless, despite the opportunity of entrants to avoid an open and obvious risk, in some circumstances a residual risk will remain. Land possessors have a duty of reasonable care with regard to those residual risks. Thus, the fact that a dangerous condition is open and obvious bears on the assessment of whether reasonable care was employed, but it does not pretermit the land possessor's liability. . . .

An entrant who encounters an obviously dangerous condition and who fails to exercise reasonable self-protective care is contributorily negligent. Because of comparative fault, however, the issue of the defendant's duty and breach must be kept distinct from the question of the plaintiff's negligence. The rule that land possessors owe no duty with regard to open and obvious dangers sits more comfortably—if not entirely congruently—with the older rule of contributory negligence as a bar to recovery.

If a danger is open and obvious, a warning ordinarily will not provide additional protection against harm. The primary purpose of a warning is to give notice of the existence of the risk. (In some circumstances, a warning plays other roles, such as providing information about alternative courses of action or how to ameliorate any harm that does occur.) Risks that are known, open, or obvious already provide notice to those who might be exposed to the risk, making a warning superfluous. Hence, if the only purpose of a warning would be to provide notice of a danger that is open and obvious, there is no liability for failing to provide such a warning.

When land is held open to the public and a high volume of

entrants can be anticipated, a reasonable possessor should anticipate greater risk, requiring greater precaution than if the land is
private or few entrants are likely. . . . In this Restatement, public
use is just one of many factors to be considered in determining
whether reasonable care was exercised. . . .

l. Child trespassers. . . . Foreseeable risk is a function of the
number and kind of persons who may be exposed to a dangerous
condition. That some of the persons likely to be exposed are children who are particularly vulnerable because of their immaturity
is relevant to the extent of the precaution required of the land
possessor. . . .

This Section [ ] begins with a default duty of reasonable care to
all trespassers. A child trespasser who is aware of a danger and
unreasonably confronts it may have his or her damages reduced,
but recovery is not barred under this Section. . . .

[T]here may be the rare child . . . whose entrance onto the
land occurs with sufficient violence to the land possessor's rights
that the child might also come within the scope of § 52, Comment
a, which defines flagrant trespassers. . . .

m. Firefighters and other professional rescuers. Some jurisdictions have a rule that firefighters—or, more broadly, professional
rescuers—cannot recover for harm they suffer as the result of
negligence that requires their services, such as when a homeowner's failure to exercise reasonable care when smoking results in a
fire. This Chapter and Restatement take no position on such a rule
or its scope. However, this Chapter does affect one of the several
alternative rationales that are employed to justify such a firefighter
rule.

Historically, professional rescuers who entered private land
were either treated as licensees or as comprising a *sui generis*
category. They had a privilege to be on the land, but because their
entrance could often not be anticipated, the duty owed to them
was the lesser one owed to licensees. With the unified duty owed to
entrants on land under this Section, there is no longer any need to
categorize separately the status of firefighters, police officers, and
other professional rescuers.

The firefighter rule developed from the categorization of professional rescuers as licensees on the land, thereby limiting the liability of a land possessor whose negligence necessitated the presence of the rescuer. However, in a number of jurisdictions the
justification for (and extent of) immunity for negligent actors for
harm to professional rescuers has evolved away from relying on
the rescuer's status on the land. Most jurisdictions today justify
limitations on liability on different principles or policies than when
the doctrine was first developed. One justification is that professional rescuers are paid by taxpayers to encounter the risks of fire

fighting or law-enforcement work, risks that can be the result of taxpayer negligence, and taxpayers should not be charged twice. A second justification is that professional rescuers are provided workers' compensation for occupational injuries, and that such insurance is provided indirectly by taxpayers. A third justification may be the principle underpinning "pre-presentment negligence," the rule that a professional who is engaged to provide a service necessitated by the client's or patient's negligence may not assert such negligence in defense of a professional-malpractice claim. Although the professional rescuer is denied a cause of action, rather than being denied a defense, the circumstances are otherwise similar. Whatever the rationale behind limiting land possessors' liability to professional rescuers injured in the course of performing their duties, the movement away from the original status-based justifications requires rethinking the firefighter rule and, if it is retained, adapting its scope to the rationale justifying its continuation. Firefighter rules can have dramatically different scopes depending on the rationale or rationales justifying them. Thus, for example, if the rationale were his avoiding double taxation of taxpayers, the firefighter rule would not extend to *private* rescuers.

To the extent that the firefighter rule has historically been grounded in the status of professional rescuers on the land, this Restatement eliminates the basis for that rationale by adopting a duty of reasonable care for all entrants on the land (with the sole exception involving flagrant trespassers under § 52). Firefighters and other professional rescuers acting within the scope of their employment are not trespassers under § 50 of this Restatement because they enter the land either with the consent of the land possessor or with the legal justification of performing their public duties. . . .

q. Recreational-use statutes. Recreational-use statutes have been enacted in many states. For specified recreational uses, these statutes immunize the land possessor from liability for negligence and instead impose a more lenient duty such as to avoid willful or malicious injury. These statutes provide the incentive of diminished liability to landowners who permit recreational use of their land, thereby making more land available for recreation. These statutes carve out an area of land-possessor liability from the common law of tort and specify instead a statutory standard for liability. Thus, the rules provided in this Restatement for land possessors apply only when a recreational-use statute (or other statute) does not provide the appropriate rule of law.

t. Former possessors' duties. A former possessor who creates a risk of harm when in possession of the land continues to be subject to the ordinary duty of reasonable care provided in § 7 for that risk, even after possession is relinquished to another. . . .

C. EXCEPTIONS AND SPECIAL RULES

§ 52. Duty of Land Possessors to Flagrant Trespassers

Restatement of the Law Third, Torts: Liability for Physical and Emotional Harm

(a) **The only duty a land possessor owes to flagrant trespassers is the duty not to act in an intentional, willful, or wanton manner to cause physical harm.**

(b) **Notwithstanding Subsection (a), a land possessor has a duty to flagrant trespassers to exercise reasonable care if the trespasser reasonably appears to be imperiled and**

(1) **helpless; or**

(2) **unable to protect him- or herself.**

Comment:

a. Flagrant trespassers. This Section, in conjunction with § 51, distinguishes among trespassers and employs the concept of "flagrant trespassers" as the basis for that distinction. "Flagrant" is used here in the sense of egregious or atrocious rather than in its alternative meaning of conspicuous. Nevertheless, no single word can capture the concept, which is further explained in this Comment. This Section leaves to each jurisdiction employing the concept to determine the point along the spectrum of trespassory conduct at which a trespasser is a "flagrant" rather than an ordinary trespasser. The critical aspect of this Section is that a distinction is made, and different duties of care are owed depending on whether a trespasser is a flagrant trespasser or an ordinary trespasser. This Section thus reflects a specific application of § 7(b), which provides for modification of the ordinary duty of care because of a countervailing principle or policy.

The idea behind distinguishing particularly egregious trespassers for different treatment is that their presence on another's land is so antithetical to the rights of the land possessor to exclusive use and possession of the land that the land possessor should not be subject to liability for failing to exercise the ordinary duty of reasonable care otherwise owed to them as entrants on the land. That is, when a trespass is sufficiently offensive to the property rights of the land possessor it is unfair to subject the possessor to liability for mere negligence. This reflects a specific application of the rule provided in § 7(b) permitting a determination that, based on an articulated principle or policy, the ordinary duty of reasonable care should not apply. The policy justifying the lesser duty owed to flagrant trespassers is protection of the rights of private-property owners, which would be unfairly diminished if possessors were subject to liability to flagrant trespassers based on ordinary negligence.

216

This Chapter does not attempt to define flagrant trespassers or prescribe the precise line on the continuum that distinguishes ordinary trespassers from flagrant trespassers. . . . [S]ignificant factors that inform the location of that line include: (1) entry that results in the commission of a crime directed at the land possessor or the land possessor's family, guests, or property; (2) entry for the purpose of committing such a crime, even if it is not accomplished; (3) entry for another illegal or improper purpose; (4) entry despite efforts by the land possessor to prevent trespass and specifically to prevent entrance by the plaintiff; (5) the extent of effort by the plaintiff to defeat the exclusion efforts of the land possessor, including such acts as ignoring no-trespassing signs and defeating gates, fences, or locks; (6) repeated trespasses by the plaintiff, especially in defiance of communication by the land possessor seeking to bar such entries; and (7) entry that results in damage to the land possessor's person, family, or property. Illustrations 1 and 2 that follow are sufficiently extreme as to be applicable regardless of where a given jurisdiction chooses to draw the line, and thus are provided to assist in clarifying the flagrant-trespasser concept. In addition, Illustrations 3 to 6 are provided to assist in illuminating the factors that might be relevant to determining whether a trespass was flagrant.

Illustrations:

1. On a dark night, John goes for a walk in a city park that winds along the coastline on a bluff above the water. While walking on a path adjacent to a stone wall marking the edge of the bluff, the ground gives way, and John falls to the bottom of the bluff, suffering physical harm. A city ordinance prohibits entry into the park from dusk until dawn, allowing entry only during daylight, but no physical barrier prevents entry during that time. John is an ordinary trespasser in the park, and the city owes him a duty of reasonable care.

2. Herman engages in a late-night burglary of the Jacob liquor store after it has closed. While leaving the store after taking cash from the store's register, Herman slips on a slick spot on the floor, falls, and breaks his arm. Herman is a flagrant trespasser, and Jacob's duties to Herman are provided by this Section.

Critical to the flagrancy of a trespass is the intrusion on the possessor's right of exclusive control of real property and the freedom to use that property as the possessor sees fit. The culpability of the entrant is relevant to the extent it infringes on the possessor's rights. However, culpable conduct—even extremely culpable conduct by an entrant—that does not infringe on the possessor's right is not relevant to whether a trespass is flagrant.

Illustrations:

3. Late one night, Rick climbs over a low decorative fence

217

surrounding Rachel's Bed and Breakfast. He lies in wait until a guest returns and then assaults the guest and snatches her purse. While escaping from the property, Rick is injured by an uninsulated electrical wire providing high-intensity lighting on the grounds. Rick's criminal assault of a customer of Rachel's on the premises is important (and sufficient) to support the determination that he is a flagrant trespasser.

4. Rick assaults Sasha on a public street and snatches her purse. After running several blocks and making his escape, he stops at a local bar for a drink. On his way home, he climbs over a low decorative fence at Rachel's Bed and Breakfast and is injured by the uninsulated wire of Illustration 3. Rick's commission of the crime is not relevant to the determination of whether his trespass on Rachel's land is flagrant.

The result in Illustration 4 may seem counterintuitive. Nevertheless, tort law does not generally provide that criminals forfeit their rights to personal security. A bank robber retains the right to sue and recover from a driver who negligently runs a red light and injures the robber.

b. Distinguishing among trespassers. . . . This Section requires that a land possessor only (a) refrain from intentional, willful, or wanton conduct that harms a flagrant trespasser and (b) exercise reasonable care on behalf of flagrant trespassers who are imperiled and helpless.

Creating different categories of trespassers based on the trespassers' activities on the land reflects the reality that a wide range of trespassers exists. Toward one end of the spectrum, it would jar common sensibilities and be unfair to require a land possessor whose negligence harms a flagrant trespasser to pay damages to that person. The reason for this is not that such trespassers are unforeseeable or more difficult to protect; that is the work of breach, not duty. Rather, it is that the presence of such trespassers on the land is so inconsistent with and offensive to the rights of the land possessor that liability should not be imposed. . . .

d. Trespassers and natural conditions on unimproved and uninhabited land. . . . [D]espite the limitation of this Section to flagrant trespassers, courts may consider adopting a similar limited duty to all trespassers for risks posed by natural conditions on uninhabited and unimproved land. . . .

g. Imperiled flagrant trespassers. Subsection (b)(2) reflects the extraordinary circumstance of an identifiable individual who is imperiled and helpless to take steps for self-protection. While there is no general duty to rescue even those whose life is at risk and who have no prospect of self-help, an imperiled individual on private property can look to a very confined group of persons for aid. This Subsection does not permit a land possessor, aware of the existence and plight of a flagrant trespasser, to ignore the situation—reasonable care, under the circumstances, must be exercised.

Illustration:

8. [Garnett, Inc., owns a large tract of unimproved land and takes significant measures to keep trespassers away. Nevertheless Willy and friends drive on the land at night to go "mudding"—an activity that involves driving off-road in soft, wet ground. Willy drives up a steep embankment and the car falls and strikes a tree.] Willy . . . is trapped in his car and bleeding profusely. A security guard employed by Garnett finds Willy in his car, ignores his plight, and leaves the scene to take a coffee break. Willy dies. Garnett is subject to liability for any enhanced harm Willy suffered that could have been prevented by the security guard taking reasonable measures on behalf of Willy, such as calling 911 or providing immediate first aid.

h. Rationale. This Section reflects the need to accommodate a conflict between the law of tort and another domain of law. . . . That other domain is property law and the rights it confers on owners and possessors of real property. Trespassers act in violation of those rights, while land possessors who act unreasonably with regard to risks on their property violate tort norms. This Section reflects a reconciliation of that conflict.

The limitation on the duty to flagrant trespassers is not that they are unforeseeable, although some may be. The tort principle that there is no negligence liability for unforeseeable harm is fully accommodated by the requirement that there be foreseeable risk before any burden of precaution is required. The limited duty to flagrant trespassers also is not based on the conclusory dictum that those who enter the land must assume any risks that exist there. Rather, consistent with § 7(b), it is based on the principle that it would be unjust to require a negligent land possessor to compensate a person whose presence on the land was highly offensive to the rights of the possessor. Thus, the principle behind this Section is like a number of privileges in tort law that absolve an actor from liability because the action of another impinges on the rights of the actor, such as the privilege of self-defense when bodily harm is threatened. . . .

k. Land possessor's privileges. Existing privileges may affect a land possessor's liability to flagrant trespassers. For example, an actor may use reasonable force in self-defense. See Restatement Second, Torts §§ 63 to 76. In addition, the privileges described in §§ 79 to 86 of the Second Restatement, which protect a land possessor's right of exclusive possession of property, are applicable in determining the liability of a land possessor to a flagrant trespasser.

l. Defenses. The conventional defenses available for tortfeasors who intentionally, willfully, or wantonly injure another, such as acting in self-defense, are also available to a land possessor. . . . Thus, a land possessor who justifiably uses deadly force to protect against a threat of death or serious bodily harm is not subject to liability under this Section. . . .

n. Personal property. The provisions in this Chapter are applicable only to the duties of possessors of real property. Nevertheless, the principle identified in this Section, justifying a modification of the duty to flagrant trespassers, might also be employed . . . in the case of a person who is injured in connection with converting the personal property of another, such as stealing a car. . . .

§ 53. Duty of Lessors

Restatement of the Law Third, Torts: Liability for Physical and Emotional Harm

Except as provided in § 52, a lessor owes to the lessee and all other entrants on the leased premises the following duties:

(a) a duty of reasonable care under § 51 for those portions of the leased premises over which the lessor retains control;

(b) a duty of reasonable care under § 7 for any risks that are created by the lessor in the condition of the leased premises;

(c) a duty to disclose to the lessee any dangerous condition that satisfies all of the following:

(1) it poses a risk to entrants on the leased premises;

(2) it exists on the leased premises when the lessee takes possession;

(3) it is latent and unknown to the lessee; and

(4) it is known or should be known to the lessor;

(d) a duty of reasonable care for any dangerous condition on the leased premises at the time the lessee takes possession if:

(1) the lease is for a purpose that includes admission of the public; and

(2) the lessor has reason to believe that the lessee will admit persons onto the leased premises without rectifying the dangerous condition;

(e) a duty of reasonable care:

(1) for any contractual undertaking; or

(2) for any voluntary undertaking, under §§ 42-43, with regard to the condition of the leased premises;

(f) a duty based on an applicable statute imposing obligations on lessors with regard to the condition of leased premises, unless the court finds that recognition of a tort duty is inconsistent with the statute;

(g) a duty of reasonable care to comply with an applicable implied warranty of habitability; and

(h) a duty of reasonable care to lessees under § 40, Comment m, as well as any other affirmative duties that may apply.

Comment:

a. History and scope. . . . Historically, lessors were not generally subject to tort liability for conditions on the leased premises. The first two Restatements adopted this broad no-liability rule but then moderated it by providing a number of exceptions. In light of the growth of lessors' obligations, especially in the residential context, this Restatement eschews the earlier approach and, instead, sets forth the positive bases for a lessor's duties to those who suffer harm on the leased premises. Lessors and their lessees are, ordinarily, in a contractual relationship. Their contract may afford the lessee certain rights in the event of a breach by the landlord that causes physical harm. This Section does not address those contractual rights and only provides for claims based on tort.

c. Retained control. Subsection (a) is a direct application of § 51 to lessors. Section 51 provides that land possessors—those in control of property—owe a duty of reasonable care to entrants on the land. This duty applies to entrants in the areas over which the lessor retains possession, such as common areas, and extends as well to entrants in other areas of the leased premises who are exposed to risks from the portion of the premises retained by the lessor. Thus, if a common roof or wall over which the lessor retains possession collapses due to the lessor's negligent maintenance, the lessor is subject to liability to anyone on the premises, subject to the flagrant-trespasser exception in § 52.

d. Conduct of the lessor creating risk to others. Subsection (b), addressing the conduct of the lessor that creates risks to those on the leased premises, is a specific application of the ordinary duty of reasonable care provided in § 7. It applies to all conditions on the leased premises for which the lessor is involved in creating a risk of harm, including the design, construction, and repair or maintenance of any structures or other artificial conditions on the premises. . . .

e. Disclosure of dangerous conditions. The duty in Subsection (c) is based on the lessor's superior knowledge of the risk posed by dangerous conditions on the land and the lessor's conduct in exposing others to that risk by leasing the premises without disclosing the dangerous condition to the lessee. The duty contained in this Subsection applies to all latent conditions on the land of which the lessor has or should have knowledge but which were not created by the lessor's conduct. Thus, it applies to natural conditions on the land as well as to artificial conditions created by persons other than the lessor. When the lessor has knowledge or should have knowledge of dangerous conditions on the leased premises and fails to disclose them to the lessee, there is an element of misrepresentation by omission. If the lessor does disclose, then once the lessee takes possession with knowledge of the dangers posed by those conditions, the lessee has a duty of reasonable care under § 51. Moreover, disclosure of dangerous conditions affords the lessor and the lessee the opportunity to address their respective responsibilities to eliminate or repair those conditions. A condition is dangerous for purposes of Subsection (c) if it poses a risk of danger to entrants on the leased premises that, through the exercise of reasonable care, could be eliminated or ameliorated.

Consistent with the foundation of this duty in the doctrine of misrepresentation, Subsection (c) applies only to dangerous conditions that are not open and obvious and thus would not be appreciated by the lessee. It is not sufficient that the *condition* be open and obvious or known; the *dangerousness* must be open and obvious or known. . . .

A lessee's failure to exercise reasonable care to discover dangerous conditions does not obviate the duty imposed by this Subsection. It does, however, constitute negligence and under comparative-responsibility principles reduces the recovery of a lessee who suffers harm or, alternatively, subjects the lessee to liability, along with the lessor, to a third-party entrant who suffers harm. . . .

Illustration:

1. Kaidan, who owns an apartment building, negligently repairs the screen door on one of the apartments; consequently, the door-closing apparatus that prevents the door from slamming shut sometimes malfunctions. Kaidan knows of this problem but decides not to fix it. Kaidan then rents the apartment to Ramona without telling her of the door's condition. Soon after, she is injured when the door slams shut behind

her, its kickplate cutting her heel and severing her Achilles tendon. Kaidan is subject to liability under both Subsections (b) and (c).

Although ordinarily a lessor's disclosure of dangerous conditions to the lessee will occur before the lessee takes possession, the lessor's duty extends to exercising reasonable care to disclose latent dangers that the lessor later discovers.

f. Leases for a purpose that includes admission of the public. . . . A lessor who leases premises for uses that include admission of the public is subject to a higher duty than the duty provided in Subsection (c). . . . [I]f the public is to be admitted onto the premises, the lessor may not discharge the duty in this Subsection merely by disclosing a dangerous condition to the lessee. The lessor must assess whether the lessee will exercise reasonable care to address the dangerous condition and, if there is reason to believe the lessee will not, then the lessor must exercise reasonable care to remedy the condition. A condition is dangerous for purposes of Subsection (d) if its risks can be eliminated or ameliorated through the exercise of reasonable care. . . .

A variety of circumstances inform the determination of whether the lessor should expect that the lessee will fail to take reasonable care with regard to a dangerous condition. From prior experience with the lessee, the lessor may know that the lessee is unreliable about making repairs or that the lessee is in a financially precarious position. The lease may be for such a short period that the lessee would lack adequate opportunity to make the condition safe or would conclude that repairs would be financially infeasible, particularly if durable precautions are required. The lease itself may contain provisions that would prevent the lessee from rectifying the danger, such as a clause barring any structural changes. . . . A provision in the lease requiring the lessee to maintain and repair the premises is relevant to whether the lessor expected the lessee to remedy a dangerous condition, but is not determinative of the lessor's duty. Both lessor and lessee may be subject to liability to an entrant on the premises.

i. Duties imposed by statute. . . . Many residential landlord-tenant statutes require the landlord to repair and maintain the premises, as well as to keep them in safe condition. In states with such statutes, unless the court finds that tort liability is inconsistent with the statutory mandate, the lessor of residential premises generally owes a duty of reasonable care with regard to the entirety of the leased premises.

m. Contractual limitations on liability. Because lessors and lessees are in a contractual relationship, leases sometimes contain provisions that limit the liability of the lessor for the consequences of its negligence. Ordinarily, parties are free to strike the bargain

223

they desire, but some contractual limitations are unenforceable because they are deemed unconscionable or otherwise to violate public policy. The types of parties and the nature of their relationship with each other are central to the determination of whether a contractual limitation is enforceable. Relevant factors include: whether one party is dependent on the other; the nature of the service or good being provided; whether the service or good is essential or elective; whether the transaction implicates the public interest; the economic setting of the transaction and whether the parties are on relatively equal footing in bargaining; whether the limitation-of-liability clause is one of adhesion; whether the parties have equal information about the subject of the contract; and whether the party obtaining the benefit of limiting liability offers to provide greater protection in exchange for an additional, reasonable charge.

In the context of residential leases, these factors present a strong case for finding contractual limitations of a landlord's liability unenforceable per se. In fact, many states have statutes that so provide, and most courts that have confronted the question have reached the same conclusion. . . . For the same reason that contractual limitations of liability in residential leases are unenforceable, so too are provisions by which a lessee is required to indemnify the lessor.

The case is different for commercial leases. If the lessee is a corporate entity, it cannot suffer personal injury, although a lessor may be liable in tort for property damage. A commercial lessee is more likely to be in an equal bargaining position with a lessor, and commercial space, however critical to business operations, is not of the same character as a residence and shelter. Commercial leases also have a wider variance with regard to the factors identified above. Hence, no hard-and-fast rule about the enforceability of a contractual limitation of liability in a commercial lease is appropriate, and the matter is left to case-by-case determinations.

o. Comprehensive duty of reasonable care for lessors. This Section enumerates several sources of duties for lessors. Together they approach a comprehensive duty of reasonable care for lessors with regard to the leased premises. Some jurisdictions have adopted just such a rule. The enumeration in this Section is not intended to impede similar reform in other jurisdictions. The form of this Section is designed to be of assistance to those courts that have not yet adopted a comprehensive duty for lessors through judicial or legislative action but is not intended to suggest the undesirability of a comprehensive duty.

§ 54. Duty of Land Possessors to Those Not on the Possessor's Land

Restatement of the Law Third, Torts: Liability for Physical and Emotional Harm

(a) The possessor of land has a duty of reasonable care for artificial conditions or conduct on the land that poses a risk of physical harm to persons or property not on the land.

(b) For natural conditions on land that pose a risk of physical harm to persons or property not on the land, the possessor of the land

(1) has a duty of reasonable care if the land is commercial; otherwise

(2) has a duty of reasonable care only if the possessor knows of the risk or if the risk is obvious.

(c) Unless Subsection (b) applies, a possessor of land adjacent to a public walkway has no duty under this Chapter with regard to a risk posed by the condition of the walkway to pedestrians or others if the land possessor did not create the risk.

Comment:

b. Duty of reasonable care for artificial conditions and conduct. Land possessors may engage in many different forms of activity on their land that will pose risks to others off the land. For example, they may build automobiles, dispense drugs, construct structures, mine coal, or engage in myriad other activities that could potentially harm others off the land. Imposing a duty of reasonable care with regard to that conduct is a special application of § 7 of this Restatement. That a land possessor engages in the conduct on the possessor's own property instead of someone else's property or public property does not affect the obligation of the actor-possessor. While it does implicate how a possessor can use the land, the infringement on freedom of activity imposed by tort law is based on the impact such activity has on others. Just as an actor on public land must take care for the safety of others, so an actor on private property is obliged to take precautions for the safety of those off the land.

Artificial conditions on land may pose risks to those off the land. A deteriorated awning on a retail shop may overhang a public walkway. An older building may collapse, causing injury to those on adjacent streets or other property. . . . Subsection (a) imposes a duty of reasonable care for all artificial conditions on the land, whether the possessor created the condition or inherited it with the land. . . .

The duty provided in Subsection (a) . . . includes reasonable efforts to investigate the existence of risk as well as to eliminate or ameliorate any discovered risk.

c. Natural conditions. . . . [A] trend exists toward expansion of the duties of land possessors to a general duty of reasonable care with regard to natural conditions. In conjunction with that development has been wariness about extending that duty fully to require reasonable care in inspecting the land to find latent dangers posed by natural conditions. . . .

Commercial land is likely to be in proximity to other property or persons, and natural conditions on commercial land will, on the whole, pose a greater risk to persons off the land than will natural conditions on residential land or unimproved land. The burden of inspecting commercial land for dangers posed by natural conditions is also more modest than for most other types of private property. Thus, a duty of reasonable care to inspect the land for latent dangers posed by natural conditions is limited to possessors of commercial land. . . .

Possessors of noncommercial land have a duty of reasonable care, but the duty is limited to known and patent risks. . . .

PART IV
EMOTIONAL HARM

———

CHAPTER 13

LIABILITY FOR EMOTIONAL HARM

Scope Note: . . . . [S]ometimes a person suffers stand-alone emotional harm, that is, the emotional harm is not caused by any physical harm to that person. . . .

Historically, courts were quite restrictive and cautious about permitting recovery for pure emotional harm. Several concerns explain this caution: (1) emotional harm is less objectively verifiable than physical harm and therefore easier for an individual to feign, to exaggerate, or to imagine; (2) emotional harm can be widespread—a single act can affect a substantial population; (3) some degree of emotional harm is endemic to living in society, and individuals must learn to accept and cope with such harm; (4) giving legal credence to and permitting recovery for emotional harm may increase its severity; and (5) related to the prior concern, while mitigation may be important in minimizing this harm, there is little a legal system can do to encourage or enforce mitigation. These policy concerns often led courts to declare that actors had "no duty" to prevent pure emotional harm, except in some narrowly defined areas. Such rules were consistent with the framework provided in § 7(b), in which no-duty determinations preclude liability.

Thus, the Second Restatement provided for no recovery when negligence caused only emotional harm. Since the publication of the Second Restatement, however, courts have become more comfortable permitting recovery for negligently inflicted emotional harm. While there remain substantial restrictions—considerably more than for physical harm—recovery for negligently inflicted emotional harm is more widely available today than when the

Second Restatement was first published. This Chapter reflects that development. . . .

Some courts have expanded recovery for negligently inflicted emotional harm when the reasons given above for restricting it do not apply. Thus, courts have been more sympathetic to liability when the circumstances are such that any reasonable person would suffer serious emotional harm, when the severity of the harm or the effect of the harm limits the victim's activities of daily life, and when the scope of liability is sufficiently limited. This Chapter reflects that liberalization of recovery for pure emotional harm. . . .

A. EMOTIONAL HARM DEFINED

§ 45. Emotional Harm

Restatement of the Law Third, Torts: Liability for Physical and Emotional Harm

"Emotional harm" [means impairment or injury to a person's emotional tranquility.]

Comment:

a. Emotional harm and bodily harm. Emotional harm is distinct from bodily harm. . . . Emotional harm encompasses a variety of mental states, including fright, fear, sadness, sorrow, despondency, anxiety, humiliation, depression (and other mental illnesses), and a host of other detrimental—from mildly unpleasant to disabling—mental conditions. The distinction between physical and emotional harm is not precise and may be difficult to determine in some cases. Most physical harm, with the exception of disease, results from traumatic impact with the human body, while emotional harm can occur without such trauma, indeed without any event that resembles a physical-harm tort. Usually the existence of bodily harm can be verified objectively while the existence and severity of emotional harm is ordinarily dependent on self-reporting.

b. Bodily harm resulting from emotional harm. When an actor's tortious conduct causes emotional harm that then produces bodily harm, the rules for liability provided for physical harm . . . govern. This Chapter is applicable only when a plaintiff seeks to recover for pure or stand-alone emotional harm. . . .

B. Intentional or Reckless Infliction of Emotional Harm

§ 46. Intentional (or Reckless) Infliction of Emotional Harm

Restatement of the Law Third, Torts: Liability for Physical and Emotional Harm

An actor who by extreme and outrageous conduct intentionally or recklessly causes severe emotional harm to another is subject to liability for that emotional harm and, if the emotional harm causes bodily harm, also for the bodily harm.

Comment:

a. Scope and history. . . . The outrage tort originated as a catchall to permit recovery in the narrow instance when an actor's conduct exceeded all permissible bounds of a civilized society but an existing tort claim was unavailable. This tort potentially encompasses a broad swath of behavior and can easily, but often inappropriately, be added as a supplement to a suit in which the gravamen is another tort or a statutory violation. The intent requirement is satisfied when an actor knows that conduct is substantially certain to cause harm. Because emotional harm is often a predictable outcome of otherwise legitimate conduct, such as terminating an employee, liability for this tort could be expansive. Courts have played an especially critical role in cabining this tort by requiring "extreme and outrageous" conduct and "severe" emotional harm. A great deal of conduct may cause emotional harm, but the requisite conduct for this claim—extreme and outrageous—describes a very small slice of human behavior. The requirement that the resulting harm be severe further limits claims. These limits are essential in preventing this tort from being so broad as to intrude on important countervailing policies, while permitting its judicious use for the occasions when it is appropriate.

b. Bodily harm distinguished. . . . This Section applies to emotional harm to a person that is not itself caused by bodily harm to that person. . . . An actor who intentionally causes bodily harm through the mechanism of emotional harm may be liable independent of this Section for intentionally causing the bodily harm and also may be liable under the rule stated in this Section for the physical consequences of the intentionally inflicted emotional harm. . . .

c. Policy or principle for precluding liability. Just as § 7(b) provides that a no-duty ruling may, in exceptional cases, preclude liability on grounds of principle or policy, so too in the area of emotional harm, a court may decide that an identified and articulated policy is weighty enough to preclude liability. Thus, a court may decide that although the First Amendment does not bar liability, the protection of speech is nonetheless a weighty enough concern in a given context that liability for intentionally inflicted emotional harm should not be imposed. A number of other policies that might dictate precluding liability are already reflected in the requirement of this Section that the actor's conduct be extreme and outrageous and that the emotional harm suffered be severe.

d. Extreme and outrageous conduct. To be held liable under this Section, an actor must do more than intentionally or recklessly cause emotional harm. The actor must act in a way that is extreme and outrageous. . . .

The adjectives "extreme" and "outrageous" are used together in a fashion that might suggest that each merely emphasizes the other, rather than serving a distinct role. However, some conduct that may be outrageous—for example, marital infidelity—is sufficiently common that it could not be characterized as extreme (although today it may also not be outrageous). Similarly, some extreme conduct—climbing Mt. Everest, for example—is not outrageous. Thus, this double limitation, "extreme and outrageous," requires both that the character of the conduct be outrageous and that the conduct be sufficiently unusual to be extreme.

Under § 1(b), an actor is charged with intending a consequence if the actor "acts knowing that the consequence is substantially certain to result." Under this definition of intent, liability could extend to a wide variety of conduct without regard to the legitimacy or social utility of the conduct. For example, a person who breaks a marriage engagement may be substantially certain that the rejection will cause severe emotional harm, but that conduct is not a proper basis for liability. Important policies support protecting the freedom to end an engagement. Indeed, the larger point is that unless liability under this Section is appropriately limited, freedom and socially productive conduct could be impeded. Individuals participating in society must be prepared to suffer emotional trauma—even as serious as that resulting from a broken engagement—without legal recourse, in order to encourage freedom and, specifically, in the case of engagement, to avoid marriages that are likely to fail. The difficulty with this tort is that the "substantially certain" element of intent does not balance the social utility of the actor's conduct against the risk of causing emotional harm.

Similarly, as a matter of policy, even if emotional harm is inflicted for no purpose other than to cause such harm, some degree of emotional harm must be expected in social interaction and tolerated without legal recourse. Under the "extreme and outrageous" requirement, an actor is liable only if the conduct goes beyond the

231

bounds of human decency such that it would be regarded as intolerable in a civilized community. Ordinary insults and indignities are not enough for liability to be imposed, even if the actor desires to cause emotional harm.

Whether an actor's conduct is extreme and outrageous depends on the facts of each case, including the relationship of the parties, whether the actor abused a position of authority over the other person, whether the other person was especially vulnerable and the actor knew of the vulnerability, the motivation of the actor, and whether the conduct was repeated or prolonged.

Illustrations:

    4. Bronwen and Helmut, who are friends, decide to live together to reduce living expenses. At first, their relationship is platonic, but a year later, Helmut, a police officer, becomes romantically interested in Bronwen. Because she does not share his interest, Bronwen moves out and establishes a separate residence. Over the course of the next two years, Helmut obsessively stalks and harasses Bronwen. He calls Bronwen at all hours of the day and night, both at work and at home; he threatens her and any other man she is dating. Helmut stalks Bronwen, frequently from his police cruiser, and sometimes runs lights and sirens to frighten her. Bronwen suffers severe emotional harm. Helmut's conduct may be found extreme and outrageous; in light of the egregiousness of Helmut's conduct, a court might even make such a ruling as a matter of law.

    5. Margaret, a sales representative for MDC, becomes pregnant at about the same time that MDC is reexamining its allocation of representatives to its sales territories. MDC concludes that Margaret's existing territory cannot support a sales representative. Dave, Margaret's supervisor, who is aware of her pregnancy, uses the occasion of an annual performance review to inform Margaret that her territory is being eliminated. Dave offers Margaret another territory; Margaret would have to relocate to accept the transfer. When Margaret does not accept the transfer, she is terminated. Margaret sues MDC, alleging employment discrimination. She also asserts a claim for intentional infliction of emotional harm. MDC has not, as a matter of law, engaged in extreme and outrageous conduct and is not liable to Margaret for her emotional harm.

Specific rules for when conduct is extreme and outrageous cannot be stated, nor can categories of conduct be identified for formulation into universal rules. Nevertheless, guidance can be found in cases in which courts have submitted defendants' conduct to the jury to determine whether it is extreme and outrageous, for example: surreptitiously videotaping a 16-year-old in various stages of undress; engaging in prolonged physical and mental abuse of another; sexually abusing another; committing suicide in another's home; and torturing or maliciously killing another's pet.

e. Conduct that exercises a legal right. An actor can intentionally or recklessly cause severe emotional harm while exercising a legal right. For example, a spouse who seeks a divorce or an employer who terminates an at-will employee might be substantially certain that the conduct will cause severe emotional harm, but neither is liable for that conduct. Otherwise, the tort of intentional infliction of emotional harm would undermine well-established principles of marital law and employment law.

Although an actor exercising legal rights is not liable under this Section merely for exercising those rights, the actor is not immunized from liability if the conduct goes so far beyond what is necessary to exercise the right that it is extreme and outrageous. A spouse who announces intimate facts in the newspaper as part of the process of obtaining a divorce or an employer who unnecessarily humiliates a fired employee goes further than is necessary to exercise the legal right and may be subject to liability if the conduct is found to be extreme and outrageous.

g. Role of judge and jury. As with all questions of fact, the court first determines whether the evidence is sufficient to permit a jury to find the actor's conduct extreme and outrageous and the harm severe, and if so, it is then for the jury to decide whether the actor's conduct was in fact extreme and outrageous and to award damages for the harm. However, the court plays a more substantial screening role on the questions of extreme and outrageous conduct and the severity of the harm, than on other questions of fact. . . .

h. Actor's intent. . . . Courts uniformly hold that reckless conduct, not just intentional conduct, can support a claim for intentional infliction of emotional harm. In this sense, the scienter requirement for this tort is more expansive than, for example, the scienter requirement for battery. Three rationales support this. First and most important, to recover for intentional infliction of emotional harm, a plaintiff must prove that the defendant's conduct was extreme and outrageous. An actor who commits a battery does not necessarily act in an extreme and outrageous manner. Because recklessness entails balancing the risk of harm with the difficulty of preventing it, a reckless actor may be more culpable than an actor who satisfies the intent requirement because emotional harm was substantially certain to occur (without regard to the difficulty of avoiding that harm). Second, unlike battery, the resulting harm must satisfy the "severe" threshold. Third, if an actor's state of mind fails to satisfy the intent requirement for intentional torts causing physical harm, the injured person may still be able to prove negligence. However, a person who cannot recover for intentional infliction of emotional harm usually faces substantial obstacles to recovering on a negligence theory. Thus, courts have good reason to include cases of recklessness within the tort of intentional infliction of emotional harm.

233

i. Conduct directed at the claimant. Actors who intend to cause severe emotional harm often direct their conduct at particular individuals. The person intended to be harmed is readily identifiable, and liability is, therefore, appropriately confined. In such cases, the concept of "transferred intent," applicable to intentionally caused physical harm as well as to assault, may be employed if, instead of harming the intended victim, the conduct harms a different person.

Illustration:

6. Caryn wants to take revenge on her ex-boyfriend, Mike. She calls his home one night with a false story that his daughter has been murdered, employing a horrific account of the events leading to her death. Unknown to Caryn, Mike's roommate, Gordie, who has a very close relationship with Mike's daughter, answers her call and suffers severe emotional harm at the news. Caryn is subject to liability under this Section even though she acted with a purpose to cause emotional harm to Mike and not to Gordie. . . .

[D]ifficulty with the use of transferred intent does arise in a context where an actor's conduct may be substantially certain to cause emotional harm to a large group of individuals ("bystanders"), such as when a beloved national leader is assassinated. Courts generally have limited the potential scope of liability for emotional harm to bystanders present at the time of the tortious conduct who are also close family members of the victim.

Illustration:

7. Same facts as Illustration 6, except that Gordie, believing Caryn's story, calls a number of Mike's relatives to relate what Caryn told him. Caryn is not subject to liability to Mike's relatives under this Section. . . .

In some "substantially certain" cases as well as in some cases of recklessness, the identity of the person at whom the conduct is directed may be unclear. For example, if a school recklessly ignores a pattern of child abuse by an employee, thereby posing a risk that some yet-unidentified children will suffer similar harm in the future, the "directed at" limitation does not shield the school from liability to those who are later abused by the offending employee. Indeed, adhering to a "directed at" requirement in such cases would largely nullify the recklessness element of this Section.

Illustrations:

8. Despite receiving numerous and repeated complaints over 18 months that Allen, employed by the Spartan Preschool, had made inappropriate sexual remarks and otherwise abused children at the school, the school supervisor takes no action. Thereafter, Allen engages in a repeated course of such abuse of

Rose, a four-year-old child, causing her severe emotional harm (although she suffers no physical harm). The Spartan Preschool is subject to liability to Rose under this Section, even though the school's reckless conduct was not directed specifically at Rose.

9. Same facts as Illustration 8, except that several members of Rose's family also seek to recover from the Spartan Preschool for their severe emotional harm resulting from the abuse of Rose. Their claims are subject to the limitations provided in Comment *m*.

Some cases arise in which there are so many indeterminate victims that scope-of-liability concerns require limits on liability. For example, the egregious mishandling of a corpse is not "directed at" any individual, but it is substantially certain to cause harm to a significant number of family and friends of the deceased. Some courts have used the "directed at" requirement to impose limits in this situation, but reliance on that requirement is not very helpful, because it does not provide any coherent basis for distinguishing among affected family and friends. Instead, controlling the number of claimants can better be performed by crafting an appropriate rule limiting the scope of liability under this Section. See Comment *m*.

j. Severe emotional harm. . . . . [T]he law intervenes only when the plaintiff's emotional harm is severe and when a person of ordinary sensitivities in the same circumstances would suffer severe harm. There is no liability for emotional harm suffered only because of the unusual vulnerability of a victim, unless the actor knew of that special vulnerability. . . .

As with the determination of whether a defendant's conduct was extreme and outrageous, courts play a more significant role than is usual in determining whether the allegations or evidence support a determination that severe emotional harm exists. . . .

l. Bodily harm. Severe emotional harm is often accompanied or followed by illness or other bodily harm, which can afford objective evidence verifying that the harm is genuine and severe. This Section is not limited, however, to cases in which bodily harm occurs. If the conduct is extreme and outrageous and results in severe emotional harm without any accompanying physical manifestation, liability is appropriate under this Section.

m. Emotional harm caused by harm to a third person. When an actor's extreme and outrageous conduct causes harm to a third person, as, for example, when a murderer kills a husband in the presence of his wife, the actor may know that the murder is substantially certain to cause severe emotional harm to the witnessing spouse. The murderer acts at least recklessly with regard to that risk. In these cases, this Section applies. . . .

Modern courts have continued to limit liability to cases in which the person seeking recovery contemporaneously perceived the event, as distinguished from those who discovered what has occurred later. This limitation may be justified by the practical necessity of drawing a line, since the number of persons who suffer emotional harm at the news of a homicide or other outrageous attack may be virtually unlimited.

The Second Restatement also limited recovery to those who were members of the third person's immediate family. This limitation is justified by the need to place manageable limits on such claims. It is also justified by the generalization that the harmed person's close family members are more likely to suffer severe emotional harm than are strangers or acquaintances. Accordingly, this Comment limits recovery for emotional harm to "bystanders" who are close family members and who contemporaneously perceive the event.

If an actor harms someone for the purpose of inflicting mental distress on another person, the limitations contained in this Comment do not apply.

Illustration:

12. Bill is awarded custody of his son, Jack, after a bitter custody battle with Rose, Jack's mother. To retaliate against Bill and cause him anguish, Rose mutilates Jack during her visitation weekend. In Bill's suit against Rose for intentional infliction of emotional harm, although Bill did not perceive the mutilation of Jack, contemporaneous perception is not required because Rose acted for the purpose of causing Bill emotional harm.

There is one category in which there has been modest judicial development toward not requiring contemporaneous perception of the event: when a minor child is sexually abused by a predator. Child abuse, by its nature, is unlikely to occur in the presence of a (non-abusive) parent, and the certainty and severity of the emotional impact of child abuse on the parents is beyond cavil. Moreover, limiting recovery in such cases to the parents of a victim of abuse avoids concerns about wide-ranging and unbounded liability. Nevertheless, because there is no emerging consensus on this expansion and because there may remain limitations to be worked out to make this exception to the "presence" requirement workable—such as might be required when one parent makes such a claim against another parent in the midst of a divorce—the Institute leaves this matter to future development.

C. NEGLIGENT INFLICTION OF EMOTIONAL HARM

§ 47. Negligent Conduct Directly Inflicting Emotional Harm on Another

Restatement of the Law Third, Torts: Liability for Physical and Emotional Harm

An actor whose negligent conduct causes serious emotional harm to another is subject to liability to the other if the conduct:

(a) places the other in danger of immediate bodily harm and the emotional harm results from the danger; or

(b) occurs in the course of specified categories of activities, undertakings, or relationships in which negligent conduct is especially likely to cause serious emotional harm.

Comment:

a. Scope. This Section limits a negligent actor's liability for emotional harm to two situations. One is when the actor's negligent conduct places the person seeking recovery in danger of bodily harm but actually causes only emotional harm. The other is when the negligent conduct occurs within certain classes of activities, undertakings, and relationships in which the conduct does not create a risk of bodily harm but nevertheless poses a significant risk of serious emotional harm. By contrast, § 48 addresses liability when an actor's negligence causes serious emotional harm to a bystander through the mechanism of bodily harm to a third person. . . .

b. History. The rules stated in this Section arose as two lines of exceptions to the general rule that an actor is not liable for negligent conduct that causes only emotional harm.

The first is based on cases in which an actor's negligent conduct created a danger of bodily harm and caused some impact, however slight, to the person seeking recovery. This exception came to be called the "impact" rule. Later, courts expanded this exception to cover cases in which the actor's negligent conduct did not actually cause impact but created a danger of bodily harm. This exception came to be called the "zone of danger" rule. The "zone of danger" rule then spawned the "bystander" rule stated in § 48, under which a bystander can recover for emotional harm caused by contemporaneously observing bodily harm to a close relative, even though the bystander is not in the zone of danger. Although the "bystander" rule is often viewed as an expansion of the "zone of danger" rule, it actually is quite different. The bystander rule addresses recovery for harm that is derivative of and based upon negligence toward a third person. The claim for emotional harm arises from the harm

237

to the third person. By contrast, the zone-of-danger rule embodied in Subsection (a) of this Section is based on an actor's negligent conduct that directly places the other person in danger of bodily harm and because of that danger causes emotional harm to that person.

The second line of cases recognizes an exception to the general no-liability rule when an actor undertakes to perform specified obligations, engages in specified activities, or is in a specified relationship fraught with the risk of emotional harm. Specifically, courts have imposed liability on hospitals and funeral homes for negligently mishandling a corpse and on telegraph companies for negligently mistranscribing or misdirecting a telegram that informs the recipient, erroneously, about the death of a loved one. Some courts have expanded this exception to cover persons engaged in other undertakings, activities, or relationships. Limiting recovery for emotional harm to those in the relationship or those for whom the undertaking or activity was being performed limits the scope of liability for negligently inflicted emotional harm, thereby avoiding concern about indeterminate and excessive liability.

d. Policy or principle for withdrawing liability. Just as § 7(b) provides that a no-duty ruling may, in exceptional cases, preclude liability on grounds of principle or policy, so too in the area of emotional harm, a court may decide that an identified and articulated policy is weighty enough to require the withdrawal of liability. Some of the policies that might dictate a withdrawal of liability are already reflected in limitations on liability in this Section, such as the requirement that the emotional harm suffered be serious.

e. "Zone of danger." Under the rule stated in Subsection (a), an actor whose negligent conduct places another in danger of immediate bodily harm is subject to liability to the other for serious emotional harm caused by reaction to the danger, even though the conduct did not cause any impact or bodily harm to the other. Exposure to a toxic substance with a significant latency period, along with subclinical effects that do not rise to the level of bodily harm, do not satisfy the zone-of-danger requirement (nor would it constitute impact); otherwise, the "immediacy" requirement in this Section would be nullified. Similarly, conduct that exposes a person to subclinical effects that do not rise to the level of bodily harm does not satisfy the zone-of-danger requirement. However, when an actor creates a risk of bodily harm that causes emotional harm in anticipation of immediate bodily harm or death, such as might occur in passengers in an apparently doomed aircraft, the emotional harm is recoverable under this Section.

Illustrations:

1. Raissa is a passenger on an Oceana Airlines flight.

Due to negligent maintenance of the airplane by Oceana, it abruptly loses altitude and begins to enter into a spin. During its uncontrolled descent, oxygen masks drop for use, and passengers are alerted to prepare for a crash landing. The pilot regains control of the airplane a few hundred feet before it would have crashed and lands the airplane safely, with no passengers suffering physical harm. As a result of reasonably fearing that injury or death was imminent, Raissa suffers serious emotional harm. Oceana Airlines is subject to liability to Raissa under Subsection (a).

2. Kapri and Laura, her passenger, are driving westbound on a freeway when a vehicle in an eastbound lane, driven by Hasan, negligently crosses the median, heading directly at Kapri and Laura. Kapri screams, anticipating the impact, and Laura puts her head between her knees. Although Kapri slams on her brakes, she cannot avoid the collision. Laura survives the impact, but Kapri is killed. As a result of her anticipation of the accident, Laura suffers from post-traumatic stress disorder ("PTSD"), a serious emotional harm. Hasan is subject to liability to Laura under Subsection (a) for Laura's PTSD. In jurisdictions that permit recovery for "pre-impact" fear in a survival action, Hasan is subject to liability for Kapri's "pre-impact" fear under Subsection (a).

f. Specific activities or undertakings. Under the rule stated in Subsection (b), an actor who negligently performs specified undertakings or activities is subject to liability for emotional harm caused by negligence in conducting the undertaking or activity. Unlike Subsection (a), recovery under this Subsection does not require that the defendant have created a risk of bodily harm to the plaintiff. Early cases were of two types: (1) delivering a telegram or other communication erroneously announcing death or illness; and (2) mishandling a corpse or bodily remains. More recently, courts have recognized the awkwardness of relying on "impact" or "zone of danger" in cases involving consumption of a food that is then found to have been contaminated with a repulsive foreign object, such as a condom or a rodent, and instead have recognized these cases as falling within the rule of Subsection (b).

Illustrations:

3. ABC Hospital negligently misidentifies a corpse, causing it to be cremated rather than sent to a funeral home for burial as directed by the family. Members of the family suffer serious emotional harm upon learning about the mistake. ABC Hospital is subject to liability under Subsection (b).

4. The Jonestown morgue negligently determines the identity of a corpse brought to it by the police department. Sadie, the sister and next of kin of the person who was errone-

ously determined to be the corpse, is contacted by the morgue, told of the death, and provided instructions about making final arrangement for disposal of the body. Sadie, who lives out of town, does so. Upon viewing the deceased, Sadie discovers that the deceased is not her sister. As a result of this episode, Sadie suffers serious emotional harm. Jonestown is subject to liability to Sadie under Subsection (b).

Some jurisdictions have also applied the rule stated in Subsection (b) to circumstances in which, for example, a physician negligently diagnoses a patient with a dreaded or serious disease; a physician negligently causes the loss of a fetus; a hospital loses a newborn infant; a person injures a fetus; a hospital (or another) exposes a patient to HIV infection; an employer mistreats an employee; or a spouse mentally abuses the other spouse.

Courts have not provided clear guidelines to identify precisely which activities, undertakings, or relationships will support liability. Even for undertakings in which there is a risk of infecting another with HIV—a circumstance fraught with the risk of emotional harm—there is considerable variation in the scope of this category, including whether there must be a scientifically valid or plausible source of infection and whether the plaintiff must demonstrate that the source was actually contaminated with HIV. Typically, the undertaking or relationship is one in which serious emotional harm is likely or where one person is in a position of power or authority over the other and therefore has greater potential to inflict emotional harm. Courts appropriately identify such categories of activities, undertakings, or relationships as giving rise to liability for emotional harm. Courts do not address liability on the mere fact that serious emotional harm was foreseeable under the facts of the specific case.

Courts sometimes inquire whether a plaintiff is a "direct victim" of the defendant's negligent conduct. This approach is employed when plaintiff has not been placed at risk of physical harm (and thus Subsection (a) is unavailable) and is unable to make out a claim for emotional harm as a bystander under § 48. The inquiry framed by Subsection (b) of this Section and this Comment addresses the same issue and may be more helpful than the "direct victim" approach.

h. Relationship between undertakings and contracts. The existence of a contract between the parties may affect a claim under this Section in several different ways. Contract law may provide the person harmed with an alternative claim. Although damages for emotional harm ordinarily are not recoverable for breach of contract, some contracts—such as burial contracts—are so intimately tied to emotional issues that they call for an exception to that general rule. . . . [Contractual] liability does not preempt tort claims, as tort law may be more liberal in permitting claims

240

and afford a remedy to a third person who is not in contractual privity with the actor. . . .

The second effect of a contract is that it may be the basis for finding an undertaking or relationship under this Section that is appropriate for permitting emotional-harm claims. Thus, a doctor who agrees to treat a patient who is suspected of having contracted a dread disease may, by entering into that contractual relationship, be subject to liability under this Section. Yet a third consequence of a contract may be that the contract allocates the risk of serious emotional harm occurring. In such a case, the court would be obliged to consult the law applicable to the interpretation and enforcement of contractual disclaimer provisions.

i. Relationship between Subsection (b) and foreseeability. Courts often state that the test for determining whether negligently caused emotional harm is recoverable is whether the actor reasonably should have foreseen the emotional harm. But foreseeability cannot appropriately be employed as the standard to limit liability for emotional harm. For example, a doctor who negligently (and incorrectly) diagnoses a popular movie star or professional athlete as having terminal cancer is not liable to the star's fans who suffer emotional harm upon hearing the diagnosis, even though such harm is clearly foreseeable. Indeed, the rules stated in this Section and in § 48 are exceptions to a general rule that negligently caused pure emotional harm is not recoverable even when it is foreseeable. Instead of relying on foreseeability to identify appropriate cases for recovery, the policy issues surrounding specific categories of undertakings, activities, and relationships must be examined to determine whether they merit inclusion among the exceptions to the general rule of no liability.

j. Physical consequences not required. Significant emotional harm may cause physical illness or other bodily harm. Some courts insist that plaintiff present with physical symptoms to ensure that the emotional harm claimed is genuine and serious. The rule stated in this Section, while requiring serious emotional harm, is not limited to cases in which there are physical manifestations. The requirements that the harm be serious, that the circumstances of the case be such that a reasonable person would suffer serious harm, and that there be credible evidence that the plaintiff has suffered such harm better serve the purpose of screening claims than a requirement of physical consequences.

k. Fear of future injury. Persons who have been exposed to toxic substances and who are at risk of future injury or disease— such as is the case from exposure to asbestos (posing risk of future asbestosis, lung cancer, or mesothelioma)—have sought recovery for emotional harm. Sometimes these claims are described as seeking recovery for "cancerphobia." Under the rule stated in Subsec-

241

tion (a), exposed persons might claim that they suffered emotional harm as a result of being placed in danger of bodily harm. However, these cases are different from others under Subsection (a), in which the risk of bodily harm has passed and no future event exists that might trigger bodily harm. By contrast, courts deny recovery in cancerphobia cases, at least during the indeterminate latency period before the person actually suffers bodily injury. The rule stated in Subsection (a), which requires that the person be placed in "immediate" danger, does not apply to these cases. One reason for this limitation is a concern that multiple lawsuits— one when the person is exposed (for "pure" emotional harm) and another, later, if bodily injury does occur (for the physical-harm tort and related emotional harm)—would result.

By way of contrast, exposure to some infectious agents, such as HIV, might create emotional harm in a way that does not raise the potential of multiple lawsuits because the person can determine within a known and relatively short interval whether or not the exposure actually did cause physical injury. These cases are akin to those in which a person is put in danger of being hit by an automobile and is not physically harmed but suffers emotional harm. In both the automobile and the HIV-exposure cases, the period during which the person is subject to risk and suffers emotional harm is (unlike the cancerphobia cases) relatively confined. Thus, Subsection (a) applies to cases in which the period between exposure and determination of no physical harm is sufficiently short. . . .

l. Serious emotional harm. The rule stated in this Section applies only when the person seeking recovery has suffered serious emotional harm. In addition, the actor's conduct must be such that would cause a reasonable person to suffer serious emotional harm. Thus, there are objective and subjective components to this requirement. Objectively, an unusually susceptible person may not recover if an ordinary person would not have suffered serious emotional harm. But if that "reasonable person" threshold is met, a person may recover for all harm subjectively suffered, even if that suffering is greater than an ordinary person's because of a predisposition or special vulnerability.

The requirement that emotional harm be serious in order to be recoverable ameliorates two concerns regarding providing a claim for negligent infliction of emotional harm. The threshold reduces the universe of potential claims by eliminating claims for routine, everyday distress that is a part of life in modern society. And at the same time, the seriousness threshold assists in ensuring that claims are genuine, as the circumstances can better be assessed by a court and jury as to whether emotional harm would genuinely be suffered. . . .

m. Property damage. Recovery for emotional harm resulting

242

from negligently caused harm to personal property is not permitted under this Section. Emotional harm due to harm to personal property is insufficiently frequent or significant to justify a tort remedy. While pets are often quite different from other chattels in terms of emotional attachment, an actor who negligently injures another's pet is not liable for emotional harm suffered by the pet's owner. This rule against liability for emotional harm secondary to injury to a pet limits the liability of veterinarians in the event of malpractice and serves to make veterinary services more readily available for pets. Although harm to pets (and chattels with sentimental value) can cause real and serious emotional harm in some cases, lines—arbitrary at times—that limit recovery for emotional harm are necessary. Indeed, injury to a close personal friend may cause serious emotional harm, but that harm is similarly not recoverable under this Chapter. However, recovery for intentionally inflicted emotional harm is not barred when the defendant's method of inflicting harm is by means of causing harm to property, including an animal.

n. Strict liability. The Products Liability Restatement does not address recovery for stand-alone emotional harm. But Subsection (a) of this Section can serve as a basis for recovery to a plaintiff who is put in danger of imminent bodily harm due to a product defect. . . . [O]ften the basis for liability in a products-liability case is a standard equivalent to negligence, rather than true strict liability. However, as with negligence, courts have not yet worked out the categories of activities or undertakings that would support recovery for emotional harm in products-liability cases under Subsection (b) of this Section, and, consequently, this Restatement leaves that matter to future development. . . .

In the case of emotional harm caused by wild animals. . . . [this Restatement] supports liability for emotional harm caused by a wild animal. . . . Similar reasoning is applicable to abnormally dangerous animals who are dangerous because of the risk of attacking human beings.

o. Respecting the domain of other torts protecting specific emotional interests. A variety of other torts protect specific aspects of emotional tranquility. They include defamation, invasion of privacy, false imprisonment, and malicious prosecution. The more general protection for emotional harm contained in this Section should not be used to dilute or modify the requirements of those torts, especially those with a communicative aspect because of the special role of communication in the American legal system. As with intentional infliction of emotional harm, when the allegedly tortious conduct is communicative, it may be subject to constitutional and common-law protection and privileges.

Similarly, when protection of an identified emotional interest is removed from tort liability, claims for infliction of emotional harm under this Chapter are unavailable for conduct that would have infringed that interest. For example, the torts of criminal conversation and alienation of affection protected a spouse's specific interest in his or her partner's remaining monogamous and a more general interest in family harmony. In jurisdictions that have abolished those torts, an actor is not subject to liability under this Chapter for conduct that would have subjected the actor to liability under those torts. However, if the actor's conduct goes beyond that comprising the abolished tort, the actor may be subject to liability.

§ 48. Negligent Infliction of Emotional Harm Resulting from Bodily Harm to a Third Person

Restatement of the Law Third, Torts: Liability for Physical and Emotional Harm

An actor who negligently causes sudden serious bodily injury to a third person is subject to liability for serious emotional harm caused thereby to a person who:

(a) perceives the event contemporaneously, and

(b) is a close family member of the person suffering the bodily injury.

Comment:

a. Scope and history. This Section reflects the rule first adopted by the California Supreme Court in Dillon v. Legg, 441 P.2d 912 (Cal. 1968) and the evolution of that rule. Before *Dillon*, American courts permitted a person to recover for negligently caused emotional harm only if the person suffered physical impact due to the defendant's negligent conduct or, later, was personally in the "zone of danger" created by the defendant's negligent conduct. In *Dillon*, the court allowed a mother who witnessed the defendant's car hit her son to recover for her own emotional harm even though the defendant's car never touched her and even though she herself was never in danger of being hit. The plaintiff's emotional harm was due solely to witnessing the accident that harmed her son, a third party. Most American courts have now adopted some version of this "bystander" rule. Liability under this Section is independent of whether liability exists under § 47. . . .

c. Policy or principle for withdrawing liability. Just as § 7(b) provides for the withdrawal of liability through a no-duty ruling in exceptional cases on grounds of principle or policy, so too in the area of emotional harm, a court may decide that an identified and articulated policy is weighty enough to require the withdrawal of liability. Some of the policies that might dictate a withdrawal of liability are already reflected in limitations on liability in this Section, such as the requirement that the emotional harm suffered be serious.

d. Bystander recovery for emotional harm: derivative claim. In addition to the requirements of this Section, a bystander's cause of action for negligently inflicted emotional harm is derivative of the physically injured person's tort claim against the tortfeasor. To recover for emotional harm under this Section, a plaintiff must prove that the physically injured person could recover from the tortfeasor. Any contributory negligence of the physically injured person is imputed to the plaintiff. . . . In addition to the physically injured person's contributory negligence, the bystander's claim is also reduced by the bystander's own contributory negligence. Thus, when a plaintiff-father's negligent supervision enables his young child to wander to a dangerous area where the defendant negligently injures the child, the father's recovery for emotional harm will be reduced because of his own negligence.

e. Contemporaneous perception. To recover under this Section, a person who suffers emotional harm must have contemporaneously perceived the events that caused physical harm to the third person. It is not enough that the person later learned about the events, later viewed a recording of them, or later observed the resulting bodily injuries. While in most cases the person will see the events, the perception required by this Section is not limited to sight.

Illustrations:

1. Thompson runs a red light and hits Rodriguez's daughter who suffers serious injury. Rodriguez sees the accident from the sidewalk and suffers serious emotional harm. Rodriguez can recover under this Section.

2. Same facts as Illustration 1, except Rodriguez does not witness the accident but instead learns about it through a phone call from the hospital treating his injured daughter. Rodriguez then goes to the hospital, sees the injuries, and suffers serious emotional harm. Rodriguez cannot recover under this Section.

3. Same facts as Illustration 2, except Rodriguez learns about the accident by seeing video footage of it two hours later on the evening news. Rodriguez suffers serious emotional harm as a result. Rodriguez cannot recover under this Section.

4. Same facts as Illustration 1, except Rodriguez is visually impaired and thus does not see the accident, but he hears the screeching of brakes, the impact of the car, and his daughter's screams. Rodriguez can recover under this Section.

The contemporaneous-perception requirement may require fine distinctions in close cases. For example, a plaintiff might first hear a crash but only later turn and see that a close family member was harmed. Or parents might witness their home burning down, knowing their child is inside the house. This Section does not provide precise rules about what constitutes contemporaneous perception or which specific events comprising an accident must be perceived. . . .

The requirement that the plaintiff contemporaneously perceive the accident reflects a recognition that courts must draw lines and that contemporaneous perception of an accident, in most instances, is a more substantial shock than learning about it later. There is an unavoidable arbitrariness to the line-drawing in this area.

Beyond the question of what aspects of an accident must be perceived, this Section leaves for future development whether the events must be perceived while the plaintiff is physically present or whether contemporaneous transmission by some medium is sufficiently equivalent to physical presence. Continuing developments in communication technology will no doubt affect the determination.

f. Close family member. To recover under this Section, a person suffering emotional harm must be a close family member of the person who suffers bodily injury.

Illustrations:

5. Same facts as Illustration 1. As the physically injured person's parent, Rodriguez can recover under this Section.

6. Wilson runs a red light and hits Walsh with his automobile. Garcia, a long-time business associate of Walsh, sees the accident and suffers serious emotional harm. Garcia cannot recover under this Section because Garcia is not related to Walsh.

As with the requirement of contemporaneous perception, individual cases can present close questions of who qualifies as a close family member. For example, a grandparent who lives in the household may have a different status from a cousin who does not. The case law in each jurisdiction will develop its own rules in this respect. . . .

The requirement that the bystander be a close family member reflects a pragmatic recognition that a line must be drawn and that witnessing physical injury to a close family member will, in general, cause a more serious shock than if the injured party is not related.

Sometimes people live functionally in a nuclear family without formal legal family ties. When defining what constitutes a close family relationship, courts should take into account changing practices and social norms and employ a functional approach to determine what constitutes a family.

246

g. Relationship to foreseeability. Many courts refer to the requirements of this Section—contemporaneous perception of the accident and a close family relationship—as indications that the emotional distress is both genuine and foreseeable. Some courts state that the actual test is foreseeability and that a person can recover even if the formal requirements are not satisfied. This approach is unsatisfactory because genuine emotional harm can occur and is foreseeable in many situations in which courts clearly would not permit recovery. For example, a negligent airline that causes the death of a beloved celebrity can foresee genuine emotional harm to the celebrity's fans, but no court would permit recovery for emotional harm under these circumstances.

The law of negligence has never applied the ordinary rules of foreseeability to emotional harm. Pure emotional harm is generally not recoverable not because the harm is not genuine or foreseeable, but because as a matter of policy it is an injury whose cost the legal system should not normally shift, even to someone who is negligent. Courts have created exceptions to this general no-liability rule, such as the rule stated in this Section. It is tempting to expand these exceptions in close cases by referring to a more general requirement such as foreseeability, but that approach would eviscerate the general rule that pure emotional harm is normally not recoverable.

Consequently, the requirements of contemporaneous perception and a close family relationship are pragmatic concessions to the need to draw lines as well as reflections of the judgment that the shock of contemporaneously perceiving bodily injury is an especially traumatic experience to a close family member. Both requirements must be satisfied; they are not merely factors to be considered in an ultimate judgment about whether liability can be imposed.

The requirements in this Section might be described or criticized as arbitrary. And they are arbitrary in the sense that they are both over-broad and under-broad (as is any rule) and that some other rules, modestly different, might equally well serve their function. . . . But the rules in this Section are not arbitrary in the more pejorative sense of the term; they serve a function and are neither random nor irrational. Limits are required for emotional harm because of its ubiquity, and an alternative to workable and effective limits for such liability could be a rule of no liability. This Section permits liability, albeit in a circumscribed class of cases.

h. Role of judge and jury. Consistent with the rejection of foreseeability as the test for recovery under this Section, determining which classes of family members are owed a duty by those who negligently cause serious physical injury to another is a question of law for the court. Those who are not within the class are not

247

owed a duty. If the class of relationships is specifically defined, ordinarily there will not be a factual dispute requiring jury determination. On the other hand, if the class is defined more generally or functionally, it may be necessary in some cases for the jury to decide whether a given plaintiff has the requisite relationship. Among those in the class permitted to maintain a claim under this Section, the quality of the relationship between the plaintiff and the accident victim will bear primarily on the measure of damages, not on the question of liability.

Illustrations:

7. John drives Jane, his 12-year-old daughter, to school. Just after Jane steps out of the car, Robert, another driver, negligently runs into Jane, causing her serious physical injury. John observes the accident. In a jurisdiction that requires a bystander to be within the second degree of consanguinity in order to satisfy the "close family member" requirement for recovery of emotional harm, the jury would have no role in determining that John satisfies the requisite relationship, as there could be no genuine dispute about the issue.

8. Carol is a good friend of Jody's and godmother of Jody's daughter, Maddy. While Carol is visiting, Maddy falls down an unlit staircase and suffers serious personal injury. Carol sues Conrad Co., the landowner who negligently failed to replace the lights in the stairwell, for serious emotional harm arising from her observation of Maddy's fall. In a jurisdiction that limits bystander recovery to those in the nuclear family of the third person, as a matter of law Conrad Co. would not be subject to liability.

9. Same facts as Illustration 8, except that the jurisdiction has decided that bystander recovery for "close family members" can be available to those in an intimate, longstanding, and emotionally significant relationship with the injured third party. If Carol introduces facts from which a reasonable person could conclude she has such a relationship with Maddy, it is for the jury to determine whether Carol is within the class that can recover for serious emotional harm under this Section.

i. No requirement of resulting physical consequences of the emotional harm. Significant emotional harm often is accompanied by illness or other bodily harm. This Section is not limited, however, to cases in which the emotional harm has caused illness or other bodily manifestations. The circumstance of contemporaneous perception of serious bodily injury or death to a close family member is sufficient to provide confidence in the genuineness of the harm.

j. No requirement of physical impact or fear for one's own safety. This Section applies to a person who suffers emotional harm from contemporaneously perceiving bodily injury to a close family member even though the actor's negligent conduct does not cause direct physical impact to the person or cause that person to have fear or apprehension for his or her own safety. . . .

l. Serious bodily injury. The requirement that the third person must suffer "serious" bodily injury is grounded in the need to provide limits on liability under this Section. It is also based on the generality that modest or minor physical injury is unlikely to produce a substantial emotional response by an observer, even one who is a close family member. Death, significant permanent disfigurement, or loss of a body part or function will almost always be sufficient for a jury to find this requirement satisfied. By contrast, bruises, cuts, single simple fractures, and other injuries that do not require immediate medical treatment will rarely be sufficient to satisfy this requirement.

m. Sudden bodily injury to third person. In addition to the third person suffering serious bodily injury, the injury must occur in a sudden and dramatic manner. Slow deterioration, even to a seriously disabling condition or death, is insufficient to support liability under this Section.

n. Strict liability. . . . [L]iability for emotional harm to a bystander by means of a product defect that causes physical harm to a third party is sufficiently confined and coherent that it has received acceptance and is endorsed by this Comment, even though the black letter is limited to negligence. Many strict-products-liability claims require proof very much akin to that required for negligence in order to prove a defect and therefore are not dramatically different from negligence claims. . . .

PART V

LIABILITY OF EMPLOYERS AND THOSE WHO HIRE INDEPENDENT CONTRACTORS

———

CHAPTER 14

DIRECT AND VICARIOUS LIABILITY OF THOSE WHO HIRE EMPLOYEES AND INDEPENDENT CONTRACTORS

A. OVERVIEW OF LIABILITY OF EMPLOYERS AND OTHER PRINCIPALS

§ 7.03. Principal's Liability—In General

Restatement of the Law Third, Agency

(1) A principal is subject to direct liability to a third party harmed by an agent's conduct when

(a) as stated in § 7.04, the agent acts with actual authority or the principal ratifies the agent's conduct and

(i) the agent's conduct is tortious, or

(ii) the agent's conduct, if that of the principal, would subject the principal to tort liability; or

(b) as stated in § 7.05, the principal is negligent in selecting, supervising, or otherwise controlling the agent; or

(c) as stated in § 7.06, the principal delegates performance of a duty to use care to protect other persons or their property to an agent who fails to perform the duty.

(2) A principal is subject to vicarious liability to a third party harmed by an agent's conduct when

(a) as stated in § 7.07, the agent is an employee who commits a tort while acting within the scope of employment; or

(b) as stated in § 7.08, the agent commits a tort when acting with apparent authority in dealing with a third party on or purportedly on behalf of the principal.

Comment:

a. Scope and cross-references. This section provides an overview of the bases on which a principal may be subject to liability for the conduct of an agent or other actor. . . .

b. Liability on basis of principal's own conduct; vicarious liability. A principal's own fault may subject the principal to liability to a third party harmed by an agent's conduct. Often termed "direct liability," such liability stems either from the principal's relationship with an agent whose conduct harms a third party or from the agent's failure to perform a duty owed by the principal to the third party. . . . An agent's tort may, separately, subject a principal to vicarious liability. . . . A principal who is vicariously liable may, additionally, be subject to liability on the basis of the principal's own conduct.

253

Significant consequences may follow from the distinction between direct and vicarious liability. In particular, a principal's vicarious liability turns on whether the agent is liable. In most cases, direct liability requires fault on the part of the principal whereas vicarious liability does not require that the principal be at fault. The distinction may also be relevant to whether a loss is insurable. Principals, not agents, are subject to vicarious liability. . . .

c. *Organizational principals.* A principal that is not an individual can take action only through its agents, who typically are individuals. Even when an agent is not an individual, its ability to act derives from its own agents. An organization's tortious conduct consists of conduct by agents of the organization that is attributable to it. An organization may breach a duty of care that it owes to a third party even though the breach cannot be attributed to any single agent of the organization. Thus, an organization's conduct may be tortious when it fails to fulfill a duty that the organization owes to a third party. For example, a custodian owes a duty of reasonable care to third parties with respect to risks created by those in its custody. A custodian that is an organization would breach its duty of reasonable care through the action or inaction of its employees and other agents, including the prescription and enforcement by managerial agents of directives and guidelines to be followed by other agents.

d. *Agents with multiple principals.* An agent who commits a tort may have more than one principal for at least some purposes. . . .

(2). *"Lent employees," or "borrowed servants."* When work requires specialized skills or equipment or requires that an actor perform a task on less than a full-time basis, it is not unusual that the actor who performs the work is employed by a firm that contracts to provide the actor's services to another firm. . . . When an actor negligently injures a third party while performing work for the firm that has contracted for the actor's services, the question is whether that firm (often termed the "special employer") or the initial employer (often termed the "general employer"), or both, should be subject to liability to the third party. Liability should be allocated to the employer in the better position to take measures to prevent the injury suffered by the third party. An employer is in that position if the employer has the right to control an employee's conduct. When both a general and special employer have the right to control an employee's conduct, the practical history of direction may establish that one employer in fact ceded its right of control to the other, whether through its failure to exercise the right or otherwise.

It is a question of fact whether a general or a special employer, or both, have the right to control an employee's conduct. Factors that a court may consider in making this determination include the extent of control that an employer may exercise over the details of an employee's work and the timing of the work; the relationship between the employee's work and the nature of the special employer's business; the nature of the employee's work, the skills required to perform it, and the degree of supervision customarily associated with the work; the duration of the employee's work in the special employer's firm; the identity of the employer who furnishes equipment or other instrumentalities requisite to performing the work; and the method of payment for the work. . . .

e. Punitive damages. When a principal is subject to vicarious liability as a consequence of a tort committed by an employee or other agent, the principal is subject to liability to the plaintiff for the entire share of comparative responsibility assigned to the agent. . . .

Punitive damages may also be awarded against a principal when the principal is subject to vicarious liability for the agent's tortious conduct if punitive damages could be awarded against the agent under applicable law in the relevant jurisdiction. . . . Jurisdictions vary, however, on the circumstances under which it is proper to award punitive damages against a principal. A slight majority of states hold that punitive damages may be awarded against a principal that is vicariously liable on the basis that an employee-agent acted within the scope of employment when committing a tort, without requiring any additional showing of culpability on the part of the employer. A substantial minority of states . . . require[ ] a showing that the tortious conduct was that of a managerial agent or that the principal was otherwise implicated in the conduct. The [latter] approach . . . is preferable because it requires consideration of circumstances relevant to a principal's culpability. . . .

Illustration:

    1. P, a landlord, employs A Ejectment Co. to dispossess a tenant. P knows that A Ejectment Co. has a reputation for using undue force in dealing with tenants. E, an employee of A Ejectment Co., in accordance with its usual methods, commits an unprovoked battery on T, a tenant, in order to induce T to leave. In an action by T against P, punitive damages can be awarded.

Although there is no rigid test to determine whether an agent is a "managerial agent" . . ., the determination should focus on the agent's discretion to make decisions that would have prevented the injury to the plaintiff or that determine policies of the organization relevant to the risk that resulted in the injury. The title that an agent holds is not dispositive, nor is the fact that the agent is not among the highest in an organization's hierarchy. If an

255

agent in fact manages a business or enterprise, the agent is a "managerial agent" of the principal on whose behalf it manages, although the agent is external to the principal's own organizational structure. . . .

B. DIRECT LIABILITY IN NEGLIGENCE OF EMPLOYERS

§ 7.05. Principal's Negligence in Conducting Activity Through Agent; Principal's Special Relationship with Another Person

Restatement of the Law Third, Agency

> **(1) A principal who conducts an activity through an agent is subject to liability for harm to a third party caused by the agent's conduct if the harm was caused by the principal's negligence in selecting, training, retaining, supervising, or otherwise controlling the agent.**

> **(2) When a principal has a special relationship with another person, the principal owes that person a duty of reasonable care with regard to risks arising out of the relationship, including the risk that agents of the principal will harm the person with whom the principal has such a special relationship.**

Comment:

a. Scope and cross-references. The rules stated in this section are specific instances of general tort-law principles. . . .

b. In general; relationship to other bases for liability. The rules stated in this section stem from general doctrines of tort law not limited in their applicability to relationships of agency. . . . A foreseeable risk of harm may be created when one person conducts an activity through another person. For example, the actor chosen for a task may lack competence to perform it without endangering others. A task may require using an instrumentality that is dangerous to others unless the user has appropriate skill or supervision. Some tasks require performance in settings that pose a foreseeable risk of criminal or other intentional misconduct against third parties or their property unless the actor is chosen with due care in reference to that risk.

Illustrations:

1. P, who owns an apartment building, employs A as its on-site manager. P knows that A is impatient and has a violent temper. T, one of P's tenants, complains to A about the lack of heat in T's apartment. Enraged, A assaults T. P is subject to liability to T. P hired A knowing that A's tempera-

ment was not suited to the foreseeable demands of on-site residential management. P's liability to T under this section is independent of whether P is subject to liability to T under § 7.07 [respondeat superior] on the basis that A's conduct was within the scope of A's employment by P.

3. P, who owns a furniture store, employs A to deliver furniture to retail customers. A's duties include entering customers' homes to situate items they have purchased. Having entered T's home to deliver a sofa, A assaults T. Prior to employing A, P conducted no check of A's background. Had P done so, P would have discovered criminal convictions for assault. Had P known of A's criminal history, P would not have employed A to make deliveries. P is subject to liability to T. . . .

c. Causation and duty. Liability under this rule is limited by basic principles of tort law, including requirements of causation and duty.

Illustration:

5. Same facts as Illustration 1, except that P reasonably believes that A's temperament is suited to the duties of on-site apartment management on the basis of P's inquiries to A's prior employers. However, P does not check with law-enforcement authorities. Had P so checked, P would have discovered that A has been convicted of income-tax evasion. P would not have viewed that conviction as material to A's duties as an on-site manager, which do not involve tax-compliance tasks, and P would have employed A had P known of A's tax-evasion conviction. P is not subject to liability to T as a consequence of A's assault on T. Even if P acted negligently in failing to check A's record with law-enforcement authorities, P's failure to detect A's tax-evasion conviction was not the factual cause of harm to T and did not increase the risk of an assault by A against T. . . .

e. Principal's special relationship to person subject to risk. General principles of tort law impose a duty of reasonable care on an actor in a special relationship with another with regard to risks that arise within the scope of the relationship. . . .

When an employee or other agent harms a person with whom the principal has a special relationship, the principal may be subject to liability although the employee or other agent acted without actual or apparent authority. An employer may be subject to liability although in harming the person an employee acted outside the scope of employment. The fact that a principal has delegated performance of its duty, whether or not the delegate is an agent, does not relieve the principal of liability.

The basis for imposing liability on a principal or employer

257

under this rule is its failure to discharge its duty of reasonable care to the person with whom it has a special relationship. A principal may fail to discharge its duty although it used reasonable care in choosing its employees and other agents. For example, in some settings and relationships, a person's vulnerability to harm may affect the measures that a principal may reasonably be required to take to safeguard against risks, including those posed by employees and other agents. In particular, relationships that expose young children to the risk of sexual abuse are ones in which a high degree of vulnerability may reasonably require measures of protection not necessary for persons who are older and better able to safeguard themselves. Such measures may include prohibiting unsupervised contact between a child and an employee. Likewise, persons of any age taken into custody by law-enforcement officers are vulnerable to risks of harm against which they may lack the ability to safeguard themselves.

C. VICARIOUS LIABILITY OF EMPLOYERS FOR TORTS COMMITTED BY EMPLOYEES

§ 2.04. Respondeat Superior

Restatement of the Law Third, Agency

>   An employer is subject to liability for torts committed by employees while acting within the scope of their employment.

Comment:

b. In general. . . . The doctrine of respondeat superior is fundamental to the operation of the tort system in the United States. The doctrine establishes a principle of employer liability for the costs that work-related torts impose on third parties. Its scope is limited to the employment relationship and to conduct falling within the scope of that relationship because an employer has the right to control how work is done. . . .

Functionally tied though the doctrine is to tort law, it has long been classified as an element of agency doctrine. In early times, a master's servants were treated as part of the household and their relation to the master made their acts his responsibility as the head of the household. . . . In the first treatise on agency published in the United States, William Paley stated, as a principle of agency law, that "[a] master is responsible for the negligence or unskillfulness of a servant acting in the prosecution of his service, though not under his immediate direction." William Paley, A Treatise on the Law of Principal and Agent, Chiefly with Reference to Mercantile Transactions 126 (3d ed. 1840). As the location of work moved outside the household and into mercantile and industrial settings, an employer's responsibility for harm caused by employee activities followed the employer's right to control how work is done.

Viewed as a doctrine within the law of agency, respondeat superior is a basis upon which the legal consequences of one person's acts may be attributed to another person. Most often the doctrine applies to acts that have not been specifically directed by an employer but that are the consequence of inattentiveness or poor judgment on the part of an employee acting within the job description. Most cases applying the doctrine involve negligence resulting in physical injury to a person or to property. But respondeat superior is not the exclusive basis on which an employer may be vicariously liable for torts committed by employees. Many employees have jobs in which they interact with third parties, as do nonemployee agents, by making transactions and statements on the employer's behalf. This activity is transactional and communicative in nature. When it is misused, for example to perpetrate a fraud for the employee's sole benefit, the employer's responsibility is often determined by whether the party injured reasonably believed the employee's activity to be authorized. The fraud is associated with a transaction, in contrast to the negligent physical actions to which respondeat superior is conventionally applied. Many cases apply the doctrine of apparent authority to determine whether an employer is liable for employee torts associated with such transactions and statements. The application of apparent-authority doctrine, and not respondeat superior, may be a consequence of the generalization that employees work with things but agents deal with people. Many employees and agents, of course, do both, and "things" are often instrumentalities for communicating with others.

Respondeat superior is inapplicable when a principal does not have the right to control the actions of the agent that makes the relationship between principal and agent performing the service one of employment. In general, employment contemplates a continuing relationship and a continuing set of duties that the employer and employee owe to each other. Agents who are retained as the need arises and who are not otherwise employees of their principal normally operate their own business enterprises and are not, except in limited respects, integrated into the principal's enterprise so that a task may be completed or a specified objective accomplished. Therefore, respondeat superior does not apply.

Respondeat superior assigns responsibility to an employer for the legal consequences that result from employees' errors of judgment and lapses in attentiveness when the acts or omissions are within the scope of employment. A firm or organization that employs individuals usually structures their work to limit the scope of discretion and individual action, thus limiting the occasions when unreasonable decisions are likely to be made. Impulsive conduct is not typical of firms or organizations. The firm as a principal may always act more rationally and reasonably than would most individuals acting by themselves because different individuals are assigned different tasks, often monitoring and checking each other. Respondeat superior creates an incentive for principals to choose employees and structure work within the organization so as to reduce the incidence of tortious conduct. This incentive may reduce the incidence of tortious conduct more effectively than doctrines that impose liability solely on an individual tortfeasor.

Respondeat superior also reflects the likelihood that an employer will be more likely to satisfy a judgment. Moreover, an employer may insure against liability encompassing the consequences of all employees' actions, whereas individual employees lack the incentive and ability to insure beyond any individual's liability or assets. . . .

D. Overview of Liability of Those Who Hire Independent Contractors

Scope Note: This Chapter addresses the liability of actors who hire independent contractors, including both the actor's direct liability in negligence as well as the actor's vicarious liability for the torts of an independent contractor. Under the traditional rule, one who hires an independent contractor was not liable when the independent contractor is a cause of harm. The rule, however, was subject to multiple exceptions, which fall into two categories. One category consists of claims relating to the hirer's own negligence. The second includes situations that, on the basis of policy, warrant subjecting the hirer to vicarious liability when the contractor tortiously causes physical harm.

[T]his Chapter addresses each category—direct negligence and vicarious liability—according to the separate analytical framework that applies to each. Direct-negligence claims against one who hires an independent contractor entail a specific application of the negligence principles of this Restatement. By contrast, the rules that historically have permitted some vicarious-liability claims against those who hire independent contractors stem from theoretical and practical considerations relating to vicarious liability in this context.

As to claims of direct negligence, §§ 55 and 56 apply the general principles of negligence in this Restatement to situations in which an actor hires an independent contractor. Under these principles, an actor who creates a risk of harm ordinarily is subject to a duty of reasonable care. See § 7(a). When an actor's conduct does not create a risk of harm, the actor does not owe a duty of care unless one of the affirmative duties in §§ 38-44 is applicable. Thus, an actor who hires an independent contractor owes a duty of care when (1) the independent contractor is hired to perform an

260

activity that creates a risk of harm or (2) the actor is subject to any of the affirmative duties provided in §§ 38-44 and hires an independent contractor to perform any of the obligations required by the affirmative duty. . . .

Sections 57-65 relate to vicarious liability. As a general rule, an actor who hires an independent contractor is not subject to vicarious liability for harm caused by the contractor's action. This general rule, however, is subject to exceptions. . . .

E. DIRECT LIABILITY IN NEGLIGENCE OF THOSE WHO HIRE INDEPENDENT CONTRACTORS

§ 55. Direct Liability in Negligence of Those Who Hire Independent Contractors

Restatement of the Law Third, Torts: Liability for Physical and Emotional Harm

> An actor:
>
> (1) who hires an independent contractor to perform an activity that creates a risk of physical harm; or
>
> (2) who is under any of the affirmative duties provided in §§ 38-44 and hires an independent contractor to perform any of the obligations required by the affirmative duty
>
> is subject to liability for physical harm when the actor's negligence is a factual cause of any such harm within the scope of liability, subject to the duty limitation in § 56 and other duty limitations under this Restatement.

Comment:

c. *Duty.* . . . This Section applies [the duty principles of this Restatement] to instances in which an actor hires an independent contractor and the actor's negligence is a factual cause of harm within the scope of liability. An actor may hire an independent contractor to carry out an activity that creates a risk of physical harm to others. Because the activity entails a risk of harm, its initiation by the actor—albeit through a decision to use an independent contractor—constitutes conduct creating a risk of harm. For instance, a person might decide to move furniture from his apartment to a new house. The actor's decision to move furniture creates risk to others when it is carried out, whether the actor or an independent contractor carries out the activity. Thus, the principles of § 7 apply. The hirer owes the ordinary duty of reasonable care unless the duty limitation in § 56 or other duty limitations in this Restatement apply. . . .

e. *Negligence.* In determining whether the actor is negligent,

261

the definition set out in § 3 applies. The actor's negligence may take various forms. These include the failure to use reasonable care to select a competent contractor; that is, a contractor who possesses the knowledge, skill, experience, equipment, and personal characteristics that a reasonable person would realize a contractor should have to perform the work without creating unreasonable risk of injury. In addition, the hirer's negligence might include giving orders or directions to the contractor without exercising reasonable care; failing to exercise reasonable care to discover dangerous conditions on the land and to eliminate or ameliorate those that are known or should have been discovered by the exercise of reasonable care; failing to use reasonable care as to artificial conditions and activities on the land that pose a risk of physical harm to those off the land; and failing to exercise reasonable care with respect to any part of the work over which the actor has retained control.

Illustrations:

1. Telephone Company lays underground cable in parts of a city. Telephone Company hires Martin as the independent contractor to perform the digging necessary for laying the cable. When the job starts, Martin has no previous digging or construction experience and only several hours of practice using a trenching machine. Telephone Company does not inquire into Martin's experience in using trenching machines or working around gas pipes. During the course of the digging, Martin negligently strikes and damages a gas line, causing an explosion that seriously injures Anthony. Telephone Company is subject to liability to Anthony under this Section for failing to use reasonable care in selecting a competent contractor.

2. Tonya hires Blue Moon Movers, a local moving company, to transport furniture and packages from her old office to her new office. Tonya is a chemist, and some of her packages contain chemical mixtures that are combustible at temperatures over 100 degrees Fahrenheit. Tonya does not advise Blue Moon Movers that several boxes contain chemicals combustible at high temperatures. The move occurs on a summer day, and the temperature inside the truck exceeds 100 degrees. An explosion results, causing a collision that injures Darren, another driver. Tonya is subject to liability to Darren under this Section for failing to warn Blue Moon about the chemicals or to take other precautions as to the chemicals. . . .

§ 56. Duty Limitation as to Work Entrusted to an Independent Contractor

Restatement of the Law Third, Torts: Liability for Physical and Emotional Harm

(a) An actor who entrusts work to an independent contractor owes no duty as to the manner in which the work is performed by the contractor, except as provided in Subsection (b).

(b) When an actor entrusts work to an independent contractor but retains control over any part of the work, the actor has a duty of reasonable care as to the exercise of the retained control.

Comment:

b. *Duty.* . . . Although an actor selects, hires, and instructs an independent contractor, the hirer generally relinquishes control of the work to the independent contractor. The contractor thus has control over the manner and means of the contracted work relinquished to it, as well as superior knowledge about risks and precautions. Generally, the hirer has little practical ability to improve the level of reasonable care as to work being performed under the control of the independent contractor. Thus, obligating the hirer to exercise reasonable care over the manner in which the contractor performs the work once the work is entrusted to the contractor would not yield safety benefits and might, indeed, interfere with safety-related decisions and actions that otherwise would be taken by the contractor, who is under a duty to use reasonable care and often has superior knowledge and ability relating to safety in the work. Over time, these insights have formed the basis of the doctrine, followed in virtually all jurisdictions, that a hirer is not subject to liability for negligence as to the manner in which a contractor performs work entrusted to the contractor and over which the hirer has retained no control. . . .

Illustrations:

1. John, a hotel owner, contacts AmeriPipe to deliver and install a hollow steel pipe 20 feet long and 8 inches in diameter to fit vertically over an existing stub of pipe secured in the ground. John plans to use the resulting structure to display a sign for the hotel. AmeriPipe's representative tells John that AmeriPipe does not ordinarily install such pipes, but only delivers them. When AmeriPipe's workers deliver the pipe, however, John renews his request that they install the pipe, offering to pay extra for the installation. AmeriPipe's workers, after contacting their supervisors, agree to go ahead with the installation. John returns to his office while the workers attempt the installation by using their truck, hooks, chains, and additional poles for stabilization. The pipe slips off, bouncing on a passing car and injuring the driver. John owes a duty of care under § 55 and is subject to liability to the injured driver for lack of reasonable care in selecting a competent contractor. The duty limitation in § 56 does not apply because the case does not involve allegations that John failed to use reasonable care as to the manner in which AmeriPipe performed the work.

2. Same facts as Illustration 1, except when John first contacts AmeriPipe, the company's representative sends John information showing that the company has extensive experience in installing pipes and is bonded for this purpose. John is not subject to negligence liability under § 55 because he has not failed to use reasonable care. Further, John does not have a duty of care with respect to the manner in which AmeriPipe performed the work because John did not retain control over any part of the work. . . .

c. *Retained control: meaning.* For Subsection (b) to apply, the hirer must retain some degree of control over the manner in which the work is done, such that the contractor is not entirely free to do the work in the contractor's own manner. The extent of control necessary to warrant a duty under Subsection (b) is less than the control deemed necessary for an employer–employee relationship. Nonetheless, the control necessary to trigger a duty under Subsection (b) requires more than merely the general right to order the work stopped or resumed, to inspect its progress or to receive reports, to make suggestions or recommendations that need not necessarily be followed, or to prescribe alterations and deviations.

In assessing control for purposes of Subsection (b), both the right to control and the actual exercise of control are relevant. . . .

F. VICARIOUS LIABILITY OF THOSE WHO HIRE INDEPENDENT CONTRACTORS

§ 57. Vicarious Liability of Those Who Hire Independent Contractors: General Rule

Restatement of the Law Third, Torts: Liability for Physical and Emotional Harm

Except as stated in §§ 58-65, an actor who hires an independent contractor is not subject to vicarious liability for physical harm caused by the tortious conduct of the contractor.

Comment:

a. *Background and scope.* This Section sets forth the general rule . . . that one who hires an independent contractor is not subject to vicarious liability for harm caused by the tortious conduct of the contractor. This general rule is subject to exceptions. . . .

c. *Rationales relating to vicarious liability for hirers of independent contractors.* Several rationales support the general rule that those who hire independent contractors are not subject to vicarious liability for harms caused by the negligence of the contractor. In employer–employee settings, vicarious liability has

264

been seen as consistent with fairness because the rule places on the employer's enterprise the costs of harms that result from activities characteristic of, and of benefit to, the enterprise. By contrast, in hirer–independent contractor settings, the independent contractor is the person or entity that regularly benefits from the risk-creating enterprise. Although the hirer obtains the gains achieved by the contractor, that alone is not sufficient to impose vicarious liability. Likewise, a corrective-justice rationale does not warrant generally imposing liability on one who, without fault and without a right of control, hired the person whose negligence caused the harm. As to deterrence, hirers of independent contractors are less able than employers to monitor or ensure safety precautions because hirers lack control over the manner and means of the work. Further, hirers of independent contractors have less knowledge than employers about the safety-related details and methods of the work.

By contrast, one consideration favoring vicarious liability for hirers is the potential for insolvent contractors. When an insolvent contractor negligently causes harm, the claimant will be unable to recover from the primarily responsible party. In addition, insolvent contractors may have inadequate incentives to use reasonable care. Subjecting the hirer to vicarious liability gives hirers the incentive to hire solvent contractors. Although this benefit is widely recognized, it is not sufficient to support a general rule of vicarious liability for those who hire independent contractors.

Over time, courts have created multiple exceptions to the general rule of no vicarious liability for those who hire independent contractors. . . . Reasons of principle and policy support limited departures from the general rule of no vicarious liability, as to each of these areas.

§ 58. Work Involving Abnormally Dangerous Activities

Restatement of the Law Third, Torts: Liability for Physical and Emotional Harm

An actor who hires an independent contractor to do work that the actor knows or should know involves an abnormally dangerous activity is subject to vicarious liability for physical harm when the abnormally dangerous activity is a factual cause of any such harm within the scope of liability.

Comment:

b. Definition of abnormally dangerous activity. "An activity is abnormally dangerous if: (1) the activity creates a foreseeable and highly significant risk of physical harm even when reasonable care is exercised by all actors; and (2) the activity is not one of common usage." Section 20(b). For discussion and Illustrations of abnormally dangerous activity, see § 20.

265

c. Rationale. An actor who engages in an abnormally dangerous activity is subject to strict liability. See § 20(a). This longstanding doctrine recognizes that, even absent negligence, liability is appropriate when an actor chooses to engage in an activity that is both uncommon within the community and imposes a highly significant risk. See § 20, Comment *d.* Similar principles apply when an actor engages an independent contractor for work that the actor knows or should know involves an abnormally dangerous activity. The hirer has chosen to conduct an activity—albeit through a contractor—that the hirer knows or should know will subject others to a highly significant risk arising from work that is uncommon among them. . . .

§ 59. Activity Posing a Peculiar Risk

Restatement of the Law Third, Torts: Liability for Physical and Emotional Harm

> **An actor who hires an independent contractor for an activity that the actor knows or should know poses a peculiar risk is subject to vicarious liability for physical harm when the independent contractor is negligent as to the peculiar risk and the negligence is a factual cause of any such harm within the scope of liability.**

Comment:

b. Definition of peculiar risk. The cases do not coalesce around a single definition of peculiar risk, in part because courts draw on and emphasize different guidelines and phrases from the Second Restatement. Under this Restatement, an activity poses a peculiar risk when, if reasonable care is not taken, the resulting risk differs from the types of risk that are usual in the community. This definition is consistent with the core features of the peculiar-risk doctrine. . . .

Illustrations:

1. Susan, an independent contractor, drives a tractor-trailer unit transporting cattle on a highway. Susan loses focus on the road and also drives at excessive speed. She loses control of the tractor-trailer, which flips over on the highway and injures John. The transportation of cattle in these circumstances in a tractor-trailer unit does not pose a peculiar risk because the risk of a truck turning over on the highway is not uncommon in the community.

2. John, attending a high-school football game, suffers a fatal electrical shock when he touches one of the light poles while he is leaning against a metal fence. The electrical conduit on the outside of the pole had become electrified because the insulation around a buried cable near the bottom of the pole

was damaged. Had a plastic bushing been installed near where the buried cable entered the metal conduit, the pole would not have been electrified. High-voltage electricity in this public place constitutes a peculiar risk because, unless reasonable precautions are taken, the risk is different from the ordinary risks to which persons in the community are ordinarily exposed.

c. *Relation to abnormally dangerous activity.* An activity posing a peculiar risk differs from an abnormally dangerous activity. An activity can pose a peculiar risk even if the risk is not especially severe; further, a peculiar risk can be avoided by the exercise of reasonable care. . . .

§ 60. Work on Instrumentalities Used in Highly Dangerous Activities

Restatement of the Law Third, Torts: Liability for Physical and Emotional Harm

An actor who hires an independent contractor is subject to vicarious liability if:

(a) the actor carries on an activity that the actor knows or should know poses a high risk of serious bodily harm or death unless the instrumentalities used are carefully constructed and maintained;

(b) the actor hires an independent contractor to construct or maintain such instrumentalities; and

(c) the independent contractor's negligence in constructing or maintaining such instrumentalities is a factual cause of harm within the scope of liability.

Comment:

b. *Application.* This Section applies if an actor engages in an activity that poses a high risk of serious bodily harm or death if the instrumentalities used in the activity have any imperfection, and if the actor hires an independent contractor for construction or maintenance of such instrumentalities. This category of activities is not the same as abnormally dangerous activities. An activity can qualify, for purposes of this Section, even if reasonable care can eliminate the danger and even if the activity is not an uncommon one. This category of activities is also not the same as activities posing a peculiar risk; the focus of this Section is the highly dangerous nature of the activity when any imperfection exists in instrumentalities involved in the activity.

Illustration:

1. Natural Gas Company supplies natural gas for the

267

county. Natural Gas Company retains Gas Supply Company to install a service line to carry gas to a new neighborhood. Gas Supply Company's employees negligently cause a slight tear in the pipe. The resulting gas leak causes an explosion that injures Sonya. Natural Gas Company is subject to vicarious liability under the rule in this Section.

§ 61. Activities Involving a Trespass, Nuisance, or Withdrawal of Support

Restatement of the Law Third, Torts: Liability for Physical and Emotional Harm

An actor who hires an independent contractor for an activity is subject to vicarious liability for physical harm if:

(a) the actor knows or should know that the activity is likely to involve a trespass, the creation of a public or private nuisance, or the withdrawal of lateral or subjacent support from the land of another;

(b) the independent contractor's activity constitutes a trespass, constitutes a public or private nuisance, or withdraws lateral or subjacent support from the land of another; and

(c) the trespass, public or private nuisance, or withdrawal of lateral or subjacent support is a factual cause of any such harm within the scope of liability.

Illustration:

1. Arnold hires Bob, an independent contractor, to construct a dam in a stream on Arnold's land. Arnold knows or should know that work on the dam makes it likely that the land upstream will be flooded if a heavy rainfall occurs. Before the completion of the dam, heavy spring rains cause flooding of Carol's land upstream. Arnold is subject to vicarious liability to Carol.

§ 62. Possessors and Lessors of Land

Restatement of the Law Third, Torts: Liability for Physical and Emotional Harm

(a) A possessor of land who hires an independent contractor for activity on the land is subject to vicarious liability for physical harm if:

(1) the possessor owes a duty of care under § 51 or § 54;

(2) the harm occurs while the possessor retains possession of the premises during the

268

activity or after the possessor has resumed possession of the land upon completion of the activity; and

(3) the independent contractor's negligence is a factual cause of any such harm within the scope of liability.

(b) A lessor of land who hires an independent contractor for activity on the land is subject to vicarious liability for physical harm if:

(1) the lessor is under a duty of care under § 53; and

(2) the independent contractor's negligence is a factual cause of any such harm within the scope of liability.

Comment:

d. Duty of care. To be subject to vicarious liability under this Section, the land possessor or lessor must owe a duty of care. Land possessors owe a duty of reasonable care to entrants on the land as set out in § 51, a duty of reasonable care to those not on the land as provided in § 54, and a limited duty to flagrant trespassers (§ 52). A lessor owes the duties set out in § 53 to the lessee and other entrants on the leased premises. When the possessor or lessor owes a duty of care and hires an independent contractor to perform work on the land, the possessor or lessor is vicariously liable for harm negligently caused by the contractor.

§ 63. Precautions Required by Statute or Regulation

Restatement of the Law Third, Torts: Liability for Physical and Emotional Harm

An actor who hires an independent contractor for an activity is subject to vicarious liability for physical harm if:

(a) a statute or administrative regulation imposes an obligation on the actor to take specific precautions for the safety of others; and

(b) the independent contractor's failure to comply with the statutory or regulatory obligation is a factual cause of any such harm within the scope of liability.

Comment:

c. Application. Under this Section, the statute or regulation must impose an obligation on the actor to take specific precautions for the protection of others. A statutory or regulatory obligation under this Section might require the exercise of reasonable care,

269

compliance with more specific requirements, or adherence to some other standard.

Illustration:

1. A city ordinance requires that all apartments be equipped with smoke detectors in each sleeping area and in or near each stairwell leading to an occupied area. Tonya, who owns an apartment building and leases apartments, hires Elise, an independent electrical contractor, to install smoke alarms in the building. Elise does not install smoke detectors in every stairwell as specified by the ordinance. Kenyon, a tenant in Tonya's building, is injured in a fire that started in a stairwell without a smoke detector; he would have escaped the fire without injury if a detector had been in place. Tonya is subject to vicarious liability to Kenyon for Elise's failure to comply with the city ordinance.

§ 64. Activities Under Public Franchise or in a Public Place

Restatement of the Law Third, Torts: Liability for Physical and Emotional Harm

(a) **An actor engaged in an activity that can be lawfully carried out only under a franchise granted by public authority is subject to vicarious liability for physical harm when the actor hires an independent contractor to carry out the activity and the independent contractor's negligence is a factual cause of any such harm within the scope of liability.**

(b) **An actor who hires an independent contractor for activity in a public place is subject to vicarious liability for physical harm if the independent contractor's negligence is a factual cause of any such harm within the scope of liability.**

(c) **An actor who hires an independent contractor for maintenance or repair of a public place is subject to vicarious liability for physical harm if:**

(1) **the actor is under a duty to maintain the public place in reasonably safe condition; and**

(2) **the independent contractor's negligence in maintaining the public place in reasonably safe condition is a factual cause of any such harm within the scope of liability.**

Comment:

c. Activity under a public franchise. The rule in Subsection (a) applies when an actor is carrying out an activity that can be law-

270

fully carried out only under a franchise granted by a public authority. Thus, the actor under Subsection (a) is not usually a government or governmental unit, but instead is a private or quasi-private actor whose right to carry out the activity requires express permission by a public authority. Coverage under this Subsection does not turn on whether the activity is conducted in a public place or on public land.

d. *Public place; activity in a public place.* Under this Section, the term "public place" denotes any place that a State or its subdivisions maintains for the use of the public. This includes highways, parks, public buildings, and other similar places. . . .

Illustration:

3. A city hires LightCo., an independent contractor, to operate and maintain the city's streetlights. Jamar is struck by a car while crossing a street near dusk. The streetlight was not operating at the time given the negligent failure of LightCo. to maintain the streetlights. The city is subject to vicarious liability to Jamar under Subsection (c).

§ 65. Work Accepted as the Hirer's Performance of the Work

Restatement of the Law Third, Torts: Liability for Physical and Emotional Harm

An actor who hires an independent contractor to perform services is subject to vicarious liability for physical harm if:

(a) the services are accepted in the reasonable belief that the actor or the actor's employees are rendering the services; and

(b) the independent contractor's negligence is a factual cause of harm to one who receives the services, and such harm is within the scope of liability.

Comment:

b. *History; relation to agency law.* The rule in this Section, as contained in the first Restatement, originated with cases in which an actor under a contractual obligation to perform services hired an independent contractor to perform the services, and the contractor's negligence harmed the promisee or a person connected to the contractual obligation. In these cases, the hirer was vicariously liable for harm that the contractor's negligence caused to the promisee or to another person receiving the services. The result in such cases could not be explained solely on the basis of the law of agency or the law of contract. A hirer could be vicariously liable on the basis of apparent agency, but the traditional plaintiff under an apparent-agency theory was the person who reasonably believed the contractor was acting as the hirer's employee or with the hirer's authorization. By contrast, in the cases relating to the rule in this Section, vicarious liability extended to persons who shared in services accepted by another as the hirer's performance.

The cases also did not rest directly on a contract theory. The actor who hired the independent contractor was subject to vicarious liability only if the contractor's negligence caused harm—not if the contractor simply failed to perform the contract. Further, recovery in the cases extended to those who shared in services, not just to the promisee or to a third-party beneficiary. Because neither agency law nor contract law fully addressed these situations, the first Restatement of Torts, in § 429, stated a rule of vicarious liability for hirers in such contexts.

The differences between the rule of this Section and the doctrine of apparent agency have diminished. . . . The rule in this Section, then, can be viewed as an application of the principle of apparent authority in contexts involving physical harm caused by an independent contractor. . . .

Illustrations:

1. Janet calls Beth, who operates a car service, asking Beth to send a seven-passenger car and driver to Janet's home. Beth discovers that her only seven-passenger car is out of service. Beth contacts David and arranges with David to use his seven-passenger car. Beth sends David and the car to Janet, who thinks the car is Beth's and that David is Beth's employee. Because the car is in bad condition (which a reasonable inspection by David would have revealed), a collision occurs and injures Janet. Beth is subject to vicarious liability to Janet under this Section.

2. Dionne, an insulin-dependent diabetic, goes to the emergency room at Harris Hospital after waking up with intense nausea that will not subside. At Harris Hospital, she is diagnosed with renal failure and undergoes surgery to implant a catheter that will assist with ongoing dialysis. The anesthesiologist for the surgery is Dr. Hudson, an employee of AA Associates, one of several anesthesiology groups that provide anesthesiology services for Harris Hospital. Before the surgery, Dr. Hudson introduces herself by name and states that she will be providing the anesthesia. Dionne receives no information from Dr. Hudson or Harris Hospital suggesting that Dr. Hudson is not an employee of the hospital. Harris Hospital's website lists Dr. Hudson as a member of its anesthesiology department and does not include any reference to AA Associates. Dionne suffers brain damage resulting from the negligence of Dr. Hudson. Harris Hospital is subject to vicarious liability to Dionne under this Section.

PART VI
STRICT LIABILITY

CHAPTER 15

STRICT LIABILITY

Scope Note: . . . . Strict liability is [ ] an analytically important alternative to liability based on intent and on negligence. Negligence is an obvious form of "fault"; absent an applicable privilege the intent to cause physical harm is generally faulty as well. . . . By contrast, strict liability signifies liability without fault, or at least without any proof of fault. . . .

There is [ ] no general rule of strict liability in tort in physical-harm cases. . . . Instead, there are a number of particular rules that impose strict liability in certain circumstances. Each of these rules has its own elements, which the plaintiff must prove in order to render the rule operational. . . . Certain [ ] rules of strict liability in tort, which apply in cases of physical harm, are addressed [not in other parts of the Restatement, as with products liability and vicarious liability but] in this Chapter. These are commonly referred to as rules of "traditional strict liability." This label distinguishes them from more modern doctrines of strict liability, including products liability. . . .

Just as there is no single rule of strict liability in tort, but rather a range of specific strict-liability doctrines, so it is appropriate to observe that there is no single theory for strict liability in tort. While a number of rationales and policies are generally available in explaining both the coverage and the limits of strict-liability doctrines, each of the particular doctrines may balance or accommodate these rationales and policies in its own distinctive way. Accordingly, the relevant strict-liability policies are discussed below in the context of the specific strict-liability doctrines. Moreover, each of these doctrines has its own history; strict liability is one area of tort law in which a page of history can be at least as rele-

274

vant as a page of logic. However, at a minimum, strict-liability doctrines do require that the defendant's conduct or activity be a factual cause of the plaintiff's injury.

. . . [S]trict liability is almost always invoked by plaintiffs and asserted against defendants based on their conduct falling within one of four specifications of strict liability provided in this Chapter. Accordingly, actors engaging in those activities are referred to as defendants with the victims of such harm identified as plaintiffs.

A. ABNORMALLY DANGEROUS ACTIVITIES

§ 20. Abnormally Dangerous Activities

Restatement of the Law Third, Torts: Liability for Physical and Emotional Harm

(a) An actor who carries on an abnormally dangerous activity is subject to strict liability for physical harm resulting from the activity.

(b) An activity is abnormally dangerous if:

(1) the activity creates a foreseeable and highly significant risk of physical harm even when reasonable care is exercised by all actors and

(2) the activity is not one of common usage.

Comment:

a. Subject to strict liability. Strict liability does not signify absolute liability. Even in cases covered by this Section, various limitations on liability apply and various defenses are available; the language of "subject to strict liability" acknowledges this. . . .

b. Relationship to negligence. The strict-liability rule set forth in this Section is concerned with activities that give rise to a highly significant risk of physical harm. The significance or magnitude of any risk relates to both the likelihood of harm and the severity of any harm that may ensue. However, even under negligence law, as the magnitude of the risk occasioned by the defendant's activity increases, so does the burden of precautions that the defendant is required to adopt while engaging in that activity in order to avoid being found negligent. If a highly significant risk of physical harm contributes to the case on behalf of strict liability under this Section, such a risk also facilitates the plaintiff's proof of the defendant's negligence under § 3 for failure to adopt appropriate precautions. Of course, in some instances the evidence will suggest that the defendant, though engaging in a highly risky activity, has adopted all reasonable precautions. In such cases, the issue of strict liability remains relevant. Indeed, a prerequisite for the strict-liability rule identified in this Section is not merely a highly significant risk associated with the activity itself, but a highly significant risk that remains with the activity even when all actors exercise reasonable care. . . .

For many activities that initially entail a highly significant risk, the risks in question can be dramatically reduced by the exercise of reasonable care by all actors. . . . Yet even if the defendant who engages in an activity has taken all reasonable precautions, one possible negligence argument remains. If all the risks entailed by an activity even when reasonable care is exercised outweigh all the advantages that the defendant and all others derive from the activity, it may be unreasonable and hence negligent for the defendant to carry on the activity at all, or at least to carry it on at the particular location. However, if the defendant's decision to engage in the activity is in fact negligent, the issue of the defendant's strict liability recedes in importance. Accordingly, this Section's discussion of strict liability tends to assume that the defendant is not negligent in engaging in the activity—that the advantages of the activity are sufficient to justify its risks.

This assumption has one problem, however. Claims that a defendant's entire activity is negligent are difficult to bring, either because of the problems involved in gathering all relevant information or because of the related duty limitations that courts might recognize. . . . Accordingly, under negligence law standing alone it is possible that a defendant who unreasonably engages in an activity will escape liability. A further point is that certain choices the defendant makes in the course of the activity in fact may be negligent, yet may lurk so far in the background as to elude the attention of courts in negligence cases. Among these are the choices as to the exact level at which the activity is conducted. When an activity is found to be abnormally dangerous, one effect of this finding is to give the defendant a stronger incentive than negligence law might provide to make wise decisions in terms of what activities to engage in and what precautions to adopt. . . .

d. *Rylands v. Fletcher.* . . . [G]iven the criteria for an abnormally dangerous activity in Subsection (b), a considerable fraction of abnormally dangerous activity cases involve neighbors suing land occupiers for activities on their land.

e. *Strict liability for blasting.* . . . Courts frequently state that blasting is a paradigm of an abnormally dangerous activity. It is useful to identify the elements of this paradigm case. First, the defendant chooses to engage in blasting for reasons of its own benefit and is almost certainly aware of the dangers associated with its blasting. Secondly, blasting is likely to cause harm, by way of debris or concussion, even though the defendant adopts all reasonable precautions in the course of conducting the blasting activity.

276

Because blasting remains dangerous even when all reasonable care is exercised, blasting is an activity whose dangerousness is "inevitable" or "inherent." The next special feature that distinguishes blasting is that blasting is an activity that causes harm essentially on its own, without meaningful contribution from the conduct of the victim or of any other actors. Typically, the victim is a passive, uninvolved third party, who is connected to the blasting only in the sense that the victim owns property in the neighborhood and suffers harm on account of the blasting. It is, then, the inevitably risky quality of the activity of blasting, the extent to which that activity is the almost exclusive cause of the resulting harm, the plaintiff's status as a wholly innocent and uninvolved third party, and the defendant's choice to engage for its own advantage in an activity that it knows to be inevitably risky, that makes blasting a paradigm case for strict liability.

The appeal of strict liability, it can be noted, does not depend on any notion that the defendant is in a better position than the plaintiff to allocate or distribute the risk of harm; indeed, the defendant may be a small business enterprise, the property damage suffered by the plaintiff may be no more than moderate, and the plaintiff as a property owner may already be insured for the loss that that damage entails. Nor does the appeal of strict liability rest on any disparagement of the social utility of the particular blasting activity. Even though blasting seems the best way to clear the land in order to erect an important structure, strict liability remains eminently appropriate.

f. The idea of strict liability for the causation of harm. Certain scholars, relying on ethical perceptions, have advocated a rule of strict liability for all harm that a defendant causes; in their view, the causation of harm is a sufficient criterion for liability. This position resonates deeply in public attitudes; if the person in the street is asked whether a party should be liable for injuries that the party causes, the person's answer is likely to be affirmative. These perceptions and attitudes can be easily explained; when a person voluntarily acts and in doing so secures the desired benefits of that action, the person should in fairness bear responsibility for the harms the action causes.

However, a common response to the recommendation of strict liability for the causation of harm is that most accidents happen at the literal or figurative intersection of two or more activities. This is a reality that often makes factual causation indeterminate and insufficient as a strict-liability criterion. When, for example, a train hits a car at a railroad crossing, the accident is caused by the operation of the train, but it is also caused by the operation of the car; and lurking in the background is the contribution of the city in building the highway that crosses the railroad tracks. Yet even though causation is frequently indeterminate as a possible stan-

277

dard for liability, it is not always indeterminate. As noted in Comment *e*, blasting may provide a useful example of largely unitary causation. When the defendant, by blasting, projects debris that damages the plaintiff's property, common parlance might lead one to observe that that damage has been almost exclusively caused by the defendant's activity. Moreover, in this situation, there may be safety-incentive reasons in addition to ethical reasons in support of strict liability; given the defendant's dominant role, it is almost certainly the defendant who is in a position to consider and implement whatever measures might reduce the risk of harm. The provisions in this Section can be understood, in part, as seeking to identify situations in which the defendant's role is sufficiently exclusive as to render the imposition of strict liability appropriate.

g. Highly significant risk of physical harm. A risk of physical harm can be highly significant for either or both of two possible reasons. The risk can be highly significant because the likelihood of harm is unusually high, even though the severity of expected harm is no more than ordinary. This is often the case with blasting; the probability of some harm occurring may be quite substantial, even though most of the time the particular harm will be only a moderate amount of property damage. Conversely, there are activities—the operation of a nuclear power plant is an extreme case—where the likelihood of a harm-causing incident when reasonable care is exercised is quite low, but where the severity of harm should there be an incident can be enormous. Both the likelihood of harm and the severity of possible harm should be taken into account in ascertaining whether an activity entails a highly significant risk of physical harm. The absence of a highly significant risk is one of several reasons that courts have been unwilling to impose strict liability for harms caused by leaks from or ruptures in water mains; the likelihood of harm-causing incidents is not especially high, and the level of harm when there is such an incident is generally not severe. . . .

h. Reasonable care as exercised by all actors. For purposes of this Section, a prerequisite for strict liability is not merely a highly significant risk in the defendant's activity overall, but a highly significant risk in that activity even when reasonable care is exercised by the defendant undertaking the activity, and likewise by other actors who contribute to the activity's safety level. . . .

The actors whose practice of reasonable care is relevant under this Section include the category of potential victims. The strict-liability rule is designed to protect "the innocent person who suffers harm as a result of" an "unavoidable risk of harm that is inherent" in the defendant's activity. However, an activity is not inherently and unavoidably dangerous if reasonable precautions by potential victims can commonly succeed in avoiding injuries; nor is a class of victims entirely innocent when their own injuries are often due to their own failure to exercise reasonable care. In general, when the accident rate is evidently due to a combination of the conduct choices made by potential defendants and the choices made by potential plaintiffs, both the ethical arguments and the deterrence arguments in favor of strict liability are weakened. As far as the transmission of electricity is concerned, even when reasonable care is exercised by the relevant companies, significant dangers remain; but so long as potential victims likewise exercise reasonable care in avoiding making inappropriate contact with power lines, the likelihood of serious injuries is very low. Similarly, as railroad trains approach highway crossings, significant risks may remain even when the railroads exercise reasonable care. However, if motorists and pedestrians who approach those crossings likewise exercise reasonable care, the likelihood of injuries is minimal. Partly for this reason, neither the transmission of electricity nor the operation of trains through highway crossings has been deemed to be an abnormally dangerous activity. Indeed, of all the activities that courts have found to be abnormally dangerous, there is none in which the accident rate ensuing from the activity is significantly influenced by the degree of reasonableness in the conduct of potential victims.

Illustration:

1. At the end of the planting season, farmer Fred needs to dispose of dry straw spread over much of his 50 acres. He therefore initiates a controlled burn fire, with the aim of using the fire to destroy the straw. For fires of this sort there are appropriate precautions, including placing various types of obstacles at the property's boundary line. However, even when all reasonable precautions are adopted, such fires escape the farmer's property approximately 10 percent of the time. Because of the size of such fires, when there is such an escape the damage done to neighboring property is likely to be substantial. When Fred's fire is in progress, the wind unexpectedly picks up. The fire spreads to the property of Emily, Fred's immediate neighbor, causing harm. Fred's activity in conducting the fire satisfies the requirements of Subsection (b)(1).

i. Foreseeability. In general, the case on behalf of strict liability is strengthened when the defendant has actual knowledge of the risky quality of the activity in which the defendant is engaging. In such a situation, it can be said that the defendant is deliberately engaging in risk-creating activity for the sake of the defendant's own advantage. . . .

However, the case for strict liability under this Section is sufficiently strong if the defendant has reason to know or should know of the riskiness of its activity. Accordingly, if a defendant disposes of chemicals under circumstances where the defendant knows or should know of their harmful or toxic quality, a finding that the activity is abnormally dangerous may be appropriate. However, if the defendant engages in conduct with neither actual nor constructive knowledge that the conduct is other than harmless, there is inadequate reason to impose strict liability. . . .

j. Common usage. Even if an activity involves a highly significant risk when reasonable care is exercised, the activity is not abnormally dangerous if it is in common usage. . . . An activity is plainly of common usage if it is carried on by a large fraction of the people in the community. For example, automobiles are in such general use that their operation is a matter of common usage. Accordingly, at least for this reason, the operation of automobiles is not an abnormally dangerous activity. On the other hand, the operation of a tank, or another motor vehicle of such size and weight as to be unusually difficult to control safely, is not a usual activity; therefore, the operation of such a vehicle may be abnormally dangerous. Whenever an activity is engaged in by a large fraction of the community, the absence of strict liability can be explained by principles of reciprocity. Even though various actors may without negligence be creating appreciable risks, the risks in question are imposed by the many on each other.

However, activities can be in common use even if they are engaged in by only a limited number of actors. Consider the company that transmits electricity through wires, or distributes gas through mains, to most buildings in the community. The activity itself is engaged in by only one party. Even so, electric wires and gas mains are pervasive within the community. Moreover, most people, though not themselves engaging in the activity, are connected to the activity; electric wires and gas mains reach their homes. Accordingly, the activity is obviously in common usage, and partly for that reason strict liability is not applicable.

The concept of common usage can be extended further to activities that, though not pervasive, are nevertheless common and familiar within the community. If in this sense the activity is normal, it is difficult to regard the activity as exceptional or abnormally dangerous. Basic public attitudes tend to be accepting of familiar and traditional risks, even while apprehensive of risks that are uncommon and novel. The law should be respectful of public attitudes of this sort. When an activity has moved beyond its initial stages and has become common and normal, this tends to allay concerns as to the acceptability of the activity itself. Moreover, the more common the activity, the more likely it is that the activity's benefits are distributed widely among the community; the appeal of strict liability for an activity is stronger when its risks are imposed on third parties while its benefits are concentrated among a few.

k. The two-criteria standard. . . . The location at which the activity is conducted does not independently determine whether the activity is abnormally dangerous. However, the location frequently has an important bearing on the two criteria in Subsection (b). For example . . . blasting in a developed area of the city creates a highly significant risk in a way that blasting on a deserted mountainside does not. As far as common usage is concerned, location can likewise be relevant; in arid rural communities, it may be a common practice for farmers to collect water in irrigation facilities, while this would not be common in communities where rainfall is plentiful.

In addition, the value that the defendant or others derive from the activity is not a direct factor in determining whether the activity is abnormally dangerous. . . . [T]his Section sets forth a rule of strict liability, not of negligence liability, and hence rests on the assumption that the activity's advantages are apparently substantial enough as to render reasonable the defendant's choice to engage in the activity. Given this assumption, the point that the activity provides substantial value or utility is of little direct relevance to the question whether the activity should properly bear strict liability. . . .

Illustration:

2. The Malloy Company produces components for computers that are essential to the modern economy. Its manufacturing plant is located in a community almost all of which is residential. Its manufacturing process generates a toxic chemical as a byproduct. Malloy stores this chemical in storage bins pending shipment of the chemical to an off-site disposal facility. This storage arrangement complies with the requirements of reasonable care and likewise with applicable public regulations. Even during normal and proper operations, it is often necessary to open the lids on these bins for periods of time. Wind conditions may then arise that can disperse the chemical from the storage bins to the property of Malloy's neighbors; over time, such dispersion is quite likely but not certain. When and if it occurs, the toxic fumes emanating from the chemicals can easily induce serious illnesses in those living on the property. Malloy's activity of storing the chemicals is not in common usage, and a court may determine that the activity creates a highly significant risk of physical harm even when reasonable care is exercised. Accordingly, the court may conclude that the activity is abnormally dangerous.

l. Function of court. Whether the activity is abnormally dangerous is determined by the court, applying the factors in Subsection (b). When appropriate, the court can rely on judicial notice in order to acquire information about a particular activity. Alternatively, that information can be provided by evidence, especially expert testimony. . . . The facts in question commonly concern an entire class of activities within society, rather than the conduct of the particular defendant. . . . In addition, the decision as to the standard of liability applicable to an activity is likely to have a broad societal impact. . . . Indeed, it is desirable for courts clearly to identify those activities that are abnormally dangerous, so as to give parties fair notice, avoid unequal results, and reduce subsequent litigation costs. . . .

B. ANIMALS

§ 21. Intrusion by Livestock or Other Animals

Restatement of the Law Third, Torts: Liability for Physical and Emotional Harm

An owner or possessor of livestock or other animals, except for dogs and cats, that intrude upon the land of another is subject to strict liability for physical harm caused by the intrusion.

Comment:

b. Animal intrusions: terminology. The rule of strict liability set forth in this Section is characterized in terms of animals that intrude upon the land of another. The rule's definition of animals is broad, including fowl, birds, and reptiles as well as mammals. Still, the vast majority of the rule's applications concerns livestock, mainly cattle and horses. . . . [Frequent] terminology implies that the defendant's livestock is itself committing the tort of trespass against a neighbor, and that the defendant is liable for the livestock's tort—either through some notion that identifies the defendant with the livestock or some intuition that principles of vicarious liability apply, rendering the defendant liable for the livestock trespass. . . . Nevertheless, the language of trespass is analytically imperfect; a cow is obviously incapable of committing a tort. For that reason, any idea of vicarious liability is also inapt; there is no tort on the part of the cow that can be imputed to the owner. Similarly, any idea identifying the livestock with the owner is a fiction that at best presents an image of the rule, but cannot serve as the rationale or foundation for the rule. . . .

c. Legal diversity. . . . [T]here are now three legal standards, each of which is adhered to by a group of jurisdictions. One standard is strict liability on the livestock owner, with no affirmative defense for a failure to fence out. The second standard is strict liability on the livestock owner, combined with such an affirmative defense. The third standard is negligence liability on the livestock owner, without any affirmative defense relating to fencing out. . . . Not only are jurisdictions divided in terms of which standard they employ, but there are also divisions within jurisdictions. . . .

d. Rationale. . . . On balance . . . in livestock-trespass cases

282

it is wiser to place upon the livestock owner the primary obligation of avoiding harm by building fences. Moreover, in the large majority of cases, if the livestock owner does exercise reasonable care in erecting and maintaining a fence, that fence will suffice in restraining the livestock. Nevertheless, in a limited number of cases in which a fence proves inadequate despite reasonable care, the choice between strict liability and negligence liability for the livestock owner becomes relevant. Overall, strict liability is desirable. Because in most instances a reasonable, nonnegligent fence will succeed in restraining the defendant's livestock, the added burden that strict liability places on the livestock owner is itself limited. In addition, strict liability sets forth a rule that is administratively easy to apply. Furthermore, perhaps because strict liability for intruding livestock is the common-law tradition, recognizing strict liability does not disturb the community's sense of justice. There is interesting evidence that American cattle owners regard their own liability as morally sound and accept strict liability in practice even in localities where it is not imposed as a matter of law. In England, strict liability has been retained largely because of lawmakers' understanding that the strict-liability rule has, over time, won the acceptance and approval of those rural interests that are primarily affected by the rule's operation.

e. Livestock and other animals. . . . [T]he rule in this Section [also] applies to animals other than livestock typically found on farms. . . .

g. Scope of liability. When conduct is identified as justifying strict liability, the rationale for strict liability generally relates to certain risks that are characteristic of the conduct. In light of this rationale, strict liability is typically limited to those harms that result from the risks justifying strict liability. Consistent with this limitation, the strict liability recognized by this Section is confined to harms that are commonly associated with the intrusion of animals upon neighbors' property. The consumption of grass is probably the most common form of harm caused by intruding livestock. . . . In other cases, the defendant's livestock, in the course of intruding upon the plaintiff's land, tramples on the plaintiff's crops or causes harm to structures or other physical objects located on that land. . . . Another such risk is that the intruding livestock may infect the plaintiff's animals with disease. When the defendant's horse or bull intrudes upon the plaintiff's land, that animal may attack an animal owned by the plaintiff; if so, the loss incurred by the plaintiff is compensable. Alternatively, the defendant's bull may impregnate the plaintiff's cow under circumstances that are economically disadvantageous to the plaintiff. The plaintiff's resulting loss is a consequence of the risk of trespass by the bull and is hence compensable in strict liability. In addition, the plaintiff or a member of the plaintiff's household may well at-

283

tempt to expel, capture, or restrain the intruding animal and in doing so may suffer physical injury. Accordingly, defendant's strict liability extends to those personal injuries. . . .

There remain, however, a considerable range of possible harms that are no appreciable part of the risk that underlies this Section's rule of strict liability. These harms are hence not covered by the rule.

Illustration:

2. Ann's goat intrudes upon the property of John at night, and is walking normally. John, taking a stroll on his property, does not see the goat and stumbles over it. Falling, John suffers an injury. Ann is not strictly liable to John.

h. Livestock and other animals straying onto highways. The strict-liability rule in this Section applies to animals that intrude onto neighboring property but not to animals that stray upon roads or highways, where they may contribute to a highway accident. The protection of the rights of real-property owners is a theme that plays a significant role in explaining the strict-liability rule; and this theme has no relevance in highway cases. Moreover, when a cow strays onto neighboring property and causes property damage, the cow is the only active entity. For highway accidents, there are at least two actors who engage in conduct that contributes to the accident; when an accident results from a combination of actions by various parties, the concept of strict liability has less appeal. In addition, for highway accidents generally, there is a strong tort-law tradition of relying on the negligence standard of liability. . . .

§ 22. Wild Animals

Restatement of the Law Third, Torts: Liability for Physical and Emotional Harm

(a) **An owner or possessor of a wild animal is subject to strict liability for physical harm caused by the wild animal.**

(b) **A wild animal is an animal that belongs to a category of animals that have not been generally domesticated and that are likely, unless restrained, to cause personal injury.**

Comment:

b. Wild animals. For purposes of this Section, "animal" includes not only mammals but also birds, fish, reptiles, and insects. . . . A category of animals is sometimes said to be "wild" if the animals typically live in a state of nature not having been domesticated. Domestication is a process by which human beings modify species of animals through breeding and through maintaining them in or near human habitations. . . .

Yet categories of animals are often said to be wild if they not only live in a state of nature but also are inherently fierce or dangerous. The wild-animal definition stated in this Section reflects this understanding and requires that each of two elements be satisfied: that the category of animals is not generally domesticated and that the category of animals if unrestrained is likely to cause physical injury. . . .

c. *Categories of animals.* This Section focuses not on the attributes of the particular animal but rather the attributes of the category of animals to which the particular animal belongs. . . . If a category of animal is wild, there is an ongoing risk that a particular animal, though seemingly tamed, will revert to the characteristics of the category itself. . . .

d. *Rationale.* . . . The basis for strict liability is partly historical; at least since the middle of the 19th century, the common law has imposed strict liability for wild animals. The rationale for strict liability continues with the point that wild animals are inherently dangerous. It also relies on the point that owning wild animals is an unusual activity, engaged in by a few, which imposes on others significant risks that are themselves unusual and distinctive. Moreover, while courts seem reluctant to entertain or affirm claims that a defendant has been negligent in bringing onto the defendant's property or into the defendant's household a wild animal such as a tiger or a boa constrictor, the reasonableness of the defendant's conduct is at least open to doubt in a way that makes the imposition of strict liability more appropriate. Strict liability gives the owner or possessor of the wild animal an incentive to consider whether removing the wild animal might be the wiser strategy. . . .

Illustration:

1. Alison keeps a young lion in her backyard in order to scare off any intruders. The lion is fastened to a post by a chain. Because of a defect in the chain that Alison could not be expected to detect, the lion breaks free and attacks Patrick on the sidewalk, injuring him. Despite her exercise of reasonable care in attempting to confine the lion, Alison is liable to Patrick for his injuries.

f. *Scope of liability.* Strict liability is justified because of the characteristic harms that are caused by wild animals. If the harm the plaintiff incurs is not a product of the risks posed by wild animals, then the strict liability set forth in this Section does not apply. Thus, if the defendant's bear, having escaped, is standing on and blocking a sidewalk when an inattentive child riding a bicycle collides into the bear, the strict-liability rule is not available. . . . In such a case, the defendant is not necessarily free of liability; rather, the defendant's liability is covered by the § 3 negligence standard, rather than by strict liability. . . .

§ 23. Abnormally Dangerous Animals

Restatement of the Law Third, Torts: Liability for Physical and Emotional Harm

An owner or possessor of an animal that the owner or possessor knows or has reason to know has dangerous tendencies abnormal for the animal's category is subject to strict liability for physical harm caused by the animal if the harm ensues from that dangerous tendency.

Comment:

b. Explanation and rationale. . . . The premise of this Section is that, apart from animals that trespass (§ 21) and wild animals that pose an inherent risk of personal injury (§ 22), most animals normally are safe, or at least are not abnormally unsafe in a way that would justify the imposition of strict liability. In addition, such animals provide important benefits to those who own or maintain possession of them. Thus, livestock such as cows, horses, and pigs are of substantial economic value, while pets such as dogs and cats provide essential companionship for households and families. Indeed, dogs and cats are frequently regarded as members of the family. Furthermore, ownership of animals such as dogs and cats is widespread throughout the public; therefore, the limited risks entailed by ordinary dogs and cats are to a considerable extent reciprocal. Accordingly, the case on behalf of strict liability for physical or emotional harms that all such ordinary animals might cause is weak. However, even though animals in such categories generally entail only a modest level of danger, particular animals may present significant and abnormal dangers. Once the owner or possessor of such an animal knows or has reason to know of such a danger, strict liability, subject to limitations and defenses, becomes appropriate. Given the defendant's knowledge, the reasonableness of the defendant's conduct in retaining the animal is at least questionable, and strict liability gives the owner an incentive to consider whether the animal should be retained. Even if that retention is itself proper, an abnormally dangerous animal is by definition unusual; owning such an animal is an activity engaged in by a few that imposes significant risks on others within the community. In these circumstances, strict liability is fairly imposed.

c. "Scienter." The strict-liability doctrine set forth in this Section is often referred to in terms of "scienter". . . . The rule in this Section calls for strict liability if the owner or possessor has actual knowledge of the animal's abnormally dangerous tendency or at least actual knowledge of facts that would enable a reasonable person to appreciate the animal's dangerous tendency. In the latter situation, it can be said that the owner or possessor "has reason to know" of the animal's dangerous tendency.

For strict liability to attach, it is not required that the animal be "vicious" or aggressive; a finding of the animal's abnormal "dangerousness" is sufficient. Thus if, in the course of play, a large dog jumps on people in ways that can cause them to fall and injure themselves, such a dog may be found abnormally dangerous. . . .

d. Statutory strict liability in the absence of scienter. In about half of all jurisdictions, statutes exist that impose strict liability in dog cases even in the absence of scienter. Almost all of these statutes are limited to dogs; many of the statutes are limited to the special problem of dog bites, but other statutes apply to a broader range of injuries and harms brought about by dogs. . . . For common-law purposes, a categorical distinction between dogs and all other animals is not justifiable. Nor is there justification for categorically distinguishing, as do many of the statutes, between dog bites and all other categories of dog-caused harms; yet to impose strict liability, without regard to scienter, to the full range of physical harms that may be caused or occasioned by the activities of dogs is also difficult to justify. . . .

f. Owners and possessors of abnormally dangerous animals. As is the case with respect to cattle that trespass and wild animals, strict liability can attach to the possessors of abnormally dangerous animals and also to their owners. . . . The definition of possessor excludes the person who merely has temporary custody of the animal. If, for example, a babysitter takes the family's dog for a walk as part of the afternoon work assignment, the babysitter's temporary possession of the dog does not subject the babysitter to strict liability, even if the babysitter has knowledge of the dog's dangerous tendency. . . . To be sure, if the babysitter is negligent in the management of the dog, the babysitter is subject to liability under § 6. . . .

h. Provocation. Provocation bears on the law relating to abnormally dangerous animals in two distinct ways. First, if an earlier incident in which an animal attacks is due to the fact that the animal was provoked, then the attack may not suffice in demonstrating the animal's abnormally dangerous tendency. If, for example, a hamster is squeezed hard enough, the hamster will bite; yet that bite does not reveal that the hamster is abnormally dangerous. Second, consider the animal whose prior behavior does reveal an abnormally dangerous tendency. If that animal, having been provoked, proceeds to bite, that bite may be attributable to the normal tendencies of ordinary animals, rather than to any abnormally dangerous tendency of the particular animal. If such an attribution is regarded as proper by the jury, then despite the animal owner's scienter, on account of Comment *g* the rule of strict liability is not applicable.

The double relevance that attaches to provocation justifies a discussion of the provocation concept. Even though they are substantially provoked, some dogs are so very docile as to respond by merely slinking away. Yet other dogs would respond with some violence to sufficient provocation, even though they cannot properly be labeled as abnormally dangerous for purposes of this Section. The issue, then, is not whether provocation would induce a violent response in every dog, but rather whether it would induce a response in dogs that are sufficiently normal as to avoid the abnormally dangerous label. Because the issue is the character of dogs rather than the goals of the provoker, findings of provocation do not depend on the intent of the provoker. If a plaintiff slips and falls and lands squarely on a dog, that can be provocation despite the plaintiff's lack of intent. Similarly, if a four-year-old jumps on a dog, that may be regarded as provocation even though the four-year-old is too young to be found contributorily negligent. . . .

i. Negligence liability. Many animals, while lacking the element of abnormal danger that justifies strict liability, still involve some level of risk, especially when the animal is brought into various societal settings. In light of that risk, the animal owner can potentially be held liable under the § 6 negligence standard for physical or emotional harms. . . . [T]he friskiness of dogs can create a variety of risks that the possessor of the dog, under negligence law, should make reasonable efforts to control. The dog's possessor might be aware that children are playing with the dog in a way that might induce in the dog a harm-causing response. If so, the owner can be found negligent for not making a reasonable effort to intervene. . . .

In many settings, however, an animal not abnormally dangerous may cause harm in circumstances that fail to show any negligence on the part of the owner or possessor. . . .

C. Scope of Liability

§ 24. Scope of Strict Liability

Restatement of the Law Third, Torts: Liability for Physical and Emotional Harm

Strict liability under §§ 20-23 does not apply

(a) if the person suffers physical or emotional harm as a result of making contact with or coming into proximity to the defendant's animal or abnormally dangerous activity for the purpose of securing some benefit from that contact or that proximity; or

(b) if the defendant maintains ownership or possession of the animal or carries on the abnormally dangerous activity in pursuance of an obligation imposed by law.

Comment:

a. Beneficiaries. The rules of strict liability in §§ 20-23 are designed largely to protect innocent third parties or innocent bystanders. This classification cannot be accorded to the plaintiff who voluntarily comes into contact with or approaches the defendant's animal or activity in order to secure some benefit that contact or proximity to the animal or the activity provides. Such a plaintiff incurs injury because the plaintiff, in order to derive some benefit, has deliberately come within the range of danger entailed by the defendant's animal or activity. While such a plaintiff may have negligence claims against the defendant, the strict-liability rules of §§ 20-23 do not apply.

[For example, in] certain wild-animal cases, the defendant is engaged in exhibiting wild animals to the public; for example, in a zoo. If an animal escapes from the cage, leaves the zoo, and injures a person living in the neighborhood, that person has a strict-liability claim against the zoo. But if the plaintiff is a patron of the zoo, exposed to wild animals because of the benefits the plaintiff secures by visiting the zoo, the plaintiff is beyond the scope of the defendant's strict liability. Similarly, if the plaintiff is a veterinarian or a groomer who accepts an animal such as a dog from the defendant, the plaintiff is deriving financial benefits from the acceptance of the animal, and is beyond the scope of strict liability, even if the dog can be deemed abnormally dangerous. . . .

The denial of strict liability in such situations confirms the relevance and appropriateness of negligence liability. . . . [A] zoo may be liable for negligence in allowing its animal to escape; the dog owner may be negligent in failing to inform the veterinarian of the dog's dangerous tendency. . . .

b. Legal obligations. . . . There are only a limited number of situations that are likely to be covered by the rule in Subsection (b). Depending on the circumstances of state law, a common carrier that makes itself generally available for the carriage of goods may be required to accept all goods offered for shipment, including wild animals, abnormally dangerous animals, or substances such as explosives. If state law does not allow the carrier to reject such goods for shipment, the carrier cannot be held strictly liable under Subsection (b). Moreover, a public official, as part of a more general set of responsibilities, may be required by the public agency to assume immediate control of an abnormally dangerous dog. Under Subsection (b), the public official is not subject to strict liability for harms caused by the dog. However, Subsection (b) does not except from strict liability the public agency that, by giving an order to its employee, chooses vicariously to engage in an abnormally dangerous activity or to possess an abnormally dangerous animal.

The exception from strict liability stated in Subsection (b) requires a legal or public mandate operating on the defendant. The exception does not apply if the defendant merely has secured the permission of a public agency to engage in a certain course of conduct. Thus, a license, permit, or franchise from the city to own an animal or engage in an activity such as blasting does not ordinarily relieve the defendant of strict liability under §§ 20-23. . . .

D. DEFENSES

§ 25. Comparative Responsibility

Restatement of the Law Third, Torts: Liability for Physical and Emotional Harm

If the plaintiff has been contributorily negligent in failing to take reasonable precautions, the plaintiff's recovery in a strict-liability claim under §§ 20-23 for physical or emotional harm is reduced in accordance with the share of comparative responsibility assigned to the plaintiff.

Comment:

a. Assumptions. The rule in this Section assumes that the plaintiff's contributory negligence is a factual cause of an indivisible injury that the plaintiff has incurred and that the defendant is initially subject to strict liability for the plaintiff's injury under §§ 20-23. Under these Sections, the applicability of strict liability may itself depend either on the conduct of the individual plaintiff or the conduct of potential victims more generally. For example, under § 23, Comment *g*, if the plaintiff provokes an abnormally dangerous animal into an attack, the attack may not give rise to strict liability, since even an animal not abnormally dangerous might have responded to the provocation in a similar way. Moreover, under § 20(b)(1) an activity is not abnormally dangerous unless it creates a highly significant risk even when reasonable care is exercised by all actors, including potential victims; accordingly, if the dangers associated with an activity can be minimized when potential victims take appropriate precautions, the activity is not abnormally dangerous. In all such cases, the conduct of victims serves not as an affirmative defense but rather as a factor bearing on whether the defendant is initially subject to strict liability. However, even if the case is of a general type that renders strict liability applicable, in the particular case the plaintiff may have failed to exercise reasonable care in a way that invites the application of the defense of comparative responsibility.

b. Forms of contributory negligence. The concept of negligence, and the related concept of contributory negligence, are explained in § 3, Comment *b*. There is a wide variety of conduct on the part of plaintiffs that might be deemed contributory negligence when the plaintiff sues the defendant under §§ 20-23. . . . [I]n a § 21 claim the plaintiff may have acted unreasonably in choosing a method by which to expel a trespassing animal from the plaintiff's property. In a case involving an abnormally dangerous activity under § 20, a wild animal under § 22, or an abnormally dangerous animal under § 23, the plaintiff may act unreasonably in coming into the area, or remaining in the area, where the plaintiff is endangered. . . . Given the breadth in the concept of contributory negligence, these examples of contributory negligence by the plaintiff are suggestive rather than exhaustive.

   c. *Effect of contributory negligence.* . . . It is widely perceived that in negligence actions comparative negligence provides an appealing compromise between, on the one hand, allowing the plaintiff's contributory negligence to defeat the plaintiff's claim and, on the other hand, regarding the plaintiff's contributory negligence as irrelevant to the defendant's liability. This appeal extends to strict-liability claims as well. Especially in the context of defendant strict liability, the term "comparative negligence" does not suffice; however, the term "comparative responsibility" is satisfactory. . . .

   The flexibility provided by comparative responsibility in responding to the equities entailed by the contributory negligence of the plaintiff is superior to the alternatives of either ignoring the plaintiff's contributory negligence altogether or allowing the plaintiff's contributory negligence to fully extinguish the plaintiff's recovery. Whether the goal of tort law is the achievement of fairness, the furnishing of incentives to both parties for safe behavior, or a combination of the two, the recognition of comparative responsibility is more sensible than the prior practice of regarding the plaintiff's contributory negligence as usually irrelevant to strict-liability claims. . . .

   d. *Assigning proportionate shares.* The apportionment of responsibility under this Section is best described as an ad hoc evaluation about the facts of a particular case; that evaluation is treated as though it were an instance of factfinding as such, and it is therefore entrusted primarily to the jury. The process is conducted pursuant to Restatement Third, Torts: Apportionment of Liability. Obviously, applying the principle of comparative responsibility in a strict-liability action is somewhat more difficult than applying it in an action in which the defendant is held liable under a theory of negligence. In the latter, it is more nearly feasible to compare the fault of the defendant to the contributory fault of the plaintiff. When the defendant is held liable under a theory of strict liability, no literal comparison of the fault of the two parties may be possible. According to Restatement Third, Torts: Apportionment of Liability § 8, Comment *a*, while "comparative responsibil-

291

ity" is the common legal term, "assigning shares of responsibility" might be a better term, "because it suggests that the factfinder, after considering the relevant factors, *assigns* shares of responsibility rather than *compares* incommensurate quantities.". . . .

  e. *Assumption of risk.* . . . As far as the plaintiff's contributory negligence is concerned, this Section provides that all forms of contributory negligence are subject to the comparative-responsibility process. No separate defense of assumption of risk is recognized. . . .

  A disclaimer of liability in a contract between the plaintiff and the defendant is often referred to as an "express" assumption of risk. In tort law generally, such disclaimers are frequently valid even though the plaintiff lacks actual knowledge of the specific risks involved in the defendant's conduct. In light of this, it might be thought that the tort terminology of assumption of risk is inappropriate; rather, disclaimers are legally effective because they are clauses in contracts that themselves are valid. Restatement Third, Torts: Apportionment of Liability, recognizes that contractual disclaimers of tort liability are legitimate and enforceable "unless barred by the substantive law governing the claim.". . . . [T]here are few cases dealing with the issue of the validity of disclaimers of strict liability for harms caused by animals and by abnormally dangerous activities. Given the scarcity of cases, the issue is left open in this Restatement.

PART VII
PRODUCTS LIABILITY

CHAPTER 16

PRODUCTS LIABILITY

A. CATEGORIES OF PRODUCT DEFECT (MANUFACTURING, DESIGN, AND WARNING DEFECT)

§ 1. Liability of Commercial Seller or Distributor for Harm Caused by Defective Products

Restatement of the Law Third, Torts: Products Liability

One engaged in the business of selling or otherwise distributing products who sells or distributes a defective product is subject to liability for harm to persons or property caused by the defect.

Comment:

a. History. This Section states a general rule of tort liability applicable to commercial sellers and other distributors of products generally. . . .

The liability established in this Section draws on both warranty law and tort law. Historically, the focus of products liability law was on manufacturing defects. A manufacturing defect is a physical departure from a product's intended design. Typically, manufacturing defects occur in only a small percentage of units in a product line. Courts early began imposing liability without fault on product sellers for harm caused by such defects, holding a seller liable for harm caused by manufacturing defects even though all possible care had been exercised by the seller in the preparation and distribution of the product. In doing so, courts relied on the concept of warranty, in connection with which fault has never been a prerequisite to liability.

The imposition of liability for manufacturing defects has a long history in the common law. As early as 1266, criminal statutes imposed liability upon victualers, vintners, brewers, butchers, cooks, and other persons who supplied contaminated food and drink. In the late 1800s, courts in many states began imposing negligence and strict warranty liability on commercial sellers of defective goods. In the early 1960s, American courts began to recognize that a commercial seller of any product having a manufacturing defect should be liable in tort for harm caused by the defect regardless of the plaintiff's ability to maintain a traditional negligence or warranty action. Liability attached even if the manufacturer's quality control in producing the defective product was reasonable. A plaintiff was not required to be in direct privity with the defendant seller to bring an action. Strict liability in tort for defectively manufactured products merges the concept of implied warranty, in which negligence is not required, with the tort concept of negligence, in which contractual privity is not required.

Questions of design defects and defects based on inadequate instructions or warnings arise when the specific product unit conforms to the intended design but the intended design itself, or its sale without adequate instructions or warnings, renders the product not reasonably safe. If these forms of defect are found to exist, then every unit in the same product line is potentially defective. . . . A product unit that fails to meet the manufacturer's design specifications [ ] fails to perform its intended function and is, almost by definition, defective. However, when the product unit meets the manufacturer's own design specifications, it is necessary to go outside those specifications to determine whether the product is defective. . . .

c. One engaged in the business of selling or otherwise

295

distributing. The rule stated in this Section applies only to manufacturers and other commercial sellers and distributors who are engaged in the business of selling or otherwise distributing the type of product that harmed the plaintiff. The rule does not apply to a noncommercial seller or distributor of such products. Thus, it does not apply to one who sells foodstuffs to a neighbor, nor does it apply to the private owner of an automobile who sells it to another. . . .

d. Harm to persons or property. The rule stated in this Section applies only to harm to persons or property, commonly referred to as personal injury and property damage. [Economic loss is governed by a separate rule].

e. Nonmanufacturing sellers or other distributors of products. The rule stated in this Section provides that all commercial sellers and distributors of products, including nonmanufacturing sellers and distributors such as wholesalers and retailers, are subject to liability for selling products that are defective. Liability attaches even when such nonmanufacturing sellers or distributors do not themselves render the products defective and regardless of whether they are in a position to prevent defects from occurring. . . .

§ 2. Categories of Product Defect

Restatement of the Law Third, Torts: Products Liability

A product is defective when, at the time of sale or distribution, it contains a manufacturing defect, is defective in design, or is defective because of inadequate instructions or warnings. A product:

(a) contains a manufacturing defect when the product departs from its intended design even though all possible care was exercised in the preparation and marketing of the product;

(b) is defective in design when the foreseeable risks of harm posed by the product could have been reduced or avoided by the adoption of a reasonable alternative design by the seller or other distributor, or a predecessor in the commercial chain of distribution, and the omission of the alternative design renders the product not reasonably safe;

(c) is defective because of inadequate instructions or warnings when the foreseeable risks of harm posed by the product could have been reduced or avoided by the provision of reasonable instructions or warnings by the seller or other distributor, or a predecessor in the commercial chain of distribution, and the omission of the instructions or warnings renders the product not reasonably safe.

Comment:

a. Rationale. The rules set forth in this Section establish separate standards of liability for manufacturing defects, design defects, and defects based on inadequate instructions or warnings. They are generally applicable to most products. Standards of liability applicable to special product categories such as prescription drugs and used products are set forth in separate sections . . . of this Chapter.

The rule for manufacturing defects stated in Subsection (a) imposes liability whether or not the manufacturer's quality control efforts satisfy standards of reasonableness. Strict liability without fault in this context is generally believed to foster several objectives. On the premise that tort law serves the instrumental function of creating safety incentives, imposing strict liability on manufacturers for harm caused by manufacturing defects encourages greater investment in product safety than does a regime of fault-based liability under which, as a practical matter, sellers may escape their appropriate share of responsibility. Some courts and commentators also have said that strict liability discourages the consumption of defective products by causing the purchase price of products to reflect, more than would a rule of negligence, the costs of defects. And by eliminating the issue of manufacturer fault from plaintiff's case, strict liability reduces the transaction costs involved in litigating that issue.

Several important fairness concerns are also believed to support manufacturers' liability for manufacturing defects even if the plaintiff is unable to show that the manufacturer's quality control fails to meet risk-utility norms. In many cases manufacturing defects are in fact caused by manufacturer negligence but plaintiffs have difficulty proving it. Strict liability therefore performs a function similar to the concept of res ipsa loquitur, allowing deserving plaintiffs to succeed notwithstanding what would otherwise be difficult or insuperable problems of proof. Products that malfunction due to manufacturing defects disappoint reasonable expectations of product performance. Because manufacturers invest in quality control at consciously chosen levels, their knowledge that a predictable number of flawed products will enter the marketplace entails an element of deliberation about the amount of injury that will result from their activity. Finally, many believe that consumers who benefit from products without suffering harm should share, through increases in the prices charged for those products, the burden of unavoidable injury costs that result from manufacturing defects.

An often-cited rationale for holding wholesalers and retailers strictly liable for harm caused by manufacturing defects is that, as between them and innocent victims who suffer harm because of defective products, the product sellers as business entities are in a better position than are individual users and consumers to insure against such losses. In most instances, wholesalers and retailers will be able to pass liability costs up the chain of product distribution to the manufacturer. When joining the manufacturer in the tort action presents the plaintiff with procedural difficulties, local retailers can pay damages to the victims and then seek indemnity from manufacturers. Finally, holding retailers and wholesalers strictly liable creates incentives for them to deal only with reputable, financially responsible manufacturers and distributors, thereby helping to protect the interests of users and consumers. . . .

In contrast to manufacturing defects, design defects and defects based on inadequate instructions or warnings are predicated on a different concept of responsibility. In the first place, such defects cannot be determined by reference to the manufacturer's own design or marketing standards because those standards are the very ones that plaintiffs attack as unreasonable. Some sort of independent assessment of advantages and disadvantages, to which some attach the label "risk-utility balancing," is necessary. Products are not generically defective merely because they are dangerous. Many product-related accident costs can be eliminated only by excessively sacrificing product features that make products useful and desirable. Thus, the various trade-offs need to be considered in determining whether accident costs are more fairly and efficiently borne by accident victims, on the one hand, or, on the other hand, by consumers generally through the mechanism of higher product prices attributable to liability costs imposed by courts on product sellers.

Subsections (b) and (c), which impose liability for products that are defectively designed or sold without adequate warnings or instructions and are thus not reasonably safe, achieve the same general objectives as does liability predicated on negligence. The emphasis is on creating incentives for manufacturers to achieve optimal levels of safety in designing and marketing products. Society does not benefit from products that are excessively safe—for example, automobiles designed with maximum speeds of 20 miles per hour—any more than it benefits from products that are too risky. Society benefits most when the right, or optimal, amount of product safety is achieved. From a fairness perspective, requiring individual users and consumers to bear appropriate responsibility for proper product use prevents careless users and consumers from being subsidized by more careful users and consumers, when the former are paid damages out of funds to which the latter are forced to contribute through higher product prices.

In general, the rationale for imposing strict liability on manufacturers for harm caused by manufacturing defects does not apply in the context of imposing liability for defective design and defects based on inadequate instruction or warning. Consumer expectations as to proper product design or warning are typically more difficult to discern than in the case of a manufacturing defect. Moreover, the element of deliberation in setting appropriate levels of design safety is not directly analogous to the setting of levels of quality control by the manufacturer. When a manufacturer sets its quality control at a certain level, it is aware that a given number of products may leave the assembly line in a defective condition and cause injury to innocent victims who can generally do nothing to avoid injury. The implications of deliberately drawing lines with respect to product design safety are different. A reasonably designed product still carries with it elements of risk that must be protected against by the user or consumer since some risks cannot be designed out of the product at reasonable cost.

Most courts agree that, for the liability system to be fair and efficient, the balancing of risks and benefits in judging product design and marketing must be done in light of the knowledge of risks and risk-avoidance techniques reasonably attainable at the time of distribution. To hold a manufacturer liable for a risk that was not foreseeable when the product was marketed might foster increased manufacturer investment in safety. But such investment by definition would be a matter of guesswork. Furthermore, manufacturers may persuasively ask to be judged by a normative behavior standard to which it is reasonably possible for manufacturers to conform. For these reasons, Subsections (b) and (c) speak of products being defective only when risks are reasonably foreseeable. . . .

c. Manufacturing defects. . . . [A] manufacturing defect is a departure from a product unit's design specifications. More distinctly than any other type of defect, manufacturing defects disappoint consumer expectations. Common examples of manufacturing defects are products that are physically flawed, damaged, or incorrectly assembled. In actions against the manufacturer, under prevailing rules concerning allocation of burdens of proof, the plaintiff ordinarily bears the burden of establishing that such a defect existed in the product when it left the hands of the manufacturer.

Occasionally a defect may arise after manufacture, for example, during shipment or while in storage. Since the product, as sold to the consumer, has a defect that is a departure from the product unit's design specifications, a commercial seller or distributor down the chain of distribution is liable as if the product were defectively manufactured. As long as the plaintiff establishes that the product was defective when it left the hands of a given seller in the distributive chain, liability will attach to that seller. Such defects are referred to in this Restatement as "manufacturing defects" even when they occur after manufacture. . . .

Illustrations:

    1. Jack purchased a bottle of champagne from the BBB

299

Liquor Mart. The champagne was bottled by AAA Inc., utiliz-
ing bottles manufactured by CCC Glass Co. While Jack was
opening the bottle it suddenly exploded, causing disfiguring
cuts to his face. The trier of fact determines that, originating
with CCC, the bottle contained a manufacturing defect and
that the defect caused the bottle to explode. AAA, BBB, and
CCC are subject to liability even though they exercised reasonable care in the preparation and distribution of the defective
bottle of AAA Champagne. The weakness in the glass structure
in the bottle that caused Jack's harm was a departure from the
product's intended design, subjecting each of the sellers in the
distributive chain to strict liability for selling a defective
product.

2. The same facts as Illustration 1, except that the trier
of fact determines that the manufacturing defect in the bottle
resulted from customer abuse of the bottle while it was on
display at the BBB Liquor Mart prior to sale to Jack. BBB is
subject to liability for selling a defective bottle of champagne to
Jack even though it exercised reasonable care in its marketing
of the champagne. Neither CCC nor AAA is subject to liability
if the trier of fact determines that the bottle was not defective
when it left CCC's or AAA's control.

⌐d.⌐ *Design defects: general considerations.* Whereas a manufacturing defect consists of a product unit's failure to meet the
manufacturer's design specifications, a product asserted to have a
defective design meets the manufacturer's design specifications
but raises the question whether the specifications themselves create unreasonable risks. Answering that question requires reference to a standard outside the specifications. Subsection (b) adopts
a reasonableness ("risk-utility balancing") test as the standard for
judging the defectiveness of product designs. More specifically, the
test is whether a reasonable alternative design would, at reasonable cost, have reduced the foreseeable risks of harm posed by the
product and, if so, whether the omission of the alternative design
by the seller or a predecessor in the distributive chain rendered
the product not reasonably safe. . . . Under prevailing rules
concerning allocation of burden of proof, the plaintiff must prove
that such a reasonable alternative was, or reasonably could have
been, available at time of sale or distribution.

Assessment of a product design in most instances requires a
comparison between an alternative design and the product design
that caused the injury, undertaken from the viewpoint of a reasonable person. That approach is also used in administering the
traditional reasonableness standard in negligence. . . .

How the defendant's design compares with other, competing
designs in actual use is relevant to the issue of whether the
defendant's design is defective. Defendants often seek to defend

their product designs on the ground that the designs conform to the "state of the art." The term "state of the art" has been variously defined to mean that the product design conforms to industry custom, that it reflects the safest and most advanced technology developed and in commercial use, or that it reflects technology at the cutting edge of scientific knowledge. The confusion brought about by these various definitions is unfortunate. This Section states that a design is defective if the product could have been made safer by the adoption of a reasonable alternative design. If such a design could have been practically adopted at time of sale and if the omission of such a design rendered the product not reasonably safe, the plaintiff establishes defect under Subsection (b). When a defendant demonstrates that its product design was the safest in use at the time of sale, it may be difficult for the plaintiff to prove that an alternative design could have been practically adopted. The defendant is thus allowed to introduce evidence with regard to industry practice that bears on whether an alternative design was practicable. Industry practice may also be relevant to whether the omission of an alternative design rendered the product not reasonably safe. While such evidence is admissible, it is not necessarily dispositive. If the plaintiff introduces expert testimony to establish that a reasonable alternative design could practically have been adopted, a trier of fact may conclude that the product was defective notwithstanding that such a design was not adopted by any manufacturer, or even considered for commercial use, at the time of sale. . . .

The fact that a danger is open and obvious is relevant to the issue of defectiveness, but does not necessarily preclude a plaintiff from establishing that a reasonable alternative design should have been adopted that would have reduced or prevented injury to the plaintiff. The requirement in Subsection (b) that the plaintiff show a reasonable alternative design applies in most instances even though the plaintiff alleges that the category of product sold by the defendant is so dangerous that it should not have been marketed at all. Common and widely distributed products such as alcoholic beverages, firearms, and above-ground swimming pools may be found to be defective only upon proof of the requisite conditions in Subsection (a), (b), or (c). . . . Absent proof of defect under [§§ 1 and 2], however, courts have not imposed liability for categories of products that are generally available and widely used and consumed, even if they pose substantial risks of harm. Instead, courts generally have concluded that legislatures and administrative agencies can, more appropriately than courts, consider the desirability of commercial distribution of some categories of widely used and consumed, but nevertheless dangerous, products.

Illustrations:
    3. ABC Co. manufactured and sold a high-speed printing

press to XYZ Printers, by whom Robert is employed. The press includes a circular plate cylinder that spins at a very high speed. On occasion, a foreign object, known in the trade as a "hickie," finds its way onto the plate of the unit, causing a blemish or imperfection on the printed page. To remove a hickie, it is customary practice for an employee to apply a piece of plastic to the printing plate while it is spinning. Robert performed this practice, known as "chasing the hickie," and while doing so suffered serious injuries to his hand. All employees, including Robert, knew that chasing the hickie was a dangerous procedure. Plaintiff's expert testifies that a safety-guard at the point of operation, which could have prevented Robert's injury, was both technologically and economically feasible and is utilized in similar machinery without causing difficulty. The fact that the danger is open and obvious does not bar the design claim against ABC.

4. XYZ Co. manufactures above-ground swimming pools that are four feet deep. Warnings are embossed on the outside of the pools in large letters stating "DANGER—DO NOT DIVE—SHALLOW WATER." In disregard of the warnings, Mary, age 21, dove head first into an XYZ pool and suffered serious injury. Expert testimony establishes that when Mary's outstretched hands hit the pool's slippery vinyl bottom her hands slid apart, causing her to strike her head against the bottom of the pool. For the purposes of this Illustration it is assumed that the warnings were adequate and that the only issue is whether the above-ground pool was defectively designed because the bottom was too slippery. All the expert witnesses agree that the vinyl pool liner that XYZ utilized was the best and safest liner available and that no alternative, less slippery liner was feasible. Mary has failed to establish defective design under Subsection (b).

e. Design defects: possibility of manifestly unreasonable design. Several courts have suggested that the designs of some products are so manifestly unreasonable, in that they have low social utility and high degree of danger, that liability should attach even absent proof of a reasonable alternative design. In large part the problem is one of how the range of relevant alternative designs is described. For example, a toy gun that shoots hard rubber pellets with sufficient velocity to cause injury to children could be found to be defectively designed within the rule of Subsection (b). Toy guns unlikely to cause injury would constitute reasonable alternatives to the dangerous toy. Thus, toy guns that project ping-pong balls, soft gelatin pellets, or water might be found to be reasonable alternative designs to a toy gun that shoots hard pellets. However, if the realism of the hard-pellet gun, and thus its capacity to cause injury, is sufficiently important to those who purchase and use such products to justify the court's limiting consideration to toy

302

guns that achieve realism by shooting hard pellets, then no reasonable alternative will, by hypothesis, be available. In that instance, the design feature that defines which alternatives are relevant—the realism of the hard-pellet gun and thus its capacity to injure—is precisely the feature on which the user places value and of which the plaintiff complains. If a court were to adopt this characterization of the product, and deem the capacity to cause injury an egregiously unacceptable quality in a toy for use by children, it could conclude that liability should attach without proof of a reasonable alternative design. The court would declare the product design to be defective and not reasonably safe because the extremely high degree of danger posed by its use or consumption so substantially outweighs its negligible social utility that no rational, reasonable person, fully aware of the relevant facts, would choose to use, or to allow children to use, the product.

Illustration:

> 5. ABC Co. manufactures novelty items. One item, an exploding cigar, is made to explode with a loud bang and the emission of smoke. Robert purchased the exploding cigar and presented it to his boss, Jack, at a birthday party arranged for him at the office. Jack lit the cigar. When it exploded, the heat from the explosion lit Jack's beard on fire causing serious burns to his face. If a court were to recognize the rule identified in this Comment, the finder of fact might find ABC liable for the defective design of the exploding cigar even if no reasonable alternative design was available that would provide similar prank characteristics. The utility of the exploding cigar is so low and the risk of injury is so high as to warrant a conclusion that the cigar is defective and should not have been marketed at all.

f. Design defects: factors relevant in determining whether the omission of a reasonable alternative design renders a product not reasonably safe. Subsection (b) states that a product is defective in design if the omission of a reasonable alternative design renders the product not reasonably safe. A broad range of factors may be considered in determining whether an alternative design is reasonable and whether its omission renders a product not reasonably safe. The factors include, among others, the magnitude and probability of the foreseeable risks of harm, the instructions and warnings accompanying the product, and the nature and strength of consumer expectations regarding the product, including expectations arising from product portrayal and marketing. The relative advantages and disadvantages of the product as designed and as it alternatively could have been designed may also be considered. Thus, the likely effects of the alternative design on production costs; the effects of the alternative design on product longevity, maintenance, repair, and esthetics; and the range of consumer

303

choice among products are factors that may be taken into account. A plaintiff is not necessarily required to introduce proof on all of these factors; their relevance, and the relevance of other factors, will vary from case to case. Moreover, the factors interact with one another. For example, evidence of the magnitude and probability of foreseeable harm may be offset by evidence that the proposed alternative design would reduce the efficiency and the utility of the product. On the other hand, evidence that a proposed alternative design would increase production costs may be offset by evidence that product portrayal and marketing created substantial expectations of performance or safety, thus increasing the probability of foreseeable harm. Depending on the mix of these factors, a number of variations in the design of a given product may meet the test in Subsection (b). On the other hand, it is not a factor under Subsection (b) that the imposition of liability would have a negative effect on corporate earnings or would reduce employment in a given industry.

When evaluating the reasonableness of a design alternative, the overall safety of the product must be considered. It is not sufficient that the alternative design would have reduced or prevented the harm suffered by the plaintiff if it would also have introduced into the product other dangers of equal or greater magnitude.

While a plaintiff must prove that a reasonable alternative design would have reduced the foreseeable risks of harm, Subsection (b) does not require the plaintiff to produce expert testimony in every case. Cases arise in which the feasibility of a reasonable alternative design is obvious and understandable to laypersons and therefore expert testimony is unnecessary to support a finding that the product should have been designed differently and more safely. For example, when a manufacturer sells a soft stuffed toy with hard plastic buttons that are easily removable and likely to choke and suffocate a small child who foreseeably attempts to swallow them, the plaintiff should be able to reach the trier of fact with a claim that buttons on such a toy should be an integral part of the toy's fabric itself (or otherwise be unremovable by an infant) without hiring an expert to demonstrate the feasibility of an alternative safer design. Furthermore, other products already available on the market may serve the same or very similar function at lower risk and at comparable cost. Such products may serve as reasonable alternatives to the product in question.

In many cases, the plaintiff must rely on expert testimony. . . . To establish a prima facie case of defect, the plaintiff must prove the availability of a technologically feasible and practical alternative design that would have reduced or prevented the plaintiff's harm. Given inherent limitations on access to relevant data, the plaintiff is not required to establish with particularity the costs and benefits associated with adoption of the suggested alternative design.

In sum, the requirement of Subsection (b) that a product is defective in design if the foreseeable risks of harm could have been reduced by a reasonable alternative design is based on the commonsense notion that liability for harm caused by product designs should attach only when harm is reasonably preventable. For justice to be achieved, Subsection (b) should not be construed to create artificial and unreasonable barriers to recovery.

The necessity of proving a reasonable alternative design as a predicate for establishing design defect is, like any factual element in a case, addressed initially to the courts. Sufficient evidence must be presented so that reasonable persons could conclude that a reasonable alternative could have been practically adopted. Assuming that a court concludes that sufficient evidence on this issue has been presented, the issue is then for the trier of fact. . . .

Illustrations:

6. Andrea, age four, suffered serious burns when she got out of bed one night to go to the bathroom and tripped on the electric cord connected to a hot-water vaporizer. When Andrea tripped on the cord, the vaporizer separated into its three component parts—a large, wide-mouthed glass jar, a metal pan, and a plastic top-heating unit. The plastic top-heating unit was not secured to the jar. When it came off, the hot water in the jar poured out, causing Andrea's burns. In an action alleging defective design of the vaporizer for not securing the top unit to the jar, the following factors are relevant: (1) the foreseeability that the vaporizer might be accidentally tipped over; (2) the overall safety provided by an alternative design that secures the heating unit to the receptacle holding the water; (3) consumer knowledge or lack thereof that the water in the glass jar is scalding hot; (4) the added cost of the safer alternative design; and (5) the relative convenience of a vaporizer with a lift-off cap. If Andrea offers expert testimony based on a reasonable analysis of these factors and such testimony is sufficient to allow reasonable persons to conclude that the omission of the alternative design renders the product not reasonably safe, the question of defectiveness is for the trier of fact. . . .

7. The same facts as Illustration 6, except that the safety feature that will secure the top-heating unit to the jar and prevent the water from spilling is a component that will add $5 to the cost of the vaporizer. Although the increase in cost to consumers is a relevant consideration, the impact of a finding of defectiveness on the general economy or on the profitability of the vaporizer manufacturer is not a factor to be considered in deciding whether the alternative safer design is reasonable. . . .

10. ABC Armour Co. manufactures bullet-proof vests for

use by police and security personnel. ABC offers several models, some providing front and back protection only, and others providing wrap-around protection. State A highway patrol officials chose to purchase the model that provides front and back protection only. They did so because that model is less expensive, allows greater flexibility of movement, and is more comfortable. Robert, a state trooper, was shot and killed while making a routine traffic arrest. The bullet entered the side of his body, where the vest did not provide protection. Robert's legal representative argues that the design of the vest is defective because it does not provide wrap-around coverage. Robert has not established a defect within the meaning of Subsection (b). The mere fact of the availability of a wrap-around vest does not render defective the vest that provides only front-and-back protection. Although the wrap-around design is somewhat safer, it is also more costly to buy and use. Moreover, the differences in advantages and disadvantages are sufficiently understood by consumers that omission of the wrap-around feature does not render the front-and-back design not reasonably safe. To subject sellers to liability based on that design would unduly restrict the range of consumer choice among products.

g. Consumer expectations: general considerations. Under Subsection (b), consumer expectations do not constitute an independent standard for judging the defectiveness of product designs. . . . Consumer expectations, standing alone, do not take into account whether the proposed alternative design could be implemented at reasonable cost, or whether an alternative design would provide greater overall safety. Nevertheless, consumer expectations about product performance and the dangers attendant to product use affect how risks are perceived and relate to foreseeability and frequency of the risks of harm, both of which are relevant under Subsection (b). . . . It follows that, while disappointment of consumer expectations may not serve as an independent basis for allowing recovery under Subsection (b), neither may conformance with consumer expectations serve as an independent basis for denying recovery. Such expectations may be relevant in both contexts, but in neither are they controlling.

h. Consumer expectations: food products and used products. With regard to two special product categories consumer expectations play a special role in determining product defect. See § 7 (food products) and § 8 (used products). On occasion it is difficult to determine whether a given food component is an inherent aspect of a product or constitutes an adulteration of the product. Whether, for example, a fish bone in commercially distributed fish chowder constitutes a manufacturing defect within the meaning of § 2(a) is best determined by focusing on reasonable consumer expectations.

Regarding commercially distributed used products, the rules set forth in § 2 are not adequate to the task of determining liability. Variations in the type and condition of used products are such that the stringent rules for imposition of liability for new products are inappropriate. . . .

i. Inadequate instructions or warnings. Commercial product sellers must provide reasonable instructions and warnings about risks of injury posed by products. Instructions inform persons how to use and consume products safely. Warnings alert users and consumers to the existence and nature of product risks so that they can prevent harm either by appropriate conduct during use or consumption or by choosing not to use or consume. In most instances the instructions and warnings will originate with the manufacturer, but sellers down the chain of distribution must warn when doing so is feasible and reasonably necessary. In any event, sellers down the chain are liable if the instructions and warnings provided by predecessors in the chain are inadequate. Under prevailing rules concerning allocation of burdens of proof, plaintiff must prove that adequate instructions or warnings were not provided. Subsection (c) adopts a reasonableness test for judging the adequacy of product instructions and warnings. It thus parallels Subsection (b), which adopts a similar standard for judging the safety of product designs. Although the liability standard is formulated in essentially identical terms in Subsections (b) and (c), the defectiveness concept is more difficult to apply in the warnings context. In evaluating the adequacy of product warnings and instructions, courts must be sensitive to many factors. It is impossible to identify anything approaching a perfect level of detail that should be communicated in product disclosures. For example, educated or experienced product users and consumers may benefit from inclusion of more information about the full spectrum of product risks, whereas less-educated or unskilled users may benefit from more concise warnings and instructions stressing only the most crucial risks and safe-handling practices. In some contexts, products intended for special categories of users, such as children, may require more vivid and unambiguous warnings. In some cases, excessive detail may detract from the ability of typical users and consumers to focus on the important aspects of the warnings, whereas in others reasonably full disclosure will be necessary to enable informed, efficient choices by product users. Product warnings and instructions can rarely communicate all potentially relevant information, and the ability of a plaintiff to imagine a hypothetical better warning in the aftermath of an accident does not establish that the warning actually accompanying the product was inadequate. No easy guideline exists for courts to adopt in assessing the adequacy of product warnings and instructions. In making their assessments, courts must focus on various factors, such as content and comprehensibility, intensity of expression, and the characteristics of expected user groups.

Depending on the circumstances, Subsection (c) may require that instructions and warnings be given not only to purchasers, users, and consumers, but also to others who a reasonable seller should know will be in a position to reduce or avoid the risk of harm. There is no general rule as to whether one supplying a product for the use of others through an intermediary has a duty to warn the ultimate product user directly or may rely on the intermediary to relay warnings. The standard is one of reasonableness in the circumstances. Among the factors to be considered are the gravity of the risks posed by the product, the likelihood that the intermediary will convey the information to the ultimate user, and the feasibility and effectiveness of giving a warning directly to the user. Thus, when the purchaser of machinery is the owner of a workplace who provides the machinery to employees for their use, and there is reason to doubt that the employer will pass warnings on to employees, the seller is required to reach the employees directly with necessary instructions and warnings if doing so is reasonably feasible.

In addition to alerting users and consumers to the existence and nature of product risks so that they can, by appropriate conduct during use or consumption, reduce the risk of harm, warnings also may be needed to inform users and consumers of nonobvious and not generally known risks that unavoidably inhere in using or consuming the product. Such warnings allow the user or consumer to avoid the risk warned against by making an informed decision not to purchase or use the product at all and hence not to encounter the risk. In this context, warnings must be provided for inherent risks that reasonably foreseeable product users and consumers would reasonably deem material or significant in deciding whether to use or consume the product. Whether or not many persons would, when warned, nonetheless decide to use or consume the product, warnings are required to protect the interests of those reasonably foreseeable users or consumers who would, based on their own reasonable assessments of the risks and benefits, decline product use or consumption. When such warnings are necessary, their omission renders the product not reasonably safe at time of sale. Notwithstanding the defective condition of the product in the absence of adequate warnings, if a particular user or consumer would have decided to use or consume even if warned, the lack of warnings is not a legal cause of that plaintiff's harm. Judicial decisions supporting the duty to provide warnings for informed decisionmaking have arisen almost exclusively with regard to those toxic agents and pharmaceutical products with respect to which courts have recognized a distinctive need to provide risk information so that recipients of the information can decide whether they wish to purchase or utilize the product.

Illustration:

11. ABC Adhesives Inc. manufactures a chemical adhe-

sive for home use. Sandra purchased a gallon for use in laying tile in her kitchen. The label on the container warned in large letters that fumes from the adhesive were flammable and toxic, that the product should be used with adequate ventilation, and that all sources of fire should be extinguished. Sandra opened the windows in her kitchen, but did not extinguish the pilot light in her gas stove. When she had partly completed laying the tile, the pilot light suddenly ignited the fumes from the adhesive, causing Sandra serious burns. In an action against ABC, Sandra contends that the warnings were inadequate in failing specifically to state that gas-stove pilot lights should be extinguished. Whether the warning actually given was reasonable in the circumstances is to be decided by the trier of fact.

j. Warnings: obvious and generally known risks. In general, a product seller is not subject to liability for failing to warn or instruct regarding risks and risk-avoidance measures that should be obvious to, or generally known by, foreseeable product users. . . .

Illustration:

12. XYZ Ladder Co. manufactures kitchen step ladders for home use. Sid used an XYZ ladder to post a sign above the door of his home office, unaware that his five-year-old son was playing in the office. While Sid was standing on the ladder, his son suddenly opened the door, which struck the ladder. Sid fell off the ladder and suffered a fractured hip. There were no warnings on the ladder, nor in the instruction booklet that came with it, not to use the ladder in front of an unlocked door. The danger should be obvious to foreseeable product users. No reasonable trier of fact would find XYZ liable for failing to warn about it and the court should rule for XYZ as a matter of law.

k. Warnings: adverse allergic or idiosyncratic reactions. . . . The general rule in cases involving allergic reactions is that a warning is required when the harm-causing ingredient is one to which a substantial number of persons are allergic. . . . Essentially, this reflects the same risk-utility balancing undertaken in warnings cases generally. But courts explicitly impose the requirement of substantiality in cases involving adverse allergic reactions. . . . When the presence of the allergenic ingredient would not be anticipated by a reasonable user or consumer, warnings concerning its presence are required. Similarly, when the presence of the ingredient is generally known to consumers, but its dangers are not, a warning of the dangers must be given. . . .

Illustration:

13. XYZ produces an over-the-counter nonprescription medicine containing aspirin, a well-known allergen to which a

substantial minority of persons are sensitive. XYZ may reasonably assume that those who are allergic to aspirin are aware of their allergy or that, if they are not aware, warnings of possible allergic reactions would not be heeded. Thus, it is necessary to warn only of the fact that the medicine contains aspirin.

l. Relationship between design and instruction or warning. . . . In general, when a safer design can reasonably be implemented and risks can reasonably be designed out of a product, adoption of the safer design is required over a warning that leaves a significant residuum of such risks. . . . However, when an alternative design to avoid risks cannot reasonably be implemented, adequate instructions and warnings will normally be sufficient to render the product reasonably safe. Warnings are not, however, a substitute for the provision of a reasonably safe design.

The fact that a risk is obvious or generally known often serves the same function as a warning. However, obviousness of risk does not necessarily obviate a duty to provide a safer design. Just as warnings may be ignored, so may obvious or generally known risks be ignored, leaving a residuum of risk great enough to require adopting a safer design.

Illustration:

14. Jeremy's foot was severed when caught between the blade and compaction chamber of a garbage truck on which he was working. The injury occurred when he lost his balance while jumping on the back step of the garbage truck as it was moving from one stop to the next. The garbage truck, manufactured by XYZ Motor Co., has a warning in large red letters on both the left and right rear panels that reads "DANGER—DO NOT INSERT ANY OBJECT WHILE COMPACTION CHAMBER IS WORKING—KEEP HANDS AND FEET AWAY." The fact that adequate warning was given does not preclude Jeremy from seeking to establish a design defect under Subsection (b). The possibility that an employee might lose his balance and thus encounter the shear point was a risk that a warning could not eliminate and that might require a safety guard. Whether a design defect can be established is governed by Subsection (b).

m. Reasonably foreseeable uses and risks in design and warning claims. Subsections (b) and (c) impose liability only when the product is put to uses that it is reasonable to expect a seller or distributor to foresee. . . . The harms that result from unforeseeable risks—for example, in the human body's reaction to a new drug, medical device, or chemical—are not a basis of liability. Of course, a seller bears responsibility to perform reasonable testing prior to marketing a product and to discover risks and risk-avoidance measures that such testing would reveal. A seller is charged with knowledge of what reasonable testing would reveal. If testing is not undertaken, or is performed in an inadequate manner, and this failure results in a defect that causes harm, the seller is subject to liability for harm caused by such defect.

Illustration:

15. ABC Adhesives Inc. manufactures a chemical adhesive for use in laying ceramic tile. Recently it has become known that prolonged use of its ceramic adhesive over many years by diabetics can cause severe aggravation of the diabetic condition. Diabetics who have been using the ABC adhesive and have suffered serious aggravation of their condition bring an action against ABC for failing to warn about the risks of prolonged product use. However, it cannot be established that, at the time ABC's product was distributed, special risks to diabetics were reasonably foreseeable or that reasonable testing of the product would have led to the discovery of the risks. ABC is not liable since the risks attendant to such product use were not reasonably foreseeable.

n. Relationship of definitions of defect to traditional doctrinal categories. . . . Negligence rests on a showing of fault leading to product defect. Strict liability rests merely on a showing of product defect. When a plaintiff believes a good claim for the negligent creation of (or failure to discover) a manufacturing defect may be established, the plaintiff may assert such a claim in addition to a claim in strict liability under Subsection (a). The plaintiff in such a case should have the opportunity to prove fault and also to assert the right to recover based on strict liability. . . .

Illustration:

16. A bottle of soda exploded in Bob's hand, causing harm. The soda was manufactured by LMN Bottlers, against whom Bob brings an action in tort. Bob's expert testifies that the bottle contained a manufacturing defect that caused the explosion. The expert also testifies that LMN's quality control efforts are below levels that reasonably prudent bottlers should maintain. Bob may rely on both strict liability and negligence theories. . . .

o. Liability of nonmanufacturing sellers for defective design and defects due to inadequate instructions or warnings. Nonmanufacturing sellers such as wholesalers and retailers often are not in a good position feasibly to adopt safer product designs or better instructions or warnings. Nevertheless, once it is determined that a reasonable alternative design or reasonable instructions or warnings could have been provided at or before the time of sale by a predecessor in the chain of distribution and would have reduced plaintiff's harm, it is no defense that a nonmanufacturing seller of such a product exercised due care. Thus, strict liability is imposed

311

on a wholesale or retail seller who neither knew nor should have known of the relevant risks, nor was in a position to have taken action to avoid them, so long as a predecessor in the chain of distribution could have acted reasonably to avoid the risks. . . .

p. Misuse, modification, and alteration. Product misuse, modification, and alteration are forms of post-sale conduct by product users or others that can be relevant to the determination of the issues of defect, causation, or comparative responsibility. Whether such conduct affects one or more of the issues depends on the nature of the conduct and whether the manufacturer should have adopted a reasonable alternative design or provided a reasonable warning to protect against such conduct. . . .

Foreseeable product misuse, alteration, and modification must also be considered in deciding whether an alternative design should have been adopted. The post-sale conduct of the user may be so unreasonable, unusual, and costly to avoid that a seller has no duty to design or warn against them. When a court so concludes, the product is not defective within the meaning of Subsection (b) or (c).

A product may, however, be defective . . . due to the omission of a reasonable alternative design or the omission of an adequate warning, yet the risk that eventuates due to misuse, modification, or alteration raises questions whether the extent or scope of liability under the prevailing rules governing legal causation allow for the imposition of liability. Moreover, a product may be found to be defective and causally responsible for plaintiff's harm but the plaintiff may have misused, altered, or modified the product in a manner that calls for the reduction of plaintiff's recovery under the rules of comparative responsibility. Thus, an automobile may be defectively designed so as to provide inadequate protection against harm in the event of a collision, and the plaintiff's negligent modification of the automobile may have caused the collision eventuating in plaintiff's harm.

It follows that misuse, modification, and alteration are not discrete legal issues. Rather, when relevant, they are aspects of the concepts of defect, causation, and plaintiff's fault. . . .

Illustration:

20. The ABC Chair Co. manufactures and sells oak chairs. The backs of the chairs have five horizontal wooden bars shaped to the contour of the human back. John, a college student, climbed up to the top bar of an ABC chair to reach the top shelf of a bookcase. The chair tipped and John fell, suffering serious harm. John brings an action against ABC, alleging that the chair should either have had the stability to support him when standing on the top bar or have had a differently designed back so that he could not use the bars for that

purpose. The ABC chair is not defectively designed. John's misuse of the product is so unreasonable that the risks it entails need not be designed against.

q. Causation. Under § 1, the product defect must have caused harm to the plaintiff.

B. WARNING DEFECT

§ 9. Liability of Commercial Product Seller or Distributor for Harm Caused by Misrepresentation

Restatement of the Law Third, Torts: Products Liability

> One engaged in the business of selling or otherwise distributing products who, in connection with the sale of a product, makes a fraudulent, negligent, or innocent misrepresentation of material fact concerning the product is subject to liability for harm to persons or property caused by the misrepresentation.

Comment:

c. The elements of materiality, causation, and contributory fault. It is important to note [Restatement Second Sections] define what constitutes a material misrepresentation; what is a material fact; the requirement that the misrepresentation be a cause in fact of the harm; the requirement that the misrepresentation be a legal cause of the harm; and the role of contributory fault and its relation to justifiable reliance.

d. No requirement of product defect. This Section does not require the plaintiff to show that the product was defective at the time of sale or distribution within the meaning of other Sections of this Restatement Third of Torts: Products Liability.

§ 10. Liability of Commercial Product Seller or Distributor for Harm Caused by Post-Sale Failure to Warn

Restatement of the Law Third, Torts: Products Liability

> (a) One engaged in the business of selling or otherwise distributing products is subject to liability for harm to persons or property caused by the seller's failure to provide a warning after the time of sale or distribution of a product if a reasonable person in the seller's position would provide such a warning.

> (b) A reasonable person in the seller's position would provide a warning after the time of sale if:

(1) the seller knows or reasonably should know that the product poses a substantial risk of harm to persons or property; and

(2) those to whom a warning might be provided can be identified and can reasonably be assumed to be unaware of the risk of harm; and

(3) a warning can be effectively communicated to and acted on by those to whom a warning might be provided; and

(4) the risk of harm is sufficiently great to justify the burden of providing a warning.

Comment:

a. Rationale. Judicial recognition of the seller's duty to warn of a product-related risk after the time of sale, whether or not the product is defective at the time of original sale within the meaning of other Sections of this Restatement, is relatively new. Nonetheless, a growing body of decisional and statutory law imposes such a duty. Courts recognize that warnings about risks discovered after sale are sometimes necessary to prevent significant harm to persons and property. Nevertheless, an unbounded post-sale duty to warn would impose unacceptable burdens on product sellers. The costs of identifying and communicating with product users years after sale are often daunting. Furthermore, as product designs are developed and improved over time, many risks are reduced or avoided by subsequent design changes. If every post-sale improvement in a product design were to give rise to a duty to warn users of the risks of continuing to use the existing design, the burden on product sellers would be unacceptably great.

As with all rules that raise the question whether a duty exists, courts must make the threshold decisions that, in particular cases, triers of fact could reasonably find that product sellers can practically and effectively discharge such an obligation and that the risks of harm are sufficiently great to justify what is typically a substantial post-sale undertaking. . . . The legal standard is whether a reasonable person would provide a post-sale warning. In light of the serious potential for overburdening sellers in this regard, the court should carefully examine the circumstances for and against imposing a duty to provide a post-sale warning in a particular case.

b. When a reasonable person in the seller's position would provide a warning. The standard governing the liability of the seller is objective: whether a reasonable person in the seller's position would provide a warning. . . . In applying the reasonableness standard to members of the chain of distribution it is possible that one party's conduct may be reasonable and another's unreasonable.

314

For example, a manufacturer may discover information under circumstances satisfying Subsection (b)(1) through (4) and thus be required to provide a post-sale warning. In contrast, a retailer is generally not in a position to know about the risk discovered by the manufacturer after sale and thus is not subject to liability because it neither knows nor should know of the risk. Once the retailer is made aware of the risk, however, whether the retailer is subject to liability for failing to issue a post-sale warning depends on whether a reasonable person in the retailer's position would warn under the criteria set forth in Subsection (b)(1) through (4).

c. Requirement that seller or other distributor knows or should know of the product-related risk. A duty to warn after the time of sale cannot arise unless the product seller or other distributor knows or in the exercise of reasonable care should know of the product-related risk that causes plaintiff's harm. . . .

As a practical matter, most post-sale duties to warn arise when new information is brought to the attention of the seller, after the time of sale, concerning risks accompanying the product's use or consumption. When risks are not actually brought to the attention of sellers, the burden of constantly monitoring product performance in the field is usually too burdensome to support a post-sale duty to warn. However, when reasonable grounds exist for the seller to suspect that a hitherto unknown risk exists, especially when the risk involved is great, the duty of reasonable care may require investigation. With regard to one class of products, prescription drugs and devices, courts traditionally impose a continuing duty of reasonable care to test and monitor after sale to discover product-related risks.

Illustration:

1. ABC manufactures and sells Model 1220 power drills used exclusively in heavy industry. Three years after the Model 1220 is first put on the market, ABC learns that when the drill is used continuously for more than four hours it overheats, causing it to fracture. ABC learns of the overheating problem when the Model 1220 is first used on a new metal alloy that was not previously available, and thus not in use, at the time of first distribution. The new alloy causes the drill to heat well beyond temperatures caused by any other metal for which the Model 1220 has ever been used. No reasonable person could have foreseen the development of the new alloy when any of the drills were sold. Because the risk of overheating was not foreseeable at the time of sale of many of the Model 1220s, those units are not defective within the meaning of § 2. Whether ABC is subject to liability for failing to issue a post-sale warning regarding the risks of overheating is determined based on the factors set forth in Subsection (b)(1) through (4).

e. Requirement that those to whom a warning might be

provided be identifiable. The problem of identifying those to whom product warnings might be provided is especially relevant in the post-sale context. . . .

g. *The seller's ability to communicate the warning effectively to those who are in a position to act to prevent harm.* For a post-sale duty to warn to arise, the seller must reasonably be able to communicate the warning to those identified as appropriate recipients. When original customer sales records indicate which individuals are probably using and consuming the product in question, direct communication of a warning may be feasible. When direct communication is not feasible, it may be necessary to utilize the public media to disseminate information regarding risks of substantial harm. . . .

h. *Requirement that those to whom a post-sale warning might be provided be able to act effectively to reduce the risk.* To justify the potentially high cost of providing a post-sale warning, those to whom such warnings are provided must be in a position to reduce or prevent product-caused harm. Such recipients of warnings need not be original purchasers of the product, so long as they are able to reduce risk effectively.

j. *Distinguishing post-sale failures to warn from defects existing at the time of sale.* . . . A seller who discovers after sale that its product was defective at the time of sale within the meaning of this Restatement cannot generally absolve itself of liability by issuing a post-sale warning. . . . Of course, even when a product is defective at the time of sale a seller may have an independent obligation to issue a post-sale warning based on the rule stated in this Section. . . .

C. Defenses and Remedies

§ 17. **Apportionment of Responsibility Between or Among Plaintiff, Sellers and Distributors of Defective Products, and Others**

Restatement of the Law Third, Torts: Products Liability

(a) A plaintiff's recovery of damages for harm caused by a product defect may be reduced if the conduct of the plaintiff combines with the product defect to cause the harm and the plaintiff's conduct fails to conform to generally applicable rules establishing appropriate standards of care.

(b) The manner and extent of the reduction under Subsection (a) and the apportionment of plaintiff's recovery among multiple defendants are governed by generally applicable rules apportioning responsibility.

316

Comment:

a. History. The rule stated in this Section recognizes that the fault of the plaintiff is relevant in assessing liability for product-caused harm. Section 402A of the Restatement, Second, of Torts, recognizing strict liability for harm caused by defective products, was adopted in 1964 when the overwhelming majority rule treated contributory negligence as a total bar to recovery. Understandably, the Institute was reluctant to bar a plaintiff's products liability claim in tort based on conduct that was not egregious. Thus, § 402A, Comment *n*, altered the general tort defenses by narrowing the applicability of contributory negligence and emphasizing assumption of risk as the primary defense. Since then, comparative fault has swept the country. Only a tiny minority of states retain contributory fault as a total bar.

A strong majority of jurisdictions apply the comparative responsibility doctrine to products liability actions. Courts today do not limit the relevance of plaintiff's fault as did the Restatement, Second, of Torts to conduct characterized as voluntary assumption of the risk.

Certain forms of consumer behavior—product misuse and product alteration or modification—have been the subject of much confusion and misunderstanding. Early decisions treated product misuse, alteration, and modification, whether by the plaintiff or a third party, as a total bar to recovery against a product seller. Today misuse, alteration, and modification relate to one of three issues in a products liability action. In some cases, misuse, alteration, and modification are important in determining whether the product is defective. In others, they are relevant to the issue of legal cause. Finally, when the plaintiff misuses, alters, or modifies the product, such conduct may constitute contributory fault and reduce the plaintiff's recovery under the rules of comparative responsibility.

§ 18. Disclaimers, Limitations, Waivers, and Other Contractual Exculpations as Defenses to Products Liability Claims for Harm to Persons

Restatement of the Law Third, Torts: Products Liability

Disclaimers and limitations of remedies by product sellers or other distributors, waivers by product purchasers, and other similar contractual exculpations, oral or written, do not bar or reduce otherwise valid products liability claims against sellers or other distributors of new products for harm to persons.

Comment:

a. Effects of contract defenses on products liability tort claims

317

for harm to persons. A commercial seller or other distributor of a new product is not permitted to avoid liability for harm to persons through limiting terms in a contract governing the sale of a product. It is presumed that the ordinary product user or consumer lacks sufficient information and bargaining power to execute a fair contractual limitation of rights to recover. For a limited exception to this general rule, see Comment *d.* The rule in this Section applies only to "sellers or other distributors of new products.". . . . Nothing in this Section is intended to constrain parties within the commercial chain of distribution from contracting inter se for indemnity agreements or save-harmless clauses.

d. Waiver of rights in contractual settings in which product purchasers possess both adequate knowledge and sufficient economic power. The rule in this Section applies to cases in which commercial product sellers attempt unfairly to disclaim or otherwise limit their liability to the majority of users and consumers who are presumed to lack information and bargaining power adequate to protect their interests. This Section does not address whether consumers, especially when represented by informed and economically powerful consumer groups or intermediaries, with full information and sufficient bargaining power, may contract with product sellers to accept curtailment of liability in exchange for concomitant benefits, or whether such consumers might be allowed to agree to substitute alternative dispute resolution mechanisms in place of traditional adjudication. When such contracts are accompanied by alternative nontort remedies that serve as an adequate quid pro quo for reducing or eliminating rights to recover in tort, arguments may support giving effect to such agreements. Such contractual arrangements raise policy questions different from those raised by this Section and require careful consideration by the courts.

D. PRINCIPLES OF GENERAL APPLICABILITY

§ 19. Definition of "Product"

Restatement of the Law Third, Torts: Products Liability

For purposes of this Restatement:

(a) **A product is tangible personal property distributed commercially for use or consumption. Other items, such as real property and electricity, are products when the context of their distribution and use is sufficiently analogous to the distribution and use of tangible personal property that it is appropriate to apply the rules stated in this Restatement.**

(b) **Services, even when provided commercially, are not products.**

318

(c) Human blood and human tissue, even when provided commercially, are not subject to the rules of this Restatement.

Comment:

a. History. . . . Apart from statutes that define "product" for purposes of determining products liability, in every instance it is for the court to determine as a matter of law whether something is, or is not, a product.

b. Tangible personal property: in general. For purposes of this Restatement, most but not necessarily all products are tangible personal property. In certain situations, however, intangible personal property (see Comment *d*) and real property (see Comment *e*) may be products. Component parts are products, whether sold or distributed separately or assembled with other component parts. An assemblage of component parts is also, itself, a product. Raw materials are products, whether manufactured, such as sheet metal; processed, such as lumber; or gathered and sold or distributed in raw condition, such as unwashed gravel and farm produce. . . .

d. Intangible personal property. Two basic types of intangible personal property are involved. The first consists of information in media such as books, maps, and navigational charts. Plaintiffs allege that the information delivered was false and misleading, causing harm when actors relied on it. They seek to recover against publishers in strict liability in tort based on product defect, rather than on negligence or some form of misrepresentation. Although a tangible medium such as a book, itself clearly a product, delivers the information, the plaintiff's grievance in such cases is with the information, not with the tangible medium. Most courts, expressing concern that imposing strict liability for the dissemination of false and defective information would significantly impinge on free speech have, appropriately, refused to impose strict products liability in these cases. One area in which some courts have imposed strict products liability involves false information contained in maps and navigational charts. In that context the falsity of the factual information is unambiguous and more akin to a classic product defect. However, the better view is that false information in such documents constitutes a misrepresentation that the user may properly rely upon.

The second major category of intangible, harm-causing products involves the transmission of intangible forces such as electricity and X rays. With respect to transmission of electricity, a majority of courts have held that electricity becomes a product only when it passes through the customer's meter and enters the customer's premises. . . .

e. Real property. Traditionally, courts have been reluctant to impose products liability on sellers of improved real property in that such property does not constitute goods or personalty. A housing contractor, building and selling one house at a time, does not fit the pattern of a mass producer of manufactured products, nor is such a builder perceived to be more capable than are purchasers of controlling or insuring against risks presented by weather conditions or earth movements. More recently, courts have treated sellers of improved real property as product sellers in a number of contexts. When a building contractor sells a building that contains a variety of appliances or other manufactured equipment, the builder, together with the equipment manufacturer and other distributors, are held as product sellers with respect to such equipment notwithstanding the fact that the built-in equipment may have become, for other legal purposes, attachments to and thus part of the underlying real property. Moreover, the builder may be treated as a product seller even with respect to the building itself when the building has been prefabricated—and thus manufactured—and later assembled on- or off-site. Finally, courts impose strict liability for defects in construction when dwellings are built, even if on-site, on a major scale, as in a large housing project.

f. The distinction between services and products. Services, even when provided commercially, are not products for purposes of this Restatement. Thus, apart from the sale of a product incidental to the service, one who agrees for a monetary fee to mow the lawn of another is the provider of a service even if the provider is a large firm engaged commercially in lawn care. . . .

PART VIII
NUISANCE

CHAPTER 17

NUISANCE

A. TYPES OF NUISANCE

§ 821A. Types of Nuisance

Restatement of the Law Second, Torts

In this Restatement "nuisance" is used to denote either

(a) a public nuisance as defined in § 821B,
or

(b) a private nuisance as defined in § 821D.

Comment:

a. This Section is intended to be exclusive. Any harm to person or property that does not fall within either of the two stated categories is not a nuisance and is not included within any of the Sections of this Chapter. It may possibly result in liability based on other grounds such as ordinary negligence, but the particular rules stated as applicable to nuisances do not apply to it.

b. *Meaning of "nuisance."* The term frequently is used in several different senses. In popular speech it often has a very loose connotation of anything harmful, annoying, offensive or inconvenient, as when it is said that a man makes a nuisance of himself by bothering others. Occasionally this careless usage has crept into a court opinion. If the term is to have any definite legal significance, these cases must be completely disregarded.

In its legal significance, "nuisance" has been employed in three different senses:

(1) It is often used to denote human activity or a physical condition that is harmful or annoying to others. Thus it is often said that indecent conduct or a rubbish heap or the smoking chimney of a factory is a nuisance.

(2) It is often used to denote the harm caused by the human conduct or physical condition described in the first meaning. Thus it may be said that the annoyance caused by loud noises or by objectionable odors is a nuisance to the person affected by them.

When the word is used in either of these two senses it does not necessarily connote tort liability. The courts that use the word in either sense will often proceed to discuss whether the particular "nuisance" is actionable and may conclude that it is not.

(3) Often, however, the term has been used to denote both the conduct or condition and the resulting harm with the addition of the legal liability that arises from the combination of the two. Thus the courts may say that a person is maintaining a nuisance, meaning that he is engaged in an activity or is creating a condition that is harmful or annoying to others and for which he is legally liable; or they may distinguish between a "nuisance per se," meaning harmful conduct of a kind that always results in liability and a "nuisance per accidens," meaning harmful conduct that results in liability only under particular circumstances.

B. PUBLIC NUISANCE

§ 821B. Public Nuisance
Restatement of the Law Second, Torts

(1) **A public nuisance is an unreasonable interference with a right common to the general public.**

(2) **Circumstances that may sustain a holding that an interference with a public right is unreasonable include the following:**

(a) **Whether the conduct involves a significant interference with the public health, the public safety, the public peace, the public comfort or the public convenience, or**

(b) **whether the conduct is proscribed by a statute, ordinance or administrative regulation, or**

(c) whether the conduct is of a continuing nature or has produced a permanent or long-lasting effect, and, as the actor knows or has reason to know, has a significant effect upon the public right.

Comment:

b. Common law public nuisances. At common law public nuisance came to cover a large, miscellaneous and diversified group of minor criminal offenses, all of which involved some interference with the interests of the community at large—interests that were recognized as rights of the general public entitled to protection. Thus public nuisances included interference with the public health, as in the case of keeping diseased animals or the maintenance of a pond breeding malarial mosquitoes; with the public safety, as in the case of the storage of explosives in the midst of a city or the shooting of fireworks in the public streets; with the public morals, as in the case of houses of prostitution or indecent exhibitions; with the public peace, as by loud and disturbing noises; with the public comfort, as in the case of widely disseminated bad odors, dust and smoke; with the public convenience, as by the obstruction of a public highway or a navigable stream; and with a wide variety of other miscellaneous public rights of a similar kind. In each of these instances the interference with the public right was so unreasonable that it was held to constitute a criminal offense. For the same reason it also constituted a tort. Many states no longer recognize common law crimes, treating the criminal law as entirely statutory. But the common law tort of public nuisance still exists, and the traditional basis for determining what is a public nuisance may still be applicable.

i. Action for damages distinguished from one for injunction. There are numerous differences between an action for tort damages and an action for an injunction or abatement, and precedents for the two are by no means interchangeable. In determining whether to award damages, the court's task is to decide whether it is unreasonable to engage in the conduct without paying for the harm done. Although a general activity may have great utility it may still be unreasonable to inflict the harm without compensating for it. In an action for injunction the question is whether the activity itself is so unreasonable that it must be stopped. It may be reasonable to continue an important activity if payment is made for the harm it is causing, but unreasonable to continue it without paying.

On the other hand an award of damages is retroactive, applying to past conduct, while an injunction applies only to the future. In addition, for damages to be awarded significant harm must have been actually incurred, while for an injunction harm need only be threatened and need not actually have been sustained at all. To maintain a damage action for a public nuisance, one must have suffered damage different in kind from that suffered by the general public; this is not necessarily true in a suit for abatement or injunction.

§ 821C. Who Can Recover for Public Nuisance

Restatement of the Law Second, Torts

(1) In order to recover damages in an individual action for a public nuisance, one must have suffered harm of a kind different from that suffered by other members of the public exercising the right common to the general public that was the subject of interference.

(2) In order to maintain a proceeding to enjoin to abate a public nuisance, one must

(a) have the right to recover damages, as indicated in Subsection (1), or

(b) have authority as a public official or public agency to represent the state or a political subdivision in the matter, or

(c) have standing to sue as a representative of the general public, as a citizen in a citizen's action or as a member of a class in a class action.

Comment:

b. Difference in kind and degree. The private individual can recover in tort for a public nuisance only if he has suffered harm of a different kind from that suffered by other persons exercising the same public right. It is not enough that he has suffered the same kind of harm or interference but to a greater extent or degree. Thus when a public highway is obstructed and all who make use of it are compelled to detour a mile, no distinction is to be made between those who travel the highway only once in the course of a month and the man who travels it twice a day over that entire period. For both there has been only interference with the public right of travel and resulting inconvenience, even though the interference and the inconvenience have been much greater in the one case than in the other. The explanation of the refusal of the courts to take into account these differences in extent undoubtedly lies in the difficulty or impossibility of drawing any satisfactory line for each public nuisance at some point in the varying gradations of degree, together with the belief that to avoid multiplicity of actions invasions of rights common to all of the public should be left to be remedied by action by public officials.

c. Difference in degree of interference cannot, however, be entirely disregarded in determining whether there has been difference in kind. . . .

d. Physical harm. When the public nuisance causes personal injury to the plaintiff or physical harm to his land or chattels, the harm is normally different in kind from that suffered by other members of the public and the tort action may be maintained.

Illustration:

2. A digs a trench across the public highway and leaves it unguarded at night without any warning light. B, driving along the highway, drives into the trench and breaks his leg. B can recover for the public nuisance.

h. Pecuniary loss. Pecuniary loss to the plaintiff resulting from the public nuisance is normally a different kind of harm from that suffered by the general public. A contractor who loses the benefits of a particular contract or is put to an additional expense in performing it because of the obstruction of a public highway preventing him from transporting materials to the place of performance, can recover for the public nuisance. The same is true when it can be shown with reasonable certainty that an established business has lost profits, as when the obstruction of the highway prevents a common carrier from operating buses over it or access to the plaintiff's place of business is made so inconvenient that customers do not come to it. If, however, the pecuniary loss is common to an entire community and the plaintiff suffers it only in a greater degree than others, it is not a different kind of harm and the plaintiff cannot recover for the invasion of the public right.

Illustration:

11. A pollutes public waters, killing all of the fish. B, who has been operating a commercial fishery in these waters, suffers pecuniary loss as a result. B can recover for the public nuisance.

j. Action to enjoin or abate. A public official who is authorized to represent the state or an appropriate subdivision in an action to abate or enjoin a public nuisance may of course maintain the action. An administrative agency may also be given this authority, whether it promulgated the administrative regulations it is seeking to enforce or not.

So also a person who has suffered damages that are different from those suffered by other members of the public and who is thus able to bring an action in tort for his damage is able to seek an injunction against the public nuisance. It has been the traditional rule that if a member of the public has not suffered damages different in kind and cannot maintain a tort action for damages, he also has no standing to maintain an action for an injunction. The reasons for this rule in the damage action are that it is to prevent the bringing of a multiplicity of actions by many members of the public and the bringing of actions for trivial injury.

C. Private Nuisance

§ 821D. Private Nuisance

Restatement of the Law Second, Torts

A private nuisance is a nontrespassory invasion of another's interest in the private use and enjoyment of land.

Comment:

b. Interest in use and enjoyment of land. The term "interest" . . . is used in this Restatement in a broad sense. It comprehends not only the interests that a person may have in the actual present use of land for residential, agricultural, commercial, industrial and other purposes, but also his interests in having the present use value of the land unimpaired by changes in its physical condition. Thus the destruction of trees on vacant land is as much an invasion of the owner's interest in its use and enjoyment as is the destruction of crops or flowers that he is growing on the land for his present use. "Interest in use and enjoyment" also comprehends the pleasure, comfort and enjoyment that a person normally derives from the occupancy of land. Freedom from discomfort and annoyance while using land is often as important to a person as freedom from physical interruption with his use or freedom from detrimental change in the physical condition of the land itself. This interest in freedom from annoyance and discomfort in the use of land is to be distinguished from the interest in freedom from emotional distress. The latter is purely an interest of personality and receives limited legal protection, whereas the former is essentially an interest in the usability of land and, although it involves an element of personal tastes and sensibilities, it receives much greater legal protection.

§ 822. General Rule

Restatement of the Law Second, Torts

One is subject to liability for a private nuisance if, but only if, his conduct is a legal cause of an invasion of another's interest in the private use and enjoyment of land, and the invasion is either

> **(a) intentional and unreasonable, or**

> **(b) unintentional and otherwise actionable under the rules controlling liability for negligent or reckless conduct, or for abnormally dangerous conditions or activities.**

Comment:

c. Liability for an invasion of interests in the use and enjoyment of land now depends upon the presence of some type of tortious conduct. Most invasions are intentional, and, with regard to the interest invaded, they are called private nuisances. These invasions have no name derived from the type of conduct involved. This circumstance naturally led to thinking of private nuisance as itself a type of liability-forming conduct and to contrasting it with negligence. But as has been said, a negligent interference with the use and enjoyment of land is private nuisance in respect to the interest invaded and negligence in respect to the type of conduct that causes the invasion. Many interests other than those in the use and enjoyment of land may be invaded by negligent, reckless or abnormally dangerous conduct, and it is only when an interest in the use and enjoyment of land is invaded that an action for private nuisance and an action based on the type of conduct involved are actions for the same cause, and are not to be distinguished but identified.

An invasion of a person's interest in the private use and enjoyment of land by any type of liability-forming conduct is private nuisance. The invasion that subjects a person to liability may be either intentional or unintentional. A person is subject to liability for an intentional invasion when his conduct is unreasonable under the circumstances of the particular case, and he is subject to liability for an unintentional invasion when his conduct is negligent, reckless or abnormally dangerous. These are the types of conduct that are stated in this Chapter as subjecting a person to liability for invasions of interests in the private use and enjoyment of land.

§ 826. Unreasonableness of Intentional Invasion

Restatement of the Law Second, Torts

An intentional invasion of another's interest in the use and enjoyment of land is unreasonable if

> **(a) the gravity of the harm outweighs the utility of the actor's conduct, or**

> **(b) the harm caused by the conduct is serious and the financial burden of compensating for this and similar harm to others would not make the continuation of the conduct not feasible.**

Comment:

b. Unreasonableness in general. The mere fact that an invasion of another's interest in the use and enjoyment of land is intentional does not mean that it is unreasonable. . . . Many invasions [ ] can be justified as reasonable although the actor knows that they are resulting or are substantially certain to result from his conduct. . . .

c. *The point of view.* The unreasonableness of an intentional invasion is determined from an objective point of view. The question is not whether the plaintiff or the defendant would regard the invasion as unreasonable, but whether reasonable persons generally, looking at the whole situation impartially and objectively, would consider it unreasonable. Consideration must be given not only to the interests of the person harmed but also for the interests of the actor and to the interests of the community as a whole. Determining unreasonableness is essentially a weighing process, involving a comparative evaluation of conflicting interests in various situations according to objective legal standards.

d. *"Gravity" of harm and "utility" of conduct.* The terms "gravity" and "utility" are used in this Restatement to express the legal evaluation of harm and conduct. . . . [T]he utility or meritoriousness of conduct from a legal standpoint is not always the same as its meritoriousness from the standpoint of the actor. One operating a factory in a populous locality and employing five thousand people might regard his activity as highly meritorious even though it produced unnecessary noise and smoke, whereas the legal merit or utility of his conduct would be greatly reduced by the fact that he was not taking all practicable measures to eliminate interference with others. . . .

e. *"Gravity" vs. "utility."* The unreasonableness of an intentional invasion of another's interest in the use and enjoyment of land is ordinarily determined in each individual case on the particular facts of that case, and the decision of whether the utility of the conduct outweighs the gravity of the harm is normally made by the trier of fact upon a thorough consideration of [ ] factors. . . . Even though the noise and smoke from a factory cannot feasibly be eliminated, the utility of the factory is not weighed in the abstract. In a suit for damages, the legal utility of the activity may also be greatly reduced by the fact that the actor is operating the factory and producing the noise and smoke without compensating his neighbors for the harm done to them. The conduct for which the utility is being weighed includes both the general activity and what is done about its consequences. . . .

D. SIGNIFICANT-HARM REQUIREMENT

§ 821F.   Significant Harm

Restatement of the Law Second, Torts

There is liability for a nuisance only to those to whom it causes significant harm, of a kind that would be suffered by a normal person in the com-

munity or by property in normal condition and used for a normal purpose.

Comment:

a. The rule stated in this Section is applicable to both public and private nuisances.

b. Liability—Damages—Injunction. The rule stated in this Section applies only to tort liability in an action for damages. A public nuisance may be prosecuted criminally although it has not yet resulted in any significant harm, or indeed any harm to anyone. . . . The recovery of damages in a tort action is, however, limited to those who have in fact suffered significant harm of the kind stated in this Section.

c. Significant harm. . . . [T]here must be a real and appreciable invasion of the plaintiff's interests before he can have an action for either a public or a private nuisance. . . .

d. Hypersensitive persons or property. When an invasion involves a detrimental change in the physical condition of land, there is seldom any doubt as to the significant character of the invasion. When, however, it involves only personal discomfort or annoyance, it is sometimes difficult to determine whether the invasion is significant. The standard for the determination of significant character is the standard of normal persons or property in the particular locality. If normal persons living in the community would regard the invasion in question as definitely offensive, seriously annoying or intolerable, then the invasion is significant. If normal persons in that locality would not be substantially annoyed or disturbed by the situation, then the invasion is not a significant one, even though the idiosyncracies of the particular plaintiff may make it unendurable to him. Rights and privileges as to the use and enjoyment of land are based on the general standards of normal persons in the community and not on the standards of the individuals who happen to be there at the time.

Thus a hypersensitive nervous invalid cannot found an action for a private nuisance upon the normal ringing of a church bell across the street from his house, on the ground that the noise has become so unbearable to him that it throws him into convulsions and threatens his health or even his life, if a normal member of the community would regard the sound as unobjectionable or at most a petty annoyance. This is true also when the harm to the plaintiff results only because of the hypersensitive condition of his land or chattels or his abnormal use of them. Thus an ordinary power line supplying electric current for household use does not create a nuisance when it interferes by induction with highly sensitive electrical instruments operating in the vicinity.

On the other hand, when the invasion is of a kind that the

normal individual in the community would find definitely annoying or offensive, the fact that those who live in the neighborhood are hardened to it and have no objection will not prevent the plaintiff from maintaining his action. For example, the noise of a boiler factory next door may be a private nuisance even though the plaintiff and others who live in the vicinity are stone deaf and cannot hear it. The deafness of the plaintiff himself will affect the damages that he can recover, but it does not prevent the existence of a genuine interference with the use and enjoyment of his land as, for example, for the purpose of entertaining guests. . . .

e. Particular community. The location, character and habits of the particular community are to be taken into account in determining what is offensive or annoying to a normal individual living in it. Thus the odors of a hen house, which would be highly objectionable in a residential area in a city, may be acceptable and normally regarded as harmless and inoffensive in a rural district.

f. Normal mental reactions. In determining whether the harm would be suffered by a normal member of the community, fears and other mental reactions common to the community are to be taken into account, even though they may be without scientific foundation or other support in fact. Thus the presence of a leprosy sanatarium in the vicinity of a group of private residences may seriously interfere with the use and enjoyment of land because of the normal fear that it creates of possible contagion, even though leprosy is in fact so rarely transmitted through normal contacts that there is no practical possibility of communication of the disease.

g. Duration or frequency of invasion. It is often said by the courts and commentators that in order to constitute a nuisance the interference must continue or recur over some period of time. These statements usually are true for the particular facts or issue giving rise to them. . . .

The decisions do not, however, support a categoric requirement of continuance or recurrence in all cases as an established rule of law. If the defendant's interference with the public right or with the use and enjoyment of land causes significant harm and his conduct is otherwise sufficient to subject him to liability for a nuisance, liability will result, however brief in duration the interference or the harm may be. Thus when a magazine of explosives, which has caused no harm, explodes and shakes the plaintiff's adjoining building to pieces, liability may be based on the ground of a private nuisance; and the same is true when the defendant, spraying his land with insecticide for five minutes, ruins the plaintiff's adjoining crops. So likewise, a public nuisance may consist of a single unlawful prize fight or indecent exposure or a two-minute obstruction of the public highway that causes particular harm such as personal injury to the plaintiff.

E. DEFENSES

§ 840D. Coming to the Nuisance

Restatement of the Law Second, Torts

> **The fact that the plaintiff has acquired or improved his land after a nuisance interfering with it has come into existence is not in itself sufficient to bar his action, but it is a factor to be considered in determining whether the nuisance is actionable.**

Comment:

b. The rule generally accepted by the courts is that in itself and without other factors, the "coming to the nuisance" will not bar the plaintiff's recovery. Otherwise the defendant by setting up an activity or a condition that results in the nuisance could condemn all the land in his vicinity to a servitude without paying any compensation, and so could arrogate to himself a good deal of the value of the adjoining land. The defendant is required to contemplate and expect the possibility that the adjoining land may be settled, sold or otherwise transferred and that a condition originally harmless may result in an actionable nuisance when there is later development.

Illustration:

1. A operates a brick kiln on his own land, which is adjacent to vacant land owned by B. The smoke, gas and fumes from the kiln do no harm to the vacant land. Before a prescriptive period has run, C buys the vacant land from B, moves in upon it and erects a dwelling and plants trees, vines and shrubbery. The operation of the brick kiln renders the occupation of the dwelling uncomfortable and kills the planted vegetation. C is not barred from recovery by the fact that he has acquired and improved the land after the defendant's activity was already in existence.

c. Although it is not conclusive in itself, the fact that the plaintiff has "come to the nuisance" is still a factor of importance to be considered in cases where other factors are involved.

Illustration:

3. A operates a brewery in a former residential area in which industrial plants are beginning to appear. The brewery noises, odors and smoke interfere with the use and enjoyment of the land of B adjoining it. C buys the land from B, moves in upon it and brings an action for the private nuisance. The fact that C has come to the nuisance, together with the changing character of the locality, may be sufficient to prevent recovery. . . .

PART IX
APPORTIONMENT OF LIABILITY

CHAPTER 18

APPORTIONMENT OF LIABILITY

A. APPORTIONING LIABILITY AMONG TWO OR MORE PERSONS

§ 1. Issues and Causes of Action Addressed by This Restatement

Restatement of the Law Third, Torts: Apportionment of Liability

This Restatement addresses issues of apportioning liability among two or more persons. It applies to all claims (including lawsuits and settlements) for death, personal injury (including emotional distress or consortium), or physical damage to tangible property, regardless of the basis of liability.

334

Comment:

a. Nomenclature and issues addressed by this Restatement. . . . This Restatement addresses issues that arise in apportioning liability among two or more persons, including the plaintiff. . . .

Comparative responsibility has a potential impact on almost all areas of tort law. Sometimes comparative responsibility directly affects apportionment, such as when it determines the *effect* of a plaintiff's negligence on his or her recovery. At other times, comparative responsibility . . . can affect other rules of tort law. For example, rules about joint and several liability can affect rules concerning fault or causation, because a court might be willing to relax liability rules when a defendant is liable only for a portion of the harm. . . .

Comparative responsibility requires courts to coordinate liability rules and defenses in ways that transcend the traditional boundaries between various torts. Tort law generally reflects two variables: the nature of the defendant's conduct and the nature of the plaintiff's injury. Apportionment issues cut across this structure. Several defendants might be subject to liability under different tort theories, but apportionment among them requires coordination. . . .

Applying different apportionment rules to different parts of a multi-party, multi-theory lawsuit poses important practical problems, but it also highlights conceptual tensions. The intellectual underpinning of having subcategories in substantive tort law—that is, of having separate torts—is that various torts raise different policy concerns. The intellectual underpinning of comparative responsibility is that a single injury is more or less unitary. . . .

[T]he core issues [around the problem of apportionment include]:

(1) the legal effects of different types of a plaintiff's conduct, such as a plaintiff's intentional self-injury, a plaintiff's negligence, and a plaintiff's voluntarily assuming a risk;

(2) joint and several liability;

(3) apportionment of damages by causation; and

(4) contribution and indemnity.

b. Bases of liability addressed by this Restatement. This Restatement applies to all claims to recover compensation for death, personal injury, or physical damage to tangible property, including intentional torts, negligence, strict liability, nuisance, breach of warranty, misrepresentation, or any other theory of liability. This Restatement takes no position on whether or under what circumstances emotional distress or consortium is recoverable. . . .

c. Special issues involving intentional torts. Intentional torts

335

present special problems of apportionment. These concerns are strongest in cases where an alleged intentional tortfeasor contends that the plaintiff's own conduct was unreasonable. They are taken into account when applying the rules of this Restatement to particular cases. In some situations, this Restatement provides special rules governing intentional tortfeasors. The basic concept is that liability should be apportioned among all legally culpable actors according to proportionate shares of responsibility, while affording appropriate redress to victims of intentional torts. Consequently, this Restatement is applicable to all bases of liability, including intentional torts, but provides courts with flexibility to fashion appropriate special rules for victims of intentional torts.

Traditionally, a plaintiff's negligence was not a defense to intentional torts. Courts and legislatures generally ignored intentional torts when they adopted comparative responsibility. Whether intentional torts should be included raises two principal issues as well as some subordinate ones. First, should a plaintiff's negligence reduce the plaintiff's recovery against an intentional tortfeasor? Second, when one of two or more defendants is liable for an intentional tort, should a percentage of responsibility be assigned to that tortfeasor? Such an allocation could affect: (a) the plaintiff's own percentage of responsibility and thereby reduce the plaintiff's recovery against other defendants, including nonintentional tortfeasors, (b) whether to impose joint and several liability on various defendants, (c) the allocation of responsibility to other defendants, (d) whether a different defendant should bear liability for responsibility assigned to the intentional tortfeasor, (e) the rules governing settlement, and (f) contribution and indemnity.

Although some courts have held that a plaintiff's negligence may serve as a comparative defense to an intentional tort, most have not. This Restatement takes no position on that issue. When substantive rules of law provide that the plaintiff's negligence is a defense to an intentional tort, it reduces but does not bar recovery. When substantive rules of law provide that the plaintiff's negligence is not a defense to an intentional tort, the plaintiff's negligence is still a comparative defense to other, nonintentional torts.

In a multiparty lawsuit in which a defendant or other relevant person is liable for an intentional tort, the factfinder assigns a percentage of responsibility to each party and each other relevant person, including the plaintiff and any intentional tortfeasor, but special rules apply to these cases. Considerations in joint and several liability change when an intentional tortfeasor is involved. Consequently, § 12 provides that an intentional tortfeasor is jointly and severally liable for a plaintiff's indivisible injury, even when joint and several liability has otherwise been abolished. Section 14 provides that a nonintentional tortfeasor is liable for the percentage of responsibility assigned to an intentional tortfeasor when the nonintentional tortfeasor has a special duty to protect the plaintiff from harm by the intentional tortfeasor. Section 23, Comment *e*, permits the nonintentional tortfeasor to recover those damages as contribution from the intentional tortfeasor.

d. Exceptions. The specific policies embodied in a particular cause of action, especially a statutory cause of action, may preclude applying a plaintiff's negligence as a comparative defense, preclude imposing joint and several liability, or preclude allowing indemnity and contribution. . . .

e. Other types of injuries. [T]his Restatement sometimes may be referred to by analogy in suits for purely nontangible economic loss caused by breach of contract or warranty, fraud, misrepresentation, nonmedical professional malpractice, or, where recognized, negligence; in suits by insureds or others against insurers for inappropriate claims-settlement practices; and in suits for breach of fiduciary relationship, interference with contractual relations, defamation, and invasion of privacy. These principles may also be referred to by analogy when a statutory system calls for apportionment, except when inconsistent with a policy of the statute. . . .

B. MULTIPLE TORTFEASORS AND INDIVISIBLE HARMS

§ 10. Effect of Joint and Several Liability

Restatement of the Law Third, Torts: Apportionment of Liability

When, under applicable law, some persons are jointly and severally liable to an injured person, the injured person may sue for and recover the full amount of recoverable damages from any jointly and severally liable person.

Comment:

a. Introductory note. This Topic concerns the apportionment of damages among multiple tortfeasors and the plaintiff, when more than one tortfeasor is liable for an indivisible injury to the plaintiff. . . . The Institute takes no position on the appropriate rule of joint and several liability for independent tortfeasors who do not act intentionally.

The reasons for leaving this matter to the law of the applicable jurisdictions include: 1) there is no majority rule on this matter extant today; 2) in addition to the lack of a majority rule, there is a farrago of arrangements in existence, most of which employ some amalgam of joint and several liability and several liability in the case of independent tortfeasors; 3) much of the law in this area is statutory; 4) different foundational perspectives on tort law justify differing resolutions of the appropriate use of joint and several or several liability; and 5) in some cases, other aspects of a local jurisdiction's law play an important role in the resolution of this question. . . .

[I]t is important to appreciate that the primary consequence of what form of joint and several or several liability is imposed is the allocation of the risk of insolvency of one or more responsible tortfeasors. Joint and several liability imposes the risk that one or more tortfeasors liable for the plaintiff's damages is insolvent on the remaining solvent defendants, while several liability imposes this insolvency risk on the plaintiff. The adoption of comparative responsibility, which permits plaintiffs to recover from defendants even though plaintiffs are partially responsible for their own damages, has had a significant impact on the near-universal rule of joint and several liability. The rationale for employing joint and several liability and thereby imposing the risk of insolvency on defendants . . . does not coexist comfortably with comparative responsibility. Joint and several liability has also been justified on the ground that each defendant's tortious conduct is a legal cause of the entirety of the plaintiff's damages. Of course, with the adoption of comparative fault, the plaintiff who is comparatively negligent is also a legal cause of the entirety of the damages. . . .

b. *Joint and several liability.* Section 10 states the consequence of a determination that a person is jointly and severally liable. . . .

A judgment should permit a plaintiff to recover the full amount of the recoverable damages for an indivisible injury from any jointly and severally liable defendant. The plaintiff may not, pursuant to the judgment for that claim, obtain more than the total of the recoverable damages, except when the plaintiff has made a favorable partial settlement. . . .

[J]oint and several liability means only that the defendant is liable for the full amount of the plaintiff's recoverable damages, regardless of whether there are other persons who are jointly and severally or, alternatively, severally liable to the plaintiff. . . .

c. *Recoverable damages.* "Recoverable damages" means the amount to which the plaintiff is entitled after reduction for any comparative responsibility of the plaintiff.

Illustration:

1. A sues B, C, and D, who are found jointly and severally liable to A. The factfinder determines that A's damages are $100,000 and assigns 20 percent responsibility to A. A may recover $80,000 from either B, C, or D. A may not recover more than $80,000 in total from B, C, and D, pursuant to any judgment against B, C, and D.

§ 11. Effect of Several Liability

Restatement of the Law Third, Torts: Apportionment of Liability

When, under applicable law, a person is sever-

ally liable to an injured person for an indivisible injury, the injured person may recover only the severally liable person's comparative-responsibility share of the injured person's damages.

Comment:

a. Several liability. Section 11 states the consequence of a determination that a person is severally liable for an indivisible injury. . . . Several implications follow from imposing several liability on independent tortfeasors. First, a defendant held severally liable is only liable for that portion of the plaintiff's damages that reflect the percentage of comparative responsibility assigned to that defendant. Second, because liability is limited to defendants' several share of damages, other nonparties may be submitted to the factfinder for an assignment of a percentage of comparative responsibility. . . . The purpose of submitting those nonparties is not to adjudicate their liability, but to enable defendants' comparative share of responsibility to be determined. . . .

[S]everal liability shifts the burden of insolvency from defendants to plaintiffs and creates a symmetrical unfairness to that existing with pure joint and several liability when a plaintiff is also comparatively responsible for the damages. Indeed, several liability is especially unfair in universally imposing the risk of insolvency on plaintiffs, even though some are not comparatively responsible for their damages.

b. Indivisible injury. The rules stated in this Topic apply to an indivisible injury suffered by the plaintiff that is legally caused by multiple tortfeasors, of which the plaintiff may be one. . . . Section 11 [ ] employs a defendant's comparative percentage of responsibility to determine that defendant's several share for an indivisible injury.

c. Contribution by severally liable defendant. When all defendants are severally liable, each one is separately liable for that portion of the plaintiff's damages. Since overlapping liability cannot occur, severally liable defendants will not have any right to assert a contribution claim.

§ 12. Intentional Tortfeasors

Restatement of the Law Third, Torts: Apportionment of Liability

Each person who commits a tort that requires intent is jointly and severally liable for any indivisible injury legally caused by the tortious conduct.

Comment:

a. Scope. The provision for joint and several liability for intentional tortfeasors in this Section applies regardless of the rule regarding joint and several or several liability for independent nonintentional tortfeasors in the jurisdiction. . . .

b. Intent. . . . Some form of intent is an element in all intentional torts, and this Section imposes joint and several liability on all intentional tortfeasors. Any culpability of a person that does not meet the standard of § 8A, such as gross negligence, recklessness, or similar conduct, does not satisfy the standard stated in this Section.

In addition, there occasionally may be cases in which, although the defendant technically has committed an intentional tort, the defendant's culpability is quite modest, for example a defendant who committed a battery based on an unreasonable, yet honest, belief that the conduct was privileged. In such situations, courts may decide that such low-culpability intentional tortfeasors should not be subject to the provisions of this Section and instead treated in accordance with the rule for nonintentional tortfeasors in the jurisdiction.

c. Separate or indivisible injuries. . . . When an injury is indivisible and legally caused by the tortious conduct of an intentional tortfeasor and one or more other persons, the intentional tortfeasor is jointly and severally liable for all damages. The rule stated in this Section does not address whether other parties whose unintentional but tortious conduct is also a legal cause of the indivisible injury are jointly and severally liable.

Illustration:

1. A breaks down the door to B's hotel room and rapes B. C, the operator of the hotel, is also found liable for the rape because of negligence in providing security. The factfinder assigns 20 percent responsibility to C and 80 percent responsibility to A. A is jointly and severally liable for all recoverable damages pursuant to this Section, regardless of . . . the governing provision on joint and several liability for independent tortfeasors who do not act with intent.

§ 13. Vicarious Liability

Restatement of the Law Third, Torts: Apportionment of Liability

A person whose liability is imputed based on the tortious acts of another is liable for the entire share of comparative responsibility assigned to the other, regardless of whether joint and several liability or several liability is the governing rule for independent tortfeasors who cause an indivisible injury.

Comment:

a. Scope. In a number of contexts, the responsibility of one actor is legally imputed to another, and vicarious liability is imposed. The most familiar is respondeat superior—the liability of a principal for the tortious acts of an agent and of a master for tortious acts of a servant. . . . The rule stated in this Section does not determine when the tortious conduct of one person is imputed to another. Rather, the rule in this Section applies when the governing law provides for such imputation. . . .

d. Single measure of responsibility for multiple parties. When one or more parties is held liable solely because of the tortious acts of another actor, the factfinder should treat the actor and all such vicariously liable parties as a single entity for the purpose of assigning comparative responsibility.

e. Scope of liability. The vicariously liable party is liable only for the share of plaintiff's damages for which the tortious actor is held liable pursuant to this Section.

Illustration:

1. A sues B, C, and D in a jurisdiction that applies several liability to independent tortfeasors who cause a single indivisible injury. C is B's employer, and the sole basis for C's liability is C's vicarious liability for B's negligence. The factfinder assigns 40 percent of the responsibility to B and C, who are considered a single entity . . . and assigns 60 percent of the responsibility to D. B and C are each liable for up to 40 percent of A's damages (although A may only recover a total of 40 percent of the damages from both B and C), but neither is liable for the other 60 percent of A's damages, for which D is severally liable.

f. Indemnity. A party held liable solely because of the tortious conduct of another may be entitled to indemnity from the latter pursuant to § 22.

§ 14. Tortfeasors Liable for Failure to Protect the Plaintiff from the Specific Risk of an Intentional Tort

Restatement of the Law Third, Torts: Apportionment of Liability

A person who is liable to another based on a failure to protect the other from the specific risk of an intentional tort is jointly and severally liable for the share of comparative responsibility assigned to the intentional tortfeasor in addition to the share of comparative responsibility assigned to the person.

341

Comment:

a. Scope. The rule in this Section applies only when a person is negligent *because* of the failure to take reasonable precautions to protect against the specific risk created by an intentional tortfeasor. . . .

Illustration:

1. A is a guest at a hotel operated by B. B neglects to provide adequate door locks on A's room, as a result of which C, an intruder, gains access to A's room, assaults A, and steals A's property. B is liable for the shares of comparative responsibility assigned both to B and to C, because the risk that made B's conduct negligent was specifically the risk that someone would assault A and steal A's property. C is jointly and severally liable for all of A's damages. See § 12 (intentional tortfeasors). . . .

The rule stated in this Section includes tortious acts of commission as well as omission. . . .

Illustrations:

2. A, a police officer, is injured when shot by B, a criminal that A was pursuing in a car chase. A is injured both by the bullet and by a sharp shard of defective glass in the windshield of A's police cruiser, manufactured by C. A was wearing a bullet-proof vest manufactured by D that, had it not been defective, would have prevented A's injuries. Assuming that the applicable rules of legal cause make B and D liable for the injury caused by the bullet and B, C, and D liable for the injury caused by the glass, D is liable for its share of comparative responsibility and B's share of comparative responsibility for the bullet damages and the glass damages, because D is liable for failing to protect against both the shooting and the risk of being assaulted with a broken bottle or other glass. This Section does not impose liability on D for C's share of comparative responsibility for the glass damages; D's joint and several or several liability with regard to C's comparative share of responsibility for the glass damages is determined by the applicable law on joint and several liability for independent tortfeasors in the jurisdiction (Tracks A-E). B is jointly and severally liable for the entirety of A's damages. See § 12 (intentional tortfeasors). D's right to contribution from B is governed by § 23, Comment *e*. B's right to contribution from D is governed by § 23 and Comment *l*.

4. A, engaged in salvage operations, locates and raises to the ocean surface a ship that had sunk many years before. A contracts with B to tow the shipwreck into port later that day. The contract between A and B provides that any damage to

the ship that occurs while B is performing its obligations will be borne by the parties according to applicable tort law. B neglects to tow the ship into dock, and, because it is sitting on the water overnight, C, a thief who pirates unoccupied ships, strips it of much of its valuable contents. If B is negligent for the delay in towing the ship only because of the risk that the ship would be harmed or resunk by adverse weather conditions, B is not liable for the share of comparative responsibility assigned to C based on the rule stated in this Section. B's joint and several liability is determined by the applicable law on joint and several liability for independent tortfeasors in the jurisdiction (Tracks A-E). If B is negligent for the delay in towing the ship because of the risk of thieves ransacking the ship (e.g., B was on notice that pirates were known to be lurking in the area looking for looting opportunities), B is liable for the share of comparative responsibility assigned to C based on the rule stated in this Section. B is liable for C's share regardless of whether B would be negligent in addition because of the risks posed by adverse weather conditions. [B's right to contribution from C and C's right to contribution from B are governed by a separate Section]. . . .

b. *Rationale.* The modification of joint and several liability and the application of comparative responsibility to intentional tortfeasors create a difficult problem. When a person is injured by an intentional tort and another person negligently failed to protect against the risk of an intentional tort, the great culpability of the intentional tortfeasor may lead a factfinder to assign the bulk of responsibility for the harm to the intentional tortfeasor, who often will be insolvent. This would leave the person who negligently failed to protect the plaintiff with little liability and the injured plaintiff with little or no compensation for the harm. Yet when the risk of an intentional tort is the specific risk that required the negligent tortfeasor to protect the injured person, that result significantly diminishes the purpose for requiring a person to take precautions against this risk.

A number of courts therefore have concluded that persons who negligently fail to protect against the specific risk of an intentional tort should bear the risk that the intentional tortfeasor is insolvent. The rule stated in this Section similarly makes such persons liable for the intentional tortfeasor's share of comparative responsibility. The negligent person may assert a contribution claim against the intentional tortfeasor. . . .

[I]n jurisdictions that retain full joint and several liability, the rule provided in this Section is unnecessary because joint and several liability applies to every tortfeasor who is a legal cause of the plaintiff's injury. However, in jurisdictions that have adopted some modification of joint and several liability, this Section makes the

343

person who tortiously fails to protect against an intentional tort liable not only for that person's own share of comparative responsibility but also for the intentional tortfeasor's share of comparative responsibility. . . .

[W]hile the rule stated in this Section is limited to a specific duty to protect against intentional torts, whether there are other limited circumstances in which the rule should be extended to those who fail to protect against nonintentional tortfeasors is a matter on which this Restatement takes no position.

§ 15. Persons Acting in Concert

Restatement of the Law Third, Torts: Apportionment of Liability

When persons are liable because they acted in concert, all persons are jointly and severally liable for the share of comparative responsibility assigned to each person engaged in concerted activity.

Comment:

a. Scope. . . . The joint and several liability of those engaged in concerted activity is for the total comparative responsibility assigned to all who engage in the concerted activity. This Restatement takes no position on whether a concerted-action tortfeasor is also jointly and severally liable for the share of comparative responsibility assigned to an independent tortfeasor who is also liable for the same indivisible injury.

Illustration:

1. A, a pedestrian, sues B, C, and D, who engaged in a drag race on a busy city street, and E, who was not involved in the drag race. B and C simultaneously collided with A, breaking A's leg. D and E also collided with A, causing a fracture of A's skull. The factfinder determines damages to be $25,000 for the broken leg and $50,000 for the fractured skull and assigns 50 percent responsibility to each of B and C for the broken leg and 50 percent responsibility to each of D and E for the fractured skull. The factfinder also determines that B, C, and D were engaged in concerted activity. B, C, and D are jointly and severally liable to A for $50,000 pursuant to the rule stated in this Section. B, C, and D are jointly and severally liable for this amount regardless of . . . the applicable law regarding the joint and several liability of independent tortfeasors. Whether B, C, and D are also jointly and severally liable for E's $25,000 comparative share of A's skull fracture is a matter on which this Restatement takes no position. E's liability for A's fractured skull depends on the governing rules regarding joint and several liability or, on the other hand, several liability for independent tortfeasors who cause an indivisible injury.

344

b. Similar activities and relationships. A number of other situations similar to concerted activity or vicarious liability may be sufficient to impose joint and several liability on tortfeasors who engage in certain conduct or have a specific relationship. Thus, one who directs tortious conduct by another, even though not technically the employer of the tortious actor, may be subject to joint and several liability for injury. . . .

§ 16. Effect of Partial Settlement on Jointly and Severally Liable Tortfeasors' Liability

Restatement of the Law Third, Torts: Apportionment of Liability

The plaintiff's recoverable damages from a jointly and severally liable tortfeasor are reduced by the comparative share of damages attributable to a settling tortfeasor who otherwise would have been liable for contribution to jointly and severally liable defendants who do not settle. The settling tortfeasor's comparative share of damages is the percentage of comparative responsibility assigned to the settling tortfeasor multiplied by the total damages of the plaintiff.

Comment:

b. History. [The] Restatement Second, Torts, provided for a credit based on a settlement with one tortfeasor of at least the amount paid by the settling tortfeasor to the plaintiff. This Section replaces [the Restatement Second Section].

c. Rationale. . . . Fairness in loss allocation [ ] requires that nonsettling tortfeasors receive a credit against the judgment for the settling tortfeasor's share of responsibility. This Section provides nonsettling tortfeasors with a credit equal to the percentage share of plaintiff's damages assigned to the settling tortfeasor. If the factfinder later determines that the settling tortfeasor bore no responsibility or on some other basis determined that the settling tortfeasor was not liable to the nonsettling tortfeasor for contribution (e.g., because of an immunity), the nonsettling tortfeasor receives no credit for that nonliable settling tortfeasor. . . .

Illustration:

1. A, a passenger in B's car, sues B for negligence in going through a stop sign and C, who also went through a stop sign at the same intersection, resulting in a collision that injured A. A settles with B for $20,000. The factfinder assigns 20 percent responsibility to A for distracting B and 45 percent and 35 percent responsibility respectively to B and C and determines that A suffered $100,000 in damages. C receives a $45,000 credit (B's 45% share of comparative responsibility × $100,000 damages) due to A's settlement with B that is ap-

plied to the total damage award by the jury, thereby reducing C's liability to $35,000.

No perfect method exists for apportioning liability among a plaintiff, a settling tortfeasor, and a nonsettling tortfeasor. . . . Nevertheless, the rule adopted in this Section provides the nonsettling tortfeasor with a credit against the judgment in the amount of the comparative share of the settling tortfeasor. The comparative-share credit is adopted rather than its primary alternative, a credit in the amount of the settlement with the settling tortfeasor, also known as a pro tanto credit because on balance it better provides for fairness in loss allocation and has administrability advantages. First, the comparative-share credit obviates the need for courts to review the bona fides of partial settlements and contributes to an equitable distribution of liability among the plaintiff, settling tortfeasors, and nonsettling tortfeasors. Second, it is more easily applied and avoids the complications of determining whether the settlement should be credited against the total damages before or after the plaintiff's share of the damages is subtracted from the total damages. Third, it has the benefit of being consistent with the treatment of partial settlements when there is only several liability. Fourth, a percentage-share credit avoids the need to value assets for which there is no ready market valuation. The United States Supreme Court, after thoroughly canvassing the respective advantages and disadvantages of these two systems, chose a comparative-share credit for Admiralty cases.

The major advantage of a pro tanto credit system is that it encourages early partial settlements, because the plaintiff is assured that all damages can be recovered from the remaining tortfeasors if the plaintiff prevails at trial. . . .

A pro tanto credit has the disadvantage of imposing any inadequacy in a partial settlement between the plaintiff and a settling tortfeasor on nonsettling tortfeasors against whom the plaintiff prevails at trial. . . . Some jurisdictions with a pro-tanto-credit rule attempt to restrict the possibility of inadequate settlements by reviewing the settlement to assure that it is reasonable or entered into in good faith. Court determination of good faith necessarily requires a satellite legal proceeding to assess the settlement, and there is reason to question the capacity of courts to make a determination on this matter. . . .

§ 17. Joint and Several or Several Liability for Independent Tortfeasors

Restatement of the Law Third, Torts: Apportionment of Liability

If the independent tortious conduct of two or more persons is a legal cause of an indivisible injury, the law of the applicable jurisdiction deter-

mines whether those persons are jointly and severally liable, severally liable, or liable under some hybrid of joint and several and several liability.

Comment:

a. Alternative versions of joint and several or several liability. The Institute takes no position on whether joint and several liability, several liability, or some combination of the two should be adopted for independent tortfeasors who cause an indivisible injury. . . . . [T]here is currently no majority rule on this question, although joint and several liability has been substantially modified in most jurisdictions both as a result of the adoption of comparative fault and tort reform during the 1980s and 1990s. Nevertheless, five different versions of joint and several, several, and combinations of the two are presented in the five separate and independent Tracks that follow this Section. These five Tracks are mutually exclusive, although modifications (or combinations of some) of them are possible.

The first Track—the "A" series—presents a rule of pure joint and several liability. The "A" Track then proceeds to resolve subsidiary issues implicated by this premise. These issues include identifying those who may be submitted to the jury for assignment of a percentage of comparative responsibility and the treatment of claims against an employer who is immune from tort liability because of the exclusive remedy bar of workers' compensation. The second Track—the "B" series—presents a pure several-liability scheme and addresses the subsidiary questions posed by that premise.

The first hybrid Track—the "C" series—begins with a rule of joint and several liability for independent tortfeasors who cause an indivisible injury to a plaintiff. However, it places the risk of a tortfeasor's insolvency on all parties who bear responsibility for the plaintiff's damages, including the plaintiff. An insolvent tortfeasor's comparative share of responsibility is reallocated to the other parties in proportion to their comparative responsibility. A very similar result is obtained by starting with a rule of several liability but then providing for reallocation in the event of insolvency. This Track also addresses which persons should be subject to an assignment of comparative responsibility and the effect of that allocation on the apportionment of liability among the parties. This Track is theoretically the most appealing in that it apportions the risk of insolvency to the remaining parties in the case in proportion to their responsibility, thereby providing an equitable mechanism for coping with insolvency. There may be administrative and practical difficulties with the reallocation provisions that are contained in this Track.

The "D" Track is another hybrid system in which joint and several liability is imposed on independent tortfeasors whose percentage of comparative responsibility exceeds a specified threshold. Thus, tortfeasors assigned a modest percentage of comparative responsibility below the threshold are severally liable, while those at or above the threshold are jointly and severally liable. The "D" Track reflects legislation in approximately a dozen states and responds to the concern that many tortfeasors whose responsibility for a plaintiff's injury is quite minimal are held liable for the entirety of the recoverable damages under a pure joint-and-several-liability scheme. However, any threshold is an imperfect way to screen out tangential tortfeasors, and often the threshold is set too high (50 percent) to serve this function well. When there are many tortfeasors, this Track does not perform well, as it virtually guarantees that several liability will be imposed, regardless of the role of any given tortfeasor in the plaintiff's injuries. This threshold series also imposes the risk of insolvency on an entirely innocent plaintiff whenever all solvent defendants are below the specified threshold. To the extent that the justification for modifying joint and several liability is the adoption of comparative responsibility so that the plaintiff may also be legally culpable, imposing the risk of insolvency on an innocent plaintiff is unwarranted.

The "E" Track represents yet another hybrid system, in which the variable that determines joint and several liability or several liability is the type of harm suffered by the plaintiff. Independent tortfeasors are jointly and severally liable for damages for certain harms (often termed "economic" or "pecuniary" harms) but are severally liable for compensatory damages for the remainder of harm (referred to as "noneconomic" or "nonpecuniary" harm). Apportioning the risk of insolvency in this fashion (i.e., defendants bear it with regard to economic harm and plaintiffs bear it with regard to noneconomic harms) thus treats the recovery of economic loss as more important to a plaintiff. In addition, damages for economic harm, being susceptible to objective proof, are subject to considerably less variance in their determination by the factfinder. The "E" Track reflects legislation in about a half-dozen states. Some critics contend that this Track works an injustice to those who are not wage earners and thereby suffer a greater proportion of noneconomic damages in a lawsuit. Others, including those that focus on deterrence, would also dispute the proposition that noneconomic damages are less important than economic damages. This Track also treats unfairly the plaintiff who is not comparatively responsible for the injury by imposing the risk of insolvency for noneconomic loss on the innocent plaintiff rather than the culpable defendants. Finally, this Track creates some administrative and practical difficulties in its operation.

REPORTERS' NOTE

Comment a. Alternative versions of joint and several or several liability.

The clear trend over the past several decades has been a move away from pure joint and several liability. Most jurisdictions have adopted some hybrid form of joint and several and several liability. As of the time this Restatement was published, pure joint and several liability was employed in 15 jurisdictions. However, only nine of those states had adopted comparative responsibility; five of the remaining joint-and-several-liability jurisdictions still retain contributory negligence and one uses a slight/gross rule to determine if a plaintiff can recover. Fifteen jurisdictions have adopted several liability. More jurisdictions have some form of a hybrid system than have either pure joint and several or pure several-liability systems. . . .

C. INDEMNITY AND CONTRIBUTION

§ 22. Indemnity

Restatement of the Law Third, Torts: Apportionment of Liability

(a) **When two or more persons are or may be liable for the same harm and one of them discharges the liability of another in whole or in part by settlement or discharge of judgment, the person discharging the liability is entitled to recover indemnity in the amount paid to the plaintiff, plus reasonable legal expenses, if:**

(1) **the indemnitor has agreed by contract to indemnify the indemnitee, or**

(2) **the indemnitee**

(i) **was not liable except vicariously for the tort of the indemnitor, or**

(ii) **was not liable except as a seller of a product supplied to the indemnitee by the indemnitor and the indemnitee was not independently culpable.**

(b) **A person who is otherwise entitled to recover indemnity pursuant to contract may do so even if the party against whom indemnity is sought would not be liable to the plaintiff.**

Comment:

b. Extinguishing liability of the indemnitor. Except when a contract for indemnity provides otherwise . . . an indemnitee must extinguish the liability of the indemnitor to collect indemnity. The indemnitee may do so either by a settlement with the plaintiff that by its terms or by application of law discharges the indemnitor from liability or by satisfaction of judgment that by operation of law discharges the indemnitor from liability. . . .

c. Indemnitor and indemnitee's liability to the plaintiff, including settlors seeking indemnity. [Subject to exceptions], an indemnitee must prove that the indemnitor would have been liable to the plaintiff in an amount equal to or greater than the amount the indemnitee seeks. An indemnitee may recover reasonable legal expenses defending the claim against the plaintiff, but not reasonable legal fees collecting indemnity. . . .

Illustration:

1. A manufactures a product and sells it to B, who is a retailer. B then sells the product to C, who is injured. C settles with B for $100,000. B sues A for indemnity. B is unable to prove that the product was defective when it left A's control and, therefore, is unable to prove that A would have been liable to C. Absent contractual indemnity, B cannot recover indemnity from A. . . .

f. Contractual indemnity. Contractual indemnity is similar to exculpatory contracts and is governed by similar rules. . . . [C]ontractual indemnity is determined by the terms of the contract. An indemnitee can recover contractual indemnity for his or her own legally culpable conduct only if the contract is clear on that point. If the contract is otherwise clear, it need not contain specific words, such as "negligence" or "fault."

i. Procedure. Indemnity may normally be recovered in a third-party claim in the suit where the indemnitee is sued by the plaintiff or in a separate lawsuit. That issue is governed by the appropriate procedural rules of each jurisdiction.

§ 23. Contribution

Restatement of the Law Third, Torts: Apportionment of Liability

(a) **When two or more persons are or may be liable for the same harm and one of them discharges the liability of another by settlement or discharge of judgment, the person discharging the liability is entitled to recover contribution from the other, unless the other previously had a valid settlement and release from the plaintiff.**

(b) **A person entitled to recover contribution may recover no more than the amount paid to the plaintiff in excess of the person's comparative share of responsibility.**

(c) **A person who has a right of indemnity against another person under § 22 does not have a right of contribution against that person and is not subject to liability for contribution to that person.**

Comment:

e. Proportionate shares. If a person is otherwise entitled to contribution, the amount of contribution is determined by the percentages of responsibility the factfinder assigns to each person.

Illustration:

> 5. A sues B and C. The factfinder finds that B and C are liable, finds that A's damages are $100,000, and assigns 10 percent responsibility to A, 30 percent responsibility to B, and 60 percent responsibility to C. In a jurisdiction that uses joint and several liability, A is entitled to collect $90,000 from B. If A collects $90,000 from B, B is entitled to recover $60,000 ($100,000 × .60) in contribution from C. . . .

f. Contribution limited to amount above the percentage share of the person seeking contribution. If a person is otherwise entitled to recover contribution, contribution is limited to the amount that person pays to the plaintiff above that person's percentage of responsibility. In a jurisdiction where a defendant is only severally liable, a defendant normally would pay no more than its own percentage share and would not be entitled to contribution. Even in a jurisdiction that does not use joint and several liability, however, a severally liable defendant might be sued with less than all of the relevant persons and be liable for more than its own percentages of responsibility, and therefore be entitled to contribution.

Illustrations:

> 10. A sues B and C. The factfinder finds that B and C are liable, finds that A's damages are $100,000, and assigns 40 percent responsibility to B and 60 percent responsibility to C. B pays A $40,000, either because the jurisdiction does not use joint and several liability, or because A chooses to recover only $40,000 from B. B cannot recover contribution from C because B did not pay more than B's percentage share of responsibility.
>
> 11. Same facts as Illustration 10, except that B pays A $50,000. B can recover $10,000 in contribution from C.

g. Contribution for more than the percentage share of the person against whom contribution is sought. In a jurisdiction that uses joint and several liability . . . a person who otherwise is entitled to contribution is entitled to recover the percentage share of liability of the person against whom contribution is sought plus that person's proportionate share of any other person's percentage share of liability.

Illustration:

> 12. A sues B, C, and D. The factfinder finds that B, C, and D are liable, finds that A's damages are $100,000, and assigns 10 percent responsibility to A, 50 percent responsibility to B, 25 percent responsibility to C, and 15 percent responsibility to D. B pays the entire $90,000 judgment and sues C for contribution. B can recover $30,000 contribution from C ($25,000 plus 25/75ths of $15,000). After C pays B $30,000 in contribution, B can recover $10,000 and C can recover $5,000 in contribution from D.

h. Contribution in favor of a settlor. A person who is otherwise entitled to contribution can recover contribution even though the person extinguished the liability of another by settlement rather than payment of judgment. A settlor need not prove that he would have been found liable to the plaintiff. A settlor must show only that the settlement was reasonable.

i. Contribution against a settlor. A person who settles with the plaintiff before final judgment is not liable for contribution to others for the injury. In contrast, settlement after final judgment, or after settlement between the plaintiff and the person seeking contribution, does not protect the settlor from contribution.

D. MULTIPLE TORTFEASORS AND DIVISIBLE HARMS

§ 26. Apportionment of Liability When Damages Can Be Divided by Causation

Restatement of the Law Third, Torts: Apportionment of Liability

(a) **When damages for an injury can be divided by causation, the factfinder first divides them into their indivisible component parts and separately apportions liability for each indivisible component part. . . .**

(b) **Damages can be divided by causation when the evidence provides a reasonable basis for the factfinder to determine:**

(1) **that any legally culpable conduct of a party or other relevant person to whom the factfinder assigns a percentage of responsibility was a legal cause of less than the entire damages for which the plaintiff seeks recovery and**

(2) **the amount of damages separately caused by that conduct.**

Otherwise, the damages are indivisible and thus the injury is indivisible. . . .

Comment:

a. Scope. This Section addresses apportionment of liability when damages can be divided by causation. Damages can be divided by causation when any person or group of persons to whom the factfinder assigns a percentage of responsibility (or any tortious act of such a person) was a legal cause of less than the entire damages. Divisible damages are first divided by causation into indivisible parts, and then each indivisible part is apportioned by responsibility. This Section addresses how these two processes work in the same case. . . .

The policies underlying division by [both] causation and apportionment by responsibility suggest solutions to [issues of blending comparative responsibility and causal apportionment]. No party should be liable for harm it did not cause, and an injury caused by two or more persons should be apportioned according to their respective shares of comparative responsibility. . . .

   c. *Employing the two-step process in Subsection (a).* Under Subsection (a), the factfinder divides divisible damages into their indivisible component parts. The factfinder then apportions liability for each indivisible component part. . . . For each indivisible component part, the factfinder assigns a percentage of comparative responsibility to each party or other relevant person. The percentages of comparative responsibility for each component part add to 100 percent. . . . The plaintiff is entitled to judgment in an amount that aggregates the judgments for each component part.

Illustrations:

   1. A negligently parks his automobile in a dangerous location. B negligently crashes his automobile into A's automobile, damaging it. When B is standing in the road inspecting the damage, B is hit by C, causing personal injury to B. B sues A and C for personal injury and property damage. B's negligent driving and A's negligent parking caused damage to B's automobile. A's negligent parking, B's negligent driving, B's negligent standing in the road, and C's negligent driving caused B's personal injuries. The factfinder determines damages separately for B's automobile and B's person. The factfinder assigns separate percentages of responsibility to A and B for damage to B's automobile, considering A's parking and B's driving. A's and B's percentages add to 100 percent. The factfinder assigns a separate percentage of responsibility to A, B, and C for B's personal injury, considering A's parking, B's driving, B's standing in the road, and C's driving. A's, B's, and C's percentages add to 100 percent. After applying the rules in Topics 1-4 [basic rules and liability, contribution, indemnity, and settlement of multiple tortfeasors for indivisible harm] to each component injury, the court determines A's and C's liability to B by adding each party's liability for each component injury.

   2. Same facts as Illustration 1. The factfinder finds that damages for B's automobile are $1,000 and that damages for B's personal injury are $10,000. For the damage to B's automobile, the factfinder assigns 70 percent responsibility to A and 30 percent responsibility to B. For B's personal injuries, the factfinder assigns 20 percent responsibility to A, 40 percent responsibility to B, and 40 percent responsibility to C. A is liable to B for $2,700: $700 ($1,000 × .70) for damage to B's automobile plus $2,000 ($10,000 × .20) for B's personal injuries. C is liable to B for $4,000 ($10,000 × .40) for B's personal

injury. Whether A and C are jointly and severally liable for B's personal injury is determined by Topic 2 [liability of multiple tortfeasors for indivisible harm].

3. Same facts as Illustration 2, except that, for B's personal injury, the factfinder assigns 20 percent responsibility to A, 60 percent responsibility to B, and 20 percent responsibility to C. Under pure comparative responsibility, A is liable to B for $2,700: $700 ($1,000 × .70) for damage to B's automobile and $2,000 ($10,000 × .20) for B's personal injuries. C is liable to B for $2,000 ($10,000 × .20) for B's personal injury. Under modified comparative negligence, A is liable to B for $700 ($1,000 × .70) for damage to B's automobile. B is barred from recovering from A or C for B's personal injury.

e. *Persons to whom the factfinder assigns a percentage of responsibility.* . . . [P]ercentages of comparative responsibility can be assigned to a plaintiff, the defendants, settling tortfeasors, and, depending on rules about joint and several or several liability, nonparty tortfeasors ("other relevant persons"). . . .

f. *Divisible damages.* Whether damages can be divided by causation is a question of fact. The fact that the magnitude of each indivisible component part cannot be determined with precision does not mean that the damages are indivisible. All that is required is a reasonable basis for dividing the damages.

Divisible damages can occur in a variety of circumstances. They can occur when one person caused all of the damages and another person caused only part of the damages. They can occur when the parties caused one part of the damages and nontortious conduct caused another part. They can occur when the nontortious conduct occurred before or after the parties' tortious conduct. They can occur in cases involving serial injuries, regardless of the length of time between the injuries. They can occur when the plaintiff's own conduct caused part of the damages.

Dividing damages by causation among different tortious acts by the same person may be required. When a person commits two or more tortious acts that cause different parts of the damages, each tortious act is treated separately.

g. *Indivisible injuries.* Damages are indivisible, and thus the injury is indivisible, when all legally culpable conduct of the plaintiff and every tortious act of the defendants and other relevant persons caused all the damages. Unless sufficient evidence permits the factfinder to determine that damages are divisible, they are indivisible.

h. *Burden of proof and sufficiency of evidence to permit damages to be divided by causation.* . . . Whether damages are divisible is a question of fact. A party alleging that damages are divisible has the burden to prove that they are divisible. Whether there is sufficient evidence to prove divisibility is determined by each jurisdiction's applicable rules. The magnitude of each divisible part is also a question of fact. The burden to prove the magnitude of each part is on the party who seeks division. . . .

i. Inconsistent jury findings. Having juries assign different sets of percentages for different parts of damages creates the possibility of inconsistent verdicts. A jury might find that specific conduct was legally culpable in one set of percentages but not in another. Similarly, a jury might compare specific conduct at different ratios of responsibility in different sets of percentages. . . .

Normally, small variations in responsibility in different sets of percentages is tolerable, especially when they do not affect thresholds for modified comparative responsibility or joint and several liability. These variations normally do not require correction or a new trial. . . . Because any inconsistency will be apparent on the face of the verdict, courts can have the jury correct the inconsistency, thereby avoiding a new trial.

j. One-step apportionment. Sometimes a court may determine that the two-step process in Subsection (a) is administratively unsuitable because the case is too complex for a jury to find the requisite facts. The complexity of apportioning liability in a two-step process increases as the number of relevant causes increases. Thus, a court may decide to use a one-step process of apportionment. The factfinder determines the total recoverable damages and then assigns percentages of responsibility to each person who caused some of the damages. These percentages add to 100 percent. When assigning percentages of responsibility, the factfinder takes into account evidence relevant to comparative responsibility, and evidence relevant to causation.

The percentages of responsibility affect liability in the same way as for an indivisible injury. . . .

PART X
DAMAGES

CHAPTER 19

DAMAGES

A. BASIC CONCEPTS

§ 901. General Principle

Restatement of the Law Second, Torts

The rules for determining the measure of damages in tort are based upon the purposes for which actions of tort are maintainable. These purposes are:

(a) to give compensation, indemnity or restitution for harms;

(b) to determine rights;

(c) to punish wrongdoers and deter wrongful conduct; and

358

(d) to vindicate parties and deter retaliation or violent and unlawful self-help.

Comment:

a. The purposes for which actions of tort are allowed explain the three types of damages awarded and, to a large extent, the rules for determining the amount awarded in each. . . . [T]he law of torts attempts primarily to put an injured person in a position as nearly as possible equivalent to his position prior to the tort. The law is able to do this only in varying degrees dependent upon the nature of the harm. . . .

b. The second purpose of the law of torts, that is, to determine or to assert rights, results from the inability of the common law to settle controversies before some wrongful act has been done. The existence of other remedies for testing rights, such as equitable proceedings and declaratory judgments, does not displace the common law remedy of granting nominal damages. These damages are a frequent consequence of actions brought merely to determine or to assert rights.

c. Finally, unlike the law of contracts or of restitution, the law of torts, which was once scarcely separable from the criminal law, has within it elements of punishment or deterrence. In certain types of cases punitive damages can be awarded; and the measure of recovery against a conscious wrongdoer may be greater than that permitted against a tortfeasor who was not aware that his act was tortious.

Originally the primary purpose of the law of torts was to induce the injured party and members of his family or clan to resort to the courts for relief, rather than taking the law into their own hands by attempting to wreak vengeance on the wrongdoer or by resorting to violent means of self-help. This purpose still has significance today, and both compensatory and punitive damages may be utilized to promote it. . . .

§ 903. Compensatory Damages—Definition

Restatement of the Law Second, Torts

"Compensatory damages" are the damages awarded to a person as compensation, indemnity or restitution for harm sustained by him.

Comment:

a. When there has been harm only to the pecuniary interests of a person, compensatory damages are designed to place him in a position substantially equivalent in a pecuniary way to that which he would have occupied had no tort been committed. When however, the tort causes bodily harm or emotional distress, the law cannot restore the injured person to his previous position. The sensations caused by harm to the body or by pain or humiliation are not in any way analogous to a pecuniary loss, and a sum of money is not the equivalent of peace of mind. Nevertheless, damages given for pain and humiliation are called compensatory. They give to the injured person some pecuniary return for what he has suffered or is likely to suffer. . . .

b. In cases in which a tortfeasor has received from the commission of a tort against another person a benefit that constitutes unjust enrichment at the expense of the other, he is ordinarily liable to the other, at the latter's election, either for the damage done to the other's interests or for the value of the benefit received through the commission of the tort. The rules on the measure of recovery when the injured person chooses the value of the benefit received by the tortfeasor are stated in the Restatement of Restitution. . . .

§ 904. General and Special Damages

Restatement of the Law Second, Torts

(1) "General damages" are compensatory damages for a harm so frequently resulting from the tort that is the basis of the action that the existence of the damages is normally to be anticipated and hence need not be alleged in order to be proved.

(2) "Special damages" are compensatory damages for a harm other than one for which general damages are given.

Comment:

a. . . . In many cases in which there can be recovery for general damages, there need be no proof of the extent of the harm, since the existence of the harm may be assumed and its extent is inferred as a matter of common knowledge from the existence of the injury as described. In other cases, however, the existence of a particular harm must be proved, although it need not be specifically alleged. Thus, if a claim is made for "great bodily harm," the plaintiff can recover damages for physical suffering and for a broken leg without proof as to the first, but only after proof of the second. . . .

c. . . . If bodily harm of any kind is alleged, physical pain and suffering resulting from it can be shown without any specific allegation. In other words, it is regarded as general damages.

§ 905. Compensatory Damages for Nonpecuniary Harm

Restatement of the Law Second, Torts

Compensatory damages that may be awarded

without proof of pecuniary loss include compensation

    (a) for bodily harm, and

    (b) for emotional distress.

Comment on Clause (a):

b. Bodily harm. Bodily harm is any impairment of the physical condition of the body, including illness or physical pain. . . . It is not essential to a cause of action that pecuniary loss result. Furthermore, damages can be awarded although there is no impairment of a bodily function and, in some situations, even though the defendant's act is beneficial.

Illustrations:

1. A tortiously strikes B heavily on the back, causing B severe but momentary pain. The blow causes a bone to slip back into place. B is entitled to compensatory damages, undiminished by the fact that the blow was beneficial, except as it prevents future suffering.

2. A is afflicted with deafness in one ear. She informs her physician, B, that she does not desire an operation upon it. Nevertheless, while A is under an anesthetic, B operates upon the ear, thereby preventing subsequent harm but causing pain for a considerable period following the operation. A is entitled to compensatory damages for the suffering, undiminished by reason of the physical benefit conferred upon her by B except as it prevents future suffering.

§ 906. Compensatory Damages for Pecuniary Harm

Restatement of the Law Second, Torts

Compensatory damages that will not be awarded without proof of pecuniary loss include compensation for

    (a) harm to property,

    (b) harm to earning capacity, and

    (c) the creation of liabilities.

Comment on Clause (b):

c. Harm to earning capacity. . . . An injured person who seeks to recover damages for loss of earnings before trial must prove by a preponderance of evidence that the defendant's act has prevented him from receiving the earnings; he is also entitled to damages for the loss of prospective earnings based upon the evidence concerning what he probably could have earned but for the harm, and as to what he probably can now earn through the earning period of his life. Damages for causing a loss of earning capacity are not necessarily based upon what the plaintiff has done or would have done or intends to do, but are based upon the amount by which the earning capacity of the plaintiff has been reduced through the conduct of the tortfeasor. Thus one who was hurt at the beginning of a vacation is not deprived of compensation for his earning capacity because he had no intention of spending his time in work, provided work was available. Likewise, one whose income is sufficient to relieve him of the necessity of working is not barred from recovering damages for loss of his earning capacity. One who was unemployed at the time of the injury may nevertheless have had a substantial earning capacity. On the other hand, in determining the losses before trial, the fact that the plaintiff could not have obtained work, even if he had not been harmed, is considered. So, too, the fact that he may not be able to obtain work in the future is a factor to be taken into consideration in determining the value of his earning capacity.

§ 908. Punitive Damages

Restatement of the Law Second, Torts

(1) **Punitive damages are damages, other than compensatory or nominal damages, awarded against a person to punish him for his outrageous conduct and to deter him and others like him from similar conduct in the future.**

(2) **Punitive damages may be awarded for conduct that is outrageous, because of the defendant's evil motive or his reckless indifference to the rights of others. In assessing punitive damages, the trier of fact can properly consider the character of the defendant's act, the nature and extent of the harm to the plaintiff that the defendant caused or intended to cause and the wealth of the defendant.**

Comment:

a. Purpose. The purposes of awarding punitive damages, or "exemplary" damages as they are frequently called, are to punish the person doing the wrongful act and to discourage him and others from similar conduct in the future. Although the purposes are the same, the effect of a civil judgment for punitive damages is not the same as that of a fine imposed after a conviction of a crime, since the successful plaintiff and not the state is entitled to the money required to be paid by the defendant. . . .

b. Character of defendant's conduct. Since the purpose of punitive damages is not compensation of the plaintiff but punishment of the defendant and deterrence, these damages can be awarded only for conduct for which this remedy is appropriate—which is to

362

say, conduct involving some element of outrage similar to that usually found in crime. The conduct must be outrageous, either because the defendant's acts are done with an evil motive or because they are done with reckless indifference to the rights of others. Although a defendant has inflicted no harm, punitive damages may be awarded because of, and measured by, his wrongful purpose or intent, as when he unsuccessfully makes a murderous assault upon the plaintiff, who suffers only a momentary apprehension. In all these cases, however, a cause of action for the particular tort must exist, at least for nominal damages. Reckless indifference to the rights of others and conscious action in deliberate disregard of them may provide the necessary state of mind to justify punitive damages.

Punitive damages are not awarded for mere inadvertence, mistake, errors of judgment and the like, which constitute ordinary negligence. And they are not permitted merely for a breach of contract. . . .

§ 910. Damages for Past, Present and Prospective Harms

Restatement of the Law Second, Torts

One injured by the tort of another is entitled to recover damages from the other for all harm, past, present and prospective, legally caused by the tort.

Comment:

b. *Time for estimating damages.* The amount of special or consequential damages to which a person is entitled is determined in the light of all the evidence that the parties present before the end of the trial concerning the total harm that has resulted or that it appears probably will result from the tortious act, assuming that there could have been recovery for the harm if it had occurred before suit was brought. The principal condition imposed on the recovery of damages for prospective harm is the requirement of reasonable certainty of proof.

Any event occurring prior to the trial that increases the harmful consequences of the defendant's tortious conduct, if it is an event for the consequences of which the defendant is responsible, increases the damages recoverable to the same extent, whether the event has occurred before suit is brought or after suit. Likewise an event that indicates that the conduct is less harmful than had been supposed prevents or diminishes damages for the consequences. This is also true of an event that prevents or diminishes harmful consequences of the tortious conduct.

Illustration:

1. A negligently operates his car so that it skids into B, a

363

pedestrian. B experiences only a slight impact and is under the doctor's care for only two days. He brings suit against A, and recovers a verdict of $5,000 for the slight harm then apparent. The verdict is set aside, on appeal, on the ground that the award is excessive. At the second trial there is evidence that the impact has caused a deterioration of the bone that began after the first trial. B is entitled to recover as damages such amount for loss of earning capacity and past and future suffering that the facts now justify and a verdict for $12,000 may not be excessive.

§ 914. Expense of Litigation

Restatement of the Law Second, Torts

(1) **The damages in a tort action do not ordinarily include compensation for attorney fees or other expenses of the litigation.**

(2) **One who through the tort of another has been required to act in the protection of his interests by bringing or defending an action against a third person is entitled to recover reasonable compensation for loss of time, attorney fees and other expenditures thereby suffered or incurred in the earlier action.**

Comment on Subsection (1):

a. The rule in this country, in contrast to that in England, is that neither party to a tort action can recover in that action his counsel fees or other legal expenses of maintaining the action itself, except to the limited extent to which he may be authorized to do so by statutes providing that he may recover his "costs" and disbursements. . . . This rule does not apply, of course, when a statute or a contract provides expressly or impliedly for the recovery of counsel fees or other expenses. Exception to the rule is also occasionally made in other cases involving the assertion of a claim or defense known to be spurious, or amounting to harassment or oppressive action, especially in suits in equity where the court traditionally has more discretion. . . .

§ 914A. Effect of Taxation

Restatement of the Law Second, Torts

(1) **The amount of an award of tort damages is not augmented or diminished because of the fact that the award is or is not subject to taxation.**

(2) **The amount of an award of tort damages is ordinarily not diminished because of the fact that although the award is not itself taxed, all or a part of it is to compensate for the loss of future benefits that would have been subject to taxation.**

Comment:

a. Taxation of tort award itself. Whether an award of tort damages is subject to taxation is controlled by statutory provisions for the jurisdiction involved, together with their interpretation. . . . It is not within the scope of this Restatement [ ] to state rules providing when an award of tort damages is subject to taxation.

That question is distinct from the question of what effect taxation of the award has upon the amount of the award. The answer to the latter question is that it has no effect. Whether or not the award is taxed, its amount should be the same.

B. DIMINUTION OF DAMAGES

§ 918. Avoidable Consequences

Restatement of the Law Second, Torts

(1) **Except as stated in Subsection (2), one injured by the tort of another is not entitled to recover damages for any harm that he could have avoided by the use of reasonable effort or expenditure after the commission of the tort.**

(2) **One is not prevented from recovering damages for a particular harm resulting from a tort if the tortfeasor intended the harm or was aware of it and was recklessly disregardful of it, unless the injured person with knowledge of the danger of the harm intentionally or heedlessly failed to protect his own interests.**

Comment: . . . .

Illustrations:

1. A intentionally strikes B, causing a slight wound on B's hand. B unreasonably delays in taking antiseptic measures and the wound becomes infected, as a result of which B is unable to use his hand for six weeks. B sues A, claiming damages, including loss of six weeks' earnings. A files an answer stating that B was neglectful in not having the wound attended to. The answer is not a defense to B's action, but B is entitled to damages only for the pain, loss of earnings and other elements of damages that B would have suffered if he had used reasonable care.

2. A, a trespasser upon B's pasture, negligently leaves open a gate in the fence. B sees that the gate is open but carelessly fails to close it, as a result of which B's cattle escape and are lost. B is not entitled to damages for the loss of his cattle. . . .

b. Amount by which damages are reduced. Except when the

365

rule stated in Subsection (2) is applicable, a person who fails to avert the consequences of a tort, which he could do with slight effort is entitled to no damages for the consequences. If harm results because of his careless failure to make substantial efforts or incur expense, the damages for the harm suffered are reduced to the value of the efforts he should have made or the amount of expense he should have incurred, in addition to the harm previously caused.

Illustration:

8. A tortiously destroys B's fence. Although B knows the facts and is able to build a temporary barrier at an expense of $20, he fails to do so and his cattle worth $500 stray from the field and are lost. B is entitled to recover only $20 in addition to the value of the destroyed fence.

§ 920. Benefit to Plaintiff Resulting from Defendant's Tort

Restatement of the Law Second, Torts

When the defendant's tortious conduct has caused harm to the plaintiff or to his property and in so doing has conferred a special benefit to the interest of the plaintiff that was harmed, the value of the benefit conferred is considered in mitigation of damages, to the extent that this is equitable.

Comment:

a. The rule stated in this Section normally requires that the damages allowable for an interference with a particular interest be diminished by the amount to which the same interest has been benefited by the defendant's tortious conduct. Thus if a surgeon performs an unprivileged operation resulting in pain and suffering, it may be shown that the operation averted future suffering. (See Illustration 1). If a surgeon has destroyed an organ of the body, it may be shown in mitigation that the operation improved other bodily functions. (See Illustration 2). Likewise one who has interfered with the physical condition of land can show in mitigation, except in cases like those dealt with in Comments *c*, *d* and *f*, that the change resulted in an improvement to the land. (See Illustration 3).

Illustrations:

1. A, a surgeon, having been directed to examine but not to operate upon B's ear, performs an operation that is painful but that averts future pain and suffering. The diminution in future pain is a factor to be considered in determining the amount of damages for the pain caused by the operation.

2. A, a surgeon, without B's consent, operates upon B's eye, causing B to lose the sight in that eye. In an action of bat-

366

tery, it may be shown in mitigation of damages for the loss of the eye that had A not operated, the sight of the other eye would have been lost.

3. A tortiously digs a channel through B's land, thereby making it impossible to grow crops upon the land through which the channel runs. It may be shown in mitigation that the digging of the channel drains the remainder of B's land, making it more valuable.

§ 920A. Effect of Payments Made to Injured Party

Restatement of the Law Second, Torts

(1) **A payment made by a tortfeasor or by a person acting for him to a person whom he has injured is credited against his tort liability, as are payments made by another who is, or believes he is, subject to the same tort liability.**

(2) **Payments made to or benefits conferred on the injured party from other sources are not credited against the tortfeasor's liability, although they cover all or a part of the harm for which the tortfeasor is liable.**

Comment:

a. *Payments by or for defendant.* If a tort defendant makes a payment toward his tort liability, it of course has the effect of reducing that liability. This is also true of payments made under an insurance policy that is maintained by the defendant, whether made under a liability provision or without regard to liability, as under a medical-payments clause. This is true also of a payment by another tortfeasor of an amount for which he is liable jointly with the defendant or even by one who is not actually liable to the plaintiff if he is seeking to extinguish or reduce the obligation. . . .

b. *Benefits from collateral sources.* Payments made or benefits conferred by other sources are known as collateral-source benefits. They do not have the effect of reducing the recovery against the defendant. The injured party's net loss may have been reduced correspondingly, and to the extent that the defendant is required to pay the total amount there may be a double compensation for a part of the plaintiff's injury. But it is the position of the law that a benefit that is directed to the injured party should not be shifted so as to become a windfall for the tortfeasor. If the plaintiff was himself responsible for the benefit, as by maintaining his own insurance or by making advantageous employment arrangements, the law allows him to keep it for himself. If the benefit was a gift to the plaintiff from a third party or established for him by law, he should not be deprived of the advantage that it confers. The law does not differentiate between the nature of the benefits, so long as

367

they did not come from the defendant or a person acting for him. One way of stating this conclusion is to say that it is the tortfeasor's responsibility to compensate for all harm that he causes, not confined to the net loss that the injured party receives. Perhaps there is an element of punishment of the wrongdoer involved. Perhaps also this is regarded as a means of helping to make the compensation more nearly compensatory to the injured party.

c. The rule that collateral benefits are not subtracted from the plaintiff's recovery applies to the following types of benefits: (1) Insurance policies. . . . (2) Employment benefits. . . . (3) Gratuities. . . . (4) Social legislation benefits. . . .

C. COMPENSATORY DAMAGES FOR SPECIFIC TYPES OF HARM

§ 924. Harm to the Person

Restatement of the Law Second, Torts

One whose interests of personality have been tortiously invaded is entitled to recover damages for past or prospective

(a) bodily harm and emotional distress;

(b) loss or impairment of earning capacity;

(c) reasonable medical and other expenses; and

(d) harm to property or business caused by the invasion.

Comment:

a. The rule stated in this Section is applicable to invasions of interests of personality. . . . Thus the rule is applied in actions for assault, battery, false imprisonment, malicious prosecution when the plaintiff is put under restraint, insulting conduct amounting to a tort, and all other acts constituting a tort because intended or likely to cause bodily harm or emotional distress, whether the harm is negligently, recklessly or intentionally caused or results from an abnormally dangerous activity. When there is an intended trespass to the person, as in the case of a battery, assault or imprisonment, harm is not essential to a cause of action and if none is suffered, nominal damages at least are awarded. However, except in a few situations, there is no liability for merely negligent conduct that threatens bodily harm but results only in emotional distress not causing bodily harm. . . .

§ 925.   Actions for Causing Death   *wrongful death*

Restatement of the Law Second, Torts

**The measure of damages for causing the death
of another depends upon the wording of the statute
creating the right of action and its interpretation.**

Comment:

   a.   In the United States also, the omission of the common law
[to allow recovery from a person who causes death] has been cor-
rected in every state by statutes colloquially known as "wrongful
death acts." . . . .

   b. Types of statutes. The American statutes creating a cause of
action for death are not uniform in their provisions with regard to
the method by which the chief elements of damages are
determined. . . .

INDEX

371

INDEX

INDEX

373

INDEX

deprivation of use of chattels, 37–38
dispossessed chattels, 34, 36

CHATTELS—Continued
Trespass to chattels—Continued
duties of possessors of personalty, 220
intent, 35
"intermeddling" with chattels, 34, 35, 36–37
liability to person in possession, 35–38
physical contact with chattel, 35
ways of committing, 34–35

CHILD ABUSE
Emotional harm to parents from, 236

CHILDREN
Comparative responsibility/contributory negligence, 78
Dangerous adult activities, 78–79
Duty of parent with dependent children, 196
Negligence
excused statutory violations, 93, 94
generally, 77–79
Negligence per se, 94
Parents' affirmative duties, 196
Trespass on land, 214

COERCION
Consent obtained by, 53
Threats. *See* THREATS

COLLATERAL-SOURCE RULE
Damages, 367–368

"COMING TO THE NUISANCE"
Defense of, 332

COMPARATIVE RESPONSIBILITY/CONTRIBUTORY NEGLIGENCE
Ameliorative doctrines for defining, 171–173
Assumption of risk, compared, 173
Avoidable consequences, 172
Burden of proof, 175
Calculation of shares of responsibility, 176–177
Causation, 176, 179–180
Children, 78
Continuing risk of actor's conduct, 191
Contractual limitations on liability, 169–170
Defendant's negligence
plaintiff's negligence same as standard for, 173–174
relationship to, 173–174
repair or treatment of condition caused by plaintiff's negligence, 177–178
Dividing damages by causation, 352–355
Effect of, 291
Factors for assigning shares of responsibility, 179–181
Foreseeability, 109–113
Forms of, 290–291
Generally, 334–335
Implied assumptions of risk, relationship to, 173–174
Indivisible injury, when plaintiff suffers an, 175–179
Intervening acts, 161–162
Judicial adjustments of, 177
Land owners and possessors, 174
Last clear chance, 172
Mitigation of damages, 172
Modified comparative responsibility, 178–179

375

G

H

I

INDEX

INDEX

INDEX

PHYSICAL HARM—Cont'd
Bodily contact/harm
   apprehension of. *See* ASSAULT
   emotional harm, bodily harm resulting from, 229, 235
   emotional harm, distinguished, 229, 230
   generally, 114
   interest in freedom from. *See* BATTERY
Definition of, 114
Emotional harm
   bodily harm, distinguished, 229, 230
   bodily harm resulting from, 229, 235
   physical consequences not required, 241
   as physical harm, 114
Factual cause. *See* FACTUAL CAUSE
Highly significant risk of, 278
Intentional harm, liability for
   affirmative defenses, 17
   generally, 15–16
   umbrella rule, 15–17
Negligence, 66–68
Prior conduct creating risk of, 189–191
Proximate cause. *See* PROXIMATE CAUSE
Restatement Third of Torts, 5–8

PHYSICIANS
Affirmative duties, 198

POISONOUS SUBSTANCES
See TOXIC SUBSTANCES AND DISEASE

PREEXISTING CONDITIONS
Proximate cause, 156–159

PRIMA FACIE CASE
Negligence, 66

PRINCIPAL'S LIABILITY
Direct liability
   generally, 253–254
   principal's negligence, 256–257
Employer liability. *See* EMPLOYER LIABILITY
Generally, 253–255
Multiple principals, agents with, 254–255
Organizational principals, 254
Principal's negligence, 256–257
Punitive damages, 255–256
Special relationship of principal with another person, 256, 257–258
Vicarious liability, 253–256

PRIVATE NECESSITY
Trespass on land, 54–56

PRIVATE NUISANCE
Generally, 327–328
"Gravity" of harm versus "utility" of conduct, 329
Independent contractors, hirer's liability for, 268
Unreasonableness of intentional invasion, 328–329

PRODUCTS LIABILITY
Affirmative defenses
   apportionment of liability, 316–317
   contractual exculpations, 317–318
   disclaimers, 317–318
   waivers, 317–318
Alteration of product, 312–313

INDEX

R

REAL PROPERTY/LAND
Defense of property. *See* DEFENSE OF PROPERTY
Nuisance invasions of. *See* NUISANCE
Owners and possessors. *See* LANDLORD AND TENANT; LAND OWNERS AND POSSESSORS
Products liability, 319–320
Trespass to. *See* TRESPASS ON LAND

REASONABLE CARE
Affirmative duties and, 186
Duty of, 190, 192. *See also* DUTY OF CARE
Generally, 59–60

RECKLESSNESS
Assumption of risk, 13
Definition of, 13
Emotional harm, 230–236
Factors considered
    likelihood of harm, 15
    magnitude of risk/burden of precautions, imbalance between, 14
    obviousness of risk, 14
    severity of harm, 15
Liability for, 13–14
Likelihood of harm, 15
Magnitude of risk/burden of precautions, imbalance between, 14

RECKLESSNESS—Continued
Obviousness of risk, 14
Risk of harm not increased, 18
Scope of liability, 17–19
Severity of harm, 15
Significance of finding, 13–14
Synonymous terminology, 13

RECREATIONAL USE STATUTES
Land owners and possessors, 215

REGULATIONS
Independent contractors, hirer's liability for, 269–270
Negligence, 187
Negligence per se, 88

RENDERING AID TO INJURED PERSONS
Affirmative duty to others, 201–205
Comparative responsibility/contributory negligence, 166–167
Joint and several liability, 166–167
Liability for enhanced harm, 165–167

RESCUERS/"RESCUE DOCTRINE"
Affirmative duty to others, 201–205
Comparative responsibility/contributory negligence, 160–161
Duty of land possessors to, 214–215
History of, 159
Limits on liability, 160
Scope of doctrine, 159–160

RES IPSA LOQUITUR
Alternative formulations of doctrine, 99–100
Causation and, 101–102
Comparative responsibility/contributory negligence, 103–104
Defendant's access to information, 104
Expert testimony, 101
Generally, 99

INDEX

T

†